Brotherhood Club's Guide to Men's Emotional Health

Kenneth Hughes

Copyright Page

This book is published by KLH Publishing

Disclaimer This guide is intended for informational and supportive purposes only. The author is not a licensed medical or mental health professional. Rather, he writes from the perspective of someone who has personally sought treatment and continues to engage in his own journey of emotional health. The content herein reflects lived experience, research, and collective wisdom, but it should not be considered a substitute for professional medical advice, diagnosis, or treatment.

Readers are encouraged to seek the guidance of qualified health providers with any questions regarding their emotional or physical well-being. Never disregard professional advice or delay seeking it because of something you have read in this book.

Table of Contents

Forward

My name is Kenneth. I've lived the majority of my life in and out of mental health care systems—sometimes searching, sometimes surviving. *Brotherhood Club's Guide to Men's Emotional Health* is more than a book. It's a mirror. A reckoning. A lifeline. It's part self-reflection, part offering—for anyone who's ever felt like they were drowning in silence.

My journey began when I was just thirteen. I had just graduated from middle school and started high school when my father passed away. That day split my life in two. I came home from school to find him collapsed in the doorway—unresponsive. I called 911 while my mother parked the car. By the time help arrived, his heart had stopped. He was rushed to the hospital, where he remained comatose for weeks. The doctors said if he woke up, he'd be brain-dead. Eventually, my mother and older brother had to make the impossible decision: they let him go.

I still carry that moment like a wound that never fully closes. I blamed myself. I thought, *If I had stayed home, maybe he'd still be here.* That guilt became the gateway to a spiral—medications that numbed me, drugs that erased me. All I wanted was to stop feeling. To disappear.

Decades have passed, but in many ways, I'm still that boy who cried after every fight. I've sat across from countless therapists. I've swallowed pills with names I can't pronounce. I've tried to find myself in diagnoses, in treatment plans, in temporary relief. And still, I ask: *Who am I?* No one has answered.

I carry a world of trauma on my back. Not metaphorically—*literally*. It shapes how I move, how I speak, how I breathe. This book is a window into that weight. Into the therapy sessions, the medications, the psychiatric check-ins that keep me emotionally stable enough to show up in the world. It's not a polished story. It's a survival map.

I've lived through things that rewired my nervous system. I've lost people I couldn't save. I've blamed myself for things no child should carry. I've been medicated into numbness, counseled into exhaustion, and still—*still*—I wake up wondering who I am beneath the trauma.

This book is for the ones who feel that too. The ones who hate themselves just for existing. The ones who can't explain the ache but feel it in their bones. The ones who are barely holding on.

I need you to see me—not because I want pity, but because visibility is survival. If you see me, maybe you'll see yourself. Maybe you'll stop pretending you're fine. Maybe you'll ask for help. Maybe you'll live.

There are answers. There are people who care. There are therapies that work. There are medications that stabilize. There are communities—like Brotherhood Club—that exist so you don't have to carry this alone.

If you're reading this, I love you. I'm proud of you for picking up this book. You didn't come here by accident. You came here because something inside you is still searching. Still fighting. Still hoping.

Let this book be your companion. Your mirror. Your mythic guide.

And before you turn the page, sit with this:

Prompt: Who are you outside of work?

Introduction – Start of Your Journey

This conversation is long overdue—one that countless men have yearned to have but never found the words to begin. If you've found your way to these pages, you're likely carrying the quiet weight of unspoken truths, the exhaustion of maintaining facades that no longer fit, and perhaps a growing awareness that something vital has been missing from your journey as a man.

You are not alone in this recognition, nor does it acknowledge how it diminishes your strength. The very act of opening this book represents a profound form of courage—the kind our culture has often discouraged, yet the kind that holds the key to authentic connection and meaningful transformation. This is your invitation into a space of genuine exploration, where your voice matters deeply and your path toward emotional wholeness isn't just possible, but essential for the fullest expression of who you were meant to be.

Why We Stay Silent

From our earliest moments, the world begins crafting invisible scripts about who we should become as men. These messages arrive disguised as guidance: "*Big boys don't cry,*" "*Man up and handle it,*" "*Don't be so sensitive.*" They echo through childhood playgrounds, resonate in locker room conversations, and weave themselves into the fabric of family expectations. Over time, these cultural whispers crystallize into an unforgiving code that governs how we navigate the vast landscape of human emotion.

This conditioning penetrates far deeper than mere social etiquette—it becomes the architecture of our identity, creating what researchers describe as "emotional armor." This protective shell promises to shield us from vulnerability while simultaneously severing our connection to the profound richness of our inner lives. We become masters of emotional translation, converting the complex symphony of human feeling into socially acceptable forms: sadness transforms into anger, fear morphs into aggression, and loneliness disguises itself as fierce independence.

Consider the profound paradox embedded within this system. We're taught that emotional expression represents weakness, yet our inability to process and communicate our feelings contributes to some of the most devastating challenges men face in our modern world. Depression rates among men continue their upward climb, suicide remains a leading cause of death for men under 35, and countless relationships fracture under the weight of emotional unavailability. The very silence that promised protection has become our greatest threat.

The cultural conditioning that demands our silence isn't serving our highest good—it's constructing a prison of our own making, reinforced by generations of well-meaning men who learned the same painful lessons and transmitted them like inherited wounds. This isn't authentic strength; it's a collective trauma that transcends cultures, families, and communities, leaving millions of men feeling profoundly isolated in their struggles.

This silence ripples outward, touching every life we encounter. When we cannot access our own emotional truth, we struggle to create meaningful connections with others. Our relationships become carefully choreographed performances rather than genuine exchanges of hearts and minds. Our children absorb these patterns, learning through our example that emotions represent dangerous territory to be avoided, perpetuating cycles of disconnection that can span generations.

Yet here lies a truth that the culture of silence rarely reveals: the very emotions we're taught to suppress serve as our internal compass, guiding us toward what matters most profoundly. Anger illuminates our boundaries and reveals our deepest values. Sadness honors our losses while connecting us to our infinite capacity for love. Fear protects what we hold dear and alerts us to precious things we cannot afford to lose. When we silence these messengers, we forfeit access to invaluable information about ourselves and our place in the world.

The silence that once promised protection has become the very force that limits our potential for joy, authentic connection, and purposeful living. But this silence need not define our destiny—it simply marks the beginning of our courageous journey toward emotional freedom and authentic strength.

Your Personal Story: A Bridge to Understanding

Allow me to share something that required years of inner work to acknowledge, even in the privacy of my own thoughts. There was an extended period when I believed I had achieved mastery over the art of emotional control. I could maintain perfect composure in any situation, solve complex problems without becoming "emotional," and project an image of unshakable strength that earned respect and admiration. I wore this ability like a badge of profound honor, convinced it made me more reliable, more trustworthy, more authentically masculine.

What I failed to recognize was that this emotional numbness was systematically eroding everything that truly mattered in my life. My relationships felt hollow and performative, as though I were participating in elaborate theatrical productions rather than engaging in genuine human connections. I could navigate surface-level conversations with remarkable ease, but when discussions ventured into deeper territory—feelings, fears, dreams, profound disappointments—I found myself instinctively reaching for familiar escape routes: deflecting with humor, changing subjects abruptly, or simply shutting down entirely.

The awakening came during what should have been one of life's most fulfilling chapters. I had achieved numerous external markers of success, yet I felt completely disconnected from any sense of joy or authentic fulfillment. It was as if I were observing my own life through thick, impermeable glass—physically present but emotionally absent, going through practiced motions without accessing the emotional richness that gives existence its deeper meaning.

The breaking point arrived not through dramatic crisis but through quiet, persistent desperation. Sitting alone one evening in the silence of my own company, I realized I couldn't recall the last time I had felt genuinely connected to another human being—including myself. The emotional armor that had once felt protective and necessary now felt suffocating and imprisoning. I was drowning in plain sight, surrounded by people who witnessed only the carefully constructed surface I had learned to present with such precision.

That moment of raw recognition launched a journey that continues to unfold today—one of gradually learning to trust my own emotional experience, to name feelings I had spent decades avoiding, and to discover that vulnerability isn't the opposite of strength but rather its most authentic and powerful expression. The path hasn't been linear or comfortable. There have been setbacks, moments of profound resistance, and countless uncomfortable growth experiences. But each courageous step toward emotional honesty has brought greater aliveness, deeper connections, and a sense of authenticity I never knew I was missing.

Your story undoubtedly differs from mine in its specific details, yet I suspect you'll recognize familiar threads woven throughout your own experience. Perhaps you've felt the bone-deep exhaustion that accompanies constantly managing your public image. Maybe you've wondered why achieving long-sought goals doesn't bring the satisfaction you anticipated. You might recognize the particular loneliness that can exist even in crowded rooms, or the frustration of yearning for deeper connections while lacking the tools to create them.

These experiences aren't character deficits or personal failures—they're the predictable outcomes of a system that taught us to sever the vital connection between our inner world and outer expression. The encouraging truth is that this disconnection can be healed, and your very presence with these words suggests you're ready to begin that profound healing process.

Your journey toward emotional wholeness represents more than personal growth—it's an act of profound courage that holds the power to transform not only your own life but the lives of everyone in your circle of influence. Each man who chooses to break the silence creates sacred space for others to follow, contributing to a collective healing that our world desperately needs.

What This Book Will and Won't Do

Let us establish clear, honest expectations about the transformative journey you're courageously beginning, grounded in both respect for your current position and genuine care for your ultimate destination. This book is not a miracle cure, a magical formula, or a simple sequence of steps that will instantly transform your emotional landscape overnight. Authentic emotional healing and sustained growth require time, patience, consistent practice, and profound self-compassion. Anyone promising immediate transformation is offering false hope, and you deserve far better than empty promises.

What this book *will* provide is a trusted companion and experienced guide through the complex, often uncharted terrain of male emotional development. Consider it a comprehensive map for territory that most of us were never taught to navigate—a thorough exploration that honors both where you've been and illuminates where you're choosing to go. It will help you understand why emotional expression feels so challenging for many men, provide practical, evidence-based tools for developing emotional awareness and vocabulary, and offer time-tested strategies for building relationships that support authentic connection and mutual growth.

You'll discover approaches to emotional regulation that have been refined in therapeutic settings and validated by research, learn to distinguish between healthy and unhealthy coping mechanisms, and explore various therapeutic modalities that can support your continued development. Most importantly, you'll discover that you're not broken, fundamentally flawed, or alone in your struggles—you're simply in the process of unlearning patterns that no longer serve your highest good while developing new skills that align with your authentic values and aspirations.

This book will guide you through understanding the deep roots of emotional suppression, help you identify the specific costs it may have extracted from your life, and provide concrete, actionable strategies for developing genuine emotional fluency. We'll explore the crucial distinction between healthy and toxic expressions of masculinity. Examine how to cultivate supportive male friendships that go beyond surface-level interaction. Navigate romantic relationships with greater authenticity and vulnerability, and consider how emotional growth can transform your approach to fatherhood, mentorship, or leadership.

We'll delve into practical tools like mindful breathwork, reflective journaling, and consciousness practices that can support your daily emotional well-being and resilience. You'll learn to recognize early warning signs of emotional overwhelm, develop healthy boundaries that protect your energy while remaining open to connection, and create meaningful rituals that support ongoing emotional health. Throughout this journey, cultural sensitivity remains paramount—recognizing that men from different backgrounds may face unique challenges and require tailored approaches to emotional healing.

What this book *will not* do is judge you for your starting point or pressure you toward any predetermined version of masculinity. There's no single correct way to embody masculine energy, and emotional health doesn't require abandoning all traditional masculine qualities that serve you well. Strength, protection, provision, and problem-solving can all remain integral parts of your identity when grounded in emotional awareness rather than emotional suppression.

This book also cannot replace professional therapy, medical treatment, or specialized intervention when those are needed for your particular situation. While the tools and perspectives offered here can be tremendously beneficial, some circumstances require the personalized attention and expertise of trained mental health professionals. Part of emotional maturity involves recognizing when to seek additional support, and this book will help you identify those moments while removing any shame that might prevent you from accessing appropriate help.

Perhaps most importantly, this book won't ask you to become someone fundamentally different from who you are. Instead, it will support you in discovering who you already are beneath the accumulated layers of conditioning and external expectations. The goal isn't to eliminate valuable masculine traits but to choose consciously which aspects of masculinity serve your authentic self-expression and which ones limit your capacity for connection, fulfillment, and joy.

This journey deeply respects your need for privacy and offers the confidential exploration you may require as you examine these sensitive aspects of your inner life. Whether you're reading in the solitude of your personal space or sharing insights with carefully chosen trusted allies, this book is designed to meet you exactly where you are in your emotional development, without judgment or pressure to move faster than feels right for you.

As we embark on this profound exploration together, I invite you to approach it with curiosity rather than harsh judgment, patience rather than urgent pressure, and deep compassion rather than critical evaluation. The silence you've maintained around your emotional life served important purposes once—perhaps protecting you from ridicule, rejection, or overwhelming pain. Honor that protective wisdom even as you prepare to move beyond its limitations.

The pages that follow contain stories from men who have walked similar paths of courage and growth, insights from researchers and therapists who deeply understand male emotional development, and practical tools that have proven effective in countless lives seeking greater authenticity and connection. Most importantly, they contain an invitation to reclaim a vital part of yourself that has been waiting patiently for permission to emerge and flourish.

Your voice carries profound importance. Your feelings hold deep validity. Your journey toward emotional health represents not just a gift to yourself but a contribution to everyone whose life you touch with your presence. Our world needs men who can access the full spectrum of their humanity—not because traditional masculinity is inherently wrong, but because authentic strength includes the courage to feel deeply, love openly, and connect genuinely with the sacred mystery of being human.

This book stands as your confidential companion on a path toward greater wholeness, offering you the support, understanding, and practical guidance you deserve as you courageously choose to break the silence that has held you back from your fullest expression. The healing begins here, and it begins with your brave decision to explore what lies beyond the boundaries of what you've always known. Welcome to the conversation that holds the power to transform everything.

Prompt: What is something people think about you that isn't true?

Chapter 1: The Cost of Emotional Armor

The protective shell we've constructed around our emotional lives wasn't forged in malice—it was crafted with the tender intention of survival, woven from threads of cultural expectation and familial wisdom passed down through generations. Yet like ancient armor that once served warriors well but now restricts movement in peacetime, our emotional defenses have become both shield and shackle, protecting us from vulnerability while simultaneously severing our connection to the profound richness of human experience.

This invisible armor feels as natural as breathing, so seamlessly integrated into our identity that we rarely pause to examine its weight or question its necessity. We've worn it so long that we've forgotten what it feels like to move freely through the world without its constraints. But every piece of armor exacts a price, and the cost of emotional suppression extends far beyond the boundaries of our individual lives, rippling outward to touch every relationship we hold dear and every dream we dare to pursue.

Understanding these costs isn't an exercise in self-blame or regret—it's an act of courageous self-discovery that illuminates the path toward authentic strength and meaningful connection. When we can clearly see what we stand to gain by choosing vulnerability over armor, the journey toward emotional freedom becomes not just possible, but irresistibly compelling.

How Emotional Suppression Manifests: The Hidden Toll

Physical Manifestations: When the Body Holds What the Mind Cannot

Your body serves as the faithful chronicler of every emotion you've ever denied, every feeling you've pushed aside, every moment of pain you've deemed too dangerous to acknowledge. When emotions find no outlet through conscious expression, they don't simply vanish into the ether—they take up residence in your nervous system, creating intricate patterns of tension, inflammation, and dysfunction that can persist for years, even decades.

The stress of maintaining emotional suppression creates what researchers call "allostatic load"—the cumulative physiological toll of chronic stress adaptation. Imagine holding your breath for just a moment too long, feeling that subtle strain building in your chest, that quiet discomfort that grows until release becomes essential. Now envision that same tension distributed throughout your entire being, sustained across years of unexpressed grief, unprocessed anger, and unacknowledged fear. Your body maintains a constant state of vigilant readiness, always prepared for the next emotional threat that might require immediate suppression.

This chronic activation manifests in remarkably consistent patterns across different men's experiences. Tension headaches become so familiar they feel like old friends rather than warning signals. Jaw pain from unconsciously clenching teeth during difficult conversations transforms into a nightly ritual of grinding that disrupts sleep and erodes enamel. Lower back pain—often the body's metaphor for carrying emotional burdens we refuse to acknowledge—becomes a constant companion that no amount of stretching or massage can fully alleviate.

Sleep becomes an elusive sanctuary as your nervous system struggles to down regulate from its perpetual state of alert readiness. The same hypervigilance that helps you maintain emotional control during waking hours makes it nearly impossible for your body to fully relax when rest is needed. You may find yourself lying awake replaying conversations, analyzing interactions for emotional threats, or simply feeling restless in ways you cannot name or address.

Digestive challenges frequently accompany emotional suppression, as the intricate gut-brain connection responds to psychological stress with physical symptoms that can seem mysteriously unrelated to their emotional origins. The phrase "gut feeling" exists for profound reasons—your intestinal tract contains more nerve cells than your spinal cord and serves as a critical processing center for emotional information your conscious mind might not yet recognize. When we consistently override these gut instincts in service of emotional suppression, digestive dysfunction often follows.

Research consistently demonstrates that men who struggle with emotional expression face elevated rates of cardiovascular disease, autoimmune disorders, and chronic pain conditions. The inflammatory processes triggered by unprocessed emotional stress create cascading effects throughout the body's systems, manifesting as high blood pressure, irregular heart rhythms, compromised immune function, and increased susceptibility to infections and illness.

Perhaps most concerning is the impact on longevity itself. Longitudinal studies following men across decades have revealed that those who struggle with emotional expression and authentic connection face significantly higher mortality rates than their more emotionally expressive counterparts. The armor that promises protection ultimately becomes a burden that diminishes both the quality and quantity of the very life it was meant to preserve.

Mental Manifestations: The Inner Landscape of Silence

The psychological costs of emotional armor reveal themselves gradually, like a slow leak that eventually floods the foundation of your mental well-being. What begins as a protective strategy designed to shield you from emotional pain eventually becomes a prison that limits your capacity for joy, creativity, and authentic self-expression.

Depression in men often bears little resemblance to the stereotypical images of overwhelming sadness and uncontrollable tears. Instead, it frequently manifests as profound numbness, persistent irritability, and a pervasive sense of emptiness that feels like living life through thick fog. When you've spent years systematically disconnecting from your emotional core, the natural consequence is a flattening of your entire emotional spectrum. Joy becomes as inaccessible as sorrow, enthusiasm as distant as despair, wonder as foreign as fear.

This emotional numbing creates what psychologists term "anhedonia"—the inability to experience pleasure in activities that once brought satisfaction and meaning. Life begins to feel like you're watching it happen to someone else, participating mechanically in experiences without accessing their emotional substance. Work loses its sense of purpose, relationships feel hollow and performative, and achievements that once brought pride now feel strangely empty and unsatisfying.

Anxiety frequently accompanies emotional suppression, though it may not be immediately recognized as such. Rather than acknowledging feelings of worry, fear, or uncertainty, many men experience anxiety as physical restlessness, difficulty concentrating, or a persistent sense of unease they struggle to identify or articulate. The energy that would naturally be used to process and express emotions becomes trapped, creating a background hum of tension that colors every interaction and decision.

Cognitive functioning also pays a price when emotional processing becomes compromised. The same neural networks involved in emotional regulation play crucial roles in executive functioning, creative problem-solving, and social cognition. When these systems are chronically suppressed, men often report feeling mentally "foggy," struggling with concentration, and finding it difficult to access their usual problem-solving abilities and innovative thinking.

Perhaps most insidiously, emotional suppression creates a feedback loop of shame and self-criticism that deepens the very patterns it seeks to address. When you notice symptoms of depression, anxiety, or cognitive impairment but lack the emotional vocabulary or cultural permission to explore their roots, these struggles begin to feel like personal failures rather than natural consequences of emotional disconnection. This self-judgment adds yet another layer of stress and further motivation to suppress whatever feelings might be contributing to your difficulties.

Memory itself becomes affected by sustained emotional suppression. Our brains are designed to encode experiences more deeply when they carry emotional significance, creating rich, textured memories that connect us to the meaning and value of our lived experiences. When we routinely disconnect from our feelings, we also disconnect from this richness, leaving behind a collection of facts and events without their accompanying emotional resonance. Many men report feeling like their past is a series of accomplishments and activities without the feelings that would make those experiences truly their own.

Relational Manifestations: The Distance Between Hearts

The relational costs of emotional armor may be the most heartbreaking of all, because they rob us of the very connections that could provide healing, support, and profound meaning. When we lose touch with our own emotional landscape, we inevitably lose the ability to navigate the emotional terrain of others, creating distance in the relationships we most want to nurture and protect.

Intimate partnerships suffer profoundly when emotional armor becomes the primary mode of relating. What appears to others as emotional unavailability or lack of caring often represents a desperate attempt to maintain the protective strategies that once felt essential for psychological survival. The cruel irony is that the very behaviors we developed to avoid emotional pain often create the relationship problems that generate even deeper emotional suffering.

Partners frequently report feeling lonely even when physically together with emotionally suppressed men. Conversations remain trapped at surface levels, focused on practical logistics, problem-solving, or external events rather than the inner experiences that create true intimacy. The deep sharing that builds authentic connection becomes impossible when one person cannot access their emotional truth, creating a cycle where partners may become frustrated or withdrawn, which then confirms the suppressed person's unconscious belief that emotions lead to rejection and abandonment.

Male friendships often develop around shared activities, interests, or professional connections rather than emotional sharing, which can provide meaningful connection while accommodating emotional suppression. However, these relationships frequently lack the depth and mutual support that could be available through more emotionally honest interaction. When crisis strikes—job loss, health challenges, relationship difficulties, or family emergencies—many men discover that their friendships, while genuinely valued, don't provide the emotional support and understanding they desperately need during difficult times.

The impact on children can be particularly profound and far-reaching. Children are natural emotional barometers who learn not just from our explicit teachings but from the patterns we model through our daily interactions. When fathers struggle with emotional expression, their children receive implicit messages about which feelings are acceptable and which must be hidden or denied. Sons may absorb the lesson that emotional suppression is an essential component of masculine identity, while daughters may learn not to expect emotional availability and vulnerability from the men in their lives. These patterns can echo across generations, creating family legacies of emotional distance that feel normal but limit everyone's capacity for authentic connection.

Professional relationships and leadership effectiveness also suffer when emotional intelligence becomes compromised. Modern workplace culture increasingly values emotional awareness, empathetic communication, and collaborative leadership—skills that require the ability to recognize, understand, and appropriately express emotions. Men who struggle with emotional awareness often find themselves at a disadvantage in situations requiring conflict resolution, team motivation, motivational communication, or innovative thinking that draws on emotional insight and interpersonal connection.

Real-World Examples: The Human Face of Emotional Suppression

Understanding the abstract concepts of emotional suppression becomes far more compelling when we witness how these patterns play out in real lives, real relationships, and real consequences. The stories that follow represent composite narratives drawn from therapeutic experiences, research findings, and the lived experiences of countless men who have courageously chosen to examine the hidden costs of their emotional armor.

Michael's Story: When Success Becomes Hollow

Michael entered therapy at forty-five, carrying the external markers of a life well-lived: a thriving legal practice, a beautiful home in an affluent neighborhood, two accomplished children, and a marriage that appeared solid from every external perspective. Yet as he sat in the therapeutic space for the first time, his carefully maintained composure couldn't mask the profound emptiness he described feeling despite his considerable achievements.

"I should be happy," Michael began, his voice carrying the measured tone of someone accustomed to boardroom presentations. *"Everything in my life is exactly what I worked for, what I thought I wanted. But I feel like I'm watching someone else's life through a window. I'm present but not really there, if that makes any sense."*

Michael's story began to unfold as a masterclass in emotional suppression disguised as strength and competence. Raised in a family where achievement equaled worth and emotional expression was viewed as weakness or self-indulgence, Michael learned early that his value lay in his ability to solve problems, meet expectations, and never burden others with his own emotional needs.

When his parents divorced during his senior year of high school—a traumatic disruption that left him reeling with confusion, sadness, and anger—Michael responded by throwing himself into his studies with renewed intensity. While his younger siblings processed their grief through tears, acting out, and seeking comfort, Michael became the family's emotional caretaker, managing logistics, providing practical support, and maintaining the facade that everything was manageable.

"I became the family's emotional Switzerland," Michael reflected. "When Mom was crying about Dad leaving, I researched divorce attorneys and organized financial documents. When my brother was struggling with grades, I found him tutors and study programs. When my sister was having social problems at school, I gave her strategies and advice. I was excellent at fixing everyone else's problems, but I never learned to acknowledge that I had feelings about any of it."

This pattern became Michael's template for navigating all challenging situations throughout his adult life. He excelled in law school not despite emotional stress but because he channeled all difficult feelings into academic achievement. He built his legal career by becoming known for his calm demeanor under pressure, his ability to think clearly during crisis situations, and his skill at helping clients navigate their most difficult moments without becoming "emotionally involved" in their struggles.

These qualities served Michael well professionally and earned him respect, financial success, and a reputation for reliability and competence. However, they came at costs he was only beginning to recognize when he sought therapeutic support.

His marriage to Rebecca had been built on mutual respect, shared goals, and genuine affection, but it lacked the emotional intimacy that could have sustained them through life's inevitable challenges and transitions. Michael loved his family deeply, but he expressed that love through provision, protection, and problem-solving rather than emotional presence and vulnerable sharing. His children learned to approach him with practical questions and achievements to share, but they rarely brought him their fears, disappointments, or emotional struggles.

The awakening came during what should have been a moment of professional triumph. After fifteen years of building toward partnership at his prestigious firm, Michael received the news he had worked tirelessly to achieve. Standing in the senior partner's office, hearing words he had dreamed about for nearly two decades, he felt absolutely nothing—no joy, no satisfaction, no sense of accomplishment or vindication. Just the same hollow numbness that had become his constant, unacknowledged companion.

That evening, when Rebecca asked about his day with excited anticipation, expecting to celebrate this long-awaited achievement, Michael delivered the news with the same emotional tone he might use to report the weather forecast. The look that crossed Rebecca's face at that moment—disappointment mixed with concern and a deep sadness he had never seen before—pierced through his emotional armor in a way that nothing else had.

"Don't you feel anything about this?" she asked quietly. *"Don't you feel anything about anything anymore?"*

The question haunted Michael because he genuinely couldn't answer it. Somewhere along the path of achieving everything he thought he wanted, he had lost access to the feelings that would make any achievement meaningful. Success without the capacity to feel satisfaction becomes just another item to check off a list, and Michael was beginning to recognize that he had been checking off items on his life's to-do list without ever accessing the emotional richness that would make any of it truly fulfilling.

Michael's therapeutic journey involved slowly learning to recognize and tolerate emotions he had been suppressing for decades. The process was neither quick nor comfortable—he experienced physical symptoms as his body began to release years of stored tension, relationship challenges as he learned to be emotionally present with his family, and professional adjustments as he discovered that emotional awareness actually enhanced rather than hindered his effectiveness as an attorney.

The transformation Michael experienced illustrates how emotional suppression can coexist with external success while creating profound internal emptiness. His story demonstrates that emotional armor doesn't just protect us from pain—it also shields us from joy, satisfaction, and the sense of authentic engagement that gives life its deeper meaning and purpose.

David's Story: The Anger That Masked Everything Else

David sought therapeutic support at thirty-eight after his wife Sarah separated from him, citing his *"anger problems"* and emotional unavailability as primary factors in their relationship breakdown. His teenage son had grown distant and uncommunicative, and his circle of friends had gradually shrunk as people grew weary of navigating his unpredictable emotional volatility.

"Everyone tells me I have anger management issues," David explained during our initial session, his jaw tight with frustration and his hands clenched despite his attempts to appear relaxed. *"But the truth is, I don't feel angry most of the time. I feel... nothing. Empty. Then something small happens—someone cuts me off in traffic, my son forgets to take out the trash, Sarah asks me about my day—and suddenly I'm exploding over things that shouldn't matter. I don't understand it, and I hate that I can't control it."*

David's story revealed how emotional suppression can create a pressure-cooker effect where all difficult emotions become converted into anger because it's the only feeling that feels active, powerful, and socially acceptable for men to express. Raised in a working-class household where his father worked multiple jobs and his mother struggled with untreated depression, David learned early that his role was to be strong, helpful, and never add to his parents' considerable burden.

When neighborhood children bullied his younger sister, David learned to fight. When money was tight and bills piled up, David got a part-time job at fourteen to contribute to household expenses. When his mother had particularly difficult days with her depression, David made dinner for his siblings, helped them with homework, and maintained the household routines that kept their family functioning.

"I learned that feelings were a luxury our family couldn't afford," David reflected as his story unfolded. *"There was always some crisis that needed immediate attention, some problem that required action rather than processing. I didn't have time to be sad about Dad never being around, or scared about Mom's crying episodes, or angry about having adult responsibilities as a kid. I just had to handle whatever came up."*

This coping strategy served David remarkably well in many contexts throughout his development. He became incredibly capable, self-reliant, and fiercely protective of others. His work ethic became legendary among his peers, his loyalty to family and friends was unwavering, and his ability to remain functional during crises made him someone others turned to for support and guidance.

However, the emotional suppression that enabled these admirable qualities also created an internal pressure system that would eventually become destructive. David had learned to convert all difficult emotions—sadness, fear, hurt, disappointment, loneliness, shame—into anger because anger felt like action, like power, like something he could use to solve problems and protect what mattered to him.

The pattern manifested clearly in his marriage and family relationships. When Sarah would attempt to discuss concerns about their relationship, David would experience something he couldn't identify—vulnerability, fear of inadequacy, hurt from perceived criticism—but these feelings would immediately transform into anger and defensive responses. *Instead of saying, "I feel scared that you're unhappy with me,"* he would respond with, *"Nothing I do is ever good enough for you."* Rather than acknowledging, *"I feel hurt when you criticize my parenting,"* he would react with, *"You think you're such a perfect mother."*

This emotional translation system created a destructive cycle that gradually eroded the very relationships David most wanted to protect. Sarah would approach him with genuine concerns, hoping for connection and collaborative problem-solving. David would feel threatened by these conversations and respond with anger and defensiveness. Sarah would then withdraw or respond defensively herself, confirming David's unconscious belief that emotional conversations were dangerous territory that should be avoided at all costs.

The physical toll of this pattern had become significant and concerning. David suffered from chronic back pain, frequent headaches, elevated blood pressure, and persistent sleep disturbances—all physical manifestations of the chronic stress created by suppressing complex emotions while maintaining constant hypervigilance for potential threats. His body was essentially living in a state of continuous battle readiness, preparing for conflicts that existed primarily in his nervous system's interpretation of emotional interactions.

David's therapeutic journey involved learning to recognize the early warning signs of emotional activation—the tightness in his chest, the tension in his shoulders, the surge of energy that preceded his angry outbursts—and developing the capacity to pause long enough to identify what he was actually experiencing beneath the anger response.

One particularly transformative session occurred when David was describing a recent conflict with his son about academic performance. As he recounted the story, his familiar pattern of emotional escalation became visible—his voice getting louder, his breathing becoming shallow, his body language becoming more aggressive and intimidating.

I invited David to pause and notice what was happening in his body at that moment. *"My chest feels tight," he said, placing his hand over his heart with surprising gentleness. "And I feel like I need to do something, to fix this problem somehow, to make sure he doesn't mess up his future."*

"What if you weren't responsible for fixing your son's academic challenges?" I asked. *"What if this wasn't a problem that required your intervention? What would you feel then?"*

For a long moment, David sat in uncharacteristic stillness, his hand remaining over his heart as he explored unfamiliar emotional territory. When he spoke again, his voice had changed—softer, more vulnerable, carrying a quality of authentic emotion rather than defensive anger.

"I would feel scared," he admitted quietly. "Terrified, actually. Scared that he's going to make the same mistakes I did, that he won't get the opportunities I never had, that he'll struggle the way I struggled. Scared that I don't know how to help him without being controlling. Scared that I'm failing as a father."

This recognition—that his anger often served as armor protecting much more vulnerable emotions like fear, sadness, and uncertainty—opened entirely new possibilities for David's relationships and emotional development. Instead of approaching his son with criticism and demands for better performance, David learned to share his concerns and fears directly. Rather than fighting with Sarah about her "complaints," he began to acknowledge when her feedback triggered his own insecurities and fears about being inadequate as a partner.

David's story illustrates how emotional suppression can create patterns where all complex emotions get filtered through the single outlet that feels acceptable, creating destructive cycles that damage the very relationships we most want to protect and nurture.

James's Story: The Loneliness of Being Everyone's Rock

James contacted therapeutic support through his employee assistance program after what he described as "the worst week of my life"—a period that had shattered his carefully maintained image as someone who could handle any crisis with calm competence. At thirty-one, James worked as a paramedic, a profession that had earned him the nickname "The Rock" among his colleagues for his ability to remain composed and effective during the most traumatic emergencies.

But when his own crisis struck—his father's sudden death from a massive heart attack—James discovered that the emotional skills he had never developed left him completely unprepared to navigate his own grief and loss.

"I've helped hundreds of families through their worst moments," James shared during our initial conversation, his voice steady but his hands trembling almost imperceptibly. "I know exactly what to say to a mother whose child has been in an accident, or a husband whose wife is fighting for her life in the ICU. I can remain calm and supportive when other people are falling apart. But I have absolutely no idea how to handle my own feelings about losing my dad."

James's professional competence had become both his greatest strength and his most significant limitation. His ability to compartmentalize emotions, remain focused under extreme pressure, and provide steady support to others in crisis had made him exceptionally effective in his work. However, the emotional suppression that served him well professionally had become his only strategy for managing difficult feelings in every area of his life.

Raised in a military family where emotional expression was seen as weakness and self-discipline was considered the highest virtue, James learned early to push through difficult feelings rather than processing or acknowledging them. When his parents divorced during his deployment in Afghanistan, he received the devastating news through an email and had to report for duty just one hour later. When his beloved grandfather passed away while James was completing paramedic training, he attended the funeral service and returned to his certification studies the following day, determined not to let personal grief interfere with his professional goals.

"I thought being strong meant never letting emotions get in the way of doing what needed to be done," James explained as his story unfolded. "Never showing weakness, never letting feelings cloud your judgment, never burdening others with your personal struggles. And it worked, for a long time. I could handle anything that came my way without falling apart."

But his father's death overwhelmed James's well-developed suppression strategies. The grief was too powerful to compartmentalize, too persistent to ignore, and too complex to resolve through action alone. For the first time in his adult life, James found himself crying uncontrollably, unable to sleep, struggling to concentrate at work, and feeling completely overwhelmed by emotions he had no tools to process or express.

The isolation James experienced during this period revealed another hidden cost of emotional suppression—the profound loneliness that comes from having relationships built around your capacity to give support rather than your ability to receive it. James had many colleagues who respected and appreciated him, as well as several close friends who genuinely cared about him, but all of these relationships were built on shared activities, mutual respect, and James' role as a dependable, consistent presence for others during their own difficult times.

When James tried to talk about his grief, conversations would quickly shift to practical concerns—funeral arrangements, his father's estate, work scheduling adjustments—rather than the emotional territory he desperately needed to explore and process. His friends and colleagues cared about him deeply, but they had no framework for supporting him emotionally because that had never been the nature of their relationships.

"I realized I had spent my entire adult life learning how to take care of other people, but I had never learned how to let other people take care of me," James reflected with painful insight. "I was great at providing support, but I had no idea how to receive it. I didn't even know what I needed, let alone how to ask for it."

This pattern of emotional self-reliance had influenced all of James's intimate relationships as well. His romantic relationships typically followed a predictable trajectory: initial attraction based on his strength, reliability, and apparent emotional stability, followed by gradual frustration from partners who felt excluded from his inner world, and eventual breakups when deeper intimacy required more emotional vulnerability than James could access or provide.

His friendships with other men, while genuine and valued, remained largely surface-level. They would exercise together, attend sporting events, help each other with practical projects, and provide companionship and shared interests, but they rarely ventured into conversations about feelings, fears, dreams, or emotional struggles. James began to recognize that he was surrounded by people who cared about him but felt fundamentally alone in his emotional experience.

The physical toll of his isolation and suppressed grief became increasingly evident. James had always maintained excellent physical fitness as part of his professional requirements, but chronic stress and emotional suppression were beginning to affect his health in ways that exercise couldn't address. He was drinking more alcohol to help him sleep, his appetite had diminished significantly, and he was getting sick more frequently than ever before—his immune system compromised by the constant stress of suppressing overwhelming emotions.

James's therapeutic journey involved learning that emotional strength isn't characterized by the absence of difficult feelings, but by the capacity to experience emotions fully while maintaining your ability to function and connect authentically with others. True strength includes the courage to be vulnerable when appropriate, the wisdom to seek support when needed, and the self-awareness to recognize and honor your own emotional needs.

One of the most transformative moments in James's healing occurred when he attended a grief support group for people who had lost parents. Initially, sitting in a circle with others who were openly crying, sharing intimate details of their relationships with their deceased parents, and expressing raw anger, confusion, and profound sadness felt completely foreign and uncomfortable. Everything in James's conditioning suggested that this was weakness, that he should be helping these people rather than joining them in their vulnerability.

But as he listened to their stories with the same compassionate attention he brought to his work, something profound shifted in his understanding. He began to recognize his own experience reflected in their narratives—the regret over conversations never had, the sudden awareness of mortality and impermanence, the complex mixture of love and loss that accompanies the death of a parent. When his turn came to share, James spoke for the first time not as a professional helper but as a son processing grief, not as someone with answers but as someone seeking understanding and connection.

"I realized that being strong enough to feel my pain without trying to fix it or escape it was actually more difficult than pushing through it," James said later, capturing the essence of his transformation. "It took more courage to sit with my grief and let others witness it than it did to handle it alone. And for the first time since Dad died, I wasn't carrying it by myself."

James's journey toward emotional health didn't require abandoning his professional competence or his ability to remain calm during emergencies. Instead, it involved developing emotional flexibility—the capacity to access different emotional skills depending on the situation and context. He could continue being The Rock for his patients and colleagues when that was what was needed professionally, while also learning to be vulnerable, authentic, and emotionally present in his personal relationships when that was what would serve connection and healing.

The Ripple Effects: Understanding the Broader Impact

These deeply personal stories illuminate how emotional suppression creates expanding circles of influence that extend far beyond individual experience, touching every relationship, every goal, every moment of potential connection and joy. What begins as a protective strategy in childhood or adolescence gradually becomes a limiting factor that constrains not only personal fulfillment but also our capacity to contribute meaningfully to the lives of others.

The physical health implications alone represent a profound cost that our healthcare system is only beginning to recognize and address effectively. The connection between emotional suppression and stress-related health conditions—cardiovascular disease, autoimmune dysfunction, chronic pain syndromes, sleep disorders, digestive problems—suggests that many men receiving treatment for physical symptoms could benefit enormously from addressing the emotional suppression that contributes to their bodily distress.

Mental health consequences create their own complex web of challenges that often go unrecognized because they don't fit traditional models of psychological distress. Depression in men frequently manifests as irritability, restlessness, and emotional numbing rather than obvious sadness. Anxiety may appear as physical tension, difficulty concentrating, or generalized restlessness rather than recognizable worry or fear. When the root cause—emotional suppression—remains unaddressed, treatment often focuses on symptoms rather than underlying patterns.

Perhaps most tragically, the relational costs of emotional armor tend to perpetuate themselves across generations, creating family legacies of emotional distance that feel normal but limit everyone's potential for authentic connection and mutual support. Children who grow up with emotionally suppressed fathers absorb implicit lessons about which emotions are acceptable, which feelings are dangerous, and what it means to be strong in a world that seems to punish vulnerability.

Yet understanding these costs also illuminates the tremendous potential for healing, growth, and positive change. When men develop the capacity for emotional awareness and authentic expression, the benefits ripple outward just as powerfully as the original suppression did. Physical health often improves dramatically, mental clarity and creativity expand, and relationships deepen in ways that seemed impossible when emotions were forbidden territory.

The journey from emotional suppression to emotional fluency isn't about abandoning strength, competence, or traditional masculine qualities that serve us well. Instead, it's about expanding our range of responses to include the full spectrum of human experience and emotional intelligence. It's about recognizing that true strength includes the courage to feel deeply, the wisdom to express emotions appropriately and constructively, and the humility to seek support and connection when it serves our highest good and the good of those we love.

In the chapters that follow, we'll explore how to begin dismantling the armor that no longer serves your authentic self-expression, not by leaving yourself defenseless, but by replacing outdated protection with more sophisticated, flexible, and effective ways of navigating our complex emotional landscape. The cost of emotional suppression is real and significant, but equally real is the possibility of profound healing, authentic connection, and a life lived with greater depth, meaning, and joy.

The awareness you've gained by recognizing these patterns in your own life represents the first courageous step toward transformation. Your emotions aren't obstacles to overcome or weaknesses to hide—they are essential sources of information, wisdom, and connection that can guide you toward your most authentic and fulfilled self. The armor that once protected you can be consciously transformed into the emotional intelligence that will empower you to create the relationships, achievements, and sense of purpose that align with your deepest values and aspirations.

Prompt: What are your typical reactions when you're feeling stressed, anxious, or low?

Chapter 2: Where It Comes From

The patterns of emotional silence that define so many men's lives didn't emerge in isolation—they were carefully cultivated through generations of unspoken teachings, shaped by the invisible hands of family legacy and cultural expectation. Like ancient rivers that carve canyons through stone, these influences have carved deep channels in our emotional landscape, creating pathways that feel as natural as breathing yet as constraining as prison walls.

Understanding the origins of emotional suppression is not an exercise in blame or victimization, but rather an act of powerful liberation. When we can see clearly how these patterns were formed, we begin to recognize that they are not immutable truths about masculinity but learned responses that can be consciously examined, honored for their protective intentions, and transformed when they no longer serve our authentic growth and connection.

Our journey of discovery takes us into the deeper understanding of ourselves, and the generations that came before us, illuminating the complex web of influences that shaped our emotional blueprint. In this exploration, we find not only the roots of our limitations but also the seeds of our potential healing and transformation.

Family Dynamics, Societal Expectations, and Gender Norms: The Architecture of Emotional Silence

The Foundation: Early Family Teachings

Your emotional education began long before you could form conscious memories, embedded in the thousand small interactions that taught you which feelings were welcome and which were dangerous. These early lessons arrived not through formal instruction but through the subtle dance of family dynamics—the slight stiffening of a parent's body when you cried, the gentle redirection away from feelings toward action, the unconscious modeling of emotional patterns that became the template for your own approach to inner experience.

Every family operates as an emotional ecosystem, with unspoken rules about which emotions can be safely expressed and which must remain hidden. In many families, these rules developed over generations, passed down like inherited traditions that nobody consciously chose but everyone unconsciously perpetuated. Perhaps your father learned from his father that sadness was something to endure privately, that fear was weakness to be conquered rather than information to be honored, that love was best expressed through provision rather than words.

The messages you received about emotions were often wrapped in loving intentions. When a parent said, "You're okay, don't cry," they were attempting to comfort you, to help you move past pain quickly. When they praised you for being "the strong one" during family difficulties, they were recognizing your resilience and capability. Yet these well-meaning responses created profound learning experiences about which emotions were valued and which were seen as problems to be solved rather than experiences to be honored.

Consider how different emotional responses were met in your family of origin. Joy and excitement might have been welcomed up to a certain point, but perhaps discouraged when they became "too much." Anger might have been acceptable if directed at appropriate targets but forbidden if it challenged family authority. Sadness might have been tolerated briefly but met with discomfort if it lingered beyond what seemed reasonable to adult perspectives.

The structure of family roles also played a crucial part in your emotional development. If you were cast as the responsible one, you learned that your job was to manage not only your own emotions but to help regulate the emotional climate for others. If you were seen as the sensitive one, you might have learned that this trait was simultaneously valued and problematic, something that made you special but also vulnerable in a world that didn't always reward sensitivity.

Birth order added another layer of complexity to your emotional learning. As an eldest child, you might have received messages about setting a good example, being strong for younger siblings, and carrying the weight of family expectations. Middle children often learned to navigate emotional territory by finding unique niches or by becoming skilled at reading and responding to others' emotional needs. Youngest children sometimes discovered that their emotions were either dismissed as less significant or that they needed to be particularly dramatic to receive attention and care.

Family trauma—whether acknowledged or hidden in silence—created particularly complex emotional learning environments. In homes where addiction, mental illness, abuse, or other serious challenges existed, children developed sophisticated early warning systems, learning to read emotional weather patterns and adjust their own expressions accordingly. You might have learned that your own sadness felt dangerous because it resembled a depressed parent's withdrawal. Your anger might have felt terrifying because it echoed an abusive parent's rage. Your fear might have seemed like a luxury the family couldn't afford when survival required constant vigilance and strength.

The Cultural Framework: Messages from the Wider World

Beyond your immediate family, the broader culture was teaching you profound lessons about masculine emotional expression through every interaction, every story, every image you encountered. These cultural messages permeated your experience so thoroughly that they felt like natural law rather than learned perspectives that could be questioned or challenged.

From the earliest ages, toys, games, and activities were subtly gendered in ways that shaped emotional development. Boys' toys often emphasized action, competition, and problem-solving rather than emotional expression and nurturing. The heroes in your childhood stories typically demonstrated strength through emotional control, solving problems through action rather than feeling, maintaining composure even in the most challenging circumstances. While these qualities have genuine value, when they become the only acceptable template for masculine behavior, they create a narrow corridor for emotional expression that excludes vast territories of human experience.

Educational environments contributed their own layers of emotional instruction, often treating boys and girls differently when it came to emotional expression. A boy who cried at school might have been told to "toughen up" or been separated from peers to prevent "disruption," while similar emotional expression from girls was more likely to be met with comfort and support. These differential responses taught powerful lessons about whose emotions were welcome in public spaces and whose needed to be managed privately or suppressed entirely.

Sports culture, which played a formative role in many men's development, reinforced these patterns through its emphasis on mental toughness, playing through pain, and maintaining focus under pressure. While these qualities can be tremendously valuable, they can also teach that acknowledging discomfort—whether physical or emotional—represents weakness, that seeking support means giving up, and that individual suffering should be endured silently for the good of the team.

Religious and spiritual communities, though often providing valuable moral guidance and community connection, sometimes transmitted messages about masculine strength that emphasized stoicism, sacrifice, and endurance over emotional processing and authentic expression. Images of suffering in silence, bearing burdens without complaint, and finding strength through suppression could become internalized as spiritual requirements rather than optional approaches to handling life's challenges.

Media representations throughout your development consistently showed male heroes who demonstrated strength through emotional control, who could endure torture without breaking, who saved others while never needing to be saved themselves. These images created powerful templates for masculine behavior that left little room for vulnerability, interdependence, or the kind of emotional expression that fosters genuine intimacy and connection.

Economic factors also shaped your emotional development in significant ways. If your family faced financial stress, you might have learned that emotions were luxuries that couldn't be afforded, that your job was to contribute to family survival rather than to process your own emotional needs. In communities where economic opportunities were limited, emotional suppression might have felt like a necessary survival strategy, a way of maintaining the strength and focus required to overcome difficult circumstances.

The Reinforcement System: Peer Relationships and Social Hierarchies

As you moved beyond your family of origin, peer relationships became increasingly influential in reinforcing or challenging the emotional patterns you had learned. The social hierarchies that emerged in childhood and adolescence often created powerful incentives to maintain emotional suppression while punishing vulnerability through teasing, exclusion, or social demotion.

Male peer groups developed their own unspoken rules about emotional expression, enforced through subtle and not-so-subtle forms of social pressure. Boys learned quickly which emotions could be safely shared (often limited to anger, excitement, or humor) and which ones invited ridicule or social rejection (sadness, fear, tenderness, or uncertainty). These peer dynamics didn't develop in isolation—they reflected and amplified the broader cultural messages about masculinity that boys had been absorbing throughout their development.

The language that boys used with each other often reinforced emotional suppression through insults that targeted perceived emotional weakness. Terms like "crybaby," "sissy," or "mama's boy" taught that emotional expression was associated with femininity and that femininity was something to be avoided at all costs. This association between emotion and femininity created a double bind where boys learned to reject not only their own emotional expression but to devalue emotional intelligence more broadly.

Adolescent romantic relationships added another layer of complexity to emotional development. Many teenage boys received conflicting messages about emotional expression in romantic contexts—they were expected to be sensitive enough to be appealing to potential partners but not so emotional that they seemed weak or unstable. This created a narrow band of acceptable emotional expression that required constant navigation and calibration, often leading to performance rather than authenticity in intimate relationships.

Academic environments continued to shape emotional patterns as boys became young men. Competitive educational systems often rewarded analytical thinking over emotional intelligence, suggesting that feelings were obstacles to clear reasoning rather than valuable sources of information and wisdom. The emphasis on objective analysis, logical problem-solving, and intellectual achievement could create an implicit hierarchy where emotional intelligence was seen as less valuable or sophisticated than cognitive abilities.

Case Studies: Generational Silence and Inherited Emotional Habits

The most profound understanding of how emotional suppression patterns perpetuate across generations comes through witnessing their transmission in real families, real relationships, and real lives. The stories that follow represent composites drawn from therapeutic work, research findings, and the lived experiences of men who have courageously chosen to examine their emotional inheritance with both appreciation and critical awareness.

The Thompson Legacy: Three Generations of Silent Strength

The Thompson family story begins with Robert Thompson, born in 1940 into a working-class family in the industrial Midwest. Robert's childhood was shaped by economic uncertainty, his father's long hours at the steel mill, and a family culture that valued hard work, personal responsibility, and emotional self-reliance above all else. In this environment, Robert learned that emotions were obstacles to overcome rather than information to honor, that his primary value lay in his ability to work hard and ask for nothing in return.

Robert's emotional education occurred primarily through observation and absence. His father, exhausted from physically demanding work, had little energy left for emotional connection when he returned home each evening. Conversations focused on practical matters—work, money, immediate problems that needed solving—rather than feelings, dreams, or inner experiences. When Robert experienced disappointment about missing school activities due to family financial constraints, he was reminded that "life isn't fair" and that dwelling on feelings wouldn't change circumstances.

This early training served Robert well in many respects as he built his adult life. His ability to work consistently without complaining, to solve problems without becoming overwhelmed by emotions, and to provide steadily for his family enabled him to achieve the economic stability his own childhood had lacked. When Robert married Dorothy and started his family in the 1960s, these qualities made him a reliable husband and father who could be counted on to meet his family's practical needs.

However, Robert's emotional suppression also created costs that would echo through subsequent generations. His marriage to Dorothy, while stable and respectful, lacked the emotional intimacy that could have sustained them through the inevitable challenges of long-term partnership. Robert loved his family deeply, but he expressed that love through provision and protection rather than affection and emotional presence. His children learned to interpret his care through his actions—the long hours he worked to provide for them, the sacrifices he made for their opportunities—rather than through direct emotional communication.

Robert's approach to fatherhood reflected his own upbringing in ways he never consciously examined. When his children came to him with emotional struggles, he responded with practical advice and problem-solving rather than emotional validation and support. If his daughter Sarah was upset about friendship difficulties at school, Robert would suggest strategies for handling the situation rather than first acknowledging and validating her emotional experience. When his son Michael struggled with anxiety about academic performance, Robert would remind him about the importance of hard work and persistence rather than exploring the underlying fears and pressures Michael was experiencing.

Robert's son Michael, born in 1965, inherited both the strengths and limitations of his father's approach while growing up in a very different cultural and economic context. The 1970s and 1980s offered Michael opportunities his father never had—higher education, professional career possibilities, and material advantages that previous generations could only dream about. Yet Michael also inherited his family's pattern of emotional suppression, adapted to new circumstances but fundamentally unchanged in its essential character.

Michael excelled academically and professionally, driven by internal standards that left little room for acknowledging struggle, uncertainty, or emotional needs. He learned to channel difficult emotions into achievement, transforming anxiety into motivation, disappointment into determination, and loneliness into focused work. These adaptations served him well in competitive academic and professional environments, but they also maintained the family pattern of emotional disconnection.

Michael's romantic relationships followed predictable patterns that reflected his emotional inheritance. He was attracted to partners who appreciated his reliability, ambition, and apparent emotional stability, but these relationships often struggled when deeper emotional intimacy was required. His first marriage ended when his wife, Jennifer, felt increasingly lonely despite being married to a successful and dependable man.

"It's like being married to a ghost," Jennifer told him during their separation. "You're physically present, but emotionally you're somewhere else entirely. I never know what you're really thinking or feeling about anything that matters."

This feedback devastated Michael in ways he initially couldn't understand or articulate. He had followed all the rules he had learned about being a good husband—working hard, providing well, being faithful and responsible—yet it hadn't been sufficient. The failure of his marriage forced Michael to confront the emotional limitations he had inherited, though he initially approached this challenge as another problem to be solved rather than a pattern to be understood and transformed.

Michael's son David, born in 1990, represents the third generation of Thompson men to inherit this complex emotional legacy. Growing up in the digital age with access to information about emotional intelligence and mental health that previous generations never had, David is more consciously aware of emotional dynamics than his father or grandfather were at his age. However, conscious awareness doesn't automatically translate into different emotional patterns, and David finds himself struggling with many of the same limitations that constrained his predecessors.

David's childhood was materially comfortable but emotionally complicated. Michael, having learned from his divorce that emotional availability mattered in relationships, made conscious efforts to be more emotionally present with his son than his own father had been with him. However, Michael's attempts at emotional connection were often awkward and inconsistent, like attempting to speak a foreign language he had studied but never become fluent in using.

The result for David has been a mixed inheritance—he received more emotional attention than previous generations of Thompson men, but that attention came filtered through his father's own emotional limitations and discomfort with vulnerable territory. David learned that emotions were important, but he didn't develop the actual skills required to navigate them effectively. He understood intellectually that vulnerability was necessary for authentic connection, but he hadn't developed the emotional resilience required to sustain genuine openness with others.

David's struggles manifest differently than his father's and grandfather's had. While they suppressed emotions through work and achievement, David suppresses them through analysis and intellectualization. He can discuss emotional concepts with sophisticated language and insight, but he struggles to actually feel and express emotions in real time with real people. His romantic relationships often begin with promise but encounter difficulties when partners discover that his emotional sophistication is more theoretical than experiential.

The Thompson family story illustrates several crucial insights about how emotional suppression patterns persist across generations. Each generation adapted the family's emotional patterns to their contemporary circumstances without fundamentally transforming them. Robert's stoic silence became Michael's achievement-oriented emotional distance, which became David's intellectual approach to emotional avoidance. The surface expressions changed, but the underlying pattern of emotional suppression remained consistent across three generations.

The Rodriguez Experience: Cultural Heritage and Emotional Complexity

The Rodriguez family's relationship with emotional expression reflects the intricate intersection between cultural heritage, immigration experiences, and generational adaptation. Carlos Rodriguez, born in 1945 in rural Mexico, grew up immersed in traditional concepts of masculinity that emphasized honor, family responsibility, and the capacity to endure hardship without complaint. These cultural values served essential functions in his community, where men's ability to maintain dignity under difficult circumstances was crucial for family survival and social cohesion.

Carlos's understanding of masculine strength was deeply rooted in cultural traditions that had evolved over centuries. Emotional suppression wasn't viewed as limitation but as a necessary skill for navigating a world where vulnerability could be dangerous. Men were expected to embody strength not just for themselves but for their entire extended family networks, serving as pillars of stability that others could depend upon during times of crisis or uncertainty.

When Carlos immigrated to the United States in 1968, these cultural patterns encountered new challenges and pressures that tested their effectiveness in different contexts. The immigration process itself required enormous emotional resilience—leaving behind family, friends, and familiar ways of life while adapting to a new culture, language, and economic system. Carlos learned to navigate discrimination and economic uncertainty while maintaining his role as family protector and provider, a responsibility that required setting aside his own fears and uncertainties for the sake of his family's stability and success.

Carlos's emotional suppression served his family remarkably well during the challenging early years in America. His ability to work multiple jobs without complaining, to endure workplace discrimination without allowing it to affect his family relationships, and to maintain optimism about his family's future despite significant obstacles helped establish the foundation for his children's opportunities and success. These qualities enabled him to achieve what many immigrants dream of—economic stability, homeownership, and educational opportunities for his children that exceeded what would have been possible in his country of origin.

However, the same strengths that enabled Carlos's success also created emotional distance within his family that would influence subsequent generations. Carlos expressed love and care primarily through sacrifice and provision rather than through verbal affection or emotional openness. His children understood that their father cared deeply about their success and well-being, but this care was communicated through actions—long work hours to pay for their education, careful saving for family goals, consistent presence at important events—rather than through direct emotional expression.

Carlos's relationship with his son Roberto, born in 1975, reflected the complex dynamics that occur when traditional cultural patterns encounter changing social expectations. Roberto grew up bilingual and bicultural, equally comfortable in his father's Mexican heritage and the broader American culture of his peers. This cultural fluidity created both opportunities and conflicts around emotional expression that his father had never had to navigate.

Within his family context, Roberto learned his father's lessons about dignity, responsibility, and emotional control. He understood that expressing weakness or vulnerability could be seen as failing to honor the sacrifices his parents had made for his opportunities. Roberto learned to interpret his father's love through actions and sacrifices rather than through words or emotional availability, and he developed his own capacity for hard work, persistence, and emotional self-reliance.

However, Roberto's school and social environments exposed him to different models of emotional expression that sometimes conflicted with his family's cultural patterns. Teachers encouraged students to express their feelings and seek help when needed. Peer relationships sometimes required emotional vulnerability that felt uncomfortable and unfamiliar. Romantic relationships with partners from different cultural backgrounds introduced expectations about emotional availability and communication that Roberto struggled to meet without feeling like he was betraying his cultural heritage.

This cultural complexity created internal tensions for Roberto that his father had never experienced. Roberto valued the strength and resilience he had learned from his family's cultural traditions, but he also recognized that these same qualities sometimes limited his capacity for the kind of intimate connection that his romantic relationships required. Roberto found himself caught between honoring his cultural heritage and developing the emotional skills necessary for success in his professional and personal relationships.

Furthermore, Roberto's approach to raising his own son, Alex, born in 2005, reflects his conscious attempt to integrate the valuable aspects of his cultural inheritance while addressing its potential limitations. Roberto deliberately maintained cultural traditions around family loyalty, hard work, and personal responsibility while also encouraging more direct emotional communication than he had experienced in his own childhood.

Alex grows up in a household where cultural pride and emotional awareness coexist in sometimes complex ways. Roberto shares stories of his grandfather's courage and perseverance while also encouraging Alex to talk about his feelings and seek support when needed. This integration creates both opportunities and challenges for Alex, who sometimes feels caught between different expectations about masculine behavior and emotional expression.

The Rodriguez family story illustrates how cultural heritage adds profound layers of meaning to emotional suppression patterns. While each generation has made conscious attempts to adapt to changing circumstances and expectations, core cultural values about masculine strength and emotional control have persisted in modified forms. The challenge for families like the Rodriguez family is learning to preserve valuable cultural traditions while also developing the emotional flexibility necessary for thriving in contemporary relationships and professional environments.

The Williams Transformation: Breaking Cycles Through Consciousness

The Williams family represents a more successful attempt to transform inherited patterns of emotional suppression, though their journey illustrates that such transformation requires conscious effort, therapeutic support, and multiple generations of committed work. Thomas Williams, born in 1950, grew up in an African American family in the rural South during an era when emotional suppression was not just culturally expected but often essential for physical safety and social survival.

Thomas's childhood was shaped by the realities of racial segregation and economic inequality, circumstances that required extraordinary emotional resilience from Black families. His parents, who had grown up during even more dangerous times, taught him that emotional expression could be hazardous, that showing anger could provoke retaliation, that demonstrating fear could invite further victimization, and that expressing sadness could be perceived as weakness that others might exploit.

The emotional suppression that Thomas learned wasn't just about masculine expectations—it was about survival in a hostile social environment. His family taught him to "keep your business to yourself," to "never let them see you sweat," and to "be twice as good to get half as much"—lessons that required enormous emotional control and self-regulation. These survival strategies enabled Thomas to navigate integrated schools where he was often the only Black student, to succeed in workplaces where racial discrimination was commonplace, and to build a stable career in education despite facing obstacles that would have defeated less emotionally resilient individuals.

Thomas's emotional suppression served crucial protective functions throughout his adult life. His ability to maintain composure under pressure helped him succeed in professional environments where any sign of anger or frustration could have been used against him. His capacity to process stress privately enabled him to shield his family from the daily indignities he faced while building a successful career. His emotional self-control allowed him to model strength and dignity for his children, teaching them that they could overcome obstacles through persistence and character.

However, Thomas's emotional suppression also created costs within his family relationships that he didn't initially recognize or understand. His wife Patricia often felt excluded from his inner experience, unable to provide emotional support because Thomas couldn't acknowledge his own emotional needs. Thomas expressed love and care through provision and protection, but he struggled to create the emotional intimacy that could have deepened his marriage and family relationships.

The transformative moment in the Williams family's emotional evolution came when Thomas's son Kenneth, born in 1980, experienced a severe depression during his senior year of college. Kenneth had inherited his father's strength and determination, but he had also inherited the family pattern of emotional suppression that left him ill-equipped to handle the pressures of academic achievement, social discrimination, and relationship challenges that accumulated beyond his capacity to manage privately.

Kenneth's depression crisis forced the entire family to confront the limitations of their emotional strategies. Initially, Thomas viewed his son's depression as weakness to be overcome through willpower and determination, an attitude that reflected his own training in emotional suppression. However, when Kenneth's depression worsened despite his efforts to "tough it out," Thomas was forced to reconsider whether the emotional patterns that had served his own survival were adequate for his son's different challenges.

The family's experience with Kenneth's therapy became a catalyst for broader emotional transformation. Through family therapy sessions, Thomas began to understand how his own emotional suppression, while adaptive in his historical context, had created limitations for his children who were growing up under different circumstances. He learned that the emotional control that had protected him from racial violence was now preventing the kind of intimate family connection that could support his son's healing.

Thomas's willingness to examine and modify his own emotional patterns, even in his fifties, created new possibilities for his family's emotional development. He began sharing more of his own experiences with discrimination and trauma, helping his children understand the historical context of his emotional reserve while also acknowledging the ways it had limited their family's emotional connection.

Kenneth's recovery involved learning to appreciate the strength and resilience he had inherited from his father while also developing emotional vocabulary and expression skills necessary for managing his mental health. Kenneth came to understand that his depression wasn't a personal failure but rather a signal that he needed different emotional tools than the ones he had inherited, tools that could honor his family's legacy of strength while also allowing for vulnerability and help-seeking when appropriate.

When Kenneth became a father to his son Marcus, born in 2010, he was determined to create a different emotional legacy while still honoring the valuable aspects of his family's heritage. Kenneth deliberately worked to maintain the values of strength, perseverance, and family loyalty he had learned from his father while also encouraging emotional expression and help-seeking when needed.

Marcus grows up knowing stories of his grandfather's courage and resilience while also learning that emotional expression is a form of strength rather than weakness. He understands that seeking help when needed honors his ancestors' struggles rather than betraying them. Most importantly, Marcus develops in a family system that values emotional honesty while maintaining deep respect for the survival strategies that enabled previous generations to overcome extraordinary challenges.

The Williams family story demonstrates that inherited patterns of emotional suppression can be consciously transformed when families are willing to examine their emotional heritage with both appreciation and critical awareness. Their journey illustrates that breaking generational cycles doesn't require rejecting everything that came before, but rather choosing consciously which patterns to maintain and which need to be adapted for contemporary circumstances and relationships.

Understanding the Inheritance: Patterns of Transmission and Transformation

These family narratives illuminate several crucial insights about how emotional suppression patterns develop, persist, and can be transformed across generations:

Adaptive Origins: Every pattern of emotional suppression originally served protective functions, whether shielding individuals from family chaos, cultural discrimination, economic uncertainty, or social rejection. Understanding these protective origins helps reduce shame and blame while creating space for conscious choice about which patterns to maintain.

Cultural Complexity: Cultural heritage adds layers of meaning to emotional patterns that can make change feel like betrayal of family values or cultural identity. Successful transformation requires honoring valuable cultural traditions while developing emotional flexibility for contemporary contexts.

Generational Adaptation: Each generation typically adapts inherited emotional patterns to their contemporary circumstances without fundamentally transforming them. Surface expressions may change while underlying suppression patterns persist in modified forms.

Conscious Interruption: Breaking inherited patterns requires conscious recognition of their existence and deliberate effort to develop alternative approaches. This transformation usually occurs gradually across multiple generations rather than within a single lifetime.

Integration Over Rejection: The most successful approaches to transforming emotional inheritance involve integrating valuable aspects of family heritage while developing new emotional skills, rather than completely rejecting everything from previous generations.

Understanding where your emotional patterns come from provides the foundation for the healing work that lies ahead. These patterns weren't chosen consciously, and they developed within family and cultural contexts that made perfect sense given the circumstances your ancestors faced. The courage required to examine and potentially transform these patterns honors both your own growth and the love that motivated previous generations to protect you in the only ways they knew how.

In the chapters that follow, we'll explore how to begin the delicate work of transformation—learning to appreciate the protective wisdom of emotional suppression while developing new capacities for emotional awareness, expression, and authentic connection. This journey doesn't require abandoning your heritage or rejecting the strength you've inherited, but rather expanding your emotional repertoire to include the full spectrum of human experience and wisdom.

Your willingness to understand these patterns represents the first step toward breaking cycles that may have limited your family for generations. This understanding creates the possibility for you to become not just the inheritor of your family's emotional legacy, but its conscious transformer, creating new patterns that honor the past while serving the fullest expression of who you're meant to become.

Reflection: What are some early emotional wounds that may still influence me today?

Chapter 3: Breaking the Cycle

The moment of recognition arrives differently for every man—sometimes as a whisper in the quiet hours of the night, sometimes as a thunderclap during a moment of crisis, and sometimes as a gentle awakening that unfolds gradually over months or years. This recognition carries within it both heartfelt challenge and extraordinary hope: the understanding that the emotional patterns you've carried for decades are not immutable truths about your nature, but learned responses that can be consciously reformed.

This chapter marks the beginning of your active journey toward emotional freedom—not the abandonment of your strength or the rejection of your masculine identity, but the expansion of your emotional repertoire to include the full spectrum of human experience and wisdom. Here, we move from understanding why emotional suppression developed to actively dismantling the barriers that separate you from authentic connection with yourself and others.

The journey you're embarking upon requires both courage and compassion—courage to face patterns that have defined your approach to life, and compassion to honor the protective intentions these patterns once served. You are not broken or deficient; you are courageously choosing to evolve beyond limitations that no longer serve your highest good or deepest aspirations.

Recognizing the Patterns: Illuminating the Invisible Architecture

The first step in breaking cycles of emotional suppression involves developing the capacity to recognize these patterns as they operate in real time within your daily experience. Like learning to see the underlying structure of a building that has always appeared solid and seamless, emotional awareness begins with identifying the subtle signs that indicate when suppression is occurring and understanding how these patterns manifest in your thoughts, feelings, physical sensations, and behaviors.

The Physical Landscape: Your Body as Emotional Messenger

Your body serves as an exquisitely sensitive instrument for detecting emotional suppression, often registering the presence of feelings long before your conscious mind recognizes them. Learning to read these physical signals creates an early warning system that can help you catch emotional patterns before they become fully entrenched in suppression or explosive release.

Pay attention to the subtle tightening that occurs in your jaw during difficult conversations—this often signals anger or frustration that you're not fully acknowledging. Notice when your shoulders creep toward your ears without conscious intention, frequently indicating stress, anxiety, or the effort required to carry emotional burdens you haven't fully recognized. Observe the shallow breathing that sometimes accompanies emotionally challenging situations, as if your body is preparing to minimize the impact of feelings that feel too dangerous to experience fully.

Your digestive system often responds to emotional stress in ways that seem mysterious until you begin recognizing the patterns. The knot in your stomach during conflict, the loss of appetite when facing difficult decisions, or the sudden need to eat when emotions feel overwhelming can all serve as valuable information about your internal emotional state. These physical responses aren't obstacles to overcome but messengers bringing important information about your inner experience.

Sleep patterns frequently reflect emotional suppression in ways that reveal the constant energy required to maintain emotional control. If you find yourself lying awake replaying conversations, analyzing interactions for potential emotional threats, or feeling restless without understanding why, your nervous system may be working overtime to process emotions you're not consciously acknowledging during waking hours.

Chronic pain or recurring physical symptoms that have no clear medical explanation sometimes indicate areas where emotional stress has taken up residence in your body. Lower back pain can reflect the weight of carrying emotional burdens; headaches may signal the mental effort required to maintain emotional control; muscle tension throughout your body might indicate the constant vigilance required to monitor and suppress unwanted feelings.

The Mental Indicators: Thoughts That Signal Suppression

Your thinking patterns provide another crucial avenue for recognizing emotional suppression, particularly in the ways your mind works to minimize, rationalize, or redirect attention away from emotional experiences. Becoming aware of these mental patterns creates opportunities to pause and explore what emotions might be seeking your attention.

Notice when you find yourself immediately jumping to problem-solving mode when faced with emotional situations—yours or others'—rather than first acknowledging and exploring the feelings involved. While problem-solving is a valuable skill, when it becomes your exclusive response to emotional territory, it can indicate a pattern of avoiding the vulnerable work of feeling and processing emotions.

Pay attention to the internal narrative that minimizes your emotional experiences: "It's not that big a deal," "I shouldn't feel this way," "Other people have it worse," or "I need to get over this and move on." While perspective can be helpful, these thoughts can also serve to shut down emotional processing before it has a chance to provide valuable information and healing.

Observe the tendency to intellectualize emotional experiences—analyzing them, categorizing them, or explaining them rather than simply feeling them. Intellectual understanding has tremendous value, but when it becomes a substitute for emotional experience rather than a complement to it, it can indicate subtle forms of emotional avoidance.

Notice patterns of comparison that either elevate you above others' emotional struggles ("At least I'm not falling apart like he is") or diminish your own experiences in relation to others' seemingly greater challenges ("I shouldn't complain when other people have real problems"). Both patterns can serve to avoid the vulnerability of acknowledging and honoring your own emotional truth.

The Behavioral Manifestations: Actions That Reveal

Emotional Patterns

Your behaviors often provide the most concrete evidence of emotional suppression patterns, particularly in how you respond to emotionally charged situations and what strategies you use to manage difficult feelings. These behavioral patterns can become so automatic that they feel like natural responses rather than choices that reflect underlying emotional dynamics.

Observe your tendency to withdraw from emotionally challenging conversations or situations. This might manifest as changing the subject when discussions become too personal, finding reasons to leave when emotions become intense, or simply shutting down and becoming silent when feelings emerge. While strategic withdrawal can sometimes be appropriate, consistent avoidance of emotional territory often indicates suppression patterns.

Notice your use of humor, especially self-deprecating humor, during emotionally vulnerable moments. While humor can be a healthy coping mechanism and a way to create connection, when it consistently serves to deflect attention away from emotional experiences—yours or others'—it may indicate discomfort with vulnerability and authentic emotional expression.

Pay attention to your relationship with substances—alcohol, drugs, food, or even activities like work, exercise, or entertainment—particularly during emotionally stressful periods. While these can be part of healthy self-care, when they consistently serve to numb, distract, or avoid emotional processing, they may indicate suppression patterns that deserve your attention and care.

Observe your responses to others' emotional expressions, particularly if you find yourself feeling uncomfortable, impatient, or compelled to fix their problems rather than simply being present with their experience. Your reactions to others' emotions often mirror your relationship with your own emotional experiences and can provide valuable insights into your suppression patterns.

The Relational Patterns: How Suppression Shapes

Connection

Perhaps the most revealing indicators of emotional suppression appear in your relationships, where the costs of emotional unavailability become most apparent and where the patterns you've developed have the greatest impact on the people you care about most.

Notice the depth and frequency of your conversations with people you care about. If most of your interactions remain focused on external topics—work, sports, politics, practical matters—while rarely venturing into personal feelings, dreams, fears, or inner experiences, this may indicate emotional suppression patterns that limit authentic connection.

Observe your comfort level with conflict and disagreement in relationships. If you find yourself going to great lengths to avoid conflict, agreeing when you actually disagree, or becoming disproportionately uncomfortable when others express dissatisfaction or criticism, these patterns often reflect underlying fears about emotional expression and its potential consequences.

Pay attention to how you handle your own needs in relationships. If you consistently prioritize others' needs over your own, struggle to ask for help or support, or find it difficult to communicate your preferences and boundaries, these behaviors often stem from suppression patterns that view your own emotional needs as less important than maintaining harmony or avoiding burden.

Notice patterns in your romantic relationships, particularly around emotional intimacy and vulnerability. If relationships tend to remain at certain levels of closeness without deepening, if partners have complained about emotional unavailability, or if you find yourself more comfortable with the physical and practical aspects of relationships than the emotional dimensions, these patterns may reflect suppression strategies that limit authentic intimacy.

Tools for Change: Practical Pathways to Emotional Freedom

Recognition alone, while essential, is insufficient for transformation. The journey from emotional suppression to emotional fluency requires practical tools and strategies that can be implemented gradually, consistently, and with patience for the natural rhythms of change and growth. These tools aren't quick fixes but rather practices that, when cultivated over time, create new neural pathways and behavioral patterns that support authentic emotional expression and connection.

The Foundation: Building Emotional Vocabulary and Awareness

The development of emotional vocabulary serves as the foundation for all other emotional growth work. Many men discover that their emotional vocabulary is surprisingly limited, often restricted to basic categories like *"good," "bad," "stressed," or "fine."* Expanding your capacity to identify and name specific emotions creates the possibility for more nuanced understanding and expression of your inner experience.

Begin by creating a daily practice of emotional check-ins—brief moments throughout the day when you pause to identify what you're feeling at that moment. This might feel awkward or artificial initially, but like any skill, emotional awareness develops through consistent practice. Start with simple questions: "What am I feeling right now?" *"Where do I notice this feeling in my body?" "What might have triggered this emotional response?"*

Consider keeping an emotion wheel or feelings chart accessible—either as a physical reference or a digital tool—to help you identify specific emotions beyond basic categories. These resources can help you distinguish between emotions that might feel similar but carry different information: distinguishing between disappointment and sadness, between anxiety and excitement, between anger and hurt.

Practice the art of emotional observation without immediate action. Often, the impulse to suppress emotions stems from the belief that feeling them requires acting on them or that emotions demand immediate resolution. Learning to observe emotions with curiosity rather than judgment creates space for understanding what information they might be providing without the pressure to fix or change them immediately.

Develop the practice of emotional granularity—the ability to make fine-grained distinctions between similar emotions. Instead of labeling everything as *"upset,"* learn to distinguish between frustration, disappointment, anger, hurt, and sadness. This refined awareness helps you respond more appropriately to different emotional experiences and communicate more effectively with others about your inner world.

Breathing and Body Awareness: Reclaiming Your Emotional Home

Your relationship with your breath and body provides a direct pathway to emotional awareness and regulation that doesn't require extensive training or complex techniques. These practices can be implemented immediately and adapted to your lifestyle, preferences, and circumstances.

Develop a regular breathing practice that helps you create space between emotional triggers and responses. This doesn't require elaborate meditation sessions—even three deep, conscious breaths can interrupt automatic emotional suppression patterns and create space for awareness and choice. Practice breathing into your belly rather than your chest, allowing your diaphragm to expand and contract naturally.

Learn to use your breath as an anchor during emotionally challenging moments. When you notice emotional activation—whether through physical tension, racing thoughts, or the impulse to withdraw or explode—return attention to your breath as a way of staying present with the experience rather than immediately suppressing or acting on it.

Cultivate body awareness practices that help you recognize emotional information as it arises. This might involve brief body scans throughout the day, noticing areas of tension or discomfort, or simply placing your hand on your heart or stomach during difficult moments as a way of maintaining connection with your physical experience.

Experiment with movement as a tool for emotional processing and expression. This doesn't require formal exercise routines—it might involve gentle stretching when you notice tension, walking when you feel restless, or simply allowing your body to move naturally when emotions feel stuck or overwhelming. Physical movement can help emotions flow through your system rather than becoming trapped in suppression patterns.

Journaling and Written Expression: Creating Safe Space for Emotional Truth

Writing provides a private, controllable environment for exploring emotions that might feel too vulnerable to express directly to others initially. This practice allows you to develop emotional awareness and expression skills at your own pace while creating a record of your growth and insights over time.

Begin with stream-of-consciousness writing—simply putting pen to paper and writing whatever comes to mind without editing, censoring, or organizing your thoughts. This practice bypasses the analytical mind that often interferes with emotional expression and allows deeper truths to emerge naturally. Set a timer for five or ten minutes and commit to writing continuously during that time, even if you think you have nothing to say.

Develop specific journaling practices that target emotional awareness and expression. You might write letters to people you've had conflict with (without necessarily sending them), explore your feelings about specific situations or relationships, or simply describe your emotional experience of each day in detail. The goal isn't to produce polished writing but to create authentic expression of your inner world.

Experiment with different styles of written expression that might feel more comfortable than traditional journaling. You might create lists of emotions you're experiencing, write poetry or song lyrics that capture your feelings, or even create fictional stories that explore themes relevant to your emotional experience. The medium matters less than the practice of translating inner experience into external expression.

Use writing as a tool for emotional processing before and after challenging conversations or situations. Before difficult interactions, you might write about your fears, hopes, or concerns. Afterward, you can process what happened, how you felt, what went well, and what you might want to do differently in similar situations. This practice helps you learn from emotional experiences rather than simply enduring them.

Mindfulness and Present-Moment Awareness: The Art of Emotional Presence

Mindfulness practices create the foundation for all emotional growth work by developing your capacity to be present with whatever is arising in your experience without immediately moving to change, fix, or escape it. This skill is particularly valuable for men who have learned to solve problems quickly rather than first understanding them fully.

Begin with brief mindfulness practices that can be integrated into your existing routine. This might involve mindful eating during one meal per day, paying attention to physical sensations during your morning shower, or simply bringing full attention to one routine activity each day. These practices develop your capacity for present-moment awareness without requiring additional time in your schedule.

Practice mindful observation of emotions as they arise, treating them as temporary visitors rather than permanent residents or dangerous invaders. When you notice an emotion emerging, you might mentally note "anger arising," "sadness present," or "anxiety here" as a way of acknowledging the feeling without immediately suppressing or acting on it.

Develop the practice of creating space around emotions rather than being consumed by them. Imagine emotions as weather patterns moving through the sky of your awareness—you can observe and experience them without believing you are them. This perspective helps reduce the fear that often accompanies emotional expression and creates more choice about how to respond to different feelings.

Use mindfulness practices during emotionally challenging moments as alternatives to suppression or explosion. Instead of immediately trying to get rid of difficult emotions or acting on them impulsively, practice bringing curious attention to what you're experiencing. What does this emotion feel like in your body? What thoughts accompany it? What information might it be providing?

Communication Skills: Finding Your Emotional Voice

Developing the capacity to express emotions authentically and constructively in relationships requires specific communication skills that many men never had the opportunity to learn. These skills can be developed gradually through practice in low-stakes situations before applying them to more challenging relationship dynamics.

Practice using *"I"* statements to express emotional experiences without blame or defensiveness. Instead of "You make me angry when you interrupt me," try *"I feel frustrated when I'm interrupted because I want to share my thoughts completely."* This shift helps you own your emotional experience while creating space for dialogue rather than conflict.

Learn to express emotions in real time rather than waiting until they build up and explode or disappear into suppression. This requires developing awareness of emotions as they arise and the courage to share them when appropriate. You might start by expressing positive emotions—excitement, appreciation, joy—before moving to more vulnerable feelings like hurt, fear, or sadness.

Develop the skill of emotional listening—the ability to hear and validate others' emotional experiences without immediately trying to solve their problems or defend yourself against their feelings. Practice reflecting what you hear others saying about their emotional experience: *"It sounds like you felt disappointed when I forgot our plans," or "I can hear that you're feeling overwhelmed by work stress."*

Create regular opportunities for emotional sharing in your close relationships. This might involve weekly check-ins with your partner where you both share something meaningful from your emotional experience, or coffee conversations with close friends where you venture beyond surface topics to explore what's really happening in your inner worlds.

The Role of Community: Healing Through Connection

The journey from emotional suppression to authentic expression cannot be traveled alone. While individual practices and self-awareness are essential foundation elements, sustainable transformation requires the support, witness, and encouragement of others who understand the challenges and possibilities of this journey. Community provides both the safety needed to risk vulnerability and the modeling necessary to see new possibilities for masculine emotional expression.

Creating Safe Spaces for Authentic Sharing

The development of emotional fluency requires environments where vulnerability is not only safe but welcomed and honored. These spaces rarely exist naturally in most men's lives, making it necessary to consciously create or seek out communities that support authentic emotional expression and mutual growth.

Consider joining or forming a men's group specifically focused on emotional growth and authentic sharing. These groups might meet regularly to discuss challenges, share experiences, and support each other's growth beyond traditional masculine stereotypes. The key is finding or creating a group where vulnerability is seen as strength and where members are committed to their own growth rather than simply commiserating about shared challenges.

Explore therapy groups or support groups that focus on men's emotional health, relationship skills, or specific challenges you're facing. Professional facilitation can provide structure and safety that helps men navigate emotional territory that feels unfamiliar or risky. These environments offer opportunities to witness other men's emotional journeys and to receive feedback and support from both peers and trained professionals.

Seek out online communities and resources that focus on men's emotional growth and healthy masculinity. While online interaction cannot fully replace face-to-face connection, it can provide access to information, perspectives, and support that might not be available in your immediate geographic area. Look for communities that emphasize growth and healing rather than those that perpetuate emotional suppression or toxic patterns.

Consider activities and environments that naturally encourage emotional expression and connection. This might include certain forms of artistic expression, spiritual communities, volunteer work that involves helping others, or adventure-based programs that create bonds through shared challenges and mutual support.

Transforming Existing Relationships

While creating new supportive communities is valuable, the transformation of existing relationships often provides the most meaningful opportunities for practicing emotional authenticity and experiencing its benefits. This process requires patience and courage, as it involves changing established patterns that others may initially find confusing or uncomfortable.

Begin by identifying one or two existing relationships where you feel some degree of safety and mutual care. These might be long-term friendships, family relationships, or romantic partnerships where there's a foundation of respect and affection. Start by sharing slightly more of your emotional experience in these relationships, testing the waters gradually rather than making dramatic changes all at once.

Practice expressing appreciation and positive emotions more freely in your existing relationships. Share when you feel grateful, proud, excited, or moved by something someone has done or said. These positive emotions are often easier to express initially and can help others adjust to a more emotionally expressive version of you while building confidence in your own capacity for emotional sharing.

Have explicit conversations with important people in your life about your journey toward greater emotional authenticity. Explain that you're working on being more emotionally aware and expressive, and ask for their patience and support as you develop these skills. Many people will appreciate your honesty and may be relieved to know that your changes reflect growth rather than problems in the relationship.

Model the kind of emotional openness you'd like to experience in relationships. Ask others about their emotional experiences, validate their feelings when they share them, and show genuine curiosity about their inner world. Often, others will begin to reciprocate this level of emotional sharing when they experience it consistently from you.

The Ripple Effects of Authentic Masculinity

As you develop greater emotional authenticity, your transformation creates ripple effects that extend far beyond your personal experience. Your willingness to be emotionally honest gives others permission to do the same, contributing to broader cultural shifts toward healthier definitions of masculinity and more authentic human connection.

Your children, if you have them, benefit enormously from witnessing emotionally aware masculinity modeled in daily life. They learn that strength includes emotional intelligence, that men can feel deeply without losing their masculine identity, and that authentic connection requires vulnerability and emotional honesty. These lessons create the foundation for healthier emotional patterns in subsequent generations.

Your friends and colleagues often feel relief and connection when you model emotional authenticity because it creates space for them to be more authentic as well. Many men are hungry for deeper connections but lack models for how to create them. Your willingness to be emotionally genuine can catalyze transformation in multiple relationships and communities.

Your romantic relationships have the potential to reach new levels of intimacy and satisfaction when emotional suppression no longer creates barriers to authentic connection. Partners often report feeling more valued, understood, and emotionally safe when their male partners develop emotional intelligence and expression skills.

Building Your Support Network: Practical Steps

The creation of an emotional support network requires intentional action and ongoing investment. Like any valuable relationship, connections that support emotional growth require time, attention, and mutual commitment to develop and maintain.

Start by identifying people in your current network who seem open to deeper connection and emotional authenticity. These might be individuals who have shared vulnerable experiences with you, who seem emotionally aware themselves, or who have expressed frustration with superficial relationships. Reach out to these people with specific invitations to connect more deeply.

Consider working with a therapist or counselor who specializes in men's emotional health and relationship issues. Professional support can provide guidance, accountability, and a safe space to explore emotions and patterns that feel too vulnerable to share with friends or family initially. Therapy can also help you develop skills and insights that enhance your capacity for authentic connection in all your relationships.

Explore workshops, retreats, or experiential programs that focus on men's emotional development, authentic masculinity, or relationship skills. These intensive experiences often provide opportunities for deep connection and significant breakthrough experiences that can accelerate your growth and introduce you to like-minded men on similar journeys.

Invest time and energy in developing and maintaining supportive relationships. This means showing up consistently, following through on commitments, and being willing to provide support to others as well as receiving it. Emotional growth communities thrive on reciprocity and mutual investment rather than one-sided support.

The journey of breaking emotional suppression cycles is not a destination you arrive at but a continuous process of choosing authenticity over armor, connection over control, and vulnerability over the illusion of invulnerability. Each step you take toward emotional honesty creates new possibilities not only for your own life but for the lives of everyone around you.

Your willingness to recognize and transform these patterns represents an act of courage that honors both your own potential for growth and your responsibility to future generations. The strength required to feel deeply, express authentically, and connect genuinely represents the highest expression of masculine power—not the power to control or dominate, but the power to create, heal, and love without limitation.

In the chapters that follow, we will continue building upon this foundation, exploring specific strategies for navigating different areas of your life with greater emotional intelligence and authenticity. The tools and insights you've gained in this chapter provide the groundwork for a transformation that extends into every aspect of your experience, creating possibilities for joy, connection, and fulfillment that may have seemed impossible when emotional suppression felt like your only option.

The cycle can be broken, and it begins with you. Your journey toward emotional freedom is not just a personal healing but a contribution to the healing of masculinity itself, creating space for future generations of men to experience the full richness of human emotional experience without shame, fear, or limitation.

Prompt: Have you ever felt shut down or dismissed when trying to open up?

Chapter 4: The Power of Vulnerability

We are venture beyond the familiar landscapes of strength and control into the sacred realm where true power resides: the courage to be seen, known, and authentically human in a world that often demands the opposite.

I ask you to consider a profound possibility—that everything you've been taught about vulnerability might be incomplete, that the very quality you've learned to fear and avoid might actually be the key to the connection, fulfillment, and authentic strength you've been seeking all along. We stand at the threshold of understanding vulnerability not as the absence of strength, but as its most refined and powerful expression.

When you are ready, engage with these ideas that represent an act of profound bravery. In a culture that equates masculine worth with invulnerability, choosing to master the power of openness requires the kind of courage that morphs not only individual lives but entire communities and generations. Countless men have walked this path before you, each one discovering that vulnerability is not the enemy of strength but its most trusted ally.

Redefining Vulnerability: The Architecture of Authentic Strength

The word *"vulnerability"* carries within our culture a weight of misunderstanding that has obscured its true nature and transformative potential. We have been taught to perceive vulnerability as exposure to harm, as weakness that invites exploitation, as the opposite of the strength and competence that define masculine worth. Yet this understanding represents one of the most profound misconceptions that limits our capacity for authentic connection and genuine fulfillment.

True vulnerability is not the absence of strength—it is strength in its most evolved and sophisticated form. It represents the courage to show up authentically when you cannot control the outcome, to engage with uncertainty while maintaining your integrity, and to remain open to connection even when that openness carries the possibility of disappointment or hurt. This kind of vulnerability requires more courage, not less, than the defensive postures we mistake for strength.

The Mythology of Invulnerability

Our cultural narrative of masculine strength rests upon a fundamental myth—that true power comes from being impervious to harm, unaffected by criticism, and independent of others' support or approval. This mythology suggests that the strongest man is the one who needs nothing, feels nothing that might compromise his judgment, and can handle any challenge through individual effort and emotional control.

This myth feels compelling because it promises a form of safety that seems attainable through personal effort and discipline. If you can just become strong enough, smart enough, successful enough, or emotionally controlled enough, the myth suggests, you can protect yourself from the fundamental uncertainties and disappointments that characterize human existence. The appeal of this promise makes it easy to overlook its fundamental impossibility and the profound costs it extracts from those who pursue it.

The mythology of invulnerability creates what psychologists call *"emotional armor"*—protective strategies that shield us from potential hurt while simultaneously cutting us off from the very experiences that make life meaningful and fulfilling. This armor becomes so familiar that we mistake it for our true identity, forgetting that underneath the protection lies our authentic self, waiting patiently for permission to emerge and connect.

The cruel irony of pursuing invulnerability is that it creates the very isolation and disconnection it promises to protect us from. When we armor ourselves against hurt, we also armor ourselves against love, joy, and the profound satisfaction that comes from being truly known and accepted by others. The protection becomes the prison, and the very strength we cultivate to avoid pain becomes the source of our deepest suffering.

Vulnerability as Emotional Courage

Authentic vulnerability represents a form of emotional courage that transcends the simplistic binary of strong versus weak. It is the willingness to experience and express the full spectrum of human emotion while maintaining your capacity to function, connect, and contribute meaningfully to the world around you. This kind of courage requires tremendous strength—the strength to tolerate uncertainty, to risk rejection or disappointment, and to remain open even when closure feels safer.

Consider the profound courage required to share your fears with someone you care about, knowing that they might not respond with understanding or support. Think about the strength needed to acknowledge when you're struggling, to ask for help when you need it, or to admit when you've made mistakes that have hurt others. These acts require far more courage than the emotional withdrawal that masquerades as independence.

Vulnerable courage also involves the willingness to feel deeply without being overwhelmed by those feelings, to experience sadness without losing hope, to acknowledge fear without being paralyzed by it, and to embrace joy without the constant worry that it will be taken away. This emotional range and flexibility represents the kind of sophisticated strength that can navigate life's complexities with grace and authenticity.

The development of vulnerable courage creates what researchers call "emotional granularity"—the ability to distinguish between subtle differences in emotional experience and to respond appropriately to different situations with emotional intelligence rather than default protective patterns. This sophistication allows for more nuanced relationships, better decision-making, and greater resilience in the face of life's inevitable challenges.

The Science of Connection

Research in neuroscience and psychology has revealed profound truths about human connection that challenge traditional notions of strength and vulnerability. These findings demonstrate that our brains are literally wired for connection, that our nervous systems co-regulate with others through emotional attunement, and that vulnerability is the mechanism through which authentic bonding occurs.

Mirror neurons in our brains automatically attune to the emotional states of others, creating unconscious connections that influence our own feelings, thoughts, and behaviors. When someone shares vulnerability authentically, our brains respond with empathy and connection, creating bonds that feel safe and meaningful. Conversely, when someone maintains emotional armor and distance, our brains register that distance and respond with their own protective strategies.

Studies of long-term relationship satisfaction consistently show that couples who can be vulnerable with each other—who can share fears, admit mistakes, express needs, and ask for support—report significantly higher levels of intimacy, satisfaction, and relationship stability than those who maintain emotional distance. The same patterns hold true for friendships, family relationships, and even professional connections where trust and collaboration are essential.

The field of positive psychology has identified vulnerability as a core component of what researchers call "authentic living"—the ability to align your external actions with your internal values and experiences. People who live authentically report higher levels of life satisfaction, better mental and physical health, and greater resilience in facing life's challenges. Vulnerability becomes the bridge between who you truly are and how you show up in the world.

Reframing Risk and Safety

One of the most significant shifts in understanding vulnerability involves reframing our concepts of risk and safety. The armor of invulnerability promises safety through control and distance, suggesting that we can protect ourselves from hurt by limiting our emotional exposure and dependence on others. Yet this apparent safety comes with hidden costs that often exceed the risks it attempts to avoid.

Emotional armor creates what psychologists call "experiential avoidance"—the attempt to avoid difficult emotions, thoughts, or experiences, even when that avoidance prevents us from pursuing meaningful goals or relationships. This avoidance might protect us from immediate discomfort, but it also prevents us from accessing the information, growth, and connection that difficult experiences often provide.

True safety, research suggests, comes not from avoiding vulnerability but from developing the capacity to navigate it skillfully. This involves building resilience—the ability to experience difficult emotions and situations while maintaining your core sense of self and your capacity for connection and growth. Resilience allows you to be vulnerable because you trust your ability to handle whatever responses your vulnerability might generate.

The paradox of vulnerability is that the willingness to risk emotional exposure often leads to greater actual safety in relationships and life circumstances. When you can be authentic about your needs, boundaries, fears, and limitations, others can respond to you more appropriately and supportively. When you hide these realities behind armor, others are left to guess what you need and how to connect with you, often leading to misunderstandings and conflicts that create the very problems the armor was meant to prevent.

Practical Steps to Embrace Vulnerability: A Roadmap for Authentic Living

Understanding vulnerability intellectually is profoundly different from practicing it in the complex landscape of daily life. The journey from conceptual appreciation to lived experience requires practical strategies that can be implemented gradually, safely, and with respect for your own pace of growth and the realities of your relationships and circumstances.

The practices that follow are invitations rather than demands, opportunities to experiment with vulnerability in ways that feel manageable and authentic to your unique situation. Like any skill worth developing, vulnerability requires practice, patience with yourself during the learning process, and the wisdom to recognize that growth often occurs in small increments rather than dramatic transformations.

Starting Small: The Graduated Practice of Openness

The development of vulnerability as a life skill begins with small, manageable acts of openness that gradually build your capacity for larger expressions of authenticity. This graduated approach respects the natural protective instincts you've developed while creating opportunities to discover that vulnerability can be both safe and rewarding when practiced skillfully.

Begin by identifying low-risk relationships and situations where you can practice expressing thoughts and feelings that you might normally keep to yourself. This might involve sharing a genuine compliment with someone, expressing appreciation for something someone has done for you, or admitting when you don't understand something rather than pretending comprehension.

Practice expressing preferences and opinions more openly in situations where the stakes feel relatively low. Instead of automatically agreeing or staying neutral, consider sharing your actual thoughts about movies, restaurants, activities, or topics of conversation. This seemingly simple practice helps you develop comfort with being seen and known for who you are rather than maintaining the safety of invisibility.

Experiment with acknowledging your emotional responses to situations as they occur rather than processing them privately later. If something makes you happy, say so. If you feel disappointed about a change in plans, express that feeling appropriately. If you're excited about something, let that excitement be visible to others. This practice helps you develop emotional transparency as a natural part of your interactions.

Create opportunities to ask for small forms of help or support from people in your life. This might involve asking a friend for advice about a decision you're making, requesting assistance with a project, or simply asking someone to listen while you think through a challenge you're facing. These requests help you practice interdependence and discover that others often appreciate opportunities to contribute to your well-being.

The Art of Authentic Self-Disclosure

Self-disclosure—the process of sharing personal information, experiences, and feelings with others—represents one of the most powerful tools for building connection and practicing vulnerability. However, effective self-disclosure requires skill, timing, and awareness of appropriate boundaries rather than simply sharing everything with everyone.

Learn to distinguish between authentic self-disclosure and emotional dumping. Authentic disclosure involves sharing aspects of your experience that are relevant to the relationship and situation, with attention to the other person's capacity to receive what you're sharing. Emotional dumping, by contrast, involves sharing without consideration for the other person's boundaries, needs, or emotional state.

Practice reciprocal disclosure in your relationships—sharing something about your experience and then creating space for the other person to share something about theirs. This back-and-forth creates the kind of mutual vulnerability that builds genuine intimacy rather than one-sided exposure that can feel uncomfortable or inappropriate.

Develop comfort with sharing your struggles and imperfections rather than only your successes and strengths. This might involve acknowledging when you're having a difficult day, sharing a mistake you made and what you learned from it, or expressing uncertainty about a decision you're facing. These disclosures help others see you as human rather than as an idealized version that keeps them at emotional distance.

Learn to share your positive emotions and experiences as openly as you share your challenges. Many men find it easier to share struggles than to express joy, excitement, pride, or love. Practice acknowledging when something makes you happy, when you feel proud of an accomplishment, or when you feel love or appreciation for someone in your life.

Navigating Conflict with Vulnerability

One of the most challenging contexts for practicing vulnerability involves situations of conflict, disagreement, or tension in relationships. These moments often trigger our strongest defensive patterns, yet they also represent some of the most powerful opportunities for deepening connection through authentic communication and mutual understanding.

Learn to express hurt feelings rather than converting them immediately into anger or withdrawal. When someone's actions affect you negatively, practice saying *"I felt hurt when..." or "It was difficult for me when..."* rather than attacking their character or motivations. This approach communicates your experience without creating additional defensiveness that escalates conflict.

Practice acknowledging your role in conflicts rather than focusing exclusively on what others have done wrong. This might involve admitting when you've been unclear in your communication, acknowledging when your expectations were unrealistic, or recognizing when your emotional state contributed to a misunderstanding. This kind of vulnerability often defuses defensiveness and creates space for resolution.

Develop the capacity to express your needs and boundaries directly rather than expecting others to guess what you require or hoping that problems will resolve themselves. This involves learning to say things like *"I need some time to think about this before we continue the conversation" or "It would help me if we could approach this differently."*

Learn to apologize authentically when your actions have hurt others, without defending your intentions or minimizing the impact of your behavior. Authentic apology involves acknowledging what happened, taking responsibility for your part, expressing genuine remorse, and making concrete commitments about how you'll handle similar situations differently in the future.

Building Emotional Vocabulary and Expression

Many men discover that their capacity for vulnerability is limited by an underdeveloped emotional vocabulary that makes it difficult to identify and express the nuances of their inner experience. Building this vocabulary creates more sophisticated options for sharing your authentic experience with others.

Expand your ability to identify and name specific emotions beyond basic categories like *"good," "bad," "fine," or "stressed."* Consider using emotion wheels or feelings charts to help you identify more precise terms for your emotional experiences. The difference between feeling disappointed versus sad, anxious versus excited, or frustrated versus angry can be crucial for effective communication.

Practice describing the physical sensations that accompany different emotions, helping others understand not just what you're feeling but how those feelings affect you. *You might say, "I feel anxious, and my chest feels tight," or "I'm feeling overwhelmed, and it's hard for me to concentrate right now."*

Learn to express the stories and meanings that accompany your emotions rather than just the emotions themselves. Instead of only saying *"I feel sad," you might share "I feel sad because this reminds me of when my father was sick, and I'm realizing how much I miss him."* This deeper sharing helps others understand your emotional experience more completely.

Develop comfort with expressing a range of emotions rather than limiting yourself to those that feel safest or most socially acceptable. Practice expressing tender emotions like love, gratitude, and compassion as openly as you express stronger emotions like anger or determination.

Creating Ritual and Structure for Vulnerable Practice

Incorporating vulnerability into your life becomes easier when you create specific contexts and structures that support authentic sharing rather than leaving it to chance or waiting for crisis situations to force openness.

Establish regular check-ins with important people in your life where you both share something meaningful about your current experience. This might be a weekly coffee with a friend where you each share the most challenging and most rewarding aspect of your week, or a nightly practice with your partner where you each share something you're grateful for and something you're struggling with.

Create or join groups specifically focused on authentic sharing and mutual support. This might involve men's groups, therapy groups, spiritual communities, or even online forums where vulnerable communication is explicitly encouraged and protected. These contexts provide practice opportunities with people who are also committed to authentic communication.

Develop personal practices that help you stay connected to your authentic experience throughout the day. This might involve brief mindfulness check-ins, journaling practices, or simply taking moments to pause and ask yourself *"What am I feeling right now?" and "What do I need at this moment?"*

Use creative expression as a pathway to vulnerability when direct verbal communication feels too challenging. This might involve writing, music, art, or other forms of creative expression that help you explore and share aspects of your inner experience that feel difficult to communicate directly.

Stories of Transformation: Witnessing Vulnerability's Power

The abstract concepts of vulnerability and authentic strength become tangible and inspiring through the lived experiences of men who have courageously chosen to embrace openness in their relationships and daily lives. These stories, drawn from therapeutic work, research, and the real journeys of men committed to emotional growth, illustrate both the challenges and the profound rewards of choosing vulnerability over armor.

Mark's Journey: From Executive Armor to Authentic Leadership

Mark entered his late thirties as the embodiment of professional success—a senior executive at a Fortune 500 company, financially secure, respected by colleagues, and apparently living the American dream that many men aspire to achieve. Yet beneath this polished exterior, Mark struggled with a profound sense of isolation that he couldn't understand or address through his usual problem-solving strategies.

"I had spent fifteen years building what I thought was strength," Mark reflected during our conversations about his transformation. *"I could handle any crisis at work, make difficult decisions without showing emotion, and maintain composure no matter how stressful the situation became. I*

thought that made me a great leader and a strong man. But I was dying inside, and I didn't even realize it."

Mark's awakening began when his team was facing a particularly challenging project deadline that required extraordinary collaboration and creativity. Despite his technical competence and strategic thinking, Mark noticed that his team seemed hesitant to bring him problems, reluctant to share creative ideas that might seem risky, and generally more comfortable working with other leaders who seemed more approachable and emotionally available.

The feedback that catalyzed Mark's journey toward vulnerability came during a 360-degree leadership review where colleagues and subordinates could provide anonymous input about his leadership style. While the feedback praised his competence and reliability, it also consistently mentioned emotional distance, difficulty connecting with him personally, and a sense that he was unapproachable when people were struggling or needed support.

"One comment hit me like a punch to the gut," Mark remembered. *"Someone wrote, 'Mark is incredibly capable, but I would never go to him if I was having a personal crisis or needed emotional support. He feels more like a robot than a human being.' That was the moment I realized that my armor wasn't just protecting me—it was isolating me from the very people I wanted to lead and serve."*

Mark's journey toward vulnerability began with small experiments in authentic sharing during team meetings and one-on-one conversations with colleagues. Instead of maintaining his usual emotional neutrality, he began acknowledging when he felt stressed about deadlines, excited about new opportunities, or uncertain about decisions that needed to be made.

The initial responses to Mark's increased openness were mixed—some colleagues seemed surprised or uncomfortable with his emotional transparency, while others responded with relief and reciprocal sharing. Mark learned to navigate these different reactions with patience, understanding that his changes required adjustment not just from himself but from others who had become accustomed to his emotional distance.

The most significant breakthrough in Mark's leadership came during a particularly challenging period when the company was facing potential layoffs. Instead of delivering the news with his usual professional detachment, Mark chose to share his own feelings about the situation—his sadness about the impact on families, his fear about the company's future, and his commitment to handling the process with as much care and dignity as possible.

"I was terrified that showing emotion would make me seem weak or incompetent," Mark recalled. *"But what happened was the opposite. People started coming to me with their concerns and ideas. They began trusting me with information they had been keeping to themselves. The quality of our collaboration improved dramatically because people felt like they were working with a human being rather than a corporate machine."*

Mark's vulnerability also transformed his personal relationships in ways he hadn't anticipated. His marriage, which had been stable but emotionally distant, began to deepen as he shared more of his inner experience with his wife. His teenage children, who had previously seen him as a provider and problem-solver but not as someone they could confide in, began bringing him their emotional struggles and seeking his guidance on personal matters.

"I thought vulnerability would make me less effective as a leader and a father," Mark reflected. *"Instead, it made me more effective than I had ever been. People started following me not just because of my position or competence, but because they trusted me and felt connected to me as a person. My children began seeing me as someone who understood the complexity of being human rather than someone who had all the answers but couldn't relate to their struggles."*

Mark's professional success actually increased as his vulnerability skills developed. His team's performance improved as trust and communication deepened. His relationships with clients became more authentic and effective as he learned to connect on human levels rather than purely transactional ones. His reputation within the company evolved from "competent but cold" to "inspiring and trustworthy," leading to additional leadership opportunities he had been seeking for years.

David's Healing: Trauma, Vulnerability, and Recovery

David's story illustrates how vulnerability can serve as a pathway to healing from significant trauma and loss. A military veteran who had served two tours in Afghanistan, David returned home carrying invisible wounds that he initially tried to handle through the emotional suppression strategies that had served him during his military service.

"In combat, emotional suppression can literally save your life," David explained. "*You can't afford to process grief when your buddy gets killed, because you need to stay focused and functional to keep yourself and your unit alive. But when I came home, I tried to keep using those same strategies in civilian life, and they almost destroyed me.*"

David's post-military experience followed a pattern familiar to many veterans—initial relief at being home and safe, followed by growing struggles with hypervigilance, emotional numbness, relationship difficulties, and a sense of disconnection from civilian life that he couldn't understand or address. His attempts to "power through" these challenges using military-trained mental toughness only deepened his isolation and despair.

The crisis that forced David to reconsider his approach to emotional coping came when his wife Sarah threatened to leave their marriage unless he sought help for what she recognized as post-traumatic stress symptoms. Sarah's ultimatum felt like a betrayal initially—David interpreted her request for him to get help as criticism of his strength and competence.

"I felt like she was calling me weak," David remembered. *"Everything in my training told me that seeking help meant I wasn't strong enough to handle my problems. I thought that if I was really tough, really disciplined, I should be able to get over my war experiences and be the husband and father my family deserved."*

David's initial resistance to therapy and vulnerability gradually gave way as he began to recognize the costs his emotional suppression was extracting from his family and his own well-being. His children had become afraid of his unpredictable anger outbursts. His wife felt like she was living with a stranger who looked like her husband but seemed emotionally unreachable. David himself was struggling with sleep disturbances, anxiety, and a pervasive sense of numbness that made it difficult to enjoy activities and relationships that had once brought him pleasure.

The therapeutic process that transformed David's life required him to gradually develop comfort with emotional vulnerability in a safe, supportive environment. Working with a therapist who specialized in trauma and military transitions, David began to explore the experiences and emotions he had been suppressing since his military service.

"Learning to talk about what happened in Afghanistan was the hardest thing I've ever done," David shared. "Harder than combat, harder than military training, harder than anything I had experienced. But it was also the beginning of getting my life back."

David's healing journey involved learning to distinguish between the emotional suppression that had been necessary for survival during combat and the emotional awareness that was necessary for thriving in civilian relationships. He discovered that he could honor his military experience and the strength it had required while also developing new emotional skills that served his post-military life.

The process of sharing his war experiences with his therapist, and eventually with his wife and close friends, created connections and understanding that David had not imagined were possible. People responded to his vulnerability not with judgment or pity, but with respect for his courage in facing difficult experiences and seeking healing.

"I thought that talking about my struggles would make people think less of me," David reflected. *"Instead, it made them think more of me. They saw the strength it took to face these experiences rather than just the fact that I was struggling with them. My wife felt like she got her husband back. My kids stopped being afraid of me because I wasn't carrying all that unexpressed pain and rage."*

David's recovery also involved reconnecting with other veterans who were on similar healing journeys. These relationships provided mutual support and understanding that helped normalize the process of seeking help and developing emotional awareness as part of post-military adaptation.

"Finding other guys who were going through similar things was huge," David explained. *"We could talk about stuff that civilian therapists and family members couldn't fully understand, but we could also support each other in developing the emotional skills we needed for civilian life. It wasn't about staying stuck in war experiences, but about integrating them into a healthy life."*

David's transformation through vulnerability extended beyond his personal healing to become service to other veterans facing similar challenges. He became involved in veteran support organizations, sharing his story and encouraging other former military personnel to seek help when needed. His willingness to be vulnerable about his struggles created permission for others to acknowledge their own needs for support and healing.

James's Connection: Single Fatherhood and Authentic Parenting

James's story demonstrates how vulnerability can transform parenting relationships and create deeper connections with children who might otherwise remain emotionally distant. As a single father raising two teenage sons after his divorce, James initially tried to maintain his role as the strong, protective parent who could handle any challenge without showing weakness or uncertainty.

"I thought that being a good father meant never letting my kids see me struggle or doubt myself," James explained. "I wanted to be their rock, their source of stability and strength. I thought that if they saw me having difficult emotions or needing help, they would lose confidence in me or feel less secure."

James's approach to single parenting reflected many men's understanding of strength and protection—the belief that children need their fathers to be invulnerable pillars of stability who can solve any problem and handle any crisis with competence and emotional control. This approach seemed to work initially, as James managed the logistics of single parenting effectively while maintaining his professional responsibilities and providing a stable home environment.

However, as his sons moved through their teenage years, James began to notice that their relationship was becoming increasingly distant and superficial. They came to him with practical problems—help with homework, transportation needs, requests for money—but they rarely shared their emotional struggles, relationship challenges, or personal fears and dreams.

"I realized that my boys were polite and respectful, but they weren't really connecting with me," James reflected. "They saw me as someone who could solve problems and provide for them, but not as someone who would understand their inner worlds or be safe to share vulnerable feelings with."

The turning point in James's parenting approach came during a particularly difficult period when his older son, sixteen-year-old Marcus, was struggling with depression and social anxiety but refused to talk about it or seek help. James's attempts to address the situation through his usual problem-solving approach—offering advice, suggesting solutions, and trying to maintain optimistic encouragement—only seemed to create more distance between them.

James's breakthrough came when he made the conscious choice to share his own struggles with his sons rather than maintaining his facade of invulnerability. During a family conversation about Marcus's difficulties, James chose to acknowledge his own experiences with anxiety and depression, his fears about making mistakes as a single parent, and his uncertainty about how to best support his sons during challenging times.

"I told them that I didn't always know what I was doing as a father, that sometimes I felt scared and overwhelmed, and that I was still learning how to navigate some of the challenges we were all facing," James remembered. "I was terrified that this would make them lose confidence in me, but what happened was the opposite."

James's vulnerability created space for his sons to share their own struggles without feeling like they were burdening him or disappointing him with their imperfections. Marcus began opening up about his social anxiety and the pressure he felt to live up to expectations at school and in social situations. James's younger son, fourteen-year-old Tyler, began sharing his own fears about high school, relationships, and his concerns about his parents' divorce.

The transformation in their family dynamic was profound and sustained. James's sons began coming to him not just with problems they needed him to solve, but with experiences they wanted to share and emotions they needed him to understand. Their conversations became deeper and more meaningful, focusing on feelings, values, dreams, and the complexities of growing up rather than just practical matters.

"My relationship with my boys became everything I had hoped it would be, but through the opposite approach from what I thought would work," James observed. "By showing them that I was human, that I had struggles and uncertainties just like they did, I became someone they could relate to and trust with their own vulnerabilities."

James's authentic parenting approach also helped his sons develop their own emotional intelligence and vulnerability skills. They learned that strength included the capacity to acknowledge difficulties, seek support when needed, and share emotions appropriately. They developed more authentic friendships and romantic relationships because they had learned these skills from their father's modeling.

"My sons are now young men who can talk about their feelings, ask for help when they need it, and support others who are struggling," James reflected with pride. "They have the emotional tools I wish I had learned at their age, and they learned them because I was willing to be vulnerable enough to show them that these skills are part of being a strong man."

The Ripple Effects of Authentic Courage

These stories of transformation illustrate several crucial insights about the power of vulnerability in men's lives:

Professional Enhancement: Rather than undermining professional effectiveness, emotional authenticity often enhances leadership capacity, team collaboration, and workplace relationships. Vulnerability creates trust and psychological safety that improve performance and innovation.

Healing Acceleration: Trauma and emotional wounds heal more effectively when they can be shared and processed with supportive others rather than carried in isolation. Vulnerability becomes a pathway to recovery rather than an obstacle to strength.

Relationship Deepening: Authentic sharing creates the kind of intimate connection that many men long for but struggle to achieve through traditional masculine approaches. Vulnerability builds bridges rather than walls between people.

Generational Impact: When men model emotional intelligence and vulnerability for their children, they break cycles of emotional suppression and create healthier templates for the next generation's relationships and emotional well-being.

Community Building: Vulnerable men often become catalysts for broader cultural change, creating environments where other men feel safe to explore emotional authenticity and mutual support.

The journey toward embracing vulnerability as a source of strength rather than a sign of weakness represents one of the most significant transformations a man can make in his relationship with himself and others. This journey requires courage, patience, and compassion for the process of unlearning patterns that once served protective functions while learning new skills that serve connection and authentic living.

Your willingness to explore these concepts and consider how they might apply to your own life represents the beginning of a transformation that can touch every aspect of your experience—your relationships, your work, your parenting, your friendships, and your sense of purpose and meaning. Vulnerability is not about becoming weak or dependent; it is about becoming fully human and fully alive in your connections with others and with yourself.

The power of vulnerability lies not in exposure for its own sake, but in the authentic connections it creates, the healing it facilitates, and the freedom it provides from the exhausting work of maintaining emotional armor. As you continue this journey, remember that vulnerability is a practice, not a destination—a skill to be developed gradually, with wisdom and discernment, in service of the connections and experiences that matter most deeply to you.

In the chapters that follow, we will continue building upon this foundation, exploring specific strategies for implementing vulnerability and emotional intelligence in different contexts and relationships. The courage you demonstrate by engaging with these ideas creates ripple effects that extend far beyond your individual experience, contributing to a cultural transformation that future generations of men will inherit as their birthright rather than having to discover through struggle and healing.

Challenge: Tell someone you love them. It doesn't need to be romantic or someone you would normally talk to. Just saying I love you can talk someone off the ledge and make their day/life better.

Chapter 5: Redefining Masculinity

As we start this liberating chapter of your journey—we examine the very foundations of what you've been taught it means to be a man and to consider the keen possibility that masculinity itself can evolve, expand, and embrace the full spectrum of human experience without losing its essential strength or power.

This journey asks you to step beyond the narrow corridors of traditional masculine definitions into a more expansive landscape where strength includes tenderness, courage embraces vulnerability, and leadership flows from emotional intelligence rather than dominance.

Redefining masculinity isn't about abandoning what makes men powerful, but about reclaiming the complete range of masculine expression that has been lost to rigid expectations and cultural limitations.

You are part of a movement of men who are choosing to expand the definition of masculine strength to include emotional wisdom, authentic connection, and the revolutionary act of living according to your deepest values rather than society's narrow expectations.

The Evolution of Masculinity: Tracing the Arc of Change

To understand where masculinity might evolve, we must first examine where it has been—recognizing that our current definitions of masculine strength and success are not timeless truths but historical constructions that have changed dramatically across cultures, eras, and circumstances. This historical perspective illuminates both the adaptive nature of masculine roles and the profound opportunity we have to consciously shape their continued evolution.

Ancient Foundations: The Warrior-Provider Archetype

The earliest expressions of masculinity were forged in the crucible of survival, where physical strength, protective capacity, and resource acquisition determined not just individual success but community survival.

Ancient masculine archetypes—the hunter, the warrior, the protector—emerged from genuine environmental pressures that required specific qualities and behaviors for human communities to thrive in dangerous and uncertain worlds.

These early masculine roles served essential functions that extended far beyond individual expression. Men who could hunt successfully fed their families and communities. Warriors who could defend against threats protected the vulnerable. Leaders who could make quick decisions under pressure preserved group cohesion during crises. The masculine qualities that emerged from these contexts—physical courage, emotional stoicism, decisive action, and sacrifice for others—represented adaptive responses to real environmental challenges.

Yet even in ancient contexts, masculinity was more complex and varied than popular mythology suggests. Archaeological and anthropological evidence reveals that successful ancient societies included men who served as healers, artists, storytellers, and spiritual guides—roles that required emotional intelligence, creativity, and interpersonal sensitivity alongside traditional masculine strength. The complete masculine archetype included both the capacity for fierce protection and the wisdom to nurture, both the ability to act decisively and the patience to listen deeply.

The reduction of this complex masculine heritage to purely warrior-provider stereotypes represents a historical oversimplification that has obscured the fuller range of masculine expression that once existed. Ancient cultures often recognized multiple pathways to masculine honor, including roles that required what we now consider *"feminine"* qualities like empathy, artistic sensitivity, and spiritual insight.

Industrial Revolution: Masculinity Mechanized

The Industrial Revolution fundamentally altered masculine roles and expectations in ways that continue to influence contemporary definitions of male strength and success. As work moved from varied agricultural and craft-based activities to factory production, masculinity became increasingly associated with mechanical precision, emotional detachment, and the capacity to perform repetitive tasks without complaint or emotional expression.

This era birthed the conception of masculinity as machine-like efficiency—men who could work long hours without emotional needs, who could separate their inner experience from their productive output, and who could find identity and worth primarily through their economic contribution to family and society. The industrial masculine ideal emphasized reliability over creativity, consistency over adaptability, and emotional suppression over authentic expression.

The benefits of this masculine evolution were significant and shouldn't be dismissed. Industrial masculine qualities enabled the rapid technological advancement, infrastructure development, and economic growth that characterize modern civilization. Men who could work steadily, think logically, and subordinate personal needs to productive goals built the foundations of contemporary prosperity and security.

However, this mechanized model of masculinity also created profound limitations that continue to constrain men's experience today. The industrial masculine ideal treated emotional needs as inefficiencies to be minimized, relationships as secondary to productivity, and personal fulfillment as luxury that successful men shouldn't require. These patterns established the foundation for the emotional suppression and relational difficulties that characterize many contemporary men's experiences.

Post-War Masculinity: The Organization Man

The period following World War II created another significant evolution in masculine expectations, as men transitioned from wartime roles requiring physical courage and sacrifice to peacetime roles emphasizing economic success, family stability, and social conformity. The "organization man" became the new masculine ideal—professionally successful, emotionally controlled, and focused on providing material security for nuclear family units within suburban communities.

This era established many of the masculine stereotypes that continue to influence contemporary expectations: the breadwinner father who expressed love through provision rather than emotional availability, the corporate executive who demonstrated strength through professional achievement and emotional detachment, and the suburban patriarch who maintained authority through emotional distance and financial control.

The organization man model served important functions during a period of rapid social and economic change, providing stability and structure that helped communities rebuild after global conflict and economic disruption. Men who could succeed within organizational hierarchies, maintain emotional composure under pressure, and focus on long-term economic goals created the prosperity and security that characterized post-war American society.

Yet this masculine model also institutionalized emotional suppression in ways that created profound costs for men, families, and communities. The organization man ideal treated emotional expression as unprofessional, vulnerability as weakness, and authentic self-expression as subordinate to social conformity and economic success. These patterns created the foundation for the widespread emotional disconnection and relationship difficulties that prompted the men's liberation movements of subsequent decades.

Contemporary Challenges: Masculinity in Transition

Contemporary masculinity exists in a state of profound transition, caught between traditional expectations that no longer serve current circumstances and emerging possibilities that have not yet been fully defined or culturally accepted. Modern men navigate complex and often contradictory expectations about emotional expression, professional success, family involvement, and personal fulfillment that previous generations never had to reconcile.

The economic and social changes of recent decades have fundamentally altered the contexts within which masculine identity develops and operates. Traditional masculine roles like primary breadwinner, family protector, and community leader have become less relevant or attainable for many men, while new expectations around emotional availability, egalitarian partnership, and work-life balance require skills and perspectives that many men were never taught to develop.

This transitional period has created both unprecedented opportunities and significant challenges for contemporary masculinity. Men today have more freedom to explore diverse expressions of masculine identity, to develop emotional intelligence alongside traditional strengths, and to create relationships based on mutual respect rather than hierarchical authority. Simultaneously, many men struggle with identity confusion, role uncertainty, and the stress of navigating competing expectations without clear cultural guidance.

The mental health challenges that disproportionately affect contemporary men—higher suicide rates, increased depression and anxiety, substance abuse problems, and relationship difficulties—often reflect the costs of this transitional period. Men who attempt to maintain traditional masculine patterns in contexts that no longer support them experience significant stress, while men who attempt to embrace new masculine possibilities without adequate support or modeling often struggle with uncertainty and isolation.

Cultural Variations: Masculine Diversity

Examining masculinity across different cultures reveals that many characteristics we consider essentially masculine are actually cultural constructions that vary significantly across societies and historical periods. This cross-cultural perspective illuminates the possibility for conscious evolution of masculine definitions while honoring the legitimate needs and values that masculine roles have traditionally served.

Mediterranean cultures often embrace more emotionally expressive forms of masculinity that include physical affection between men, emotional intensity in relationships, and artistic sensitivity as components of masculine strength. Scandinavian societies have evolved masculine ideals that emphasize work-life balance, active fatherhood, and emotional intelligence alongside traditional masculine qualities. Many Indigenous cultures recognize multiple pathways to masculine honor, including roles as healers, visionaries, and community facilitators that require emotional sensitivity and spiritual insight.

These cultural variations demonstrate that masculine strength can be expressed through diverse behaviors and characteristics without losing its essential power or effectiveness. They suggest that the narrow definitions of masculinity that dominate contemporary Western cultures represent choices rather than biological necessities, opening possibilities for conscious evolution toward more inclusive and flexible masculine ideals.

The globalization of contemporary culture creates opportunities to learn from diverse masculine traditions while adapting them to current circumstances and needs. This cross-cultural perspective can inform the development of new masculine models that honor traditional strengths while incorporating emotional intelligence, relational skills, and personal authenticity as essential components of masculine maturity.

Healthy Masculinity: A Vision for Integration and Wholeness

Healthy masculinity represents not the abandonment of masculine strength but its evolution toward greater sophistication, integration, and effectiveness in contemporary contexts. This vision of masculinity embraces traditional masculine virtues like courage, strength, and protectiveness while expanding to include emotional intelligence, authentic vulnerability, and collaborative leadership as essential components of mature masculine expression.

The Foundation: Strength Through Integration

Healthy masculinity rests upon the recognition that true strength comes from integrating the full spectrum of human capacities rather than limiting masculine expression to narrow stereotypes that exclude essential aspects of human experience. This integration involves developing both traditionally masculine qualities and characteristics that have been labeled feminine, recognizing that the most effective and fulfilled men possess the flexibility to access different aspects of their humanity depending on what each situation requires.

Integrated masculine strength includes the capacity for fierce protection when loved ones are threatened and gentle nurturing when tenderness is needed. It encompasses decisive leadership in crisis situations and collaborative facilitation when group wisdom is more valuable than individual authority. Healthy masculinity involves the ability to compete intensely when competition serves valuable purposes and to cooperate generously when collaboration creates better outcomes for everyone involved.

This integration requires moving beyond the binary thinking that has characterized traditional masculinity—the belief that men must choose between strength and sensitivity, between independence and connection, between leadership and service. Healthy masculinity recognizes these as false dichotomies that limit masculine potential rather than enhance it, embracing paradox and complexity as sources of strength rather than sources of confusion.

The development of integrated masculine strength involves conscious cultivation of qualities and skills that traditional masculine socialization may have neglected. This might include developing emotional vocabulary and expression skills, learning to seek and receive support from others, cultivating empathy and interpersonal sensitivity, and creating the capacity for authentic intimacy in relationships. These developments enhance rather than diminish masculine effectiveness by providing more sophisticated tools for navigating complex contemporary challenges.

Emotional Intelligence as Masculine Strength

One of the most significant aspects of healthy masculinity involves recognizing emotional intelligence—the ability to understand, manage, and effectively express emotions—as a core component of masculine strength rather than a feminine characteristic that diminishes masculine identity. This recognition transforms emotional awareness from weakness to be hidden into a powerful skill set to be developed and utilized.

Emotionally intelligent masculinity includes the capacity to recognize and name emotional experiences as they arise, understanding that emotions provide valuable information about yourself, your relationships, and your environment. This emotional awareness serves decision-making, relationship-building, and personal growth in ways that emotional suppression cannot match, creating more sophisticated and effective approaches to life's challenges.

The development of emotional expression skills allows men to communicate authentically about their inner experience, creating the kind of intimate connections that provide genuine support, understanding, and mutual growth. Men who can share their fears, hopes, disappointments, and joys create relationships characterized by depth and mutual vulnerability rather than surface-level interaction based on shared activities alone.

Emotional regulation—the ability to experience intense emotions without being overwhelmed by them or acting on them impulsively—represents perhaps the most sophisticated form of masculine strength. Men who can feel anger without becoming destructive, experience sadness without becoming depressed, and acknowledge fear without being paralyzed possess tremendous power to respond effectively to challenging situations while maintaining their integrity and values.

Empathy and emotional attunement to others enhance masculine effectiveness in leadership, parenting, partnership, and friendship by providing information about others' needs, motivations, and responses that purely analytical approaches cannot access. Men who can understand and respond appropriately to others' emotional states create more successful collaborations, more satisfying relationships, and more effective solutions to complex interpersonal challenges.

Authentic Vulnerability as Courage

Healthy masculinity reframes vulnerability from weakness to be avoided into courage to be cultivated—the strength required to show up authentically when you cannot control the outcome, to risk rejection or disappointment in service of genuine connection, and to maintain openness even when closure feels safer. This understanding of vulnerability as courage expands masculine strength to include the capacity for authentic intimacy and mutual interdependence.

Authentic vulnerability involves the willingness to acknowledge your limitations, mistakes, and areas where you need support or growth, recognizing that this honesty creates opportunities for learning, connection, and collaborative problem-solving that denial and defensive posturing cannot provide. Men who can admit when they don't know something, when they've made mistakes, or when they need help access resources and relationships that enhance their effectiveness rather than diminishing it.

The practice of vulnerable courage includes sharing your authentic thoughts and feelings even when they might not be received favorably, expressing needs and boundaries clearly rather than expecting others to guess what you require, and acknowledging the impact of others' actions on your emotional experience. These practices create the foundation for relationships characterized by mutual understanding and respect rather than guesswork and assumption.

Vulnerable masculinity also involves the courage to pursue goals and activities that align with your authentic interests and values rather than those that conform to external expectations about masculine behavior. This might include exploring creative expressions, developing spiritual practices, engaging in care giving roles, or pursuing careers that prioritize personal fulfillment over traditional markers of masculine success.

Collaborative Leadership and Service

Healthy masculinity evolves beyond dominance-based models of leadership toward collaborative approaches that harness collective wisdom and create shared ownership of outcomes. This leadership style recognizes that the most effective solutions to complex contemporary challenges require diverse perspectives, mutual cooperation, and the kind of trust that emerges from authentic relationship rather than hierarchical authority.

Collaborative masculine leadership involves creating environments where others feel safe to contribute their ideas, express disagreement, and take creative risks, recognizing that psychological safety enhances rather than threatens effective leadership. Men who can facilitate group processes, synthesize diverse viewpoints, and empower others to contribute their unique strengths create more innovative and sustainable outcomes than those who rely primarily on individual authority and decision-making.

This leadership approach includes the humility to recognize when others possess greater expertise, insight, or wisdom about specific situations, and the confidence to defer to that expertise while maintaining overall responsibility for outcomes. Healthy masculine leadership knows when to lead from the front and when to support from behind, when to make decisive individual decisions and when to facilitate collaborative problem-solving.

Service-oriented masculinity recognizes that true masculine strength is measured not by what you can take or control, but by what you can contribute to the well-being of others and the health of communities. This service orientation might express itself through mentorship of younger men, volunteer work that addresses community needs, environmental stewardship, or professional work that creates genuine value rather than merely personal advancement.

Conscious Relationships and Authentic Intimacy

Healthy masculinity embraces relationship skills as essential masculine competencies rather than optional feminine concerns, recognizing that the capacity to create and maintain authentic intimate connections enhances every aspect of life experience. This involves developing the communication skills, emotional awareness, and interpersonal sensitivity required for mutual, respectful, and deeply satisfying relationships.

Conscious relationship skills include the ability to engage in conflict constructively rather than avoiding it or allowing it to become destructive, recognizing that disagreement and tension can strengthen relationships when handled with skill and mutual respect. Men who can navigate difficult conversations, acknowledge their role in relationship problems, and work collaboratively toward resolution create partnerships characterized by growth and deepening intimacy rather than stagnation and resentment.

Authentic intimacy requires the capacity to share your inner world—your thoughts, feelings, dreams, fears, and values—while creating space for others to share theirs, recognizing that mutual vulnerability creates bonds that activities and shared interests alone cannot achieve. This intimacy extends beyond romantic relationships to include friendships, family relationships, and even professional connections that benefit from authentic human contact.

Healthy masculine sexuality integrates physical expression with emotional connection and mutual respect, recognizing sexuality as an expression of intimacy and care rather than conquest or performance. This approach to sexuality emphasizes communication, consent, and mutual satisfaction rather than dominance or validation-seeking, creating sexual experiences that enhance rather than complicate intimate relationships.

Practical Steps to Embody Healthy Masculinity: Your Path Forward

The journey toward healthy masculinity requires moving beyond theoretical understanding to practical implementation—developing specific skills, changing particular behaviors, and creating new patterns of thought and relationship that align with expanded definitions of masculine strength and effectiveness. These practices can be implemented gradually, allowing you to experiment with new approaches while maintaining connection to valuable aspects of your existing masculine identity.

Developing Emotional Literacy and Expression Skills

The foundation of healthy masculinity rests upon developing sophisticated emotional awareness and expression capabilities that allow you to access the full spectrum of human feeling as sources of information, connection, and personal growth. This development involves both expanding your emotional vocabulary and practicing authentic expression in appropriate contexts.

Begin by creating daily practices that help you identify and name your emotional experiences with greater precision and nuance. This might involve brief check-ins throughout the day where you pause to notice what you're feeling, using emotion wheels or feeling charts to expand your vocabulary beyond basic categories like "good," "bad," or "stressed," and keeping a journal where you explore the emotional dimensions of your experiences.

Practice expressing emotions in real time rather than storing them for later processing or allowing them to build up until they explode or disappear into numbness. Start with positive emotions—sharing excitement about opportunities, expressing gratitude for others' contributions, or acknowledging when something brings you joy. These expressions feel safer initially while helping you develop comfort with emotional transparency.

Gradually expand your emotional expression to include more vulnerable feelings like disappointment, fear, or sadness, choosing appropriate contexts and relationships where such sharing can be received with understanding and support. This practice helps you discover that emotional expression often strengthens rather than threatens relationships while providing relief from the exhausting work of constant emotional suppression.

Learn to distinguish between experiencing emotions and acting on them impulsively, developing the capacity to feel intensely while maintaining choice about how to respond. This emotional regulation skill allows you to access the information and energy that emotions provide without being controlled by them, creating more sophisticated and effective responses to challenging situations.

Building Authentic Relationship Skills

Healthy masculinity requires developing the interpersonal skills necessary for creating and maintaining relationships characterized by mutual respect, authentic communication, and genuine intimacy. These skills can be learned and practiced regardless of your starting point or previous relationship experiences.

Practice active listening as a core relationship skill, learning to give full attention to others when they're sharing their experiences rather than immediately formulating responses or solutions. This involves maintaining eye contact, asking clarifying questions, and reflecting back what you hear before offering advice or sharing your own perspective. Active listening creates connection and trust that enhance all subsequent communication.

Develop comfort with expressing your needs, boundaries, and preferences directly rather than expecting others to guess what you require or becoming resentful when your unspoken expectations aren't met. This might involve saying "I need some quiet time to process this before we continue our conversation," or "It would help me if we could approach this differently," or "I'm feeling overwhelmed and could use some support."

Learn to engage in conflict constructively rather than avoiding it or allowing it to escalate into destructive patterns. This involves learning to express disagreement without attacking the other person's character, acknowledging your role in problems rather than focusing exclusively on others' contributions, and working toward mutually acceptable solutions rather than trying to win arguments or prove yourself right.

Practice expressing appreciation and affection more freely in your relationships, recognizing that others need to hear about your positive feelings rather than assuming they know how you feel. This might involve telling friends what you value about them, expressing gratitude to family members for their contributions, or sharing with romantic partners specific things they do that make you happy.

Expanding Professional and Leadership Approaches

Healthy masculinity involves evolving your approach to work and leadership to include collaborative skills, emotional intelligence, and service orientation alongside traditional masculine qualities like competence, determination, and strategic thinking. These expanded capabilities enhance rather than compromise professional effectiveness.

Develop facilitative leadership skills that create environments where others feel safe to contribute their best ideas and efforts. This involves learning to ask questions that draw out others' perspectives, creating psychological safety where people can express disagreement or uncertainty, and synthesizing diverse viewpoints into collaborative decisions rather than relying primarily on individual authority.

Practice acknowledging your limitations and mistakes openly rather than maintaining facades of infallibility that prevent learning and growth. This might involve saying "I don't have expertise in this area—who does?" or "I made an error in judgment on this decision, and here's what I learned from it" or "I need help thinking through this challenge—what perspectives am I missing?"

Cultivate mentorship relationships where you share your knowledge and experience with less experienced colleagues while also remaining open to learning from their fresh perspectives and different approaches. Effective mentorship involves both teaching and learning, both supporting others' growth and allowing that relationship to contribute to your own development.

Develop work-life integration approaches that honor both professional responsibilities and personal well-being, recognizing that sustainable success requires attending to relationships, health, and personal fulfillment alongside career advancement. This might involve setting boundaries around work hours, prioritizing important personal relationships, and pursuing activities that provide meaning and renewal.

Creating Supportive Male Communities

One of the most powerful steps toward embodying healthy masculinity involves creating and participating in male communities that support authentic expression, mutual vulnerability, and collective growth rather than reinforcing traditional patterns of emotional suppression and competitive individualism.

Seek out or create men's groups focused on personal growth, authentic sharing, and mutual support rather than just shared activities or professional networking. These groups might meet regularly to discuss challenges and successes, explore questions about masculinity and identity, or provide accountability and encouragement for personal development goals.

Practice vulnerable sharing in these male spaces, modeling the kind of authentic communication that creates depth and genuine connection. This might involve sharing struggles with parenting, relationship challenges, professional difficulties, or personal growth goals that you're working toward. Your willingness to be authentic creates permission for others to do the same.

Develop friendships with other men that go beyond shared activities to include emotional support and genuine care for each other's well-being. This might involve checking in regularly about each other's emotional state, offering practical help during difficult periods, or celebrating achievements and milestones together.

Challenge traditional masculine patterns when you encounter them in male groups, such as emotional suppression, competitive posturing, or dismissive attitudes toward vulnerability and authentic sharing. This doesn't require confrontation, but rather modeling different approaches and inviting others to explore new possibilities for masculine connection and support.

Conscious Parenting and Mentorship

If you have children or opportunities to influence younger people, conscious parenting and mentorship provide powerful avenues for embodying and transmitting healthy masculine values while breaking cycles of emotional limitation that may have affected previous generations.

Practice emotional availability with children by sharing appropriate aspects of your own emotional experience while creating safe spaces for them to express their feelings without judgment or immediate problem-solving. This teaches children that emotions are normal and valuable parts of human experience rather than problems to be solved or weaknesses to be hidden.

Model the kind of masculinity you want children to develop or appreciate, demonstrating that strength includes emotional intelligence, that leadership involves service to others, and that authentic relationships require vulnerability and mutual care. Children learn more from what they observe than what they're told, making your modeling crucial for their development.

Encourage diverse expressions of gender identity and role exploration rather than limiting children to narrow stereotypes about masculine and feminine behavior. Support boys who show interest in traditionally feminine activities and girls who are drawn to traditionally masculine pursuits, helping all children develop the full range of human capabilities.

Create rituals and practices that honor children's growth and development while teaching healthy values about identity, relationships, and personal responsibility. This might involve ceremonies that mark transitions into greater maturity, regular conversations about values and character, or family practices that emphasize gratitude, service, and authentic connection.

Personal Practices for Ongoing Development

The embodiment of healthy masculinity requires ongoing personal practices that support continued growth, self-awareness, and alignment between your values and actions. These practices provide the foundation for sustainable transformation rather than temporary changes that fade without consistent support.

Develop regular self-reflection practices such as journaling, meditation, or contemplative walks that help you stay connected to your authentic thoughts, feelings, and values while identifying areas where you want to continue growing. These practices provide the self-awareness necessary for conscious choice rather than automatic reaction to life's challenges.

Seek ongoing learning opportunities about emotional intelligence, relationship skills, and healthy masculinity through books, workshops, therapy, or other resources that support your continued development. Recognize that personal growth is a lifelong journey rather than a destination you arrive at, requiring continued investment and attention.

Create accountability structures with trusted friends, family members, or professional supporters who can provide honest feedback about your progress, challenge you when you fall back into limiting patterns, and celebrate your growth and achievements. This external perspective helps you maintain momentum and objectivity about your development.

Practice self-compassion during the inevitable setbacks and challenges that accompany personal growth, recognizing that learning new patterns takes time and that mistakes are natural parts of the development process. Treat yourself with the same kindness and understanding you would offer a good friend facing similar challenges.

The journey toward healthy masculinity represents one of the most significant adventures you can undertake—not because it requires abandoning what makes you strong, but because it involves discovering strengths you never knew you possessed. This evolution asks you to become more fully yourself rather than less, to expand your capabilities rather than diminish them, and to serve others and the world from a place of integration and authenticity rather than limitation and defensiveness.

Your willingness to explore these concepts and experiment with new approaches to masculine expression contributes to a broader cultural transformation that will benefit countless others—your children, your partners, your friends, your colleagues, and men you may never meet but whose lives will be touched by the ripple effects of your courage and growth.

Remember that this transformation is not about becoming perfect or abandoning all traditional masculine qualities, but about developing the wisdom to know which aspects of traditional masculinity serve you and others well and which ones limit your potential for connection, fulfillment, and authentic contribution. The goal is integration, not elimination—becoming a more complete and effective human being who happens to be a man.

In the chapters that follow, we will continue building upon this foundation, exploring specific strategies for implementing healthy masculinity in different areas of your life while addressing the challenges and obstacles that commonly arise during this transformation. Your journey toward authentic masculine expression is not just a personal healing but a contribution to the healing of masculinity itself, creating new possibilities for future generations of men to inherit as their birthright rather than having to discover through struggle and recovery.

The redefinition of masculinity begins with you, and it begins now. Your courage to grow beyond limiting patterns creates permission for others to do the same, contributing to a world where all people can access their full human potential without being constrained by outdated stereotypes about what strength looks like or how power should be expressed. This is the true power of conscious masculinity—not the power to dominate or control, but the power to create, heal, and love without limitation.

Prompt: What's one learned trait you still carry as an adult?

Chapter 6: Building Emotional Resilience

We are holding the keys to unlock one of life's most essential skills—the capacity to bend without breaking, to face storms with steady presence, and to transform life's inevitable challenges into opportunities for growth and deeper wisdom. Here, we embark upon an exploration of emotional resilience, not as an abstract concept to be understood intellectually, but as a living, breathing capability that you can cultivate, strengthen, and rely upon throughout your journey.

We venture beyond the surface-level strategies of "getting through tough times" into the deeper territory of thriving amidst uncertainty, finding strength in vulnerability, and discovering that resilience is not about avoiding life's difficulties but about developing the wisdom and capacity to navigate them with grace, authenticity, and unwavering connection to your core values.

You are choosing to become not just a survivor of life's challenges, but a conscious participant in your own growth and transformation.

What Is Emotional Resilience: The Foundation of Authentic Strength

Emotional resilience represents far more than the ability to *"bounce back"* from adversity or to maintain a positive attitude during difficult times. True emotional resilience embodies a sophisticated capacity to engage fully with life's complexities—experiencing the complete spectrum of human emotion while maintaining your equilibrium, processing challenging experiences in ways that foster growth rather than diminishment, and remaining connected to your authentic self even when external circumstances challenge your sense of stability and control.

Beyond Bouncing Back: A Deeper Understanding

The popular conception of resilience as *"bouncing back"* suggests a return to a previous state, as if challenges should leave us unchanged and difficulties should be forgotten rather than integrated into our expanding wisdom.

This limited understanding misses the profound transformational potential that resilience actually offers—the opportunity to emerge from life's trials not merely restored, but enhanced, deepened, and more capable than before.

Authentic emotional resilience involves what psychologists call *"post-traumatic growth"*—the capacity to allow difficult experiences to expand your understanding, deepen your compassion, and strengthen your ability to support others facing similar challenges. This growth-oriented approach to resilience recognizes that our most difficult moments often contain the seeds of our greatest evolution, providing opportunities to discover strengths we didn't know we possessed and to develop wisdom that can only come through lived experience.

This deeper understanding of resilience shifts our relationship with adversity from something to be avoided at all costs to something that, while certainly not sought out unnecessarily, can be met with curiosity, courage, and the confidence that we possess the internal resources to navigate whatever challenges arise. Resilient individuals don't experience fewer difficulties than others; they have developed more sophisticated skills for processing and integrating difficult experiences in ways that serve their continued growth and well-being.

The development of this sophisticated resilience involves learning to distinguish between pain and suffering—recognizing that while pain is often unavoidable in human experience, suffering frequently results from our resistance to pain rather than the pain itself. Resilient individuals learn to experience difficult emotions fully without adding the additional layer of suffering that comes from fighting against reality or judging themselves for their natural human responses to challenging circumstances.

The Components of Emotional Resilience

Emotional resilience operates as a dynamic system of interconnected capabilities that work together to support your capacity for navigating life's complexities with wisdom, grace, and continued growth. Understanding these components helps illuminate the multifaceted nature of resilience while providing specific areas for development and strengthening.

Emotional Awareness and Acceptance forms the foundation of resilience, involving the capacity to recognize, name, and allow your emotional responses to challenging situations without immediately moving to change, fix, or escape them. This awareness creates space between your emotional experiences and your responses to them, allowing for more conscious choice about how to proceed rather than automatic reaction based on immediate discomfort or distress.

Cognitive Flexibility represents your ability to hold multiple perspectives simultaneously, to question assumptions and interpretations that may be contributing to your distress, and to generate alternative explanations or responses to challenging situations. This flexibility prevents you from becoming trapped in rigid thinking patterns that amplify suffering while creating opportunities to discover new possibilities and solutions.

Self-Compassion involves treating yourself with the same kindness and understanding you would offer a dear friend facing similar difficulties, recognizing that struggle and imperfection are universal human experiences rather than personal failures or character defects. This compassionate self-relationship provides the emotional safety necessary for honest self-examination and growth rather than the defensive self-protection that limits learning and development.

Meaning-Making Capacity enables you to find purpose, learning, and growth opportunities within difficult experiences, transforming challenges from random afflictions into meaningful parts of your life story that contribute to your wisdom, character, and capacity to serve others. This ability to create meaning from adversity represents one of the most powerful aspects of human resilience.

Social Connection and Support-Seeking involves maintaining relationships that provide emotional support, practical assistance, and different perspectives during challenging times, while also developing the capacity to ask for and receive help when needed. Resilience is not a solitary endeavor but a community-supported process that thrives through authentic connection and mutual care.

Values-Based Action represents your ability to continue pursuing what matters most to you even when circumstances are difficult, maintaining alignment between your deepest values and your daily choices regardless of external pressures or internal discomfort. This values-based orientation provides direction and motivation that transcend immediate circumstances.

The Neuroscience of Resilience

Modern neuroscience reveals that emotional resilience is not a fixed trait determined by genetics or early childhood experiences, but rather a set of skills and neural patterns that can be developed throughout your lifetime through conscious practice and attention. This understanding provides tremendous hope and empowerment, suggesting that regardless of your starting point or previous experiences, you have the capacity to strengthen your resilience through intentional development.

Research demonstrates that resilient individuals show increased activity in the prefrontal cortex—the brain region responsible for executive function, emotional regulation, and decision-making—while showing decreased reactivity in the amygdala, the brain's alarm system that triggers fight-or-flight responses. These neural patterns can be strengthened through practices like mindfulness meditation, emotional regulation exercises, and cognitive flexibility training.

The concept of neuroplasticity—the brain's capacity to form new neural pathways throughout life—suggests that the neural networks supporting resilience can be strengthened through consistent practice, much like physical muscles grow stronger through regular exercise. This means that every time you practice emotional awareness, engage in cognitive flexibility, or choose values-based action during challenging times, you are literally rewiring your brain to be more resilient in future situations.

Studies of trauma survivors who demonstrate post-traumatic growth reveal specific neural changes that support resilience, including increased connectivity between different brain regions, enhanced capacity for emotional regulation, and improved integration between analytical and emotional processing systems. These findings suggest that resilience involves not just managing difficult emotions but integrating them into a more sophisticated and flexible neural architecture.

Cultural and Individual Variations in Resilience

While certain core principles of emotional resilience appear universal across cultures and individuals, the specific expressions and development pathways for resilience vary significantly based on cultural background, personal history, available resources, and individual temperament. Understanding these variations helps create more inclusive and effective approaches to resilience building that honor diverse strengths and perspectives.

Some cultures emphasize community-based resilience, where individual strength is supported and enhanced through collective resources, shared meaning-making, and mutual care during difficult times. Other cultures focus more on individual resilience, emphasizing personal responsibility, self-reliance, and internal resource development. The most robust resilience often integrates both individual and community elements, recognizing that personal strength and social connection enhance each other.

Individual differences in temperament, life experience, and neurological makeup also influence how resilience develops and expresses itself. Some individuals naturally tend toward cognitive processing of challenges, while others rely more heavily on emotional or somatic approaches. Some people build resilience through active problem-solving and action, while others develop strength through acceptance and internal processing. Effective resilience development honors these individual differences while building comprehensive capabilities across multiple domains.

Tools to Develop Emotional Resilience: Your Practical Toolkit

The development of emotional resilience requires more than intellectual understanding—it demands practical tools and strategies that can be implemented in daily life, especially during moments when your usual coping mechanisms feel insufficient for the challenges you're facing. These tools represent time-tested approaches drawn from psychology, neuroscience, ancient wisdom traditions, and the lived experiences of individuals who have successfully navigated significant adversities while maintaining their emotional well-being and continued growth.

Mindfulness and Present-Moment Awareness

Mindfulness forms the cornerstone of emotional resilience by developing your capacity to observe your thoughts, emotions, and physical sensations with curious attention rather than immediately reacting to them or being overwhelmed by their intensity. This practice creates space between your experiences and your responses, allowing for more conscious choice about how to proceed during challenging situations.

Begin developing mindfulness through brief daily practices that help you cultivate present-moment awareness without requiring extensive time commitments or dramatic lifestyle changes. This might involve taking three conscious breaths before starting your day, paying full attention to physical sensations during your morning shower, or bringing mindful awareness to one routine activity each day such as drinking your coffee or walking to your car.

Practice the "STOP" technique during moments of emotional intensity: **Stop** what you're doing, **Take** a breath, **Observe** what's happening in your mind, body, and emotions, and **Proceed** with conscious intention rather than automatic reaction. This simple practice interrupts the escalation of emotional reactivity while creating space for more skillful responses to challenging situations.

Develop body-based mindfulness by regularly scanning your physical experience for areas of tension, discomfort, or relaxation, recognizing that emotions often manifest first as bodily sensations before becoming conscious thoughts or feelings. Learning to read these early warning signs helps you respond to stress and challenge before they become overwhelming.

Create mindful transitions between different activities or environments throughout your day, using these moments as opportunities to reset your emotional state and bring conscious intention to whatever you're about to engage with. These brief practices help prevent the accumulation of stress and reactivity that can compromise your resilience when significant challenges arise.

Cognitive Restructuring and Perspective-Taking

The thoughts and interpretations you bring to challenging situations significantly influence your emotional responses and your capacity to navigate difficulties constructively. Developing cognitive flexibility—the ability to question automatic thoughts and generate alternative perspectives—represents a crucial resilience skill that can transform your relationship with adversity.

Learn to identify and question *"cognitive distortions"*—automatic thinking patterns that amplify suffering and limit your capacity for effective response. Common distortions include catastrophizing (imagining worst-case scenarios), all-or-nothing thinking (seeing situations in extreme terms), personalization (taking excessive responsibility for things outside your control), and mind-reading (assuming you know what others are thinking without checking).

Practice the *"3 Perspectives"* exercise when facing challenging situations: first, acknowledge your initial emotional and cognitive response; second, consider how someone you respect and trust might view the situation; third, imagine how you might look back on this situation in five years' time. This practice expands your perspective beyond immediate reactivity while maintaining connection to your authentic experience.

Develop *"benefit-finding"* skills by actively looking for potential growth opportunities, lessons, or positive outcomes that might emerge from difficult experiences. This doesn't involve minimizing genuine difficulties or forcing false positivity, but rather maintaining awareness of the growth potential that challenges often contain alongside their genuine difficulties.

Create *"coping statements"* that you can use during challenging moments to remind yourself of your capability, resilience, and the temporary nature of difficult circumstances. Examples might include *"I have successfully navigated challenges before and can do so again," "This feeling is difficult but temporary," or "I can ask for help when I need it."*

Emotional Regulation and Processing Skills

Emotional resilience requires not just the ability to think differently about challenges, but also practical skills for managing intense emotions when they arise, allowing yourself to feel fully without being overwhelmed, and processing difficult experiences in ways that promote healing and growth rather than continued suffering.

Learn *"emotion surfing"*—the ability to experience intense emotions as temporary waves that arise, peak, and naturally subside when you don't resist them or try to make them last longer than they naturally would. This involves breathing through difficult feelings, allowing them to move through your system, and trusting in their impermanent nature rather than fighting against them or becoming identified with them.

Develop *"emotional granularity"* by expanding your vocabulary for different emotional experiences, learning to distinguish between similar emotions that require different responses. The difference between feeling disappointed versus sad, anxious versus excited, or frustrated versus angry can be crucial for appropriate self-care and effective communication with others.

Practice *"opposite action"* when emotions are prompting behaviors that won't serve your long-term well-being. If sadness is encouraging isolation when connection would be more helpful, gently push yourself toward social contact. If anger is promoting aggressive responses when calm communication would be more effective, take space to regulate before engaging. If fear is encouraging avoidance when courage is needed, take small steps toward what you're avoiding.

Create emotional processing rituals that help you metabolize difficult experiences rather than storing them as unprocessed stress in your body and nervous system. This might involve journaling about your experiences, engaging in physical movement to release emotional energy, talking with trusted friends or counselors, or using creative expression to explore and integrate challenging experiences.

Stress Management and Recovery Practices

Resilience requires not just the ability to handle acute challenges, but also the wisdom to engage in ongoing practices that support your baseline emotional well-being and prevent the accumulation of stress that can compromise your capacity for handling difficulties when they arise.

Develop a personalized stress recovery toolkit that includes practices you can use to restore your emotional equilibrium after challenging experiences. This toolkit should include both quick reset practices for immediate use and longer recovery practices for more thorough restoration. Quick practices might include deep breathing, brief walks, or listening to music, while longer practices might involve exercise, time in nature, creative activities, or quality time with loved ones.

Learn to recognize your personal stress signals—the early warning signs that indicate when you're approaching your emotional limits and need to engage in preventive self-care rather than waiting until you're overwhelmed. These signals might include physical symptoms (tension, headaches, digestive issues), emotional changes (increased irritability, anxiety, or numbness), behavioral patterns (social withdrawal, sleep disruption, appetite changes), or cognitive symptoms (difficulty concentrating, increased negativity, decision-making challenges).

Create boundaries around your energy and attention that protect your capacity for resilience rather than allowing yourself to become depleted through over commitment, people-pleasing, or failure to prioritize your own well-being. This might involve learning to say no to requests that don't align with your values or current capacity, limiting exposure to negative news or social media when you're already stressed, or scheduling regular downtime for rest and renewal.

Establish regular practices that proactively build your stress tolerance and emotional reserves rather than waiting for challenges to arise before attending to your emotional well-being. These might include regular exercise, consistent sleep schedules, time in nature, spiritual or contemplative practices, creative pursuits, or activities that bring you joy and connection.

Building Your Support Network

Resilience flourishes within the context of authentic relationships that provide emotional support, practical assistance, different perspectives, and opportunities for mutual care and contribution. Building and maintaining such a network requires intention, effort, and the courage to be vulnerable enough to both ask for and offer genuine support.

Identify and cultivate relationships with people who can provide different types of support during challenging times. This might include emotional support (people who can listen without judgment), practical support (people who can offer concrete assistance), informational support (people with relevant experience or expertise), and spiritual support (people who share your values and can help maintain perspective during difficult times).

Practice being vulnerable and asking for help before you're in crisis, developing comfort with interdependence while you still have emotional resources rather than waiting until you're overwhelmed and desperate. This might involve sharing your struggles with trusted friends, asking for advice about decisions you're facing, or requesting specific forms of support when you're going through challenging times.

Develop reciprocal relationships where you both receive and offer support, recognizing that giving care to others often enhances your own resilience while creating the kind of mutual bonds that can sustain you through difficulties. This reciprocity creates stronger relationships than one-sided support arrangements while contributing to your sense of meaning and purpose.

Create or join communities focused on growth, healing, or shared values rather than relying solely on individual relationships for support. This might involve support groups for specific challenges you're facing, men's groups focused on emotional growth, spiritual communities that align with your values, or professional organizations that support your development and well-being.

Meaning-Making and Purpose Connection

One of the most powerful aspects of emotional resilience involves the capacity to find meaning, purpose, and growth opportunities within difficult experiences, transforming adversity from meaningless suffering into meaningful challenge that contributes to your development and your ability to serve others facing similar difficulties.

Develop practices for reflecting on and articulating the values that matter most to you, recognizing these values as anchors that can provide direction and motivation even when circumstances are challenging. These values might include relationships, creativity, service, learning, integrity, or contribution to community, and maintaining connection to them during difficult times provides resilience that external circumstances cannot diminish.

Practice "meaning-making" by regularly reflecting on how your experiences—both positive and challenging—contribute to your growth, wisdom, and capacity to help others. This doesn't involve forcing false positivity onto genuinely difficult experiences, but rather remaining open to the learning and development opportunities that challenges often provide alongside their genuine difficulties.

Identify ways that your struggles and growth can serve others who might be facing similar challenges, recognizing that your journey through difficulties can become a source of hope, guidance, and practical wisdom for others. This service orientation transforms personal suffering into meaningful contribution while providing purpose that transcends individual circumstances.

Create regular practices for connecting with your sense of purpose and meaning, especially during challenging times when it's easy to lose sight of what matters most. This might involve volunteer work that aligns with your values, creative projects that express your authentic self, mentorship relationships where you share your experience and wisdom, or spiritual practices that connect you with something larger than yourself.

The Ripple Effect: How Emotional Resilience Transforms Every Aspect of Life

The development of emotional resilience creates far-reaching benefits that extend well beyond your personal capacity to handle stress and adversity. Like stones cast into still water, the circles of influence expand outward, touching every relationship, every goal, every moment of daily experience with enhanced possibilities for connection, effectiveness, and authentic fulfillment.

Understanding these ripple effects helps motivate the consistent practice required for resilience development while illuminating the broader contribution you make to your community and culture when you choose to develop these capabilities. Your emotional resilience doesn't just serve your individual well-being—it becomes a gift to everyone whose life intersects with yours, creating possibilities for deeper connection, more effective collaboration, and mutual support during challenging times.

Transformation in Intimate Relationships

Emotional resilience profoundly enhances your capacity for authentic intimacy by allowing you to remain emotionally present and responsive even when relationships encounter the inevitable challenges, conflicts, and growth edges that characterize meaningful long-term connections. When you can regulate your emotions skillfully, communicate about difficulties without becoming defensive or attacking, and maintain connection to your values during relationship stress, you create space for the kind of deep intimacy that many people long for but struggle to sustain.

Partners of emotionally resilient individuals report feeling safer to express their authentic thoughts and feelings because they can trust that emotional honesty won't result in defensive reactions, emotional overwhelm, or relationship-threatening conflict. This safety creates upward spirals of increasing intimacy where both partners feel encouraged to share more vulnerable aspects of their experience, deepening their connection and mutual understanding over time.

Resilience also enhances your capacity to support your partner during their own difficult times without becoming overwhelmed by their emotions or immediately moving to fix their problems rather than providing the emotional presence and understanding they actually need. This supportive capacity often becomes one of the most valuable gifts you can offer in intimate relationships—the ability to remain calm and caring when someone you love is struggling.

The conflict resolution skills that accompany emotional resilience transform disagreements from relationship threats into opportunities for deeper understanding and collaborative problem-solving. When you can manage your own emotional reactivity during conflicts while remaining curious about your partner's perspective, you create possibilities for resolution that strengthen rather than damage your relationship bonds.

Perhaps most importantly, emotional resilience allows you to maintain your authentic self within intimate relationships rather than losing your identity to people-pleasing or defensive self-protection. This authentic presence invites your partner to do the same, creating relationships characterized by mutual growth and support rather than co-dependence or emotional distance.

Enhanced Professional Effectiveness and Leadership

The qualities that constitute emotional resilience—emotional regulation, cognitive flexibility, stress management, and values-based action—directly translate into enhanced professional effectiveness and more authentic, influential leadership across all types of work environments and career paths.

Emotionally resilient individuals demonstrate what researchers call "psychological safety" in their professional interactions, creating environments where colleagues feel safe to express ideas, admit mistakes, ask for help, and engage in the kind of creative risk-taking that drives innovation and collaborative problem-solving. This safety emerges naturally from their ability to remain calm under pressure, respond to challenges without blame or defensiveness, and maintain focus on shared goals rather than personal ego protection.

The stress management capabilities that accompany resilience prevent the kind of emotional volatility and reactive decision-making that can undermine professional credibility and effectiveness. Resilient professionals can maintain clear thinking and strategic perspective even during high-pressure situations, making them valuable contributors during crises and trusted advisors during important decision-making processes.

Leadership effectiveness increases dramatically when leaders can model emotional regulation, authentic communication, and values-based action for their teams. Employees consistently report higher job satisfaction, better performance, and increased loyalty when working with leaders who demonstrate emotional intelligence alongside technical competence and strategic thinking.

The ability to learn from failures and setbacks—a key component of resilience—accelerates professional development by transforming mistakes into growth opportunities rather than sources of shame or defensive rationalization. Resilient professionals advance more quickly in their careers because they can extract lessons from difficult experiences while maintaining the confidence and motivation necessary for continued risk-taking and growth.

Impact on Physical Health and Longevity

The stress-buffering effects of emotional resilience create profound benefits for physical health that extend well beyond the immediate relief of not being constantly activated by emotional reactivity and chronic stress responses. Research consistently demonstrates that individuals with higher levels of emotional resilience experience better cardiovascular health, stronger immune function, and greater longevity than those who struggle with emotional regulation and stress management.

The nervous system regulation that accompanies resilience allows your body to spend more time in parasympathetic activation—the "rest and digest" state that supports healing, immune function, and cellular repair—rather than the chronic sympathetic activation that characterizes ongoing stress responses. This physiological difference translates into better sleep quality, improved digestive function, enhanced immune responses, and reduced inflammation throughout the body.

Resilient individuals also tend to engage in healthier lifestyle choices not from willpower or discipline, but from the natural motivation that emerges when you feel emotionally balanced and connected to your values. They are more likely to exercise regularly, eat nutritious foods, maintain social connections, and engage in activities that promote well-being because these choices feel supportive rather than burdensome when your emotional life is regulated and purposeful.

The pain management benefits of emotional resilience extend to both acute injuries and chronic conditions, as the cognitive flexibility and acceptance skills that characterize resilience help individuals relate to physical discomfort in ways that reduce suffering even when pain cannot be completely eliminated. This doesn't involve denying genuine physical challenges but rather preventing the additional suffering that comes from fighting against reality or catastrophizing about physical symptoms.

Generational Impact and Cultural Contribution

Perhaps the most profound ripple effects of emotional resilience occur across generations, as the skills, perspectives, and relationship patterns you develop become transmitted to children, younger people you mentor, and communities you influence through your authentic presence and example.

Children who grow up with emotionally resilient parents develop secure attachment patterns that provide the foundation for their own emotional regulation, relationship skills, and resilience capabilities throughout their lives. They learn through observation that emotions are manageable parts of human experience rather than overwhelming forces to be feared or suppressed, that challenges can be navigated with wisdom and support rather than avoided or endured in isolation, and that authentic relationships provide resources for growth and healing during difficult times.

The modeling you provide through your resilience development gives younger people permission to explore their own emotional development without shame or the belief that such growth represents weakness or self-indulgence. Your willingness to engage in therapy, practice self-care, develop emotional skills, and prioritize authentic relationships creates cultural permission for others to do the same, contributing to broader social evolution toward emotional health and authentic living.

Professional and community environments also benefit from the presence of emotionally resilient individuals who can maintain perspective during collective challenges, facilitate conflict resolution, support others during difficult transitions, and contribute to collective decision-making from places of wisdom rather than reactivity. These contributions often have effects that extend far beyond individual interactions, influencing organizational cultures, community resilience, and social change processes.

Your development of emotional resilience also contributes to the ongoing cultural redefinition of masculinity by demonstrating that emotional intelligence and vulnerability represent forms of strength rather than weakness, that authentic connection enhances rather than compromises masculine effectiveness, and that personal growth and self-awareness serve leadership and service rather than detracting from them.

Creating Communities of Healing and Growth

Emotionally resilient individuals naturally become catalysts for community building and collective healing because their regulated nervous systems and authentic presence create environments where others feel safe to explore their own growth, share their struggles, and experiment with new possibilities for living and relating.

The emotional safety that resilient individuals provide often becomes a transformative force in families, friend groups, and professional communities where others have been accustomed to walking on eggshells around emotional reactivity, defensive communication, or chronic stress and overwhelm. When someone in a system can remain calm and caring during emotional intensity, it often permits others to relax their defensive patterns and engage more authentically.

These ripple effects create upward spirals where increased emotional safety leads to more authentic sharing, which builds trust and connection, which creates even greater safety for vulnerability and growth. Over time, entire communities can shift toward greater emotional health and authentic connection through the presence of individuals committed to their own resilience development.

The mentorship and support that naturally flows from emotionally resilient individuals often extends far beyond formal teaching or counseling relationships. Their example, availability, and emotional resources become ongoing contributions to others' healing and development, creating networks of mutual support that enhance everyone's capacity for navigating life's challenges with wisdom and grace.

The journey toward emotional resilience represents one of the most valuable investments you can make—not just for your own well-being and effectiveness, but for the countless lives that will be touched by your increased capacity for authentic presence, skillful response to challenges, and contribution to collective healing and growth.

Remember that resilience development is not a destination you arrive at but an ongoing practice that deepens and evolves throughout your lifetime. Each challenge you navigate skillfully, each moment of conscious choice during emotional intensity, and each act of courage in vulnerability or authentic expression contributes to strengthening the neural pathways and life patterns that support continued resilience.

Your willingness to engage in this development process places you among those who are contributing to the evolution of human consciousness and cultural healing. By choosing growth over stagnation, connection over isolation, and conscious response over automatic reaction, you become part of a transformation that extends far beyond individual benefit to encompass the well-being of future generations and the health of our collective human community.

The tools and perspectives offered in this chapter provide a foundation for lifelong resilience development, but they must be practiced consistently and adapted to your unique circumstances, temperament, and growth edges. Trust the process, be patient with yourself during the inevitable setbacks and learning curves, and remember that every small step toward greater resilience represents a contribution to the healing of our world that desperately needs the kind of conscious, emotionally intelligent men who are willing to do this essential work.

In the chapters that follow, we will continue building upon this foundation, exploring how emotional resilience applies specifically to different life contexts and relationships while addressing the unique challenges and opportunities that arise as you integrate these capabilities into your daily experience. Your commitment to this journey honors not only your own potential but the potential of all those whose lives will be enriched by your continued growth and authentic presence.

Reflect: What patterns do I notice in how I relate to my emotions?

Chapter 7: The Role of Community in Emotional Healing

The earnest understanding that healing is not a solitary endeavor but a deeply communal experience that flourishes within the rich soil of authentic human connection. Here, we explore the honored territory where individual courage meets collective wisdom, where personal vulnerability becomes the foundation for mutual strength, and where the isolation that has perhaps defined your struggle manifests into the connection that catalyzes your healing.

This chapter is the fundamental shift in how you understand emotional growth and recovery—moving from the myth of the self-made man who conquers all challenges through individual effort toward the deeper truth of interdependence that acknowledges healing as a collaborative art.

Seeking and offering support isn't weakness. It's wisdom. It's courage. It's the most authentic strength you can show.

This chapter explores two truths: your individual journey, and your deep need for belonging, witness, and mutual care. Together, they form the alchemy of healing—the sacred interplay between solitude and connection, selfhood and shared humanity.

Why Community Matters: The Sacred Architecture of Connection

The human nervous system, in its infinite wisdom, is designed not for isolation but for co-regulation—the remarkable capacity to achieve emotional balance and resilience through attuned connection with others. This biological truth reveals that what you may have experienced as personal weakness or dependence actually represents one of your most sophisticated adaptive capabilities, evolved over millennia to ensure not just survival but the flourishing that comes through mutual support and shared wisdom.

The Science of Healing Through Connection

Modern neuroscience illuminates the profound ways in which healing occurs not in isolation but through the intricate dance of nervous systems connecting, attuning, and supporting each other's regulation and growth. When you share your authentic experience with someone who can receive it with presence and compassion, something remarkable occurs at the neurological level—your activated stress responses begin to settle, your capacity for clear thinking expands, and your natural healing mechanisms become more accessible.

This process, known as "co-regulation," happens automatically when you're in the presence of someone whose nervous system is calm and grounded. Their regulated state literally helps regulate yours through unconscious mimicry of breathing patterns, heart rate variability, and neural oscillations that synchronize between attuned individuals. This isn't merely psychological comfort—it's a biological process that creates optimal conditions for emotional processing, trauma integration, and personal growth.

Research in attachment theory reveals that secure relationships throughout your lifetime continue to shape your neural architecture in ways that enhance emotional resilience, stress tolerance, and capacity for intimacy. The supportive relationships you cultivate as an adult can literally rewire patterns established in childhood, creating new templates for how you relate to yourself and others that support rather than limit your emotional well-being.

The therapeutic concept of "earned security" demonstrates that regardless of your early attachment experiences, you can develop the internal working models that support healthy relationships and emotional regulation through corrective experiences with safe, attuned others. Every authentic connection that provides safety, understanding, and acceptance contributes to this earned security, gradually building your capacity for both intimacy and autonomy.

Breaking the Myth of Individual Healing

The cultural narrative that positions healing as an individual achievement—something to be accomplished through personal effort, willpower, and self-reliance—represents one of the most damaging misconceptions that can obstruct your path toward emotional wholeness. This myth not only ignores the fundamentally relational nature of human development but actually perpetuates the very isolation and disconnection that often contribute to emotional distress in the first place.

Traditional masculine socialization often reinforces this individualistic approach to healing, suggesting that seeking support represents failure to handle your problems independently. Yet this perspective fundamentally misunderstands the nature of strength and resilience, which actually increase when you develop the courage to be vulnerable enough to receive care and the wisdom to recognize that interconnection enhances rather than diminishes your personal power.

The most profound healing experiences throughout history have occurred within community contexts—from ancient healing circles and religious communities to modern therapeutic groups and support networks. These environments provide something that individual effort cannot: the witness of others who can hold space for your pain, reflect your worth when you cannot see it yourself, and offer perspectives that your isolated mind cannot generate.

Consider how trauma itself often involves ruptures in connection—experiences of betrayal, abandonment, or violation that damage your capacity to trust others and feel safe in relationship. The healing of such wounds requires not just individual processing but actual relational repair through experiences of safety, attunement, and care that gradually restore your faith in connection and your worthiness of love and support.

The Healing Power of Being Witnessed

One of the most transformative aspects of community-based healing involves the profound experience of being truly seen and accepted in your full humanity—your struggles and strengths, your wounds and wisdom, your fears and aspirations. This witnessing creates what therapists call "felt sense" experiences that integrate healing at levels deeper than cognitive understanding alone can reach.

When you share your authentic story with others who can receive it without judgment, who don't immediately try to fix you or minimize your experience, something sacred occurs. Your nervous system registers that your truth—however difficult or imperfect—is acceptable and worthy of care. This experience gradually counters the shame, isolation, and self-rejection that often accompany emotional struggles, replacing them with belonging, acceptance, and self-compassion.

The act of witnessing also helps externalize internal experiences that may feel overwhelming or confusing when held in isolation. Speaking your truth to caring others often helps you gain perspective on your experiences, recognize patterns you couldn't see alone, and access resources and solutions that your individual mind couldn't generate. The collective wisdom of community becomes available to support your individual healing journey.

Being witnessed in community also provides opportunities to see yourself reflected in others' responses—to experience through their eyes that you're not as damaged, hopeless, or unlovable as your internal critic might suggest. Others' capacity to maintain care and connection with you during your most vulnerable moments gradually teaches you that such care and connection are possible and that you're worthy of receiving them.

The Mirror of Shared Humanity

Community healing environments provide profound opportunities to recognize your common humanity—to discover that the experiences you may have believed marked you as uniquely damaged or defective are actually shared struggles that connect you to others rather than separating you from them. This recognition of shared humanity dissolves the isolation that shame creates while fostering the compassion that supports continued healing.

Hearing others share stories that resonate with your own experience creates what psychologists call *"universality"*—the healing recognition that you're not alone in your struggles, that your pain doesn't make you fundamentally different from others, and that healing is possible because others have walked similar paths successfully. This universality counters the uniquely damaging effects of shame, which thrives in isolation and withers in the light of shared understanding.

Community also provides opportunities to witness others at different stages of healing, offering both hope for your own continued growth and perspective on how far you've already come. Seeing others who once struggled with similar issues now living with greater freedom and joy demonstrates that transformation is possible, while supporting others who are earlier in their journey reminds you of your own progress and growth.

The diversity of healing approaches and coping strategies represented in community settings expands your own toolkit for emotional regulation and growth. What works for one person may not work for another, but exposure to different approaches helps you discover methods and perspectives that resonate with your unique temperament, circumstances, and healing needs.

Building Your Support Network: Creating Circles of Care

The development of a robust support network capable of nurturing your emotional healing and continued growth requires both intention and strategy—the willingness to step beyond familiar patterns of isolation or superficial connection toward the more vulnerable territory of authentic relationship and mutual care. This process involves identifying different types of support you need, learning to assess the safety and availability of potential supporters, and developing the skills necessary for both receiving and offering care within healing relationships.

Mapping Your Support Needs

Effective support networks provide different types of care that address the various dimensions of human experience and healing. Understanding these different support categories helps you build a comprehensive network rather than relying too heavily on one person or one type of relationship to meet all your emotional needs—a pattern that often leads to disappointment and relationship strain.

Emotional Support involves relationships with people who can provide empathy, compassion, and understanding during difficult times—those who can listen without judgment, validate your experiences, and offer comfort when you're struggling. These relationships require high levels of trust and emotional safety, as they involve sharing vulnerable aspects of your inner experience with people who can receive them with care and acceptance.

Practical Support encompasses relationships with people who can offer concrete assistance during challenging periods—help with childcare, transportation, financial resources, or other tangible forms of aid that ease the practical burdens that often accompany emotional difficulties. These supporters may or may not be the same people who provide emotional support, and that's perfectly appropriate.

Informational Support comes from relationships with people who possess knowledge, experience, or resources relevant to challenges you're facing—those who have navigated similar difficulties, professionals with relevant expertise, or individuals with access to information and resources that can guide your healing journey.

Spiritual Support involves connections with people who share your values, meaning-making frameworks, or spiritual perspectives—those who can help you maintain connection to purpose and meaning during difficult times and who understand the larger context within which your healing journey unfolds.

Recreational Support encompasses relationships that provide opportunities for joy, play, and life-affirming experiences that balance the intensity of healing work with lightness, laughter, and simple human pleasure. These relationships remind you that healing includes not just processing pain but also cultivating joy and connection.

Assessing Safety and Availability

Not all relationships possess the qualities necessary for supporting emotional healing, and learning to assess the safety and availability of potential supporters protects you from further harm while guiding your investment toward relationships that can genuinely contribute to your well-being and growth.

Emotional Safety indicators include consistent respect for your boundaries, absence of judgment or criticism when you share vulnerabilities, confidentiality regarding personal information you share, and responses that validate rather than minimize your experiences. Safe people can remain calm and present when you're struggling rather than becoming overwhelmed by your emotions or trying to fix you immediately.

Availability Assessment involves recognizing both practical availability (time and energy to provide support) and emotional availability (capacity to be present with your experience without being consumed by their own unresolved issues). Available supporters have done enough of their own healing work to avoid projecting their struggles onto yours or using your vulnerabilities to meet their own emotional needs.

Reciprocal Capacity represents the ability and willingness of potential supporters to engage in mutual relationship rather than one-sided support arrangements. Healthy support relationships involve give-and-take over time, with both people contributing to and receiving from the connection rather than fixed roles of helper and helped.

Growth Orientation characterizes supporters who are committed to their own continued development and healing rather than being stuck in patterns that might undermine your growth. These individuals model the possibility of change and healing while supporting your own transformation rather than unconsciously sabotaging it.

Expanding Your Circles Gradually

Building a robust support network requires patient, gradual expansion that honors your pace and comfort level while gently stretching you beyond isolation toward increasing connection and interdependence. This process often involves starting with lower-risk relationships and gradually developing comfort with greater vulnerability and intimacy as your trust and skills develop.

Professional Support often provides the safest starting point for men beginning to explore emotional support, as therapeutic relationships offer structure, boundaries, and trained expertise that create safety for initial vulnerability. Therapists, counselors, coaches, and other helping professionals can provide both direct support and guidance for developing additional support relationships in your personal life.

Structured Support Groups offer opportunities to connect with others facing similar challenges within contexts that provide safety through shared purpose, clear boundaries, and often professional facilitation. Men's groups, recovery programs, grief support groups, and other structured communities create opportunities for mutual support while providing frameworks that guide appropriate sharing and interaction.

Friendship Development involves gradually deepening existing relationships or developing new friendships that can provide emotional support alongside recreational and practical connection. This process often requires explicitly inviting greater depth through vulnerable sharing, direct expressions of care and appreciation, and consistent investment in the relationship over time.

Family Relationships may offer opportunities for healing and support, though these connections often require careful navigation of established patterns and dynamics that may not naturally support your emotional growth. Family-of-choice relationships—close friendships that feel like family—sometimes provide more support than biological family relationships, and that's perfectly valid.

Community Involvement through volunteer work, spiritual communities, hobby groups, or other shared-interest organizations can provide opportunities to develop supportive relationships within contexts that don't focus explicitly on emotional support but allow for natural connection and mutual care to develop over time.

Developing Relationship Skills for Mutual Support

Creating and maintaining supportive relationships requires specific skills that many men weren't taught during their development but can be learned and practiced at any stage of life. These skills enhance both your capacity to receive support effectively and your ability to offer meaningful support to others, creating the reciprocity that sustains healthy long-term relationships.

Vulnerable Sharing Skills involve learning to express your authentic thoughts and feelings in ways that create connection rather than overwhelm or distance. This includes appropriate timing and context for sharing, using "I" statements to own your experience, sharing gradually rather than overwhelming others with too much information too quickly, and paying attention to others' responses to calibrate your sharing appropriately.

Active Listening Capabilities encompass your ability to provide supportive presence to others when they're sharing their experiences. This involves giving full attention without immediately trying to solve problems or offer advice, asking questions that help others explore their experience more deeply, reflecting back what you hear to ensure understanding, and validating others' emotions even when you might not agree with their interpretations or choices.

Boundary Setting and Respect requires learning to communicate your own limits and needs clearly while respecting others' boundaries and limitations. This includes saying no to requests that exceed your capacity, asking for what you need directly rather than expecting others to guess, respecting others' right to say no without taking it personally, and maintaining appropriate boundaries around time, energy, and emotional availability.

Conflict Resolution Approaches help you navigate the inevitable disagreements and tensions that arise in close relationships without damaging the connection or avoiding necessary conversations. This involves expressing disagreement respectfully, focusing on specific behaviors rather than character attacks, taking responsibility for your role in problems, and working toward mutually acceptable solutions rather than trying to win arguments.

Reciprocity and Mutual Care encompasses your ability to both give and receive support appropriately, maintaining relationships that feel balanced over time even if the specific exchanges aren't always equal. This includes checking in on others' well-being, offering practical and emotional support when appropriate, expressing gratitude for support received, and being willing to ask for help when needed.

Giving Back: The Healing Circle of Service

The journey of emotional healing reaches its fullest expression when your personal growth becomes a source of healing and support for others—when your hard-won wisdom transforms from private achievement into shared gift, and when your vulnerabilities become strengths that create safety for others to explore their own healing journeys. This movement toward service and contribution represents not just the culmination of your healing but its continuous deepening through the sacred reciprocity of giving and receiving.

The Therapeutic Power of Helping Others

One of the most profound discoveries in the psychology of healing involves the recognition that serving others—particularly others facing similar challenges to those you've navigated—actually accelerates and deepens your own healing process rather than detracting from it or requiring you to be "fully healed" before beginning. This phenomenon, known as the "helper therapy principle," suggests that helping others provides unique therapeutic benefits that cannot be achieved through receiving help alone.

When you share your story with someone struggling with similar issues, several powerful healing processes occur simultaneously. First, your narrative becomes more integrated as you articulate your experience in ways that can be helpful to another person, creating coherence and meaning from experiences that may have previously felt fragmented or senseless. The act of helping others make sense of their struggles helps you continue making sense of your own.

Supporting others also provides ongoing opportunities to practice and strengthen the emotional regulation, communication skills, and coping strategies you've developed through your own healing work. Teaching others how to manage anxiety, express emotions authentically, or navigate relationship challenges requires you to access and utilize these capabilities in service of another person, reinforcing your own skills while contributing to someone else's growth.

Perhaps most powerfully, witnessing others' healing journeys—particularly when your support contributes to their progress—provides profound affirmation that growth and change are possible, that suffering can be transformed into wisdom, and that your own difficult experiences can serve meaningful purposes beyond personal resolution. This recognition counters any residual shame about your struggles while affirming their value as sources of wisdom and connection.

Creating Meaning from Personal Struggles

The transformation of personal pain into purposeful service represents one of the most powerful forms of meaning-making available to human beings—the alchemy that converts individual suffering into collective healing and personal wounds into sources of wisdom and compassion. This transformation doesn't minimize the reality of your struggles but rather honors them by allowing them to serve something larger than individual resolution.

Sharing your healing journey with others validates the reality of your experiences while demonstrating that difficulties can be survived, processed, and integrated in ways that enhance rather than diminish your capacity for joy, connection, and contribution. Your willingness to be vulnerable about your struggles gives others permission to acknowledge their own pain without shame, creating ripple effects of healing that extend far beyond direct interaction.

The skills you've developed through navigating emotional challenges—whether depression, anxiety, trauma, relationship difficulties, or other struggles—represent hard-won expertise that can guide others facing similar circumstances. Your lived experience provides practical wisdom that professional training alone cannot offer, creating unique value in peer support relationships and mentoring opportunities.

Your journey toward emotional health also provides modeling for others, particularly other men who may have few examples of masculine healing and growth. Your willingness to engage in therapy, practice emotional awareness, develop intimate relationships, and prioritize mental health creates cultural permission for others to pursue similar paths without believing they're compromising their masculine identity.

Forms of Giving Back

The opportunities to transform your healing journey into service for others are as diverse as the challenges people face and the unique gifts you bring to your relationships and communities. Exploring different forms of giving back helps you discover approaches that align with your interests, capabilities, and circumstances while contributing meaningfully to others' healing and growth.

Peer Support and Mentoring involves sharing your experience directly with others facing similar challenges, either through formal programs or informal relationships that develop naturally. This might include sponsoring others in recovery programs, mentoring younger men in your profession or community, or simply being available to friends and colleagues who are navigating difficult transitions or emotional struggles.

Advocacy and Awareness encompasses efforts to reduce stigma, increase resources, and create cultural change around the issues you've faced. This might involve sharing your story publicly through speaking, writing, or social media to challenge misconceptions about men's mental health, advocating for policy changes that improve access to mental health resources, or supporting organizations that address issues relevant to your healing journey.

Community Building involves creating or contributing to environments that provide ongoing support for others' healing and growth. This might include starting or facilitating support groups, organizing community events that foster connection and reduce isolation, or contributing to online communities where people can share experiences and resources safely.

Professional Integration represents opportunities to incorporate your healing experience into your professional life in ways that serve others while honoring your own journey. This might involve pursuing career changes that allow you to work directly in helping fields, integrating your understanding of mental health into your current profession, or using your leadership positions to create more psychologically safe and supportive work environments.

Creative Expression and Sharing encompasses using artistic, literary, or other creative mediums to share your experience in ways that can touch and inspire others. This might involve writing, music, visual arts, performance, or other creative expressions that communicate the universality of struggle and the possibility of healing and growth.

Maintaining Boundaries While Serving

The desire to help others heal from struggles you've faced yourself can sometimes lead to over extension, boundary violations, or the tendency to take on more responsibility for others' healing than is healthy or sustainable. Learning to serve others while maintaining appropriate boundaries protects both your own continued healing and your capacity to provide genuine support rather than becoming depleted or resentful.

Recognizing Your Limitations involves honest assessment of your current emotional resources, skills, and capacity for providing support without compromising your own well-being. This includes acknowledging when others' needs to exceed your ability to help effectively, recognizing when professional referral is more appropriate than peer support, and maintaining awareness of your own triggers and vulnerable areas that might be activated through helping others.

Professional vs. Personal Support requires clear understanding of the differences between peer support based on shared experience and professional therapeutic intervention based on training and expertise. While your lived experience provides valuable perspectives and support, it doesn't qualify you to provide professional mental health services, and maintaining this distinction protects both you and those you're helping.

Self-Care While Serving encompasses ongoing practices that maintain your emotional and physical well-being while engaged in helping others. This includes regular check-ins with your own support network, continued engagement in personal therapy or growth work as needed, and activities that replenish your energy and joy rather than constantly giving to others.

Reciprocity and Mutual Growth involves maintaining helping relationships that provide opportunities for your own continued learning and development rather than one-sided arrangements where you're always the helper. The most sustainable and meaningful service relationships often involve mutual exchange where you both contribute to and learn from others, preventing helper-helper dynamics that can become unbalanced or codependent.

The Ripple Effects of Conscious Service

When you engage in service motivated by genuine care for others' well-being rather than need for recognition, control, or validation, your contributions create expanding circles of influence that extend far beyond the individuals you help directly. These ripple effects multiply the impact of your healing journey while contributing to broader cultural shifts toward greater emotional health and authentic masculinity.

Others who witness or benefit from your service often become inspired to engage in similar contributions, creating networks of mutual support and service that strengthen entire communities. Your willingness to be vulnerable about your struggles and generous with your wisdom creates permission for others to do the same, fostering cultures of openness and mutual care that benefit everyone involved.

The men you influence through your service—whether directly or indirectly—often become better partners, fathers, friends, and community members as their own emotional health improves. These improvements ripple through their relationships and families, potentially affecting generations of people who will benefit from the enhanced emotional awareness and authentic connection that your service helped make possible.

Your contributions to reducing stigma around men's mental health create cultural changes that make it easier for other men to seek help when needed, engage in emotional growth work, and develop the kinds of supportive relationships that enhance their well-being and effectiveness.

Every story you share, every person you support, and every example you provide of healthy masculinity contributes to this broader transformation.

The recognition that healing flourishes within community represents a profound homecoming—a return to the fundamental truth that human beings are designed for connection and that your struggles and strengths are meant to be shared in service of collective growth and mutual support. This understanding transforms your healing journey from individual achievement into community contribution, creating meaning that extends far beyond personal resolution.

Your willingness to explore community-based healing and service represents courage that honors both your individual needs and your responsibility to others who share similar struggles. By opening yourself to support and extending care to others, you participate in the ancient and ongoing human work of transforming suffering into wisdom and isolation into connection.

Remember that building community and engaging in service are not destinations you arrive at but ongoing practices that evolve throughout your lifetime. Every small step toward connection, every vulnerable sharing that creates understanding, and every act of service that draws from your own healing contributes to a transformation that extends far beyond individual benefit to encompass the healing of families, communities, and culture itself.

The journey you've undertaken by reading these words places you among those who are actively contributing to the evolution of human consciousness and emotional health. Your commitment to your own healing becomes a gift to everyone whose life you touch, and your willingness to share that healing in service of others creates possibilities for connection and growth that future generations will inherit as their birthright rather than having to discover through struggle and pain.

In the chapters that follow, we will continue exploring how these principles apply to specific life contexts and relationships, but the foundation remains constant: healing happens in community, strength grows through vulnerability, and service transforms both the giver and receiver in ways that honor the profound interconnection that defines our shared human experience.

Prompt: How were you taught to express emotions during childhood?

Chapter 8: The Journey Ahead

You stand at a threshold—not of completion, but of conscious beginning. The pages you have turned, the insights you have gathered, and the courage you have summoned to reach this point represent not an ending but a sacred commencement. At what might seem like a conclusion, we discover the profound truth that authentic emotional healing is not a destination to be reached but a dynamic, ever-evolving journey of becoming more fully who you were meant to be.

Within these pages, you'll find the wisdom and strategies necessary to sustain your commitment to this transformative path, along with glimpses of the extraordinary ripple effects that await as your healing touches every relationship, every goal, every moment of your lived experience.

Your journey represents an act of profound courage that honors not only your own potential but the countless lives that will be enriched by your continued growth and authentic presence. You are stepping into a legacy that extends far beyond personal healing to encompass the transformation of masculinity itself, creating new possibilities for future generations of men to inherit emotional wisdom as their birthright rather than having to discover it through struggle and recovery.

Embracing the Ongoing Process: The Sacred Art of Becoming

At the heart of meaningful change lies the realization that emotional healing is not a single event, but a living process—one marked by openness, renewal, and the willingness to revisit familiar ground with deeper understanding. Countless men have stepped onto this path, transforming their lives in ways both quiet and profound. Their journeys bring the principles of ongoing emotional growth, spiraling healing, and the embracing of complexity vividly to life.

Elliot's Story: Answering the Call, Again and Again

Elliot spent years building an image of unshakable success and steadfastness. For decades, he was the anchor for his family and friends—trustworthy, resilient, always composed. It was not until a season of emptiness and growing frustration unsettled his foundation that Elliot realized true strength meant more than holding it together; it meant allowing himself to unravel and rebuild in honest ways. Through therapy and support groups, he learned that facing his inner storms was not a step backward, but a return to the heart of growth. Each time an old pattern resurfaced—withdrawal, impatience, longing—he chose compassion over self-judgment, reframing setbacks as invitations to heal at greater depth. With time, Elliot became both softer and stronger, discovering that every spiral through old challenges was a movement toward greater authenticity and joy.

Malik's Journey: Embracing a Lifelong Ascent

Malik, once convinced that healing had a final summit, found reality far richer. A family crisis unexpectedly awakened old wounds, and Malik's first urge was disappointment—had he not already conquered this pain? Yet as he leaned into mindfulness and compassion, supported by a circle of men walking similar journeys, Malik recognized the wisdom in the spiral. By drawing on skills honed over years—naming his emotions, sharing vulnerably, and seeking support—he moved through his pain with new grace. Malik let go of seeking perfection, finding instead the deeper gift: life would continue presenting opportunities to practice, deepen, and grow.

Javier's Healing Spiral: Grieving with Open Hands

Javier, a devoted father and partner, believed he had come to terms with grief from his childhood. Years after processing that loss, sadness returned unexpectedly at a friend's funeral. Rather than hiding his tears, Javier shared his feelings with his family, modeling healthy vulnerability for his children. This willingness to re-encounter grief with fresh presence not only deepened Javier's own wisdom but allowed those around him to see that emotional growth is never quite finished. Each cycle brought a more profound acceptance and a growing capacity to hold both sorrow and gratitude.

Tom's Season of Rest: Honoring the Pause

Ambitious and eager for change, Tom poured himself into every self-help strategy he could find, convinced constant effort was the key to wholeness. Over time, exhaustion set in. A trusted mentor encouraged him to trust in cycles, giving himself permission to rest and integrate. During this gentle season, Tom learned that healing also happens in silence, in ordinary routines, and in the loving presence of family. By releasing the need for relentless progress, he discovered that rest itself was transformative.

Arjun's Integration: Allowing All His Colors

Arjun, both a disciplined educator and an expressive poet, long struggled to reconcile these facets of his identity. His turning point came when, rather than sidelining one in favor of the other, he invited every part of himself to the table. Through self-inquiry and courageous authenticity, Arjun found his leadership in the classroom was enriched by his emotional openness, while his poetry gained new depth from his sense of responsibility. His story became a living testament that wholeness is not about uniformity, but the seamless embrace of complexity.

These men remind us: the process of emotional growth is not a straight line, but a dance that circles back, climbs higher, carries us through seasons of striving and rest, contraction and expansion. Their transformations illuminate a universal truth—we are all travelers along a spiraling path, each revolution offering another chance to integrate wisdom, compassion, and the unique constellation of gifts and challenges that make us whole.

The journey of emotional growth is illuminated by countless stories of men who, despite setbacks and doubts, continued to prioritize their healing, each in their own unique way. Let us ground these principles by stepping into the experiences of men who have sustained their emotional development over the years—showing us what steady commitment truly looks like, and how setbacks can be woven into stories of renewal and transformation.

Stories of Sustained Growth

James: Building Resilience Through Small Steps

After experiencing burnout from years of repressing difficult emotions and striving for perfection, James realized that monumental changes weren't sustainable for him. Instead, he committed to simple daily micro-practices: three mindful breaths in the morning, a gratitude note each evening, and short check-ins with trusted friends. When stress spiked during a difficult job transition, James found himself slipping back into old habits of self-criticism and withdrawal. Instead of viewing this as failure, he reached out to his therapist—a support he'd built into his routine—and shared his struggle with his peer group. James credits his ability to return to his practices not to willpower, but to the gentle structures he created: friends who model compassion, a flexible schedule, and rituals of reflection that met him where he was.

Michael: Redefining Accountability

Michael, having grown up with rigid ideas about masculinity, struggled initially with any kind of accountability—he associated it with punishment, not support. When he joined a men's support circle, he was surprised by the nonjudgmental atmosphere. Members celebrated each step forward, no matter how small, and responded to setbacks with empathy rather than criticism. Michael found enormous relief in journaling honestly during setbacks, moving away from self-blame and instead reflecting on what triggered old patterns. Being held in this compassionate space gradually shifted his inner dialogue, allowing him to approach challenges with curiosity and patience. Today, Michael's accountability system is rooted in connection: he checks in with his mentor monthly and maintains a quarterly progress review that's more about alignment with his values than ticking off accomplishments.

David: Learning from Regression and Navigating Plateaus

For David, the road was not linear. After years of steady growth, a family crisis brought old defense mechanisms roaring back—anger, withdrawal, and isolation. Initially, he was frustrated, convinced that all his past work had been undone. Through therapy and group dialogue, he learned to reinterpret regression as an opportunity for deeper healing. By openly acknowledging his struggle in his support network, David found commonality with others and received fresh perspectives. During plateaus—those periods when progress seemed invisible—he shifted his focus from striving to integrating, trusting that the quieter seasons had their own lessons. It was through these cycles that he discovered each plateau was a quiet preparation for his next breakthrough.

Rohan: Evolving Approaches with Life's Seasons

Rohan approached emotional growth with vigor in his thirties—reading, group work, and mindfulness retreats. But as career and fatherhood reshaped his priorities, he couldn't maintain the same level of intensity. Rather than see this as failure, he adapted his practices: meditation gave way to mindful walks with his child, and therapy sessions shifted to occasional check-ins or family-focused support. Embracing what he calls his "beginner's mind," Rohan has welcomed new tools and adjusted his expectations with each season of life. He now sees his journey as an evolving spiral—never static, always open to learning.

These men remind us that sustaining emotional growth over time isn't about grand gestures or perfect routines, but about developing adaptable, compassionate practices rooted in support and authenticity. They show that real transformation endures setbacks, embraces change, and is nourished by relationships that honor both progress and vulnerability.

Building Sustainable Practices Rather Than Perfect Systems

The difference between sustainable emotional health practices and unsustainable perfectionist approaches often determines whether your growth momentum continues over years and decades or burns out during the first major life challenge or period of decreased motivation. Sustainable practices integrate naturally into your existing life rhythms rather than requiring dramatic lifestyle changes that become difficult to maintain over time.

Micro-Practices represent small, manageable actions that support your emotional well-being without requiring significant time investment or perfect conditions. These might include taking three conscious breaths before important conversations, expressing gratitude for one thing each day, checking in with your emotional state during routine transitions, or taking brief walks when you notice stress building.

These seemingly minor practices often provide more consistent benefit than elaborate routines that require perfect conditions and extensive time commitments. Their power lies not in their intensity but in their consistency and accessibility, creating steady support for your emotional development regardless of changing life circumstances.

Flexible Frameworks involve creating structures that can adapt to different seasons of your life while maintaining core elements that support your continued growth. Rather than rigid daily schedules that break down under pressure, these frameworks might include weekly check-ins with supportive friends, monthly therapy sessions, seasonal retreats or intensive experiences, and annual assessments of your growth goals and priorities.

Integration Approaches focus on weaving emotional awareness and healthy practices into activities you're already engaged in rather than adding entirely new requirements to your schedule. This might involve bringing mindful attention to routine activities, using work challenges as opportunities to practice emotional regulation, or approaching physical exercise as both fitness and stress management.

Creating Accountability Without Shame

Effective accountability systems support your continued commitment to emotional growth while honoring your humanity and the natural fluctuations that accompany any long-term development process. These systems provide gentle structure and support rather than harsh judgment or punishment when you fall short of your intentions.

Compassionate Self-Monitoring involves developing the capacity to observe your emotional patterns, behavior choices, and growth progress with the same kindness and objectivity you would offer a good friend facing similar challenges. This includes celebrating small victories, learning from setbacks without harsh self-judgment, and maintaining realistic expectations about the pace and nature of change.

External Support Systems might include trusted friends who can provide honest feedback about your growth and well-being, therapy relationships that offer professional guidance and accountability, support groups that provide community encouragement, or mentors who can offer perspective based on their own healing journeys.

Values-Based Accountability focuses on alignment between your daily choices and your deepest values rather than arbitrary rules or external expectations. This approach helps you stay motivated by connecting specific practices to larger purposes that matter to you, such as being a more present father, creating healthier relationships, or contributing to your community in meaningful ways.

Progress Tracking without obsession involves occasional assessment of your growth and well-being that provides information for course correction without becoming another source of stress or self-judgment. This might include periodic journaling about your emotional state, annual check-ins about your goals and priorities, or informal conversations with trusted friends about changes they've noticed in you.

Navigating Setbacks and Plateaus

Every authentic growth journey includes periods of apparent stagnation, temporary regression to old patterns, and challenges that test your commitment to continued development. Understanding these experiences as natural parts of the process rather than signs of failure helps you navigate them with grace while maintaining long-term momentum toward healing and growth.

Normalizing Difficulty involves recognizing that setbacks often occur during periods of significant stress, major life transitions, or when you're attempting to heal deeper layers of experience that require more time and support to address. These challenges don't indicate that you're not growing or that your previous work was ineffective—they often signal that you've developed sufficient strength to address more complex aspects of your healing.

Learning from Regression transforms temporary returns to old patterns into opportunities for deeper understanding about your triggers, stress responses, and areas where additional support or skill development would be beneficial. Rather than judging these experiences as failures, you can explore what circumstances contributed to the regression and what adjustments might prevent similar patterns in the future.

Plateau Navigation recognizes that periods of apparent stagnation often precede significant breakthroughs and serve important functions in consolidating previous growth before new expansion becomes possible.

During these times, maintaining basic practices while trusting the process often proves more effective than pushing harder or trying to force progress that isn't ready to emerge naturally.

Support Seeking during challenging periods demonstrates wisdom rather than weakness, recognizing that temporary increases in professional support, community connection, or self-care practices can help you navigate difficulties while maintaining your overall trajectory toward healing and growth.

Evolution of Practices Over Time

The specific practices, approaches, and resources that support your emotional development will naturally evolve as you grow, as your life circumstances change, and as you discover new tools and perspectives that serve your continued journey. Maintaining openness to this evolution prevents your growth work from becoming stagnant while honoring the foundation you've established.

Beginner's Mind involves approaching your emotional development with curiosity and openness to learning, even after years of growth work. This perspective keeps you receptive to new insights, tools, and approaches while preventing the arrogance or complacency that can limit continued development.

Seasonal Adjustments recognize that different life phases require different types and intensities of emotional work. The growth practices that serve you during times of major transition might differ from those that support maintenance and integration during stable periods. The approaches that work during your thirties might need modification during your fifties as your priorities, responsibilities, and life circumstances evolve.

Depth Progression acknowledges that as you develop greater emotional capacity and skill, you become ready to address more complex aspects of your experience and to serve others in more sophisticated ways. This progression might involve moving from individual therapy to group work, from receiving support to providing mentorship, or from focusing on personal healing to engaging in community service.

Integration with Life Purpose represents the gradual weaving together of your emotional growth work with your broader life purpose and contribution to the world. As your healing deepens, you often discover ways that your personal journey can serve larger goals around family, community, professional contribution, or social change.

A Vision for the Future: The Ripple Effects of Your Courage

As you continue walking this path of emotional growth and authentic living, extraordinary transformations begin to unfold—not just within your personal experience, but throughout every relationship, community, and context your life touches. These ripple effects extend far beyond what you might initially imagine, creating positive change that can span generations and inspire others to embark upon their own journeys of healing and growth.

Personal Transformation: The Flowering of Your Authentic Self

The man you become through sustained commitment to emotional growth bears little resemblance to the person you were when you first recognized the need for change. This transformation occurs gradually, almost imperceptibly, until one day you realize that the anxiety that once dominated your decisions has become manageable background noise. The relationships that once felt impossible have become sources of joy and mutual support. The work that once drained you now provides meaning and satisfaction. The future that once seemed threatening now appears full of possibility and adventure.

Your relationship with yourself undergoes perhaps the most profound transformation. The harsh inner critic that once dominated your mental landscape becomes a wise advisor who can offer constructive feedback without destroying your self-worth. The shame that once colored every perceived failure transforms into self-compassion that allows you to learn from mistakes while maintaining confidence in your fundamental worth and capacity for growth.

This internal transformation manifests in countless daily moments—the ease with which you navigate conflict without losing yourself or attacking others, the natural expression of appreciation and love that flows from your heart, the comfortable silence you can maintain without needing to fill every space with activity or distraction, the graceful way you handle disappointment without it defining your entire emotional state.

You discover a resilience you never knew you possessed—not the brittle toughness that requires constant vigilance to maintain, but a flexible strength that can bend with life's storms while maintaining connection to your core values and authentic truth. This resilience allows you to take risks in service of what matters most to you, to love deeply without guarantees, and to pursue meaningful goals even when success isn't certain.

Perhaps most remarkably, you develop the capacity to hold paradox and complexity without needing to resolve everything into simple categories. You can be strong and vulnerable simultaneously, confident and humble in the same moment, independent and interdependent as the situation requires. This sophistication allows you to respond to life's nuances with wisdom rather than reacting from rigid patterns or defensive positions.

Relationship Renaissance: Intimacy Without Walls

The evolution of your relationships often provides the most tangible evidence of your emotional growth, as the skills you develop for understanding and expressing your inner experience naturally enhance your capacity for authentic connection with others. These improvements ripple through every type of relationship in your life, creating unprecedented levels of intimacy, satisfaction, and mutual support.

Romantic Partnerships reach depths of connection and satisfaction that may have seemed impossible during earlier stages of your emotional development. You become capable of the vulnerable honesty that creates true intimacy while maintaining the emotional regulation that allows conflicts to strengthen rather than threaten your bond. Your partner experiences the safety that comes from being with someone who can remain present and caring even during difficult conversations, who can take responsibility for their own emotional state while offering genuine support during challenging times.

The physical intimacy in your romantic relationships often improves dramatically as emotional walls come down and authentic presence replaces performance anxiety or emotional distance. When you can share your fears, hopes, dreams, and struggles openly, this vulnerability naturally extends into physical connection that feels deeply meaningful rather than superficial or disconnected.

Friendships with Men evolve beyond shared activities and surface conversation to include the kind of authentic sharing and mutual support that creates lifelong bonds. You discover the profound satisfaction that comes from being truly known by other men who understand your struggles, celebrate your victories, and provide companionship during difficult times. These friendships often become some of the most valuable relationships in your life, providing perspective, accountability, and joy that enhance every other aspect of your experience.

Family Relationships often undergo healing transformations as your increased emotional intelligence allows you to navigate complicated family dynamics with greater skill and compassion. You may find yourself becoming a bridge between family members, a source of stability during family crises, or an example of emotional growth that inspires others to address their own patterns and limitations.

Your relationships with your children—whether biological, step, or chosen—become characterized by the kind of authentic connection that allows you to be both strong and vulnerable, both protective and nurturing. Children who grow up with emotionally healthy male figures develop secure attachment patterns and emotional intelligence that serve them throughout their lives.

Professional Excellence Through Emotional Intelligence

The emotional skills you develop through your healing journey translate directly into professional effectiveness and leadership capacity that distinguish you in increasingly competitive and collaborative work environments. Employers and colleagues consistently report higher satisfaction and better performance when working with emotionally intelligent men who can navigate workplace challenges with wisdom, integrity, and authentic communication.

Leadership Effectiveness multiplies exponentially when you can create psychological safety for teams, navigate conflicts constructively, and make decisions that account for both analytical factors and human dynamics. Your ability to remain calm under pressure, communicate vision effectively, and support others' development makes you a natural choice for increased responsibility and influence.

Collaborative Capacity improves dramatically when you can engage in creative tension without becoming defensive, share credit generously without feeling diminished, and contribute your unique strengths while appreciating others' different approaches and perspectives. These collaboration skills become increasingly valuable as work environments become more team-based and innovation-focused.

Stress Management abilities allow you to maintain high performance levels even during challenging periods, to make clear decisions under pressure, and to support colleagues during difficult transitions or crisis situations. This resilience makes you a stabilizing influence in work environments while protecting your own well-being and preventing burnout.

Communication Sophistication enables you to convey complex ideas clearly, to listen deeply to understand others' perspectives, and to navigate sensitive conversations with skill and diplomacy. These abilities serve you whether you're managing conflicts, presenting ideas to executives, or mentoring junior colleagues.

Community Impact: Becoming a Healing Presence

As your emotional growth deepens, you naturally become a source of healing and positive influence within your broader community, often without conscious effort or deliberate intention. Your regulated nervous system, authentic presence, and emotional wisdom create ripple effects that extend far beyond your immediate relationships to touch countless lives in ways you may never fully recognize.

Cultural Contribution occurs as you model healthy masculinity for younger men, demonstrate emotional intelligence in public settings, and challenge toxic patterns through your example rather than confrontation. Every authentic interaction, every moment of vulnerable strength, and every response that chooses connection over dominance contributes to cultural evolution toward healthier definitions of masculine power and success.

Mentorship Opportunities arise naturally as your growth becomes visible to others who recognize something different about your presence and approach to life's challenges. You may find younger men seeking your guidance, colleagues asking for advice about personal challenges, or community members looking to you for leadership during difficult times.

Service Capacity expands as your own healing creates space and motivation to contribute to causes that matter to you, whether through volunteer work, professional service, creative contribution, or simple acts of kindness that brighten others' days. This service often provides some of the deepest satisfaction available through emotional growth work.

Collective Healing occurs through your participation in communities, organizations, and relationships where your emotional health contributes to the overall well-being of the group. Healthy individuals create healthy systems, and your personal growth becomes an investment in the collective health of every community you participate in.

Generational Legacy: Breaking Cycles for Future Generations

Perhaps the most profound impact of your emotional growth extends to future generations who will inherit healthier patterns because of your courage to break cycles of emotional limitation, relationship dysfunction, and masculine disconnection that may have characterized your family history for generations.

Children's Development benefits immeasurably from growing up with emotionally healthy male figures who can model authentic strength, vulnerability, emotional intelligence, and healthy relationships. These children develop secure attachment patterns, sophisticated emotional regulation skills, and relationship capabilities that serve them throughout their lives while positioning them to create healthy families and communities of their own.

Family Patterns undergo healing transformations as your emotional growth influences extended family dynamics, challenges dysfunctional patterns, and creates new possibilities for authentic connection and mutual support. You may become the first person in your family lineage to seek therapy, to develop emotional intelligence, or to create truly intimate relationships, establishing new patterns that future generations can build upon.

Social Influence extends through your professional networks, friendship circles, and community connections where your example of healthy masculinity creates permission for others to explore their own emotional growth and relationship enhancement. Each person you influence directly may influence countless others, creating expanding circles of positive change.

Cultural Evolution occurs as your individual healing contributes to broader social transformation toward emotional intelligence, authentic relationships, and healthy definitions of strength and success. You become part of a movement of men who are actively redefining masculinity for current and future generations.

As we close this chapter and this exploration together, we stand not at an ending but at a commencement—the beginning of a journey that will continue evolving throughout your lifetime, touching every relationship, every goal, every moment of your experience with the wisdom and authenticity you've chosen to cultivate.

Your commitment to this path places you among the healers and pioneers who are actively contributing to the transformation of masculinity itself, creating new possibilities for emotional intelligence, authentic connection, and purposeful living that future generations will inherit as their birthright rather than having to discover through struggle and recovery.

The tools, insights, and perspectives you've gathered through these pages provide a foundation for lifelong growth, but they must be lived to become truly yours. Every moment of conscious choice during emotional intensity, every act of vulnerable courage in relationships, and every step toward greater authenticity contributes to a transformation that extends far beyond personal benefit to encompass the healing of our collective human experience.

Remember that this journey unfolds in its own perfect timing, honoring both your need for growth and your need for rest, both your desire for change and your need for stability. Trust the process, be patient with yourself during inevitable challenges, and celebrate the courage you demonstrate by choosing growth over stagnation, connection over isolation, and authenticity over the comfort of familiar limitations.

Your willingness to break the silence—within yourself and in your relationships—creates ripple effects of healing that touch countless lives and contribute to a future where emotional intelligence and authentic connection are recognized as the highest expressions of human strength and wisdom. This is your legacy, your gift to the world, and your invitation to a life lived with unprecedented depth, meaning, and joy.

The journey ahead sparkles with infinite possibility, and it begins with your next conscious breath, your next authentic choice, your next moment of courage in the face of whatever life offers. Welcome to the adventure of becoming fully, authentically, powerfully yourself—not despite your humanity, but because of it.

Reflection: What does healing look like for me, specifically as a man?

Chapter 9: Overcoming Trauma

Perhaps the most sacred chapter of your journey—the profound weight of what you may have carried and the extraordinary resilience that has brought you to this moment of seeking healing. This chapter requires the utmost compassion, patience, and reverence for the courage it takes to face experiences that may have shaped your understanding of safety, trust, and your place in the world.

Consider trauma not as a life sentence or permanent limitation, but as a survivable experience that, while painful and significant, can become the very foundation upon which you build deeper wisdom, authentic strength, and a capacity for connection that transforms both your own life and the lives of those you touch. Within these pages, you'll discover that healing from trauma is not about forgetting or minimizing what happened, but about reclaiming your power to choose how these experiences inform rather than control your path forward.

Whatever you've endured, you possess an inherent capacity for healing that no trauma can destroy.

Understanding Trauma: The Intersection of Experience and Impact

Trauma represents one of the most misunderstood aspects of human experience—often minimized, stigmatized, or oversimplified in ways that can leave survivors feeling isolated, ashamed, or hopeless about their capacity for healing. Yet understanding trauma in its full complexity opens pathways to recovery that honor both the profound impact these experiences can have and the remarkable resilience that characterizes the human spirit's response to adversity.

Defining Trauma: Beyond Simple Categories

Trauma occurs when we encounter experiences that overwhelm our natural capacity to process, integrate, and make meaning from what has happened to us. These experiences exceed our nervous system's ability to maintain equilibrium, creating lasting changes in how we perceive safety, relationship, and our fundamental sense of self in the world. Understanding trauma in this way moves us beyond simplistic categories of "big T" and "little t" trauma toward a more nuanced appreciation of how different experiences can profoundly affect individuals based on their unique circumstances, resources, and developmental stage.

The essence of trauma lies not necessarily in the objective severity of an event but in the subjective experience of overwhelm, helplessness, and isolation that accompanies it. A child who experiences emotional neglect may carry trauma responses that are as profound and lasting as those experienced by someone who survives a natural disaster or violent crime. What matters is not whether others would consider your experience traumatic, but whether it left you with lasting changes in how you relate to yourself, others, and the world around you.

Trauma often involves what researchers call "betrayal trauma"—experiences where those who were supposed to provide safety and care instead became sources of harm or failed to protect when protection was desperately needed. These experiences can be particularly devastating because they shatter fundamental assumptions about trust, safety, and worth that form the foundation of healthy human development. For many men, such experiences create lasting struggles with vulnerability, intimacy, and the capacity to seek or receive support from others.

Complex trauma results from repeated, ongoing experiences of harm, often occurring during crucial developmental periods when your sense of self and relationship patterns were still forming. This type of trauma can affect not just specific memories or responses but the entire architecture of how you understand yourself, others, and what it means to be safe in the world. Recovery from complex trauma often requires comprehensive approaches that address not just specific symptoms but the fundamental patterns of thought, emotion, and relationship that developed as adaptations to chronic threat.

The Neurobiology of Trauma: How Experience Changes the Brain

Modern neuroscience reveals that trauma creates specific changes in brain structure and function that help explain many of the symptoms and struggles that survivors experience. These changes represent your brain's intelligent attempt to adapt to threatening circumstances, even when those adaptations later create difficulties in contexts where such hypervigilance or emotional numbing is no longer necessary or helpful.

Trauma affects the amygdala—your brain's alarm system—causing it to become hyperactive and hypersensitive to potential threats. This hyperactivation can result in being easily startled, feeling constantly on edge, or experiencing intense emotional reactions to situations that others might not find particularly stressing. Your brain becomes exquisitely attuned to potential danger, sometimes at the expense of being able to recognize and appreciate safety when it exists.

The hippocampus, responsible for memory formation and integration, often becomes impaired through trauma, leading to fragmented memories, difficulty placing traumatic experiences in proper temporal context, and challenges integrating traumatic memories with your overall life narrative. This can result in trauma feeling like it's happening in the present even when the actual events occurred years or decades ago.

The prefrontal cortex—the brain region responsible for executive function, emotional regulation, and rational decision-making—can become less accessible during states of trauma activation. This explains why survivors often feel like they "should" be able to think their way through trauma responses but find themselves overwhelmed by emotions and reactions that seem to bypass logical analysis entirely.

Perhaps most importantly, trauma affects the brain's capacity for integration—the ability to connect different regions and functions in ways that support coherent, flexible responses to current circumstances. This lack of integration can result in feeling fragmented, experiencing yourself as divided between different states or identities, or struggling to maintain consistent emotional regulation across different situations and relationships.

Trauma's Impact on Identity and Relationships

Trauma profoundly affects not just individual symptoms but the entire fabric of how you understand yourself and relate to others. These impacts often extend far beyond the original traumatic events, influencing career choices, relationship patterns, parenting approaches, and fundamental beliefs about what is possible or safe in your life.

Identity Formation can be significantly affected by trauma, particularly when it occurs during crucial developmental periods. You may have organized your sense of self around survival strategies that were necessary during traumatic periods but that now limit your capacity for authentic self-expression and growth. This might manifest as identifying primarily as a protector, survivor, provider, or problem-solver while losing touch with other aspects of your personality and potential.

Attachment Patterns developed through early traumatic experiences often create templates for all subsequent relationships, leading to patterns of either avoiding intimacy entirely or becoming enmeshed in relationships that recreate familiar but unhealthy dynamics. These patterns can persist even when you consciously desire healthier connections, creating frustrating cycles of relationship difficulty that seem to repeat despite your best efforts to change them.

Emotional Regulation challenges stemming from trauma can affect every aspect of daily life, from work performance to parenting capacity to social interactions. You might experience emotions as overwhelming and dangerous forces to be avoided at all costs, or you might feel emotionally numb and disconnected from the full spectrum of human feeling. Both responses represent intelligent adaptations to traumatic circumstances that may now limit your capacity for authentic living.

Trust and Safety assessments become skewed by traumatic experiences, often resulting in either hypervigilance that sees danger everywhere or dissociation that disconnects you from legitimate warning signals about actual threats. Learning to calibrate your threat detection system appropriately becomes a crucial aspect of trauma recovery that affects everything from career choices to romantic partnerships.

Cultural and Gender-Specific Trauma Responses

Men's responses to trauma are often complicated by cultural expectations about masculine strength, emotional expression, and help-seeking behavior that can interfere with natural healing processes while creating additional layers of shame and isolation around traumatic experiences.

Masculine Socialization often teaches boys and men that trauma responses like fear, vulnerability, or emotional expression represent weakness or failure rather than normal human responses to abnormal situations. This socialization can lead to trauma symptoms being expressed through anger, substance use, risk-taking behavior, or emotional withdrawal rather than being recognized and addressed as trauma responses requiring appropriate care and support.

Stigma Around Male Victimization creates particular challenges for men who have experienced trauma, especially trauma involving interpersonal violence, sexual abuse, or other experiences that challenge cultural narratives about masculine strength and invulnerability. This stigma can prevent men from seeking help, sharing their experiences, or even acknowledging to themselves that they have been affected by traumatic events.

Expression Differences mean that trauma symptoms in men often manifest differently than stereotypical presentations, potentially leading to misdiagnosis or lack of recognition. Men may experience trauma through increased aggression, emotional numbing, workaholism, substance abuse, or risky behavior rather than through more recognized symptoms like anxiety, depression, or emotional volatility.

Cultural Variations in trauma response and healing approaches mean that effective treatment must account for diverse backgrounds, values, and healing traditions. Some cultures emphasize individual resilience and self-reliance, while others prioritize community healing and collective support. Understanding your own cultural background can inform your approach to healing while honoring the wisdom of your heritage.

Pathways to Healing: Navigating Your Journey to Wholeness

Healing from trauma is not a linear process with a clear beginning, middle, and end, but rather a dynamic journey of discovering your inherent capacity for resilience, integration, and growth. The pathways to healing are as diverse as the individuals who walk them, requiring approaches that honor your unique circumstances, resources, and healing style while providing the safety, support, and tools necessary for genuine transformation.

Professional Therapeutic Approaches

Professional therapy provides structured, evidence-based approaches to trauma healing that can offer safety, expertise, and specialized tools for processing and integrating traumatic experiences. Understanding different therapeutic modalities helps you make informed decisions about what types of professional support might best serve your healing journey.

Trauma-Focused Therapy approaches like Cognitive Processing Therapy (CPT) and Prolonged Exposure (PE) help you process traumatic memories in safe, controlled environments where you can examine the impact of these experiences on your thoughts, feelings, and behaviors. These approaches often involve gradually approaching traumatic memories or situations that you've been avoiding, building confidence in your capacity to handle difficult emotions and thoughts without being overwhelmed by them.

Eye Movement Desensitization and Reprocessing (EMDR) utilizes bilateral stimulation (typically through guided eye movements) while processing traumatic memories, helping your brain integrate these experiences in ways that reduce their emotional charge and intrusive impact on daily life. Many individuals find EMDR particularly helpful for processing specific traumatic incidents that feel "stuck" in their nervous system.

Somatic Experiencing and Body-Based Approaches recognize that trauma is stored not just in memories and thoughts but in the body's nervous system and muscle memory. These approaches help you develop awareness of physical sensations, learn to regulate your nervous system, and release trauma-related tension and energy that may be stored in your body. This work can be particularly valuable for men who struggle with traditional talk therapy approaches.

Internal Family Systems (IFS) therapy helps you understand different aspects of your personality as parts of an internal system, some of which may carry traumatic experiences while others developed to protect or manage these wounded aspects. This approach can be especially helpful for understanding how different parts of yourself might have different needs and responses related to your traumatic experiences.

Dialectical Behavior Therapy (DBT) provides specific skills for emotional regulation, distress tolerance, mindfulness, and interpersonal effectiveness that can be particularly valuable for managing trauma symptoms in daily life. These skills offer practical tools for handling intense emotions, navigating relationship challenges, and maintaining stability during the healing process.

Self-Directed Healing Practices

While professional support often provides crucial safety and expertise for trauma healing, self-directed practices can complement therapeutic work while providing ongoing tools for managing symptoms, building resilience, and maintaining progress over time. These practices empower you to take active role in your healing journey while developing internal resources you can access whenever needed.

Mindfulness and Grounding Practices help you develop the capacity to remain present with your experience without being overwhelmed by traumatic memories or emotional activation. Simple techniques like focusing on your breath, noticing physical sensations, or using your senses to connect with your immediate environment can interrupt dissociation or flashback experiences while building your tolerance for staying present during challenging moments.

Breathing Techniques specifically designed for trauma survivors can help regulate your nervous system and provide immediate relief during moments of activation or overwhelm. Techniques like box breathing (inhaling, holding, exhaling, and holding for equal counts) or extending your exhale longer than your inhale can activate your parasympathetic nervous system and promote greater calm and clarity.

Journaling for Trauma Processing provides safe opportunities to explore and express thoughts and feelings related to your traumatic experiences. Different journaling approaches serve different purposes—stream-of-consciousness writing can help process emotions, structured prompts can help explore specific aspects of your experience, and gratitude or progress journaling can help maintain perspective on your healing journey.

Physical Movement and Exercise can help discharge trauma-related energy stored in your body while building confidence in your physical strength and capability. Whether through structured exercise, martial arts, dance, or simply walking in nature, movement can help you reconnect with your body in positive ways while providing natural stress relief and mood enhancement.

Creative Expression offers pathways for processing and integrating traumatic experiences that don't require verbal articulation. Art, music, writing, or other creative pursuits can help you explore and express aspects of your experience that might be difficult to communicate directly while providing outlets for complex emotions and insights.

Building Your Support Network

Healing from trauma occurs most effectively within the context of safe, supportive relationships that provide the consistency, understanding, and care necessary for genuine recovery. Building this network requires intentional effort while honoring your pace and comfort level with vulnerability and connection.

Professional Support Team might include therapists, psychiatrists, medical doctors, and other helping professionals who understand trauma and can provide different types of expertise and support throughout your healing journey. Having multiple professionals who communicate with each other (with your permission) can provide comprehensive care that addresses different aspects of your recovery.

Peer Support Groups connect you with others who have faced similar experiences and can provide understanding, validation, and practical guidance based on their own healing journeys. These groups might focus on specific types of trauma, general trauma recovery, or broader topics like men's emotional health or personal growth. The universality and hope that emerge from connecting with others who understand your experience can be profoundly healing.

Trusted Friends and Family who can provide emotional support, practical assistance, and consistent care throughout your healing process represent crucial resources for recovery. These relationships may require education about trauma and its effects, as well as clear communication about what types of support are most helpful for your specific needs and circumstances.

Spiritual or Religious Community can provide meaning-making frameworks, ritual support, and community connection that complement clinical approaches to trauma healing. Many individuals find that spiritual practices and communities offer resources for forgiveness, purpose, and hope that enhance their recovery process.

Online Communities and Resources can provide access to information, support, and connection that might not be available in your immediate geographic area. These resources can be particularly valuable for men who are hesitant to seek face-to-face support initially or who want to explore different perspectives and approaches to trauma healing.

Integrative Healing Approaches

Effective trauma healing often requires approaches that address not just psychological symptoms but the whole person—including physical health, spiritual well-being, social connection, and life purpose. These integrative approaches recognize that trauma affects every aspect of human experience and that healing must therefore be comprehensive rather than focused solely on symptom reduction.

Nutrition and Physical Health support provides the biological foundation necessary for psychological healing. Trauma can affect sleep patterns, appetite, immune function, and overall physical health in ways that interfere with recovery if not addressed. Working with healthcare providers who understand trauma's physical effects can optimize your body's capacity for healing while ensuring that medical issues don't complicate your psychological recovery.

Sleep Optimization becomes particularly important for trauma survivors, as sleep disturbances often both result from and contribute to ongoing trauma symptoms. Developing good sleep hygiene, addressing nightmares or night terrors, and creating safe, comfortable sleeping environments can significantly enhance your overall healing progress.

Spiritual Exploration can provide frameworks for meaning-making, forgiveness, and transcendence that complement psychological approaches to healing. This exploration might involve traditional religious practices, meditation and contemplative traditions, nature-based spirituality, or other approaches that help you connect with something larger than yourself while finding purpose and meaning in your experiences.

Life Purpose and Contribution often emerge as crucial elements of trauma recovery, as survivors discover ways that their experiences and healing can serve others facing similar challenges. This service orientation can transform personal suffering into meaningful contribution while providing ongoing motivation for continued healing and growth.

Lifestyle Design involves creating daily routines, environments, and activities that support your healing while minimizing triggers and stressors that might interfere with recovery. This might involve changes in work situations, living arrangements, relationship patterns, or recreational activities that align better with your healing needs and goals.

Reclaiming Your Power: The Transformation from Survivor to Thriver

The journey of healing from trauma ultimately leads to a profound change in how you understand yourself and your place in the world—a shift from seeing yourself primarily as someone who was wounded by circumstances beyond your control to recognizing yourself as someone who possesses the capacity to create meaning, connection, and contribution despite and because of what you have endured.

Redefining Your Narrative

One of the most powerful aspects of trauma recovery involves developing a new relationship with your story—not denying or minimizing what happened, but expanding your identity beyond the traumatic experiences to include your resilience, your growth, and your capacity to create a meaningful future that honors both your pain and your potential.

From Victim to Survivor to Thriver represents a natural progression in how you might relate to your traumatic experiences over time. Initially, recognizing yourself as someone who was victimized by circumstances beyond your control can be an important step in releasing self-blame and acknowledging the reality of what occurred. Identifying as a survivor recognizes your strength in enduring and beginning to heal from traumatic experiences. The identity of thriver encompasses using your experiences as sources of wisdom, strength, and contribution that enhance rather than limit your capacity for joy, connection, and purpose.

Integration Rather Than Elimination means learning to hold your traumatic experiences as part of your complete life story without allowing them to define or limit your future possibilities. This integration acknowledges that what happened to you was significant and real while recognizing that you are larger than your trauma and capable of creating a future that includes healing, growth, and fulfillment.

Post-Traumatic Growth represents the scientifically documented phenomenon where individuals develop greater resilience, deeper relationships, enhanced appreciation for life, stronger spiritual connections, and clearer life purpose as a result of working through their traumatic experiences. This growth doesn't minimize the reality or impact of trauma but recognizes that human beings possess remarkable capacity to transform even the most difficult experiences into sources of wisdom and strength.

Meaning-Making Processes involve discovering or creating purposes, values, and contributions that give your experiences significance beyond personal pain. Many trauma survivors find that their healing journeys enable them to help others facing similar challenges, to advocate for social changes that prevent trauma, or to develop capacities for compassion and resilience that serve them throughout their lives.

Developing Trauma-Informed Strengths

The process of healing from trauma often reveals and develops personal strengths that might not have emerged under normal circumstances. These trauma-informed strengths represent gifts that emerge from your healing journey—capacities that serve not only your own well-being but also your ability to contribute meaningfully to others and to the world.

Emotional Intelligence and Regulation skills developed through trauma recovery often exceed those of individuals who have not faced similar challenges. Your journey through intense emotional experiences while learning to manage and integrate them can result in sophisticated emotional awareness and regulation capabilities that serve you in all areas of life.

Empathy and Compassion for others facing difficulties often develops naturally through your own healing process. Having navigated intense suffering and recovery, you often develop exceptional capacity to understand, support, and provide hope for others facing their own challenges and healing journeys.

Resilience and Adaptability skills honed through surviving and healing from trauma create confidence in your ability to handle whatever life presents. This resilience isn't about being tough or invulnerable, but about knowing that you can navigate difficulties while maintaining connection to your values and your capacity for growth and joy.

Authenticity and Vulnerability capacities often develop through trauma recovery as you learn that hiding or denying your experiences creates more suffering than sharing them appropriately with safe, supportive people. This authenticity can lead to deeper, more meaningful relationships and greater sense of integrity in all areas of your life.

Purpose and Service Orientation frequently emerges as trauma survivors discover that their experiences and healing can serve others facing similar challenges. This service transforms personal suffering into meaningful contribution while providing ongoing motivation for continued healing and growth.

Creating Safety and Agency

Reclaiming your power after trauma involves gradually developing confidence in your ability to create safety, make choices, and influence your environment in ways that support your well-being and goals. This process requires patience as you rebuild trust in yourself, others, and the possibility that you can have positive influence over your life circumstances.

Internal Safety Development involves learning to regulate your own emotional states, to self-soothe during moments of distress, and to maintain connection to your strengths and resources even during challenging times. This internal safety provides a foundation that external circumstances cannot shake, creating resilience that travels with you wherever you go.

Environmental Safety Creation encompasses making choices about living situations, work environments, relationships, and activities that support your well-being while minimizing exposure to triggers or harmful situations. This might involve significant life changes as you prioritize your healing and well-being over other considerations.

Boundary Setting and Enforcement skills become crucial for maintaining the safety and space necessary for continued healing and growth. Learning to say no to requests that would compromise your well-being, to communicate your needs clearly, and to enforce limits when others don't respect your boundaries provides ongoing protection for your healing process.

Choice and Agency Recognition involves developing awareness of the many areas where you do have choice and influence, even if trauma experiences may have created feelings of helplessness or powerlessness. Recognizing and exercising these choices, even in small ways, gradually rebuilds confidence in your capacity to shape your life according to your values and goals.

Building a Trauma-Informed Life

As you progress in your healing journey, you develop the wisdom to structure your life in ways that honor both your traumatic experiences and your healing needs while pursuing goals and relationships that provide meaning, satisfaction, and continued growth.

Career Integration might involve pursuing work that utilizes your trauma-informed strengths, whether in helping professions, advocacy roles, creative pursuits, or leadership positions where your empathy and resilience serve others. Alternatively, it might involve finding ways to integrate your healing insights into whatever profession you choose, bringing greater authenticity and wisdom to your professional contributions.

Relationship Patterns often transform as you develop greater capacity for intimacy, authentic communication, and healthy boundaries. Your relationships may deepen as you become more capable of vulnerability and emotional presence, while unhealthy relationships may naturally fall away as you prioritize connections that support your well-being and growth.

Parenting and Mentorship opportunities allow you to share the wisdom you've gained through your healing journey while helping break cycles of trauma in future generations. Whether through biological parenting, mentoring relationships, or community involvement, you can contribute to creating safer, more emotionally intelligent environments for others.

Community Contribution often becomes a natural expression of your healing as you discover ways to use your experience and wisdom in service of others. This might involve formal volunteer work, professional service, advocacy activities, or simply being a source of hope and support for others facing similar challenges.

Legacy Creation involves living in ways that honor both your traumatic experiences and your healing journey while contributing to positive change that extends beyond your individual life. This legacy might involve the relationships you build, the people you influence, the work you do, or the example you provide of what healing and growth are possible even after significant trauma.

As we conclude this exploration of trauma and healing, we honor both the profound courage it takes to face traumatic experiences and the extraordinary capacity for growth and transformation that characterizes the human spirit. Your willingness to engage with this material represents a crucial step in reclaiming your power to create a life of meaning, connection, and contribution that honors both your pain and your potential.

Remember that healing from trauma is not about forgetting or minimizing what happened, but about developing the wisdom, skills, and support necessary to live fully despite and because of your experiences. Your journey of recovery contributes not only to your own well-being but to the healing of others who will benefit from your example, your support, and your transformed understanding of what strength and resilience truly mean.

The path ahead may include continued challenges and opportunities for growth, but it also holds unprecedented possibilities for joy, connection, and contribution that seemed impossible when your wounds were fresh. Your commitment to healing honors both your own worth and your responsibility to others who share similar struggles, creating ripple effects of hope and transformation that extend far beyond your individual experience.

Trust in your capacity for healing, be patient with the natural rhythms of recovery, and remember that every step toward wholeness represents a victory not just for yourself but for everyone whose life will be touched by the authentic strength and wisdom you're developing through your courageous journey of transformation.

Prompt: How do you cope with feelings you don't fully understand?

Chapter 10: Living Authentically

Here, we enter the sacred space where your deepest truth meets your daily existence. This is not about arrival, but alignment. The wisdom you've earned through reflection and emotional growth now becomes a lived reality—one that honors your scars, your strength, and your quiet survival.

Authenticity is not a destination. It's a dynamic way of being. It infuses every choice, every interaction, and every breath with integrity. It's the moment your external life begins to echo your internal truth—not perfectly, but honestly.

Authentic living is not about eliminating complexity. It's about showing up with courage in a world that rewards performance and punishes vulnerability. It's about honoring your full self—flawed, resilient, and real. To live authentically is not indulgence. It's responsibility. Not selfishness. But service. Not ease. But the sacred weight of truth. Your willingness to engage with this work is an act of unreal bravery. And it's time.

What It Means to Live Authentically: The Architecture of Truth

Authentic living represents the harmonious integration of your inner truth with your outer expression—a way of being where your values guide your choices, your emotions inform your responses, and your genuine self becomes the foundation from which you engage with the world. This integration creates a life of coherence and integrity that provides profound satisfaction even amidst life's inevitable challenges and uncertainties.

Beyond the Mask: Understanding Your True Self

Authenticity begins with the recognition that beneath the various roles, expectations, and adaptations you've developed throughout your life lies an essential core—a fundamental truth about who you are that transcends temporary circumstances and external definitions. This true self encompasses your deepest values, your natural gifts and inclinations, your genuine emotional responses, and the unique perspective you bring to the world through your particular combination of experiences and insights.

For many men, discovering this authentic core requires peeling away layers of conditioning that may have obscured their genuine nature for decades. These layers might include professional identities that don't reflect your actual interests or values, relationship patterns that require you to suppress aspects of your personality, or social personas that feel increasingly exhausting to maintain. The process of uncovering your authentic self often involves both grief for time spent living in authentically and excitement about the possibilities that emerge when you align with your truth.

Your authentic self is not a fixed entity waiting to be discovered once and for all, but rather a dynamic, evolving expression that grows and deepens as you gain wisdom, heal from wounds, and expand your understanding of yourself and the world. This fluidity means that living authentically requires ongoing attention and adjustment rather than a single moment of self-discovery that provides permanent clarity about who you are and how you should live.

The authentic self encompasses paradox and complexity rather than seeking simple, consistent definitions. You might be simultaneously strong and vulnerable, confident and uncertain, introverted and socially engaged, depending on the situation and what feels most genuine in each moment. Authenticity includes the wisdom to access different aspects of your personality appropriately while maintaining connection to your core values and fundamental truth.

The Dimensions of Authentic Living

Authentic living expresses itself across multiple dimensions of human experience, each offering opportunities to align your external choices with your internal truth while creating a life of increasing coherence and satisfaction.

Emotional Authenticity involves honoring and expressing your genuine feelings rather than performing emotions that seem more socially acceptable or strategically advantageous. This includes allowing yourself to feel sad when grief arises, expressing excitement when genuine enthusiasm emerges, and acknowledging anger when your boundaries are violated. Emotional authenticity doesn't mean expressing every feeling indiscriminately, but rather developing the wisdom to know which emotions deserve expression and the skills to communicate them constructively.

Relational Authenticity encompasses showing up genuinely in your connections with others—sharing your real thoughts and feelings, expressing your actual needs and preferences, and maintaining relationships that honor your authentic self rather than requiring you to pretend to be someone you're not. This dimension often requires courage to risk rejection or disapproval in service of genuine connection and the wisdom to distinguish between relationships that support your authenticity and those that require you to compromise your truth.

Professional Authenticity involves aligning your work life with your values, interests, and natural strengths rather than pursuing career paths that conflict with your authentic self simply for external rewards or societal approval. This might mean making significant career changes, finding ways to infuse your current work with greater meaning and personal expression, or setting boundaries that protect your well-being and integrity in work environments that might not naturally support authentic living.

Creative Authenticity represents the expression of your unique perspective, talents, and creativity in whatever forms feel most natural and meaningful to you. This might involve traditional artistic pursuits like music, writing, or visual arts, or it might manifest through innovative approaches to problem-solving, unique contributions to your profession, or creative ways of participating in your community and relationships.

Spiritual Authenticity encompasses living in alignment with your deepest sense of meaning, purpose, and connection to something larger than yourself. This dimension might express itself through traditional religious practice, nature-based spirituality, service to others, or simply the cultivation of presence and gratitude in daily life. Spiritual authenticity requires honest exploration of what actually provides meaning and connection for you rather than what you think should or what others expect.

The Paradox of Authenticity

One of the most sophisticated aspects of authentic living involves navigating the apparent contradictions that emerge when you commit to honoring your truth while also maintaining healthy relationships and social responsibilities. These paradoxes require wisdom and flexibility rather than rigid adherence to simple rules about authentic behavior.

The paradox of **Authenticity and Adaptation** recognizes that being true to yourself sometimes requires adapting your expression to different contexts without compromising your core integrity. You might communicate differently at work than you do with close friends, not because you're being fake, but because authentic communication honors both your truth and the needs of different relationships and situations. The key lies in adaptation that serves authentic connection rather than self-betrayal or manipulation.

The tension between **Individual Truth and Collective Harmony** emerges when your authentic choices might conflict with others' needs or expectations. Authentic living sometimes requires disappointing others, setting boundaries that create temporary discomfort, or pursuing paths that others don't understand or support. This doesn't mean disregarding others' feelings, but rather finding ways to honor your truth while maintaining compassion and respect for those who might be affected by your choices.

The balance of **Present Authenticity and Future Growth** acknowledges that your authentic self includes your capacity for growth and change rather than just your current preferences and comfort zones. Sometimes authentic living requires pushing beyond familiar patterns, taking risks that feel scary but aligned with your deeper truth, or pursuing growth experiences that temporarily destabilize your sense of certainty about who you are.

The Neuroscience of Authentic Living

Modern brain science reveals that living authentically creates specific neural patterns that support mental health, emotional regulation, and overall well-being in ways that performing inauthentic roles cannot match.

Understanding these neurological benefits provides additional motivation for the often challenging work of aligning your life with your truth.

When you live authentically, your brain demonstrates increased coherence between different regions, particularly improved communication between the prefrontal cortex (responsible for decision-making and self-awareness) and the limbic system (responsible for emotions and motivation). This integration creates greater emotional intelligence, better decision-making capacity, and reduced internal conflict that exhausts cognitive resources when different parts of your brain are working at cross-purposes.

Authentic living also activates reward centers in the brain in sustainable ways that don't create addiction or tolerance patterns. Unlike external rewards that provide temporary satisfaction requiring constant escalation, authentic expression creates intrinsic rewards that remain satisfying over time while contributing to long-term well-being and life satisfaction.

Research demonstrates that people living authentically show decreased activity in brain regions associated with threat detection and social anxiety while showing increased activity in areas associated with self-compassion and social connection. This neurological shift supports the capacity for genuine intimacy and reduces the chronic stress that accompanies constant vigilance about how others perceive you.

Overcoming Barriers to Authenticity: Navigating the Obstacles

The path toward authentic living, while ultimately liberating, often encounters significant obstacles that can derail your progress or convince you to retreat to familiar but inauthentic patterns. Understanding these barriers and developing strategies for navigating them empowers you to persist through challenges while building the resilience necessary for sustained authentic living.

Fear of Judgment and Rejection

Perhaps the most universal barrier to authentic living involves the fear that showing your true self will result in judgment, rejection, or loss of important relationships. This fear often stems from early experiences where authentic expression was met with criticism, punishment, or withdrawal of love, creating unconscious associations between vulnerability and danger that persist into adulthood.

Social Conditioning around masculine expression creates particular challenges for men seeking to live authentically, as cultural messages about acceptable masculine behavior often conflict with emotional authenticity, vulnerability, and the full range of human expression. You may fear that showing sensitivity, uncertainty, or emotional depth will result in loss of respect or social status, leading to continued performance of narrow masculine stereotypes even when they don't reflect your authentic nature.

Perfectionism represents a sophisticated form of authenticity avoidance that disguises fear of judgment as high standards or achievement orientation. When you believe that your authentic self must be perfect before it deserves expression, you create impossible conditions that justify continued hiding while appearing to pursue growth and excellence.

Catastrophic Thinking amplifies the fear of judgment by imagining worst-case scenarios that are unlikely to occur but feel terrifyingly real to your nervous system. This mental habit can convince you that authentic expression will result in complete rejection, career destruction, or social exile when the actual consequences are typically much less severe and often include positive responses you hadn't anticipated.

Overcoming the fear of judgment requires gradual exposure to authentic expression in increasingly challenging contexts, starting with safe relationships and low-stakes situations before moving toward more vulnerable territory. This process builds evidence that authentic expression often leads to deeper connection rather than rejection, while also building confidence in your capacity to handle whatever responses you do encounter.

Distinguishing Safe from Unsafe People becomes a crucial skill for managing judgment fears appropriately. Some individuals in your life may indeed respond poorly to your authentic expression, not because you're doing anything wrong, but because your authenticity triggers their own discomfort with genuineness or threatens relationships built on mutual performance rather than mutual truth. Learning to identify and limit your investment in relationships that cannot support your authenticity while deepening connections with those who appreciate your genuineness reduces the emotional stakes around judgment.

Societal Expectations and Cultural Pressures

The culture you live within creates powerful, often unconscious pressures toward conformity that can make authentic living feel selfish, irresponsible, or dangerous even when your authentic choices would serve both your well-being and your capacity to contribute meaningfully to others.

Professional Expectations in many industries reward conformity, emotional suppression, and image management over authentic expression, creating environments where genuine self-expression might feel risky or inappropriate. These pressures can be particularly intense in competitive fields, leadership positions, or industries with strong cultural norms around acceptable behavior and self-presentation.

Family Systems often have unspoken rules about acceptable roles, emotional expression, and life choices that can make authentic living feel like betrayal of family loyalty or tradition. These systems may have developed around managing family trauma, maintaining social status, or preserving cultural heritage in ways that inadvertently limit individual authenticity while serving other important functions.

Economic Pressures can make authentic living feel like a luxury you cannot afford, particularly when authentic choices might involve career changes, lifestyle modifications, or other decisions that affect financial security. The relationship between authenticity and economic survival represents a genuine tension that requires careful navigation rather than simple solutions.

Community Belonging needs can create pressure to maintain personas that fit within your social groups even when those personas don't reflect your evolving authentic truth. This challenge becomes particularly complex when your authentic growth takes you in directions that differ from your community's values or when your healing journey reveals aspects of yourself that don't align with your historical identity within your social circles.

Navigating societal pressures requires developing **Internal Authority**—the capacity to trust your own wisdom and judgment even when they conflict with external expectations or demands. This internal authority develops gradually through experience with making authentic choices and witnessing their outcomes, building confidence in your ability to navigate social complexity while maintaining integrity.

Strategic Authenticity involves learning to express your authentic self in ways that honor both your truth and your practical needs for safety, belonging, and economic security. This might mean gradual revelation of your authentic self in professional settings, finding communities that support your growth while maintaining connections with existing relationships, or pursuing authentic living in stages that allow for practical adjustments along the way.

Internal Barriers: Self-Doubt and Inherited Patterns

Often the most challenging obstacles to authentic living come from within—internalized messages about your worth, capabilities, and right to express yourself genuinely that create self-sabotage even when external circumstances would support your authenticity.

Impostor Syndrome creates persistent doubt about whether your authentic self is valuable, interesting, or worthy of expression, leading to continued performance of roles that feel safer but increasingly hollow. This syndrome often develops when your authentic qualities differ from cultural definitions of success or value, creating internalized beliefs that your genuine interests, perspectives, or ways of being are somehow inadequate or embarrassing.

Shame-Based Identity involves organizing your self-concept around perceived flaws, mistakes, or inadequacies rather than your inherent worth and unique contributions. When shame becomes a fundamental lens through which you view yourself, authentic expression feels dangerous because it might reveal the inadequacies you believe define you, leading to continued hiding behind roles and performances that protect you from exposure.

Inherited Family Patterns often include unconscious rules about emotional expression, ambition, relationships, and life choices that limit authenticity even when your conscious mind recognizes these limitations. These inherited patterns might involve family loyalties that require you to maintain certain roles, emotional styles learned from parents who couldn't model authenticity, or cultural beliefs about appropriate behavior that conflict with your natural inclinations.

Trauma-Related Protective Patterns developed during difficult experiences often persist long after the original threats have passed, creating ongoing barriers to authentic expression even in safe contexts. These patterns might include hypervigilance about others' reactions, emotional numbing that disconnects you from your authentic preferences, or people-pleasing behaviors that prioritize others' comfort over your own truth.

Working with internal barriers requires **Compassionate Self-Awareness** that can observe limiting patterns with curiosity rather than judgment while gradually creating new neural pathways that support authentic expression. This work often benefits from therapeutic support, particularly approaches that address both conscious patterns and unconscious dynamics that might be operating outside your immediate awareness.

Reparenting Work involves developing the internal supportive voice that perhaps you didn't receive consistently during your developmental years—a voice that encourages authentic expression, validates your inherent worth, and provides the emotional safety necessary for genuine self-revelation. This internal support system becomes the foundation for external authentic expression.

The Courage to Disappoint Others

One of the most challenging aspects of authentic living involves accepting that your genuine choices will sometimes disappoint, confuse, or upset people you care about. This reality requires developing a different relationship with others' approval and learning to distinguish between caring about others and needing their approval to feel worthy or safe.

People-Pleasing Recovery involves recognizing the ways you may have organized your life around managing others' emotions and reactions rather than honoring your own truth and needs. This pattern often develops in childhood as a strategy for maintaining safety and connection, but it can become a barrier to authentic living when carried into adult relationships where such management isn't necessary or healthy.

Boundary Setting becomes essential for authentic living because it protects your energy, time, and emotional resources for choices that align with your values rather than constantly accommodating others' expectations or demands. Learning to say no to requests that don't serve your authentic path while maintaining care and respect for others requires skill development and practice.

Guilt Tolerance involves developing the capacity to feel guilty about disappointing others without changing your authentic choices simply to relieve that discomfort. Guilt often arises when you make choices that serve your authentic truth but conflict with others' expectations, and learning to experience this guilt as information rather than a command can be crucial for sustained authentic living.

Relationship Evolution recognizes that some relationships may change or end as you become more authentic, not because you're doing anything wrong, but because some connections were based on your inauthentic performance rather than your genuine self. Grieving these relationship changes while remaining open to the deeper connections that become possible through authenticity represents a necessary part of authentic living.

Practical Steps to Embrace Authenticity: Your Path to Genuine Living

The journey toward authentic living requires more than intellectual understanding—it demands practical strategies that can be implemented gradually, compassionately, and sustainably as you navigate the complex territory of aligning your external life with your internal truth. These steps provide a roadmap for transformation that honors both your need for growth and your need for safety and stability during transition periods.

Self-Discovery Practices: Reconnecting with Your Truth

The foundation of authentic living rests upon developing intimate familiarity with your own inner landscape—your values, preferences, dreams, fears, and the unique perspective you bring to the world through your particular combination of experiences and insights.

Values Clarification Exercises help you identify what matters most deeply to you beneath the layers of conditioning, expectation, and adaptation you may have accumulated over years of focusing primarily on external achievement or others' approval. This process might involve exploring moments when you felt most alive and engaged, identifying times when you compromised your integrity and examining the cost, or imagining how you would live if external approval and financial concerns were guaranteed.

Consider dedicating regular time to **Solitude and Reflection** practices that create space for authentic thoughts and feelings to emerge without the influence of others' reactions or expectations. This might involve daily meditation, weekly solo walks in nature, monthly personal retreats, or simply creating quiet moments throughout your day when you can check in with your authentic experience without immediately needing to act on it or share it with others.

Life Review Processes can help you identify patterns in your choices, relationships, and responses that reflect authentic versus inauthentic living, providing information about what serves your genuine well-being and what drains your energy or creates internal conflict. This review might explore career decisions, relationship patterns, recreational activities, or daily routines that either support or compromise your authentic expression.

Creative Exploration often provides pathways to authentic self-discovery that bypass analytical thinking and allow deeper truths to emerge through artistic expression, creative writing, music, or other forms of imaginative engagement. These creative practices can reveal aspects of your personality, interests, and perspective that you might not access through purely verbal or cognitive exploration.

Body-Based Awareness Practices help you reconnect with physical sensations, intuitions, and gut feelings that often provide valuable guidance about authentic choices but may have been suppressed through years of prioritizing mental analysis over embodied wisdom. This might involve yoga, dance, martial arts, massage, or simply practices of paying attention to how different choices, environments, and relationships feel in your body.

Gradual Implementation: Small Steps Toward Authentic Living

Sustainable authenticity develops through consistent small choices rather than dramatic life overhauls that might create unnecessary chaos or trigger defensive reactions from yourself or others. This gradual approach respects the natural pace of change while building confidence and skills necessary for larger authentic choices.

Daily Authenticity Practices involve incorporating small expressions of your genuine self into routine interactions and decisions, creating momentum toward more significant authentic choices over time. This might mean expressing genuine preferences about restaurants or activities, sharing real thoughts during casual conversations, wearing clothing that reflects your actual style rather than what you think others expect, or choosing recreational activities based on your interests rather than social obligations.

Incremental Boundary Setting helps you develop the skill and confidence necessary for protecting your authentic choices by starting with low-stakes situations and gradually applying boundary-setting skills to more challenging contexts. This progression might begin with declining social invitations that don't interest you, setting limits on work responsibilities that exceed your capacity, or expressing disagreement about minor issues before addressing more significant conflicts.

Authentic Communication Experiments involve practicing genuine self-expression in progressively challenging situations, building your capacity for vulnerable sharing while developing discernment about appropriate contexts and recipients for different levels of authenticity. You might start by sharing more of your actual thoughts with trusted friends before risking greater vulnerability in professional or family contexts.

Values-Based Decision-Making can be implemented gradually by applying your authentic values to increasingly significant choices, starting with daily decisions and building toward major life choices as your confidence and skill develop. This might involve choosing how to spend your leisure time based on your interests, selecting professional opportunities that align with your values, or making financial decisions that reflect your priorities rather than others' expectations.

Feedback Integration Practices help you learn from the responses you receive to authentic expression, distinguishing between feedback that serves your growth and reactions that reflect others' discomfort with genuineness rather than problems with your choices. This skill becomes crucial for maintaining authentic living without becoming defensive or retreating to inauthentic patterns when your choices generate unexpected responses.

Creating Supportive Environments and Relationships

Authentic living flourishes within contexts that provide safety, understanding, and encouragement for genuine expression. Creating and maintaining these supportive environments often requires intentional effort to build relationships and participate in communities that value authenticity while minimizing exposure to environments that punish or discourage genuine self-expression.

Relationship Audit Processes help you assess which connections in your life support your authentic expression and which require you to compromise your truth to maintain harmony or acceptance. This assessment provides information for investing more energy in supportive relationships while potentially limiting your emotional investment in connections that consistently require inauthentic performance.

Community Building involves actively seeking and participating in groups, organizations, or activities where authenticity is valued and encouraged rather than merely tolerated. This might include men's groups focused on emotional growth, spiritual communities that honor diverse expressions of seeking, professional organizations that support innovative thinking, or recreational groups centered around activities that genuinely interest you.

Mentor and Role Model Relationships provide examples of authentic living while offering guidance and encouragement during challenging aspects of your authenticity journey. These relationships might involve formal mentorship arrangements, therapeutic relationships, friendships with individuals who model authentic living, or even following the examples of public figures whose approaches to authenticity inspire your own development.

Family System Navigation requires developing strategies for maintaining authentic expression within family contexts that might not naturally support such expression, either due to established patterns or cultural factors that prioritize different values. This navigation might involve setting boundaries around family expectations, finding allies within your family system who support your authenticity, or developing the capacity to maintain your genuine self even in challenging family dynamics.

Professional Environment Assessment helps you evaluate whether your work context supports or hinders authentic expression and what modifications might be possible to better align your professional life with your authentic values and strengths. This assessment might lead to conversations with supervisors about role modifications, career changes that better reflect your interests and values, or strategies for maintaining authenticity within existing professional constraints.

Maintaining Authenticity Through Life Transitions

Authentic living requires ongoing attention and adjustment as you encounter new circumstances, relationships, and stages of life that present fresh opportunities and challenges for genuine expression. Developing systems for maintaining authenticity during transitions prevents regression to inauthentic patterns during periods of stress or uncertainty.

Transition Planning Practices involve preparing for anticipated changes—career shifts, relationship changes, geographic moves, or life stage transitions—by identifying how to maintain authentic expression during periods of adjustment and uncertainty. This planning might include identifying support resources, clarifying values that will guide decision-making during transition, or developing coping strategies that honor your authentic needs during stressful periods.

Regular Authenticity Check-ins provide ongoing assessment of whether your life choices continue to align with your evolving authentic truth, recognizing that both you and your circumstances will continue changing throughout your lifetime. These check-ins might occur during regular personal reflection times, therapy sessions, conversations with trusted friends, or annual personal retreats where you assess your current alignment and make adjustments as needed.

Flexibility Within Authenticity recognizes that genuine self-expression requires adaptability rather than rigid adherence to fixed ideas about who you are or how you should express yourself. This flexibility allows for growth, learning, and evolution while maintaining connection to your core values and authentic truth.

Integration Practices help you weave lessons learned through authentic living into your ongoing approach to life, relationships, and decision-making. These practices might include journaling about insights gained through authentic choices, sharing your learning with others who might benefit, or developing personal philosophies and approaches that reflect your accumulated wisdom about authentic living.

Legacy Considerations involve thinking about how your commitment to authentic living serves not only your own well-being but contributes to cultural change that makes authenticity easier for others, particularly future generations who will inherit the social changes that result from individuals choosing genuine expression over conformity and performance.

As we conclude this exploration of authentic living, we celebrate the extraordinary courage it takes to align your external life with your internal truth while navigating a world that often rewards conformity over genuineness. Your commitment to authenticity represents more than personal development—it's a contribution to cultural evolution that creates space for others to explore their own genuine expression and connection.

Living authentically doesn't guarantee a life free from challenge or conflict, but it offers something far more valuable: the deep satisfaction that comes from integrity, the energy that emerges when you stop performing roles that drain your spirit, and the profound connections that become possible when you show up genuinely in your relationships and communities.

Remember that authenticity is not a destination you arrive at but a dynamic practice that evolves throughout your lifetime, requiring ongoing attention, courage, and compassion for yourself during inevitable moments of uncertainty or regression. Your willingness to embrace this practice honors both your individual potential and your responsibility to model genuine living for those whose lives you touch.

The ripple effects of your authentic choices extend far beyond your personal experience, touching every relationship, every community, and every context where your presence creates permission for others to explore their own truth. Through your commitment to genuine living, you participate in the transformation of human consciousness itself, contributing to a world where authenticity becomes not a rare courage but a natural expression of what it means to be fully, magnificently human.

Your journey toward authentic living continues with each conscious choice, each moment of vulnerable courage, and each decision to honor your truth even when easier options present themselves. This is your invitation to a life of unprecedented meaning, connection, and contribution—not despite your humanity but because of your willingness to embrace and express it fully.

Reflection: What kind of support—professional, relational, spiritual—could help me grow emotionally?

Chapter 11: The Power of Reflection

Reflection isn't the beginning. It's the reckoning. This chapter doesn't ask you to start. It asks you to return—to the raw material of your life, to the moments you buried, to the truths you almost named.

Here, reflection becomes more than thought. It becomes ritual.

A practice that doesn't just illuminate, but reclaims.

A companion that doesn't just comfort, but clarifies. You'll learn how to turn inward without fear. To trace the shape of your survival. To convert pain into pattern, and memory into meaning. This is not a mirror. It's a map. And it leads to the architecture of your emotional wholeness.

Your willingness to engage with these concepts represents an act of profound courage—the recognition that within the landscape of your own consciousness lies everything needed for healing, growth, and the discovery of your most authentic self. You are stepping into an understanding that honors both the complexity of your inner world and your inherent capacity to navigate that complexity with increasing wisdom, compassion, and grace.

Why Reflection Matters: The Sacred Mirror of Self-Understanding

Reflection serves as the bridge between living and learning, between experiencing and understanding, between the unconscious patterns that may have shaped your life and the conscious choices that can transform your future. This practice offers something that external analysis, advice, or even professional guidance cannot provide—direct, intimate access to the wisdom that emerges when you turn your attention inward with genuine curiosity and compassionate awareness.

The Architecture of Inner Knowing

Within the vast landscape of your consciousness lies an intricate network of experiences, insights, emotions, and understanding that can only be accessed through the patient, gentle art of self-reflection. This inner architecture contains not only the patterns and wounds that may have created suffering, but also the seeds of healing, the resources for resilience, and the blueprint for becoming who you're truly meant to be.

Reflection creates the conditions necessary for accessing this inner wisdom by quieting the external noise that often drowns out your most authentic insights. In our fast-paced world, where immediate reactions and quick solutions are often valued over deep understanding, the practice of reflection offers a radical alternative—the courage to pause, to listen deeply, and to allow your inner knowing to emerge in its own perfect timing.

This inner knowing encompasses more than intellectual understanding; it includes the embodied wisdom that lives in your nervous system, the emotional intelligence that flows through your heart, and the spiritual insight that connects you to something larger than yourself. Reflection provides access to this multidimensional wisdom by creating space for all aspects of your being to contribute to your understanding and growth.

The process of reflection also serves as a form of internal witnessing that can be profoundly healing, particularly for men who may have spent years suppressing, avoiding, or disconnecting from their inner experience. When you offer yourself the gift of genuine self-reflection, you provide the witnessing presence that transforms experiences from isolated incidents into meaningful parts of your evolving story of growth and understanding.

The Neuroscience of Reflective Practice

Modern brain science reveals that reflection creates specific neural changes that enhance emotional intelligence, self-awareness, and the capacity for conscious choice rather than automatic reaction. These neurological benefits provide compelling evidence for reflection as not just a pleasant practice but an essential tool for optimal brain function and emotional health.

When you engage in reflective practices, your brain demonstrates increased activity in the prefrontal cortex—the region responsible for executive function, emotional regulation, and self-awareness—while showing decreased reactivity in the amygdala, your brain's alarm system.

This neurological shift creates greater emotional balance, improved decision-making capacity, and enhanced ability to respond thoughtfully rather than react impulsively to challenging situations.

Reflection also strengthens neural connections between different brain regions, particularly improving communication between analytical and emotional processing centers. This integration enables you to access both rational thinking and emotional intelligence when navigating complex life situations, rather than being limited to purely analytical or purely emotional responses.

Regular reflective practice literally rewires your brain for greater resilience, emotional regulation, and self-compassion. Each time you pause to reflect on your experiences with curiosity rather than judgment, you strengthen neural pathways that support mental health while weakening patterns associated with rumination, self-criticism, and emotional overwhelm.

The Difference Between Reflection and Rumination

Understanding the crucial distinction between beneficial reflection and harmful rumination helps ensure that your self-examination practices serve healing rather than perpetuating cycles of self-criticism or emotional stagnation. While both involve thinking about your experiences, their intentions, methods, and outcomes differ dramatically.

Reflection approaches your experiences with curiosity, compassion, and the intention to learn and grow. It maintains a balanced perspective that acknowledges both challenges and strengths, seeks to understand patterns and connections, and focuses on insights that can inform future choices. Reflective practice feels expansive, offering new perspectives and possibilities for growth.

Rumination, by contrast, tends to be repetitive, critical, and focused on problems without moving toward solutions. It often involves rehashing the same concerns repeatedly, emphasizing what went wrong without exploring what could be learned, and maintaining a narrow focus that intensifies negative emotions rather than transforming them into wisdom.

Healthy reflection also includes the body's wisdom, paying attention to physical sensations and emotional responses as sources of information rather than focusing exclusively on mental analysis. This embodied approach prevents reflection from becoming purely intellectual while ensuring that insights integrate at multiple levels of your being.

The timeline orientation also differs significantly between reflection and rumination. Reflection acknowledges the past while remaining oriented toward learning that serves your present and future growth. Rumination tends to trap you in past experiences, replaying them without progression toward resolution or understanding.

Cultural Barriers to Male Reflection

Many men encounter cultural and social barriers to developing reflective practices, as traditional masculine socialization often emphasizes action over contemplation, external achievement over internal development, and quick solutions over deep understanding. Recognizing these barriers helps you navigate them consciously rather than allowing them to prevent you from accessing the profound benefits of reflective practice.

Action-Oriented Culture frequently portrays reflection as passive or unproductive, suggesting that "real men" solve problems through action rather than contemplation. This cultural bias overlooks the reality that effective action often requires the wisdom and self-awareness that emerge through reflective understanding, making reflection not an alternative to action but its essential foundation.

Emotional Suppression Messages embedded in masculine socialization may make the internal focus required for reflection feel uncomfortable or threatening. Years of learning to avoid, suppress, or quickly resolve emotional experiences can create resistance to the vulnerable self-examination that characterizes meaningful reflection.

Productivity Pressure in contemporary culture can make reflection feel like an indulgence or waste of time rather than a valuable investment in your emotional health and decision-making capacity. This pressure often fails to recognize that reflection actually enhances productivity by improving the quality of your choices and reducing time spent correcting mistakes that arise from unreflective action.

Vulnerability Stigma may make the honest self-examination required for reflection feel risky or exposing, particularly for men who have learned that acknowledging uncertainty, mistakes, or areas for growth represents weakness rather than wisdom and courage.

Overcoming these cultural barriers requires recognizing reflection as an act of strength rather than weakness—the courage to face yourself honestly, the wisdom to prioritize understanding over immediate action, and the intelligence to invest in practices that enhance your long-term effectiveness and well-being.

Tools for Effective Reflection: Pathways to Self-Discovery

The practice of reflection encompasses diverse approaches and techniques, each offering unique pathways to self-understanding while honoring different learning styles, preferences, and life circumstances. Mastering multiple reflective tools provides flexibility and depth in your self-examination practice while preventing any single approach from becoming stale or ineffective.

Journaling: Writing Your Way to Wisdom

Written reflection offers perhaps the most accessible and flexible approach to self-examination, providing a private, controllable environment where you can explore your thoughts and feelings without external pressure or judgment. The act of writing engages multiple cognitive processes simultaneously, often revealing insights that remain hidden during purely mental reflection.

Stream-of-Consciousness Writing involves setting aside dedicated time—perhaps 10-20 minutes—to write continuously without editing, censoring, or organizing your thoughts. This approach bypasses your internal critic and analytical mind, allowing deeper truths and authentic insights to emerge naturally. Simply write whatever comes to mind, letting your thoughts flow onto the page without concern for grammar, spelling, or logical organization.

This unstructured approach often reveals patterns, concerns, or insights that your conscious mind might not recognize, as the continuous writing requirement prevents you from suppressing or redirecting thoughts that might feel uncomfortable or unexpected. Many men discover that stream-of-consciousness writing provides access to emotional awareness and creative insights that feel blocked during more structured reflection.

Prompted Journaling utilizes specific questions or themes to guide your reflection toward particular areas of growth or understanding. These prompts might explore recent experiences ("What did I learn about myself this week?"), relationship patterns ("How did I handle conflict in my relationships recently?"), or emotional responses ("What emotions have I been avoiding or suppressing?").

Effective journaling prompts encourage both honest assessment and compassionate self-examination. Rather than leading toward self-criticism, they invite curiosity about your patterns, motivations, and growth edges while maintaining a focus on learning and development rather than judgment or blame.

Gratitude and Appreciation Journaling specifically focuses on recognizing positive aspects of your experience, relationships, and personal growth. This practice isn't about forced positivity but rather about training your attention to notice and appreciate elements of your life that might be overshadowed by challenges or areas needing improvement.

Regular gratitude practice has been scientifically shown to improve mood, enhance relationships, increase life satisfaction, and build resilience during difficult periods. For men working through emotional challenges or healing from trauma, gratitude journaling can provide important balance to heavier emotional work while building resources for continued growth.

Process Journaling involves writing about specific experiences, relationships, or challenges you're navigating, using the writing process to explore your thoughts, feelings, and options more thoroughly than mental reflection alone allows. This approach can be particularly valuable for working through conflicts, major decisions, or emotional responses that feel confusing or overwhelming.

When process journaling, include not just what happened externally but also your internal responses—thoughts, feelings, physical sensations, and intuitions that accompanied the experience. This comprehensive approach helps you understand your full response to situations while identifying patterns that might inform future choices.

Meditation and Mindful Awareness: The Art of Present-Moment Reflection

Meditative practices offer pathways to reflection that emphasize present-moment awareness, embodied wisdom, and the spacious perspective that emerges when you step back from the constant stream of thoughts and reactions that characterize daily experience. These approaches complement written reflection by accessing non-verbal insights and developing the capacity for witnessing your experience with compassionate detachment.

Mindfulness Meditation develops your capacity to observe thoughts, emotions, and sensations as they arise without immediately reacting to them or becoming identified with their content. This observational stance creates space between you and your experiences, allowing for greater choice about how to respond while providing valuable information about your habitual patterns and reactions.

Begin with brief meditation sessions—even 5-10 minutes—focusing simply on observing your breath while noticing whatever thoughts, feelings, or sensations arise without trying to change or fix them. When you notice your attention has wandered to thoughts or worries, gently return focus to your breath without self-criticism, treating each return as a moment of mindful awareness rather than a failure.

As your practice develops, you can expand mindfulness meditation to include specific reflection on experiences, relationships, or challenges you're facing. Bring a particular situation to mind during meditation, observing your thoughts and feelings about it with the same non-judgmental awareness you apply to breath observation.

Body-Based Reflection recognizes that your physical experience contains valuable information about your emotional state, stress levels, and authentic responses to different situations. Your body often knows things about your experiences that your mind hasn't yet recognized, making embodied reflection a crucial complement to mental analysis.

Practice scanning through your body during reflection, noticing areas of tension, relaxation, discomfort, or ease while exploring what these sensations might communicate about your emotional state or recent experiences. Pay attention to your gut feelings, heart sensations, and overall energy levels as sources of wisdom about your authentic responses to different people and situations.

Walking Meditation combines gentle physical movement with reflective awareness, often making meditation more accessible for men who find sitting meditation challenging or restless. Choose a quiet route—whether indoors or in nature—and walk at a slower pace than usual while maintaining attention on physical sensations, surroundings, and whatever thoughts or insights arise.

Walking meditation can be particularly effective for processing emotional experiences, working through decisions, or simply creating space for insights to emerge naturally. The combination of movement and reflection often helps release mental and emotional stagnation while providing the gentle stimulation that supports creative thinking and problem-solving.

Loving-Kindness Meditation specifically cultivates compassion and care, first toward yourself and then extending outward to others in your life. This practice can be particularly valuable for men who struggle with self-criticism or harsh judgment, gradually developing the internal supportive voice that enables honest self-reflection without self-attack.

Begin by offering yourself genuine wishes for well-being: "May I be happy, may I be healthy, may I be at peace, may I live with ease." Notice any resistance or discomfort that arises with self-directed compassion, exploring these responses with curiosity rather than judgment. Gradually extend these same wishes to others—loved ones, neutral people, and eventually even those who have caused you difficulty.

Feedback-Seeking and External Perspectives

While reflection primarily involves internal examination, seeking feedback from trusted others provides external perspectives that can illuminate blind spots, confirm insights, or challenge assumptions that might limit your self-understanding. Learning to seek and integrate feedback effectively becomes a crucial component of comprehensive reflective practice.

Trusted Confidants represent people in your life who know you well, care about your well-being, and can provide honest perspective about your patterns, growth, and areas for continued development. These might include close friends, family members, romantic partners, or mentors who have witnessed your behavior across different contexts and time periods.

When seeking feedback, ask specific questions rather than general requests for input: "Have you noticed changes in how I handle stress over the past year?" or "What patterns do you observe in my relationships?" or "Where do you see my biggest areas for continued growth?" Specific questions help others provide more useful information while demonstrating that you're genuinely interested in their observations rather than seeking validation or compliments.

Professional Guidance from therapists, coaches, or other helping professionals provides structured feedback from trained observers who can recognize patterns and dynamics that might be difficult for you or your personal relationships to identify. Professional feedback often includes not just observations about your behavior but insights about underlying dynamics and suggestions for continued growth.

Consider regular check-ins with a therapist or coach as investment in your reflective practice rather than indication of problems or inadequacy. Many successful, emotionally healthy individuals maintain ongoing professional relationships specifically to support their continued self-awareness and growth rather than waiting for crises to seek professional guidance.

360-Degree Feedback approaches involve seeking input from multiple people who interact with you in different contexts—work colleagues, friends, family members, and others who can provide perspectives on how you show up in various aspects of your life. This comprehensive approach helps identify patterns that might be invisible in any single relationship context.

When gathering 360-degree feedback, create specific questions about behaviors, communication styles, emotional patterns, or other areas you want to understand better. Assure participants that you're seeking honest input for your own growth rather than looking for confirmation of your self-perceptions or fishing for compliments.

Feedback Integration Practices help you process and learn from external perspectives without becoming overwhelmed by criticism or dismissed by praise that doesn't serve your development. Effective feedback integration involves looking for patterns across multiple sources, distinguishing between observations about your behavior and others' judgments or interpretations, and identifying specific areas for continued attention and growth.

Remember that feedback represents others' perceptions rather than absolute truth about who you are. Some feedback will resonate strongly and provide valuable insights, while other input might reflect the giver's biases, limitations, or relationship dynamics rather than accurate observations about your behavior. Learning to discern which feedback serves your growth requires developing trust in your own inner knowing alongside openness to external perspectives.

Creative and Embodied Reflection Practices

Beyond traditional approaches like journaling and meditation, creative and embodied reflection practices offer alternative pathways to self-understanding that can be particularly valuable for men who find verbal or analytical approaches limiting or inaccessible.

Artistic Expression provides opportunities to explore and communicate aspects of your experience that might be difficult to access through words alone. Drawing, painting, music, poetry, or other creative pursuits can reveal insights about your emotional state, life experiences, or growth edges while providing satisfying outlets for self-expression.

You don't need artistic skill or training to benefit from creative reflection—the process matters more than the product. Set aside time to create something that represents your current experience, feelings about a particular situation, or vision for your future growth. Allow whatever emerges without judging its aesthetic value or comparing it to others' creative work.

Movement and Dance offer embodied approaches to reflection that can help release stuck emotions, explore different aspects of your personality, or simply create space for insights to emerge through physical expression. This might involve structured dance, martial arts, yoga, or simply moving your body in whatever ways feel natural and authentic.

Pay attention to how different types of movement affect your emotional state and what insights or releases occur through physical expression. Many men discover that movement-based reflection accesses wisdom and emotional release that sitting practices cannot reach, making embodied approaches valuable complements to mental reflection.

Nature-Based Reflection utilizes time in natural settings as both container and catalyst for self-examination and insight. Natural environments often provide the peace, beauty, and perspective that support deep reflection while offering metaphors and inspiration for understanding your own growth and development.

Consider regular solo time in nature specifically designated for reflection—hiking trails, sitting by water, gardening, or simply spending quiet time outdoors while contemplating your experiences, challenges, and aspirations. Many individuals find that natural settings provide clarity and insight that indoor reflection cannot match, while the rhythm of natural cycles offers perspective on their own processes of growth and change.

Integrating Reflection into Daily Life: Making Wisdom a Way of Being

The true power of reflection emerges not from occasional intensive practices but from weaving reflective awareness throughout the fabric of your daily existence, creating a life characterized by increasing consciousness, intentionality, and alignment with your deepest values and authentic truth.

Creating Reflective Rhythms and Routines

Sustainable reflective practice requires integration with your existing life rhythms rather than addition of burdensome new requirements that compete with other important priorities. The most effective approaches become natural extensions of activities you're already engaged in, making reflection feel supportive rather than demanding.

Daily Transition Moments offer built-in opportunities for brief reflection without requiring additional time in your schedule. These might include the few minutes after waking up before checking your phone, the transition between work and home, or the period before sleep when your mind naturally reviews the day's experiences.

Use these natural transition times for brief check-ins with yourself: "How am I feeling right now?" "What did I learn today?" "What am I grateful for?" or "What do I need to release before moving into my next activity?" These micro-reflections build awareness and intentionality throughout your day while requiring minimal time investment.

Weekly Review Practices provide opportunities for more comprehensive reflection on patterns, progress, and priorities that might not be visible during daily awareness. Set aside 20-30 minutes each week to review your experiences, decisions, emotional responses, and alignment with your values and goals.

Weekly reviews might include examining how you handled challenges, celebrating growth and positive choices, identifying areas for continued attention, and setting intentions for the coming week. This practice helps maintain awareness of larger patterns and progress that daily reflection alone cannot provide.

Monthly and Quarterly Deeper Dives allow for more extensive reflection on significant themes, relationship patterns, professional direction, and personal growth goals that require longer time perspectives to recognize and address effectively. These sessions might involve longer journaling sessions, extended meditation practices, or conversations with trusted friends or professional supports about your ongoing development.

Seasonal and Annual Reflection Retreats provide opportunities for major reflection on your life direction, value priorities, relationship health, and areas for significant growth or change. These might involve personal retreat days, participation in organized retreat programs, or simply extended time away from routine responsibilities for deep self-examination and life planning.

Building Reflective Capacity Gradually

Like any skill, reflective capacity develops through consistent practice and gradual challenge rather than through sporadic intensive efforts that might feel overwhelming or unsustainable. Building your reflection abilities gradually ensures that the practice remains supportive rather than becoming another source of pressure or self-criticism.

Start Small and Consistent rather than attempting dramatic changes that might prove difficult to maintain over time. Begin with just five minutes of daily reflection, gradually increasing duration and complexity as the practice becomes natural and enjoyable rather than effortful.

Experiment with Different Approaches to discover which reflective methods feel most natural and beneficial for your temperament, learning style, and life circumstances. Some individuals thrive with written reflection, others prefer meditative practices, and still others find embodied or creative approaches most accessible.

Notice Resistance with Curiosity rather than forcing yourself through reflective practices that feel consistently difficult or unpleasant. Resistance often contains valuable information about your patterns, fears, or areas that might benefit from gentler approaches or professional support.

Celebrate Small Insights and progress rather than waiting for major breakthroughs or dramatic revelations. The cumulative effect of small insights and increased awareness often creates more significant transformation than sporadic intense experiences followed by long periods without reflection.

Reflection-Informed Decision-Making

One of the most practical benefits of regular reflective practice involves enhanced decision-making capacity that draws upon both analytical thinking and inner wisdom to navigate complex choices with greater confidence and alignment with your authentic values.

Values-Based Decision Frameworks emerge naturally from reflective practice as you develop clearer understanding of what matters most deeply to you and how different choices either support or compromise your fundamental priorities and authentic expression.

Before making significant decisions, engage in reflective exploration of how different options align with your core values, support your long-term well-being and growth, and honor both your needs and your responsibilities to others. This process often reveals options or considerations that purely analytical decision-making might overlook.

Emotional Wisdom Integration involves paying attention to your emotional responses to different possibilities as valuable information rather than obstacles to rational decision-making. Your emotions often contain intelligence about potential outcomes, alignment with your authentic self, and likely satisfaction with different choices.

Notice how you feel when contemplating different options—which choices generate excitement, energy, and sense of rightness versus those that create anxiety, depletion, or internal conflict. While emotions shouldn't be the only factor in decision-making, they provide crucial data that pure logic cannot access.

Timeline Reflection Practices help you consider how decisions might affect your future self and relationships rather than focusing exclusively on immediate benefits or consequences. Reflection naturally extends your temporal perspective, helping you make choices that serve your long-term well-being rather than just short-term comfort or convenience.

Consider how you might feel about different choices in one year, five years, or at the end of your life. This expanded timeline often clarifies which options align with your deeper aspirations and values while revealing potential consequences that immediate analysis might not recognize.

Sharing Reflective Insights: Community and Connection

While reflection is inherently internal, sharing appropriate insights with trusted others can deepen your self-understanding while strengthening relationships through vulnerable authenticity and mutual growth.

Reflective Partnerships with friends, family members, or colleagues who are also committed to personal growth create opportunities for mutual sharing, accountability, and support that enhance everyone's reflective capacity. These partnerships might involve regular check-ins about insights, challenges, and growth goals.

Men's Groups and Communities focused on emotional growth and authentic sharing provide contexts where reflective insights can be shared and witnessed by others facing similar challenges and growth opportunities. These communities often provide validation, different perspectives, and encouragement that support continued reflective practice.

Professional Processing with therapists, coaches, or spiritual directors provides structured opportunities to explore and integrate insights from personal reflection while receiving professional guidance about patterns, blind spots, and areas for continued attention.

Family and Relationship Integration involves sharing appropriate reflective insights with partners, children, or family members who can benefit from understanding your growth process while supporting the kinds of relationships that honor authenticity and mutual development.

Remember that sharing reflective insights requires discernment about appropriate contexts, recipients, and levels of detail. Not all insights need to be shared with others, and some reflection is best kept private while it develops and integrates. Learning to distinguish between insights that serve sharing and those that require continued private reflection represents an important aspect of reflective wisdom.

As we conclude this exploration of reflection's transformative power, we celebrate your willingness to turn inward with curiosity and courage, recognizing that within your own consciousness lies everything needed for healing, growth, and the discovery of your most authentic path forward. Your commitment to reflective practice represents more than personal development—it's an investment in wisdom that serves not only your own well-being but enhances every relationship and community you're part of.

Remember that reflection is not about achieving perfect self-understanding but about cultivating the ongoing relationship with yourself that supports conscious living, authentic choices, and continued growth throughout your lifetime. The insights you gain through reflective practice become living wisdom that informs your responses to new challenges while providing the self-compassion necessary for navigating life's inevitable difficulties with grace and resilience.

Your willingness to engage in honest self-examination creates ripple effects that extend far beyond personal benefit, modeling for others the courage and wisdom required for authentic living while contributing to cultural transformation toward greater emotional intelligence and conscious awareness. Through your commitment to reflection, you participate in the evolution of human consciousness itself, helping create a world where inner wisdom is valued alongside external achievement.

The journey of reflection continues with each conscious pause, each moment of curious self-examination, and each choice to honor the wisdom that emerges when you create space for your deepest truth to reveal itself. This is your invitation to a life of unprecedented awareness, authenticity, and contribution—not despite your humanity but because of your willingness to embrace and explore it fully through the sacred practice of reflective awareness.

Reflection: What would it mean to me to live more emotionally aligned with my values?

Chapter 12: Cultivating Emotional Intelligence

This is where the real work begins.

Not with performance. Not with perfection.

But with the quiet mastery of emotional clarity. This chapter marks your entry into the sacred terrain of emotional intelligence—not as theory, but as ritual. Here, you'll learn to read the subtle currents of feeling, to navigate the storms beneath silence, and to wield emotional wisdom as a compass for deeper connection, sharper discernment, and enduring fulfillment.

Emotional intelligence isn't a concept. It's a survival skill.

A living architecture that shapes how you lead, love, and endure. Within these pages, you'll build the foundation for authentic relationships, trauma-aware leadership, and a life anchored in truth—not applause.

Your willingness to embrace this journey represents an act of profound courage—the recognition that emotional intelligence is not a luxury for the sensitive few, but an essential life skill that enhances every interaction, every choice, and every moment of your human experience. You are stepping into an understanding that honors both the complexity of emotional life and your inherent capacity to navigate that complexity with increasing grace, wisdom, and authentic strength.

What Is Emotional Intelligence: The Architecture of Emotional Wisdom

Emotional intelligence represents far more than simply being aware of feelings—it embodies a sophisticated constellation of skills that enables you to perceive, understand, manage, and effectively utilize emotions as powerful sources of information, motivation, and connection. This multifaceted capability serves as the foundation upon which all meaningful human interaction and personal growth ultimately rest.

The Four Pillars of Emotional Intelligence

Modern psychology recognizes four fundamental domains of emotional intelligence, each contributing essential capabilities that work together to create a comprehensive framework for emotional competence and wisdom. Understanding these components provides a clear roadmap for developing the emotional skills that can transform your relationships, enhance your decision-making, and deepen your sense of authentic fulfillment.

Self-Awareness forms the foundation of emotional intelligence, representing your capacity to recognize and understand your own emotional states as they arise, along with their triggers, patterns, and effects on your thoughts and behavior. This awareness extends beyond simply noticing when you feel "good" or "bad" to include sophisticated recognition of emotional nuances, the ability to distinguish between similar feelings, and understanding of how your emotions influence your perceptions and choices.

Developing self-awareness involves cultivating what researchers call "emotional granularity"—the ability to make fine-grained distinctions between different emotional experiences. Rather than experiencing a vague sense of being "upset," emotionally aware individuals can distinguish between disappointment, frustration, sadness, anxiety, or anger, recognizing that each emotion carries different information and may require different responses.

This foundational skill also encompasses awareness of your emotional triggers—the specific situations, interactions, or internal experiences that tend to generate strong emotional responses. Understanding these triggers empowers you to prepare for challenging situations, develop appropriate coping strategies, and choose responses that align with your values rather than being driven by unconscious emotional reactions.

Self-Regulation represents your capacity to manage your emotional responses in ways that serve your long-term well-being and authentic goals rather than being controlled by immediate emotional impulses. This skill involves neither suppressing emotions nor allowing them to dictate your behavior, but rather developing the sophisticated ability to experience feelings fully while maintaining choice about how to respond.

Effective self-regulation includes emotional flexibility—the ability to shift between different emotional states as situations require, rather than becoming stuck in particular feelings or moods. This might involve moving from anger to curiosity during conflicts, from anxiety to excitement when facing challenges, or from sadness to gratitude when processing losses or disappointments.

Self-regulation also encompasses impulse control and the capacity to delay gratification when immediate emotional satisfaction might conflict with longer-term goals or values. This skill proves essential for everything from maintaining healthy relationships during conflicts to pursuing career goals that require sustained effort despite temporary setbacks or frustrations.

Empathy involves your ability to recognize, understand, and appropriately respond to others' emotional experiences, creating the foundation for authentic connection and effective collaboration. This capacity extends beyond simple sympathy or emotional contagion to include sophisticated understanding of others' perspectives, motivations, and needs.

Cognitive empathy represents your intellectual ability to understand others' emotional experiences even when they differ from your own, while affective empathy involves actually feeling with others in ways that create genuine emotional connection. Both forms of empathy serve important functions in relationships, leadership, and community building.

Empathetic accuracy—the ability to correctly perceive and interpret others' emotional states—requires careful attention to verbal and non-verbal cues, understanding of individual differences in emotional expression, and awareness of how cultural, personal, and situational factors influence how people communicate their feelings.

Social Skills encompass your ability to use emotional information effectively in interpersonal interactions, creating positive outcomes for both yourself and others through skillful communication, conflict resolution, and relationship building. These skills integrate self-awareness, self-regulation, and empathy into practical capabilities that enhance every aspect of social interaction.

Effective social skills include the ability to express your own emotions appropriately while creating space for others to do the same, to navigate conflicts in ways that strengthen rather than damage relationships, and to influence others through authentic connection rather than manipulation or coercion.

These skills also involve what researchers call "emotional contagion management"—the ability to recognize when you're being influenced by others' emotional states and to choose whether to mirror those emotions or maintain your own emotional equilibrium depending on what serves the situation best.

The Neuroscience of Emotional Intelligence

Modern brain research reveals that emotional intelligence involves specific neural networks and can be developed throughout your lifetime through conscious practice and attention. Understanding the neurological basis of emotional intelligence provides both motivation for development and practical insights about how to enhance these crucial capabilities.

The prefrontal cortex—your brain's executive control center—plays a crucial role in emotional intelligence by integrating information from emotional centers with rational analysis, enabling you to make decisions that account for both thinking and feeling. Strengthening connections between the prefrontal cortex and limbic system enhances your capacity for emotional regulation and wise decision-making.

The anterior cingulate cortex helps monitor conflicts between different sources of information—including conflicts between rational thoughts and emotional responses—enabling you to recognize when emotions might be influencing your perceptions in ways that require conscious attention and potential adjustment.

Mirror neurons throughout your brain automatically attune to others' emotional states, creating the neurological foundation for empathy and social connection. Developing awareness of mirror neuron activation helps you distinguish between your own emotions and those you're picking up from others, enhancing both self-awareness and empathetic accuracy.

The insula processes bodily sensations and emotions, contributing to your ability to feel emotions in your body and to recognize emotional information through physical sensations. Strengthening insula function through mindfulness and body awareness practices enhances your emotional self-awareness and regulation capabilities.

Cultural and Gender Considerations

Emotional intelligence develops within cultural contexts that shape how emotions are expressed, interpreted, and valued, creating both opportunities and challenges for men seeking to develop these skills in contemporary society. Understanding these cultural factors helps you navigate potential barriers while honoring both your heritage and your growth goals.

Traditional masculine socialization often emphasizes emotional control over emotional intelligence, potentially creating gaps in empathy development, emotional expression skills, or comfort with vulnerability that characterizes authentic connection. Recognizing these gaps as learned limitations rather than inherent deficits creates opportunities for conscious development.

Different cultures vary significantly in their approaches to emotional expression, with some emphasizing emotional restraint and others encouraging more open feeling sharing. Understanding your cultural background helps you distinguish between valuable cultural wisdom and potentially limiting patterns that might interfere with emotional intelligence development.

Contemporary workplace and relationship expectations increasingly value emotional intelligence alongside traditional masculine strengths, creating opportunities for men who develop these skills while potentially disadvantaging those who rely exclusively on analytical or task-focused approaches to interaction and problem-solving.

Benefits of Emotional Intelligence: The Transformative Power of Emotional Wisdom

The development of emotional intelligence creates profound benefits that extend throughout every aspect of your life experience, enhancing not only your personal well-being but your capacity to contribute meaningfully to relationships, communities, and professional endeavors. These benefits compound over time, creating upward spirals of increased effectiveness, satisfaction, and authentic fulfillment.

Enhanced Relationship Quality and Depth

Perhaps the most immediately noticeable benefit of emotional intelligence involves dramatic improvements in the quality and depth of your relationships across all contexts—romantic partnerships, friendships, family connections, and professional collaborations. These improvements create more satisfying personal connections while building the social support networks that enhance resilience and life satisfaction.

Romantic Relationships flourish when both partners possess emotional intelligence, as the skills of self-awareness, empathy, and emotional regulation create the foundation for authentic intimacy and effective conflict resolution. Partners with high emotional intelligence can share their authentic feelings without overwhelming each other, navigate disagreements without damaging their connection, and support each other's growth while maintaining their individual identities.

Emotionally intelligent men often discover that their romantic relationships become characterized by deeper intimacy, more effective communication, and greater mutual satisfaction as they develop the capacity to understand and respond appropriately to their partner's emotional needs while expressing their own needs clearly and constructively.

The ability to repair relationship ruptures—to acknowledge mistakes, take responsibility for your role in conflicts, and work collaboratively toward resolution—proves essential for long-term relationship success and satisfaction. Emotional intelligence provides the skills necessary for these repair processes, transforming inevitable relationship challenges into opportunities for deeper connection and mutual understanding.

Friendships develop greater depth and mutual support when emotional intelligence allows for authentic sharing, empathetic listening, and the kind of vulnerable connection that creates lasting bonds between individuals. Men with developed emotional skills often report friendships characterized by genuine care, mutual vulnerability, and the ability to provide meaningful support during difficult times.

Family Relationships often undergo healing transformations as increased emotional intelligence enables better boundary setting, more effective communication during conflicts, and the capacity to maintain love and connection even when family dynamics become challenging or complicated.

Parenting Capacity improves dramatically when emotional intelligence allows you to remain calm and responsive during children's emotional storms, to model healthy emotional expression and regulation, and to create the kind of emotionally safe family environment that supports children's healthy development.

Superior Decision-Making and Problem-Solving

Emotional intelligence significantly enhances decision-making capacity by providing access to emotional information that purely analytical approaches cannot access, while also preventing emotional overwhelm from compromising rational thinking. This integration of thinking and feeling leads to more effective, satisfying, and sustainable choices across all life domains.

Values-Based Decision-Making becomes natural when emotional intelligence allows you to recognize how different choices align with your deepest values and authentic priorities rather than making decisions based purely on external expectations or short-term considerations. Your emotional responses to potential choices provide valuable information about long-term satisfaction and alignment with your genuine goals.

Risk Assessment improves when you can access both rational analysis and emotional wisdom about potential outcomes, recognizing that emotions often contain important information about situations that logical analysis might miss. Fear might signal genuine dangers that require attention, while excitement might indicate opportunities that align with your authentic interests and capabilities.

Creative Problem-Solving is enhanced when emotional intelligence allows you to access intuitive insights, to remain open to unexpected solutions during challenging situations, and to maintain the emotional regulation necessary for innovative thinking even under pressure or stress.

Timing and Context Sensitivity develop naturally as emotional intelligence helps you recognize when others are receptive to particular conversations or proposals, when situations are ripe for change or intervention, and when patience or action serves your goals better than alternative approaches.

Collaborative Decision-Making becomes more effective when emotional intelligence allows you to understand and integrate others' perspectives, to navigate group dynamics skillfully, and to facilitate processes that harness collective wisdom rather than being limited by individual viewpoints or biases.

Professional Success and Leadership Effectiveness

In contemporary work environments that increasingly value collaboration, innovation, and authentic leadership, emotional intelligence often proves more predictive of professional success than technical skills or traditional measures of intelligence. These capabilities become particularly important in leadership roles that require inspiring and coordinating others' efforts toward shared goals.

Leadership Presence emerges naturally from emotional intelligence as self-awareness creates authentic confidence, emotional regulation enables calm effectiveness under pressure, and empathy allows for connecting with diverse team members in ways that inspire trust and commitment.

Team Building and Management skills improve dramatically when emotional intelligence enables you to understand team members' individual motivations, communication styles, and work preferences while creating group dynamics that bring out everyone's best contributions rather than creating competitive or defensive interpersonal patterns.

Conflict Resolution becomes a strength rather than a dreaded responsibility when emotional intelligence provides the skills necessary to understand all parties' perspectives, to facilitate conversations that address underlying concerns rather than just surface disagreements, and to guide groups toward solutions that work for everyone involved.

Change Management proves more successful when emotional intelligence allows you to understand and address the emotional dimensions of organizational change, to communicate vision in ways that inspire rather than threaten, and to support individuals and teams through the uncertainty and adjustment that change inevitably requires.

Client and Stakeholder Relations improve when emotional intelligence enables you to understand others' needs and concerns more accurately, to communicate in ways that build trust and confidence, and to navigate complex professional relationships with wisdom and authenticity.

Physical and Mental Health Benefits

The stress-reduction and relationship-enhancement effects of emotional intelligence create significant benefits for both physical and mental health, as improved emotional regulation reduces chronic stress while enhanced social connections provide the support networks that contribute to resilience and well-being.

Stress Management improves dramatically when emotional intelligence provides tools for recognizing stress signals early, for responding to stressors in ways that address root causes rather than just symptoms, and for maintaining perspective during challenging periods that might otherwise become overwhelming.

Immune Function benefits from reduced chronic stress and enhanced social connections, both of which support optimal immune system operation and resistance to illness and disease. The physiological benefits of emotional regulation and positive relationships extend throughout your body's systems.

Cardiovascular Health improves when emotional regulation reduces the chronic activation of stress response systems that contribute to heart disease, high blood pressure, and other cardiovascular problems. The social connections that emotional intelligence facilitates also provide cardiovascular benefits through community support and shared positive experiences.

Mental Health Resilience develops naturally as emotional intelligence provides tools for processing difficult experiences, maintaining perspective during challenges, and accessing support when needed rather than struggling with emotional difficulties in isolation or denial.

Sleep Quality often improves as emotional regulation skills help resolve daytime stresses before bedtime while reducing the rumination and anxiety that interfere with restful sleep and recovery.

Practical Strategies to Build Emotional Intelligence: Your Development Roadmap

The cultivation of emotional intelligence requires consistent practice and attention across multiple domains, implemented gradually and sustainably rather than through intensive short-term efforts that might prove overwhelming or unsustainable. The following strategies provide a comprehensive framework for developing these essential capabilities while honoring your individual learning style and life circumstances.

Developing Self-Awareness: The Foundation Practice

Self-awareness forms the cornerstone of all other emotional intelligence skills, making its development a priority that supports all subsequent growth in emotional sophistication and effectiveness. These practices help you develop intimate familiarity with your own emotional landscape while building the observational skills that serve all aspects of emotional intelligence.

Emotional Check-In Practices involve creating regular moments throughout your day when you pause to notice and name what you're feeling, developing the habit of emotional awareness that prevents emotions from building up unconsciously or being expressed inappropriately. Set gentle reminders to ask yourself "What am I feeling right now?" during transitions between activities, before important conversations, or when you notice physical tension or discomfort.

Begin with simple emotional categories before developing more sophisticated emotional vocabulary. Notice the difference between feeling "good" and feeling specifically content, excited, grateful, proud, or peaceful. Similarly, expand beyond feeling "bad" to recognize whether you're experiencing disappointment, frustration, anxiety, sadness, or anger, as each emotion carries different information and may require different responses.

Body-Based Emotional Awareness recognizes that emotions manifest first as physical sensations before becoming conscious feelings, making bodily awareness a crucial component of emotional intelligence development. Practice scanning through your body regularly, noticing areas of tension, heaviness, lightness, or energy while exploring what emotional information these sensations might contain.

Pay particular attention to your breathing patterns, heart rate, stomach sensations, and muscle tension as indicators of emotional states. Rapid breathing might signal anxiety or excitement, while a tight stomach might indicate fear or anticipation. Learning to read these physical signals provides early warning systems for emotional activation that allow for more conscious responses.

Trigger Identification and Pattern Recognition help you understand the specific situations, interactions, or internal experiences that tend to generate strong emotional responses, empowering you to prepare for challenging circumstances and choose responses that align with your values rather than being driven by unconscious reactions.

Keep a simple journal noting situations that generate significant emotional responses, looking for patterns in timing, people, topics, or circumstances that tend to be emotionally activating. This awareness doesn't necessarily mean avoiding these triggers but rather approaching them more consciously and skillfully.

Values Clarification Exercises help you understand the deeper principles and priorities that drive your emotional responses, recognizing that strong emotions often arise when your values are either supported or threatened by particular situations or choices.

Identify the five values that matter most deeply to you—such as integrity, family, creativity, service, or growth—and notice when your emotional responses relate to these values being honored or compromised. This awareness helps distinguish between emotions that deserve attention and action versus those that might reflect temporary circumstances or misunderstandings.

Building Self-Regulation: Mastering Emotional Responses

Self-regulation skills enable you to experience emotions fully while maintaining choice about how to respond, preventing both harmful emotional suppression and impulsive reactions that might damage relationships or compromise your authentic goals and values.

Pause and Breathe Techniques provide immediate tools for creating space between emotional activation and response, allowing for conscious choice rather than automatic reaction during challenging moments. When you notice strong emotions arising, practice taking three deep breaths before speaking or acting, using this brief pause to access your values and intentions for the situation.

Develop the habit of saying "Let me think about that" or "I need a moment to process this" when conversations or situations feel emotionally overwhelming, giving yourself permission to respond thoughtfully rather than reactively. This approach often improves outcomes while demonstrating emotional maturity and self-respect.

Cognitive Reframing Practices involve examining the thoughts and interpretations that accompany emotional responses, recognizing that emotions often follow from our interpretations of situations rather than from the situations themselves. Learning to question and potentially modify these interpretations can dramatically alter emotional experiences.

When experiencing strong negative emotions, practice asking yourself: "What story am I telling myself about this situation? Are there other ways to interpret what's happening? What would I tell a good friend facing this same situation?" These questions often reveal alternative perspectives that reduce emotional intensity while maintaining appropriate responsiveness to genuine concerns.

The STOP Method provides a structured approach to emotional regulation during intense moments: **S**top what you're doing, **T**ake a breath, **O**bserve what you're thinking and feeling, and **P**roceed with conscious intention rather than automatic reaction. This simple framework can be applied in seconds during emotionally challenging situations.

Emotional Surfing involves learning to ride out intense emotions without being overwhelmed by them or trying to make them disappear immediately. Like ocean waves, emotions have natural rhythms of arising, peaking, and subsiding when we don't resist them or try to extend them beyond their natural duration.

Practice staying present with difficult emotions while reminding yourself that "this feeling is temporary and will pass naturally." Notice how emotions change when you observe them with acceptance rather than fighting against them or identifying completely with their content.

Values-Based Response Selection helps you choose responses that align with your deeper principles rather than immediate emotional impulses, ensuring that your actions during emotionally intense moments serve your long-term well-being and authentic relationships rather than just providing temporary emotional relief.

Before responding to emotionally charged situations, briefly connect with your core values and ask: "What response would align with who I want to be? How can I honor both my feelings and my values in this situation? What would serve the relationship and my integrity best?"

Enhancing Empathy: Understanding Others' Emotional Worlds

Empathy development requires both intellectual understanding of others' perspectives and emotional attunement that allows for genuine connection and appropriate responsiveness to others' needs and experiences.

Active Listening Practices form the foundation of empathy development by creating the attentional focus necessary to truly understand others' experiences rather than immediately planning your response or assuming you already know what they mean. Practice giving complete attention to others when they're sharing important experiences, maintaining eye contact, and asking clarifying questions that demonstrate genuine interest in understanding their perspective.

Resist the urge to offer immediate advice or solutions unless specifically requested, instead focusing on understanding the emotional content of what others are sharing. Reflect back what you hear them saying about their feelings: "It sounds like you felt really frustrated when that happened" or "I can hear how excited you are about this opportunity."

Perspective-Taking Exercises involve deliberately attempting to understand situations from others' viewpoints, considering their background, current circumstances, personality differences, and values that might influence their responses to particular situations.

When conflicts or misunderstandings arise, practice asking yourself: "What might this situation look like from their perspective? What needs or concerns might be driving their response? What experiences from their background might be influencing how they're interpreting this situation?" This intellectual empathy often reduces defensive reactions while creating space for genuine understanding.

Emotional Attunement Practices help you develop sensitivity to others' emotional states through attention to non-verbal cues, energy levels, and subtle changes in expression or behavior that might indicate emotional responses they haven't verbally communicated.

Pay attention to others' body language, tone of voice, energy levels, and overall demeanor as sources of information about their emotional state. Notice when someone seems withdrawn, agitated, excited, or sad even when their words might not directly express these feelings. This attunement allows for more appropriate and supportive responses.

Cultural Empathy Development recognizes that emotional expression and interpretation vary significantly across cultural backgrounds, requiring conscious effort to understand others' emotional communications within their cultural context rather than assuming universal emotional languages.

Learn about different cultural approaches to emotional expression, conflict resolution, and relationship building, particularly for cultures represented among people important in your life. This cultural sensitivity enhances empathy while preventing misunderstandings that might arise from different emotional communication styles.

Strengthening Social Skills: Emotional Intelligence in Action

Social skills integrate self-awareness, self-regulation, and empathy into practical capabilities that enhance every interpersonal interaction while building the kinds of relationships that provide mutual support, satisfaction, and growth.

Emotional Communication Skills involve expressing your own emotions in ways that create understanding and connection rather than defensiveness or overwhelm, while also creating space for others to share their emotional experiences authentically and safely.

Practice using "I" statements to share your emotional experiences: "I felt concerned when I didn't hear from you" rather than "You never call me back." This approach communicates your emotional truth while avoiding blame or accusation that might trigger defensive responses.

Learn to express appreciation and positive emotions as frequently as you share concerns or difficulties, recognizing that relationships thrive on positive emotional exchanges while being able to withstand occasional conflicts when the overall emotional balance remains positive.

Conflict Resolution Techniques transform disagreements from relationship threats into opportunities for deeper understanding and collaborative problem-solving when approached with emotional intelligence and genuine care for all parties' well-being.

During conflicts, practice acknowledging others' perspectives before sharing your own: "I can understand why you would feel that way" or "That makes sense from your point of view." This validation often reduces defensiveness and creates space for productive dialogue.

Focus on underlying needs and concerns rather than just surface positions, asking questions like: "What's most important to you about this issue?" or "What would need to happen for you to feel good about this situation?" This approach often reveals solutions that address everyone's core concerns.

Influence and Persuasion Through Connection recognizes that lasting influence occurs through authentic relationship and understanding rather than manipulation or coercion, creating outcomes that serve everyone involved rather than just advancing your immediate agenda.

Before attempting to influence others, invest time in understanding their perspectives, concerns, and values, demonstrating genuine interest in their well-being rather than just trying to get them to agree with you. This foundation of care and understanding makes people more receptive to your ideas and proposals.

Present your ideas in terms of others' values and interests rather than just your own, showing how your proposals might address their concerns or support their goals. This values-based approach to influence creates sustainable agreements rather than temporary compliance.

Group Dynamics and Team Emotional Intelligence involve recognizing and responding skillfully to the emotional climate of groups, teams, and communities while contributing to collective emotional health that supports everyone's best contributions.

Pay attention to group energy levels, underlying tensions, and emotional undercurrents that might not be explicitly discussed but significantly influence group effectiveness and satisfaction. Address these dynamics appropriately through skilled facilitation or private conversations with key individuals.

Model emotional intelligence in group settings by remaining calm during heated discussions, acknowledging different perspectives with respect, and maintaining focus on shared goals and values rather than getting drawn into personality conflicts or power struggles.

As we conclude this comprehensive exploration of emotional intelligence development, we celebrate your commitment to cultivating these essential life skills that enhance every aspect of human experience while contributing to the collective evolution of emotional wisdom in our world.

Remember that emotional intelligence develops gradually through consistent practice rather than through dramatic overnight transformations, requiring patience with yourself during the learning process while celebrating small improvements and insights that accumulate over time into significant enhancement of your emotional capabilities and life satisfaction.

Your willingness to develop emotional intelligence represents more than personal improvement—it's a contribution to cultural healing that creates more emotionally intelligent families, communities, and organizations for current and future generations. Through your commitment to emotional growth, you participate in the transformation of human consciousness toward greater wisdom, compassion, and authentic connection.

The journey of emotional intelligence continues with each conscious choice to pause and reflect rather than react automatically, each moment of empathetic attention to others' experiences, and each decision to respond from your values rather than your immediate emotional impulses. This is your invitation to a life of unprecedented emotional wisdom, authentic relationships, and meaningful contribution—not despite the complexity of emotional life but because of your willingness to embrace and navigate that complexity with increasing skill, grace, and love.

Prompt: How do you cope with feelings you don't fully understand?

Chapter 13: The Role of Vulnerability in Leadership

A marvelous transformation in contemporary leadership—the sacred intersection where authentic strength meets courageous openness, where traditional authority evolves into inspirational influence, and where the very qualities you may have learned to hide become the foundation of your most powerful impact. This territory will challenge everything you might have believed about what it means to lead with true effectiveness and lasting influence.

This exploration extends into a comprehensive understanding of leadership—not as the projection of invulnerability and certainty, but as the embodiment of authentic humanity that inspires others to discover their own courage, creativity, and capacity for extraordinary contribution. You will discover how the integration of vulnerability into your leadership approach becomes not a liability to be managed, but your greatest asset for creating environments where innovation flourishes and human potential is unleashed.

The world desperately needs leaders who can model authentic humanity while maintaining the strength and vision necessary to guide others through complexity and uncertainty. Step into an understanding that honors both your inherent worth as a human being and your magnificent potential to influence positive change in every life you touch through conscious, vulnerable leadership.

Redefining Leadership: The Evolution Toward Authentic Influence

The landscape of effective leadership has undergone a profound transformation in recent decades, moving away from command-and-control models based on authority and dominance toward approaches that recognize influence through authenticity, connection, and the courage to be genuinely human in positions of responsibility. This evolution reflects not a weakening of leadership but its maturation into forms that can navigate contemporary complexity while inspiring sustained excellence and innovation.

Beyond the Myth of the Invulnerable Leader

Traditional leadership mythology has long perpetuated the image of the leader as someone who possesses all the answers, never doubts their decisions, and maintains emotional equilibrium regardless of circumstances. This archetype suggests that effective leadership requires the projection of unwavering confidence and the suppression of any uncertainty, fear, or struggle that might compromise others' faith in your capability.

Yet this mythology creates profound disconnection between leaders and those they serve, establishing relationships based on performance and image management rather than trust and mutual respect. When leaders feel compelled to project invulnerability, they create environments where others also feel pressure to hide their authentic experiences, resulting in cultures of pretense that stifle creativity, innovation, and genuine engagement.

The invulnerable leader myth also places impossible burdens on individuals in leadership positions, requiring them to suppress their natural human responses to stress, uncertainty, and complexity while making decisions that affect multiple lives without acknowledging their own learning edges or areas where input and collaboration might improve outcomes.

Modern research consistently demonstrates that the most effective leaders are those who can integrate strength with authenticity, confidence with humility, and decisiveness with openness to learning and adjustment. These leaders create psychological safety that enables others to contribute their best thinking and effort rather than spending energy managing impressions or avoiding mistakes.

Vulnerability as Strategic Strength

Understanding vulnerability in leadership requires distinguishing between appropriate professional disclosure and emotional overwhelm that might compromise others' sense of safety and confidence in your leadership. Strategic vulnerability involves sharing your authentic human experience in ways that serve the team, organization, or mission rather than simply unburdening yourself of personal struggles.

Admitting Knowledge Limitations represents one of the most powerful forms of vulnerable leadership, as it creates space for others' expertise to contribute while modeling intellectual humility that encourages continuous learning and improvement. When leaders can say "I don't know, but let's figure this out together" or "This is outside my area of expertise—who can help us understand this better?" they demonstrate the kind of secure confidence that invites collaboration rather than defensive competition.

This admission of limitations doesn't diminish leadership authority but rather redirects it from omniscience toward the more realistic and sustainable foundation of orchestrating collective intelligence and creating conditions where the best ideas can emerge and be implemented effectively.

Acknowledging Mistakes and Learning openly demonstrates the kind of growth mindset that organizational success requires in rapidly changing environments. When leaders can own their errors, extract learning from failures, and adjust approaches based on new information, they model the adaptability and resilience that teams need to navigate uncertainty and innovation challenges.

This vulnerability around mistakes also creates cultures where others feel safe to take appropriate risks, admit their own errors, and contribute to collective learning rather than spending energy on blame avoidance or defensive posturing that prevents organizational growth and adaptation.

Sharing Appropriate Struggles can humanize leadership while inspiring others who face similar challenges, provided the sharing serves the team's development rather than seeking emotional support that might be more appropriately found elsewhere. This might involve acknowledging the difficulty of particular decisions, expressing concern about challenging circumstances, or sharing how you're working through leadership development areas.

The key lies in sharing struggles that others can relate to and learn from while maintaining the emotional regulation and forward-focused perspective that leadership responsibility requires. This balance demonstrates both humanity and competence, creating the combination of relatability and confidence that inspires followership.

The Neuroscience of Trust and Influence

Modern brain science reveals that trust—the foundation of all effective leadership—develops through neurological processes that respond specifically to authenticity, consistency, and the kind of emotional attunement that vulnerable leadership naturally provides. Understanding these mechanisms helps explain why vulnerable leadership proves more effective than authoritarian approaches in creating sustained influence and engagement.

When leaders demonstrate appropriate vulnerability, followers' brains register safety signals that reduce defensive activation while increasing the oxytocin production that creates bonds of trust and cooperation. This neurochemical shift enhances creativity, problem-solving capacity, and willingness to take risks in service of shared goals rather than focusing energy on self-protection.

The mirror neuron systems that enable empathy and social connection activate more strongly when leaders show authentic emotional responses rather than maintaining rigid professional personas. This activation creates the emotional resonance that transforms leadership from compliance-based relationships to inspiration-based connections that sustain motivation even during challenging periods.

Research also demonstrates that teams working with vulnerable leaders show increased activity in brain regions associated with innovation and creative problem-solving, while teams with authoritarian leaders show patterns more consistent with threat response and conservative, risk-averse thinking.

Cultural Shifts Demanding Authentic Leadership

Contemporary organizational and social contexts create unprecedented demands for leadership approaches that can navigate complexity, inspire innovation, and maintain human connection in increasingly diverse and rapidly changing environments. These demands favor leaders who can integrate traditional strengths with emotional intelligence and authentic humanity.

Generational Expectations particularly among younger workers and community members, increasingly prioritize authenticity, purpose, and psychological safety over traditional markers of authority and status. These generations respond more positively to leaders who can share their values, admit their imperfections, and demonstrate genuine care for others' growth and well-being.

Global Interconnectedness requires leadership that can build bridges across diverse cultures, perspectives, and approaches, demanding the kind of cultural humility and openness to learning that characterizes vulnerable leadership. Leaders who can acknowledge their limitations while remaining curious about others' experiences prove more effective in international and multicultural contexts.

Rapid Change Demands create environments where no individual can possess all necessary knowledge or anticipate all challenges, making collaborative leadership approaches more effective than those based on individual authority and decision-making. Vulnerable leaders who can orchestrate collective intelligence prove more adaptive than those trying to maintain illusions of individual omniscience.

Innovation Requirements in most contemporary organizations depend on psychological safety, creative risk-taking, and the kind of experimental mindset that flourishes under vulnerable leadership that normalizes learning from failure rather than avoiding it at all costs.

The Benefits of Vulnerable Leadership: Transforming Organizations Through Authentic Influence

When leaders courageously integrate appropriate vulnerability into their approach, extraordinary transformations occur that extend far beyond individual relationships to encompass entire organizational cultures, team dynamics, and collective capacity for innovation and adaptation. These benefits create upward spirals of trust, engagement, and performance that distinguish organizations with vulnerable leaders from those maintaining traditional authoritarian approaches.

Fostering Psychological Safety and Innovation

Perhaps the most significant benefit of vulnerable leadership involves creating what researchers call "psychological safety"—the shared belief that team members can speak up, ask questions, admit mistakes, and propose new ideas without fear of punishment, humiliation, or negative consequences. This safety becomes the foundation upon which all innovation and high performance ultimately rest.

Creative Risk-Taking flourishes when vulnerable leaders model the kind of experimental mindset that innovation requires, demonstrating through their own example that learning from failure represents strength rather than weakness. When team members observe leaders admitting mistakes, adjusting approaches based on new information, and remaining curious rather than defensive when challenged, they develop confidence to propose unconventional solutions and pursue creative approaches.

Teams with vulnerable leaders consistently outperform those with authoritarian leadership on measures of innovation, creative problem-solving, and adaptation to changing circumstances because psychological safety enables the kind of intellectual risk-taking that breakthrough thinking requires.

Open Communication Channels develop naturally when vulnerable leadership creates cultures where authentic sharing is valued over impression management. Team members feel safe to bring forward concerns, suggest improvements, and share information that might be uncomfortable but necessary for organizational learning and adaptation.

This open communication prevents the kind of information hoarding and defensive communication patterns that create blind spots and prevent organizations from recognizing and addressing problems before they become crises. Vulnerable leaders receive more accurate and timely information because their authenticity invites others' honesty in return.

Collective Intelligence emerges when psychological safety enables diverse perspectives to be shared and integrated rather than suppressed in favor of what seems safest or most politically acceptable. Vulnerable leaders who acknowledge their limitations naturally create space for others' expertise to contribute, resulting in decisions and solutions that draw upon collective wisdom rather than individual knowledge.

Building Deeper Trust and Engagement

Trust represents the currency of effective leadership, and vulnerable leaders consistently demonstrate higher levels of trust from their teams, colleagues, and stakeholders because authenticity creates the predictability and safety that trust requires. This trust translates into increased engagement, loyalty, and discretionary effort that drives superior performance.

Predictable Authenticity allows others to understand how you'll respond to various situations, creating the consistency that trust requires. When leaders hide behind professional personas, others must constantly guess about their true motivations, reactions, and intentions, creating uncertainty that undermines trust and effective collaboration.

Vulnerable leaders who share their values, acknowledge their limitations, and demonstrate consistent emotional responses become predictable in their authenticity, allowing others to develop confidence in their character and intentions even when specific decisions or directions might not be immediately understood.

Reciprocal Vulnerability develops when leaders model appropriate emotional sharing and authentic communication, inspiring others to respond with similar openness that deepens relationships and creates the kind of mutual understanding that sustains collaboration through difficult periods.

This reciprocal vulnerability creates bonds between leaders and team members that transcend transactional relationships, resulting in the kind of mutual investment and care that motivates extraordinary effort and loyalty during challenging times.

Emotional Contagion Benefits occur when vulnerable leaders' authentic emotional responses—their genuine excitement about possibilities, their appropriate concern about challenges, their visible commitment to shared values—inspire similar emotional engagement from others rather than the compliance-based responses that authoritarian leadership typically generates.

Research consistently shows that teams led by emotionally authentic leaders demonstrate higher levels of engagement, creativity, and resilience than those led by emotionally controlled or manipulative leaders, because authentic emotions create the kind of inspirational influence that motivates intrinsic rather than extrinsic performance.

Developing Others' Leadership Potential

Vulnerable leaders naturally become catalysts for developing leadership capacity in others because their authenticity creates environments where people feel safe to take risks, learn from mistakes, and develop their own authentic leadership approaches rather than simply mimicking authoritarian styles that don't align with their personalities or values.

Mentorship Through Modeling occurs when vulnerable leaders demonstrate how to integrate strength with humanity, confidence with humility, and decisiveness with openness to learning. Others observe these leaders navigating challenges with grace and authenticity, learning leadership approaches that they can adapt to their own circumstances and styles.

Safe Learning Environments created by vulnerable leadership enable others to experiment with leadership responsibilities, make mistakes, and receive feedback in contexts that support growth rather than punishment. This safety accelerates leadership development because people can focus on learning and improvement rather than defensive self-protection.

Empowerment and Delegation feel natural when vulnerable leaders acknowledge their limitations and recognize others' strengths, creating opportunities for distributed leadership that develops capacity throughout organizations rather than concentrating all authority in single individuals.

Succession Planning becomes more effective when vulnerable leaders prioritize developing others rather than protecting their own positions, recognizing that their legacy depends more on the leaders they develop than on their individual achievements or the authority they accumulate.

Organizational Culture Transformation

The influence of vulnerable leadership extends beyond immediate teams to transform entire organizational cultures in ways that enhance performance, adaptability, and human flourishing across all levels and departments.

Values-Driven Culture emerges when vulnerable leaders demonstrate alignment between their stated values and actual behavior, inspiring others to prioritize integrity and authenticity over political maneuvering or impression management. This values alignment creates the kind of cultural coherence that sustains performance during stressful periods while attracting and retaining high-quality team members.

Learning Organization Development occurs naturally when vulnerable leadership models curiosity, adaptability, and the kind of growth mindset that organizational success requires in rapidly changing environments. These cultures become characterized by continuous improvement, innovation, and the kind of intellectual agility that creates competitive advantages.

Diversity and Inclusion Enhancement results from vulnerable leadership that acknowledges limitations and actively seeks diverse perspectives, creating environments where different backgrounds, experiences, and approaches are valued rather than merely tolerated. This inclusion enhances decision-making quality while creating the kind of belonging that enables everyone's best contributions.

Crisis Resilience develops when vulnerable leadership has created the trust, communication patterns, and collective problem-solving capabilities that enable organizations to navigate unexpected challenges with unity and effectiveness rather than fragmenting under pressure.

Practical Steps to Lead with Vulnerability: Your Implementation Roadmap

The integration of vulnerability into your leadership approach requires thoughtful implementation that balances authenticity with appropriate professional boundaries, ensuring that your openness serves others' development and organizational goals rather than simply expressing your personal emotional needs. These practical strategies provide a framework for developing vulnerable leadership skills gradually and sustainably.

Starting with Self-Awareness and Intentionality

Before sharing vulnerability with others, effective leaders develop clear understanding of their own emotional patterns, triggers, and motivations to ensure that their authenticity serves leadership effectiveness rather than undermining it through inappropriate emotional expression or boundary violations.

Leadership Values Clarification involves identifying the principles and purposes that guide your leadership approach, creating the foundation for authentic expression that remains aligned with your responsibilities and commitments to others. These values become filters for determining when and how to share vulnerable experiences in ways that serve your leadership mission.

Consider what matters most deeply to you as a leader: Is it developing others' potential, creating innovative solutions, building inclusive communities, or serving particular causes? These values help determine which personal experiences and emotions deserve sharing because they connect with and support your leadership purposes.

Emotional Trigger Identification helps you recognize the situations, interactions, or stressors that tend to generate strong emotional responses, enabling you to prepare for these moments and choose conscious responses rather than reactive expressions that might compromise your leadership effectiveness.

Keep a brief leadership journal noting situations where you felt particularly activated, stressed, or emotionally reactive, looking for patterns in circumstances, people, or topics that tend to trigger intense responses. This awareness doesn't mean avoiding these triggers but approaching them more consciously and skillfully.

Support System Development ensures that you have appropriate outlets for processing your personal struggles and emotional needs that don't depend on your team members or organizational relationships. Vulnerable leaders need strong support systems that allow them to maintain emotional regulation and clear boundaries in their leadership roles.

This might include professional coaching or therapy relationships, peer leader support groups, trusted mentors, or personal friends who can provide emotional support and perspective without the complications that mixing personal and professional relationships often creates.

Intention Setting Practices help you approach vulnerable leadership moments with clear purposes rather than unconscious emotional expression that might confuse or burden others. Before sharing personal experiences or emotions, briefly consider: "What do I hope to accomplish with this sharing? How might this serve others' development or our shared goals?"

Graduated Vulnerability Practices

Developing comfort with vulnerable leadership requires starting with lower-risk situations and gradually building the skills and confidence necessary for more challenging expressions of authenticity that maintain appropriate boundaries while creating deeper connection and trust.

Acknowledging Knowledge Gaps represents perhaps the safest starting point for vulnerable leadership, as intellectual humility typically feels less emotionally exposing than sharing personal struggles while providing immediate benefits for team collaboration and collective problem-solving.

Practice saying "I don't know" when faced with questions outside your expertise, followed by curiosity about who might have relevant knowledge or how the group might approach learning together. This intellectual vulnerability demonstrates secure confidence while inviting others' contributions.

Sharing Learning Experiences allows you to model growth mindset and continuous improvement while maintaining appropriate professional boundaries around more personal emotional content. This might involve sharing books, courses, or experiences that have influenced your leadership thinking, including what you're still learning or developing.

Expressing Appropriate Concerns about organizational challenges, industry changes, or team development needs demonstrates emotional investment in shared success while maintaining the forward-focused perspective that leadership requires. This might involve acknowledging difficulty of decisions you're facing while emphasizing your commitment to finding good solutions.

Celebrating Others' Contributions authentically allows you to express genuine emotions like gratitude, excitement, and pride while focusing attention on others' growth and achievements rather than your personal experiences. This emotional authenticity builds connection while maintaining appropriate professional focus.

Creating Safe Spaces for Team Vulnerability

Vulnerable leadership becomes most effective when it creates environments where others also feel safe to share authentically, ask questions, admit mistakes, and contribute their full selves to shared goals rather than maintaining defensive personas that limit engagement and creativity.

Regular Check-In Practices create structured opportunities for team members to share their current state, challenges, and needs in ways that build mutual understanding and support while maintaining focus on collective goals and individual development within professional contexts.

These check-ins might occur at the beginning of team meetings, through brief one-on-one conversations, or via structured team reflection sessions that invite authentic sharing about work experiences, learning edges, and areas where additional support would be helpful.

Mistake Normalization Processes involve creating explicit cultural expectations that mistakes represent learning opportunities rather than failures, beginning with your own modeling of mistake acknowledgment and learning extraction before expecting others to follow suit.

When errors occur—whether your own or others'—practice responding with curiosity rather than blame: "What can we learn from this? How might we prevent similar problems in the future? What additional support or resources might be helpful?" This approach transforms mistakes into growth opportunities while maintaining accountability.

Decision-Making Transparency involves sharing appropriate aspects of your decision-making processes, including the factors you're considering, the advice you're seeking, and the uncertainties you're navigating. This transparency helps others understand your thinking while inviting their input and perspective.

Feedback Culture Development creates environments where giving and receiving feedback becomes normal and safe rather than threatening, beginning with your own requests for input about your leadership effectiveness and areas for continued development.

Model receiving feedback gracefully, asking clarifying questions, thanking others for their perspectives, and following up on changes you make based on input received. This demonstrates that feedback serves growth rather than representing criticism or attack.

Managing Boundaries and Professional Appropriateness

Effective vulnerable leadership requires clear boundaries that ensure your authenticity serves others' development and organizational goals rather than burdening others with emotional content that exceeds appropriate professional relationships or compromises their sense of safety and confidence in your leadership.

Professional vs. Personal Distinction involves developing discernment about which personal experiences and emotions connect with and serve your leadership mission versus those that are better processed in personal relationships or professional support contexts outside your work environment.

Generally, experiences that relate to your leadership learning, professional development challenges, or struggles that team members might face themselves represent appropriate professional vulnerability, while personal relationship issues, family problems, or mental health challenges that don't directly connect to work contexts typically require other outlets.

Timing and Context Sensitivity help you choose appropriate moments for vulnerable sharing that don't overwhelm others or compromise their sense of safety and confidence during critical periods when they need strong, steady leadership more than authentic emotional expression.

During crisis situations, major organizational changes, or high-stress periods, vulnerable leadership might emphasize acknowledgment of difficulty and commitment to finding solutions rather than sharing personal emotional struggles that might increase others' anxiety or uncertainty.

Reciprocity Balance ensures that vulnerable leadership creates opportunities for others to share authentically rather than becoming one-sided emotional expression that makes others uncomfortable or creates inappropriate caretaking dynamics within professional relationships.

Pay attention to whether your vulnerable sharing invites others to respond with their own authenticity or whether it seems to create pressure for others to manage your emotions or provide support that exceeds appropriate professional boundaries.

Cultural and Individual Sensitivity recognizes that comfort with emotional expression and vulnerable sharing varies significantly across cultural backgrounds and individual personalities, requiring adaptation of your approach to honor diverse communication styles and preferences within your team or organization.

Some team members may appreciate emotional authenticity while others prefer more task-focused communication, and effective vulnerable leaders learn to read these differences and adapt their approach while maintaining their authentic leadership style.

Measuring Impact and Adjusting Approach

Vulnerable leadership requires ongoing attention to its effects on others and on organizational outcomes, allowing for continuous refinement of your approach to ensure that authenticity consistently serves leadership effectiveness rather than becoming self-indulgent or counterproductive.

Feedback Seeking on Leadership Style involves regularly requesting specific input about how your vulnerable leadership approach affects others' experience, comfort level, and ability to contribute effectively to shared goals. This feedback helps you calibrate appropriate levels and types of vulnerability for different contexts and relationships.

Team Engagement Monitoring tracks whether vulnerable leadership correlates with increased participation, creative contribution, risk-taking, and general team satisfaction versus signs that your approach might be creating discomfort or uncertainty that interferes with performance.

Innovation and Risk-Taking Measurement assesses whether psychological safety created through vulnerable leadership translates into the kind of creative problem-solving, initiative-taking, and experimental approaches that organizational success requires in rapidly changing environments.

Trust and Relationship Quality Assessment involves paying attention to whether vulnerable leadership deepens relationships and increases trust versus creating dependency, discomfort, or inappropriate boundary crossing that compromises professional effectiveness.

Use regular one-on-one conversations to check in about relationship health, asking questions like: "How is our working relationship serving your development and success? Is there anything about my leadership approach that you find particularly helpful or challenging?"

As we conclude this exploration of vulnerable leadership, we celebrate your courage to consider leadership approaches that honor both your humanity and your responsibility to create environments where others can flourish and contribute their best efforts to shared goals and meaningful purposes.

Remember that vulnerable leadership represents not a destination you arrive at but a dynamic practice that evolves throughout your leadership journey, requiring ongoing attention to balance authenticity with appropriate boundaries while continuously developing the emotional intelligence and interpersonal skills that effective vulnerability demands.

Your willingness to integrate vulnerability into your leadership approach contributes to a profound transformation in how power and influence operate in our world, creating possibilities for more humane, effective, and sustainable approaches to guiding collective efforts toward positive change and meaningful contribution.

The journey of vulnerable leadership continues with each conscious choice to model authenticity over performance, each decision to acknowledge limitations while maintaining confidence, and each moment when you choose connection over control in service of bringing out the best in yourself and others. This is your invitation to leadership that serves not only immediate goals but contributes to the evolution of human consciousness toward greater wisdom, compassion, and collaborative potential.

Through your commitment to vulnerable leadership, you participate in creating organizational cultures and social systems that honor human dignity while achieving extraordinary results, demonstrating that strength and authenticity are not opposing forces but complementary aspects of the kind of leadership our world desperately needs.

Challenge: For 7 days, give one **genuine, specific compliment or affirmation** each day — to a colleague, friend, partner, or yourself. Avoid vague praise; focus on effort, growth, or character (e.g., "I admire how you handled that stressful moment today").

Goal: Practice reinforcing positivity in yourself and others.

Chapter 14: The Strength in Asking for Help

Asking for help has to be one of the hardest things to do as a man. We are raised to be self-reliant and told that asking for help is somehow weakness or embarrassing. Let's venture into territory that challenges one of the most deeply ingrained myths of our time: that true strength means standing alone, that authentic power requires self-reliance, and that asking for help represents a fundamental weakness to be avoided at all costs.

Let's look at a radical reimagining of what it means to be truly strong—not as an isolated fortress weathering every storm in solitude, but as a wise architect of connection who understands that the most magnificent structures are built through collaboration, support, and the courageous vulnerability of recognizing when expertise beyond your own is needed. It's in these pages where you'll learn that reaching out for help is not a surrender of your power but its most sophisticated expression.

We live in a world that often celebrates individual achievement above collective support, choosing to explore interdependence and mutual aid places you among the pioneers of authentic strength. These steps take practice understanding both your inherent capability and your fundamental humanity, which flourishes through connection rather than in isolation.

Redefining Strength: The Architecture of Courageous Connection

The conventional understanding of strength—as individual fortitude that requires no external support or guidance—represents one of the most limiting and ultimately destructive myths that contemporary culture perpetuates. True strength, as we shall discover, involves the sophisticated wisdom to recognize when collaboration serves your goals better than solitary effort, and the emotional intelligence to seek appropriate support without diminishing your essential capability or worth.

Dismantling the Myth of Self-Reliance

The mythology of complete self-reliance suggests that mature, capable individuals should be able to handle all of life's challenges through personal resources alone—that needing help indicates failure, immaturity, or fundamental inadequacy that marks you as somehow less capable than those who appear to navigate difficulties without external support or guidance.

This myth creates a profound disconnection from reality, as even a cursory examination of human achievement throughout history reveals that every significant accomplishment has emerged through collaboration, mentorship, community support, and the wisdom of individuals who were humble enough to seek guidance from others with relevant experience or expertise.

Consider the greatest leaders, artists, innovators, and healers throughout history—none achieved their contributions in isolation. They sought mentors, collaborated with peers, built upon the work of predecessors, and often received crucial support during their most challenging moments. What distinguished them was not their ability to avoid needing help, but their wisdom in recognizing when help could accelerate their growth and their courage in seeking it appropriately.

The self-reliance myth particularly damages men, as cultural messages about masculine strength often equate emotional or practical support-seeking with weakness, creating internal shame and external stigma around the natural human need for guidance, encouragement, and collaborative problem-solving during life's inevitable challenges and transitions.

This mythology also ignores the reality that human beings are fundamentally social creatures whose nervous systems are designed for co-regulation, whose learning accelerates through modeling and mentorship, and whose resilience develops most effectively within supportive community contexts that provide both challenge and encouragement.

Understanding Interdependence as Wisdom

Recognizing interdependence—the reality that all human flourishing occurs within webs of mutual support and collaboration—represents a sophisticated understanding of how life actually works rather than a compromise of individual strength or capability. This recognition allows you to access resources and perspectives that exponentially expand your capacity for growth, contribution, and authentic fulfillment.

Strategic Resource Utilization involves understanding that seeking appropriate help allows you to focus your energy and attention on areas where your unique gifts and capabilities can make the greatest contribution while accessing expertise in areas that lie outside your natural strengths or current knowledge base.

A master carpenter doesn't hesitate to consult with an electrician when wiring is needed, not because the carpenter is incapable of learning electrical work, but because accessing specialized expertise allows the project to be completed more effectively while the carpenter focuses on what they do best. This same principle applies to emotional, psychological, and spiritual aspects of human development.

Collective Intelligence emerges when individuals have the wisdom to recognize that groups often generate better solutions than any single person could develop in isolation, particularly when facing complex challenges that benefit from diverse perspectives, varied experiences, and different areas of expertise working in collaboration.

Mentorship and Modeling represent forms of help-seeking that accelerate learning by accessing the accumulated wisdom of others who have navigated similar challenges successfully. Every master in any field began as a student seeking guidance from those with greater experience and skill.

Community Resilience develops when individuals understand their place within larger systems of mutual support, recognizing that their individual strength both contributes to and is enhanced by the collective capacity of their communities to provide care, resources, and encouragement during difficult times.

The Neuroscience of Support-Seeking

Modern brain science reveals that seeking appropriate help creates specific neurological benefits that enhance learning, emotional regulation, and problem-solving capacity while reducing the chronic stress that accompanies attempting to handle overwhelming challenges in isolation.

When you receive appropriate support, your nervous system registers safety signals that reduce threat-response activation while increasing access to the prefrontal cortex regions responsible for clear thinking, creative problem-solving, and emotional regulation. This neurological shift enhances your capacity to learn from difficult experiences rather than simply surviving them.

Co-regulation occurs when your nervous system synchronizes with others who are calm and grounded, automatically improving your own emotional state and cognitive function. This biological process demonstrates that seeking support from regulated individuals literally enhances your own capacity for effective response to challenges.

Social Connection Benefits include increased oxytocin production that reduces stress hormones while enhancing immune function, cardiovascular health, and overall resilience. These benefits accumulate over time, creating significant health advantages for individuals who maintain supportive relationships compared to those who attempt to handle life's challenges in isolation.

Mirror Neuron Activation during supportive interactions provides unconscious learning opportunities that enhance your own coping strategies, emotional intelligence, and problem-solving approaches through observation and modeling of how others navigate similar challenges effectively.

Cultural Healing Through Redefined Strength

When you courageously choose to seek help when appropriate, you participate in a broader cultural transformation that makes it safer for others to acknowledge their own needs for support while challenging the toxic aspects of individualistic culture that create isolation, shame, and preventable suffering.

Masculine Evolution occurs when men model help-seeking as a form of strength rather than weakness, creating permission for other men to explore interdependence and mutual support without compromising their sense of masculine identity or social standing.

Stigma Reduction happens through visible examples of capable, successful individuals who openly acknowledge the role that support, therapy, mentorship, and community have played in their growth and achievements, demonstrating that seeking help correlates with rather than contradicts strength and success.

Community Healing emerges when individuals understand their responsibility to both receive support when needed and offer it to others facing similar challenges, creating networks of mutual aid that enhance everyone's resilience and capacity for contribution.

Generational Change occurs when children grow up witnessing adults seek help appropriately, learning that support-seeking represents wisdom and strength rather than weakness or failure, breaking cycles of isolation and unnecessary suffering that have characterized previous generations.

The Benefits of Asking for Help: The Transformative Power of Connection

When you develop the courage and wisdom to seek appropriate help during life's challenges and transitions, extraordinary benefits emerge that extend far beyond the immediate resolution of specific problems to encompass profound enhancements in personal growth, relationship quality, and your overall capacity for resilience and authentic contribution.

Accelerated Personal Growth and Learning

Perhaps the most significant benefit of help-seeking involves the dramatic acceleration of personal development that occurs when you access the wisdom, perspective, and expertise of others rather than attempting to figure everything out through isolated trial and error.

Compressed Learning Curves result when mentors, therapists, coaches, or experienced friends share insights that would take years to develop independently, allowing you to benefit from others' mistakes and successes while focusing your energy on implementation rather than basic discovery of effective approaches.

Professional therapy can provide decades of research-backed insights about human psychology and emotional healing in months of focused work, while business mentorship can help you avoid costly mistakes and identify opportunities that individual exploration might never reveal.

Expanded Perspective emerges when others help you see situations from angles you hadn't considered, challenging assumptions that might be limiting your options while revealing possibilities that isolation couldn't generate. Fresh eyes often identify solutions that familiarity has rendered invisible.

Emotional Processing Support allows you to work through difficult experiences with trained professionals or trusted friends who can provide the witnessing, validation, and guidance that transforms painful experiences into wisdom rather than unresolved trauma that continues affecting your life negatively.

Skill Development accelerates when you have access to individuals who can teach, model, and provide feedback about capabilities you want to develop, whether technical skills, emotional intelligence, communication abilities, or leadership approaches.

Accountability and Motivation emerge naturally within supportive relationships where others encourage your growth while providing gentle accountability that helps you maintain momentum toward your goals even during periods when internal motivation feels insufficient.

Enhanced Emotional Intelligence and Self-Awareness

Seeking help provides unique opportunities to develop sophisticated understanding of your own emotional patterns, triggers, strengths, and growth edges through the mirror of others' observations and the safety of supportive relationships where honest self-examination can occur without judgment.

Blind Spot Illumination occurs when trusted others can observe patterns in your behavior, communication, or emotional responses that you cannot see from inside your own experience, providing invaluable information for personal development and relationship improvement.

Emotional Vocabulary Expansion develops naturally in therapeutic or coaching relationships where professionals help you identify and name complex emotional experiences with greater precision, enhancing your capacity for self-awareness and communication with others.

Pattern Recognition improves when supportive others help you identify recurring themes in your relationships, career challenges, or personal struggles, enabling conscious change rather than unconscious repetition of limiting patterns.

Values Clarification often emerges through conversations with wise counselors, mentors, or spiritual guides who help you distinguish between authentic personal values and inherited expectations that might be driving choices that don't serve your genuine well-being.

Trauma Integration requires professional support in most cases, as the specialized knowledge and safe container that therapists provide enable processing and healing of painful experiences that might otherwise remain unresolved and continue affecting your life negatively.

Improved Relationship Quality and Social Connection

The vulnerability required for appropriate help-seeking naturally enhances your capacity for authentic connection while providing models and practice for the kind of interdependent relationships that create mutual support, satisfaction, and growth.

Intimacy Development accelerates when you practice the vulnerable sharing that help-seeking requires, developing comfort with emotional authenticity that translates into deeper, more satisfying personal relationships characterized by mutual understanding and support.

Communication Skills improve through practice in therapy, coaching, or support group contexts where you learn to express your needs, feelings, and experiences clearly while also developing capacity to listen deeply to others' experiences without immediately trying to fix or minimize them.

Boundary Setting abilities develop naturally when working with professionals who model appropriate limits while helping you identify and communicate your own boundaries in relationships that may have been characterized by overgiving, people-pleasing, or other patterns that compromise mutual respect.

Trust Building occurs through positive experiences of receiving support, care, and guidance from others without exploitation or judgment, gradually healing any previous relational trauma while building confidence in your ability to identify trustworthy people.

Reciprocity Skills develop as you learn to receive support gracefully while also identifying appropriate opportunities to contribute to others' well-being, creating the balanced give-and-take that sustains healthy long-term relationships.

Increased Resilience and Stress Management

Building a network of appropriate support resources dramatically enhances your capacity to navigate life's inevitable challenges with greater ease, effectiveness, and recovery speed while preventing the accumulation of stress that can lead to burnout, health problems, or relationship difficulties.

Crisis Navigation becomes more manageable when you have established relationships with professionals and trusted friends who can provide guidance, perspective, and practical assistance during emergency situations rather than facing overwhelming challenges in complete isolation.

Preventive Care emerges when regular check-ins with therapists, coaches, or supportive friends help you recognize and address developing problems before they become crises, similar to how regular medical checkups prevent minor health issues from becoming serious conditions.

Stress Distribution occurs when you have multiple sources of support that can share the emotional and practical burdens of challenging periods rather than carrying everything alone or overwhelming any single relationship with all your support needs.

Recovery Acceleration happens when appropriate support helps you process difficult experiences more quickly and completely than would be possible in isolation, preventing the kind of unresolved stress accumulation that compromises immune function, sleep quality, and overall health.

Coping Strategy Expansion develops through exposure to how others effectively handle similar challenges, expanding your toolkit of responses beyond the limited strategies you might have developed independently.

Professional and Creative Enhancement

Access to mentorship, coaching, and professional development support often proves crucial for career advancement, creative expression, and the development of leadership capabilities that serve both personal fulfillment and contribution to others.

Career Acceleration frequently results from mentorship relationships that provide industry insights, networking opportunities, and guidance about professional development strategies that individual effort alone cannot access as effectively.

Leadership Development benefits enormously from coaching and feedback that help you understand your impact on others while developing the emotional intelligence and communication skills that contemporary leadership requires.

Creative Breakthrough often emerges when artistic or creative mentors help you push beyond familiar approaches while providing encouragement during the vulnerable periods when creative growth requires experimentation and risk-taking.

Innovation Support develops through collaboration with others who can contribute different perspectives, skills, and resources to projects that exceed what individual effort could accomplish.

Performance Optimization occurs when coaches, trainers, or consultants help you identify and address limiting factors in your professional or creative performance while building on existing strengths more effectively.

Practical Steps to Seek Support: Your Roadmap to Connection

Developing the ability to seek appropriate help requires both practical strategies for identifying trustworthy resources and emotional skills for navigating the vulnerability that authentic support-seeking involves. These concrete steps provide a framework for building the support networks that can transform your capacity for growth, resilience, and contribution.

Recognizing When Help Is Needed

The first crucial skill in effective help-seeking involves developing awareness of your own limits, signs of overwhelm, and circumstances where external support could significantly improve outcomes compared to continuing individual efforts alone.

Early Warning Signal Recognition helps you identify the physical, emotional, and behavioral indicators that suggest you're approaching the edges of your current capacity and could benefit from additional resources or perspective before situations become overwhelming or crisis-oriented.

Physical signs might include persistent fatigue, sleep disruption, appetite changes, increased susceptibility to illness, or chronic tension and pain. Emotional indicators could involve increased irritability, anxiety, depression, numbness, or feeling overwhelmed by routine responsibilities. Behavioral changes might include social withdrawal, decreased performance, increased conflict in relationships, or abandoning activities you usually enjoy.

Complexity Assessment involves recognizing when situations exceed your current knowledge, skills, or emotional capacity in ways that suggest professional or peer support could provide significant benefits rather than continuing to struggle with challenges that have appropriate external resources available.

Career transitions, relationship difficulties, parenting challenges, grief and loss, trauma recovery, addiction issues, and mental health concerns represent common areas where professional support often proves more effective than individual effort alone.

Growth Edge Identification helps you distinguish between challenges that represent natural learning opportunities within your capacity and those that would benefit from guidance, mentorship, or professional support to navigate effectively and safely.

Stuck Pattern Recognition enables you to identify when you're repeating the same approaches to problems without making progress, suggesting that fresh perspectives or different strategies might be needed to create breakthrough rather than continued frustration.

Identifying Appropriate Resources and Support Types

Different types of challenges require different forms of support, and developing discernment about which resources best serve specific needs prevents both under-utilizing available help and expecting inappropriate support from people or services that aren't designed to address your particular circumstances.

Professional Support Categories include various types of trained helpers who specialize in different aspects of human development and challenge resolution, each offering specific expertise and approaches that serve particular needs.

Licensed therapists provide professional support for mental health concerns, trauma recovery, relationship difficulties, and personal development issues requiring specialized training and clinical expertise. Different therapeutic approaches serve different needs, from cognitive-behavioral therapy for anxiety and depression to trauma-focused approaches for PTSD and complex trauma recovery.

Coaches offer guidance for goal achievement, career development, leadership enhancement, and life transitions, focusing on forward movement and skill development rather than healing from past difficulties. Life coaches, career coaches, and executive coaches provide different specializations within the coaching field.

Medical professionals address physical health concerns that may be affecting emotional well-being, while psychiatrists can evaluate and treat mental health conditions that benefit from medication alongside therapeutic approaches.

Peer Support Resources connect you with others facing similar challenges or who have successfully navigated circumstances you're currently experiencing, providing understanding, encouragement, and practical wisdom that professional support alone cannot offer.

Support groups for specific challenges—grief, addiction recovery, divorce, parenting, career transition—provide community connection with others who understand your experience firsthand while offering practical strategies and emotional support from people who have walked similar paths.

Men's groups focused on emotional development, authentic masculinity, or general personal growth create opportunities for male community and support that addresses the particular challenges men face in contemporary culture.

Online communities and forums can provide 24/7 access to support and information, particularly valuable for men who may be hesitant to seek face-to-face support initially or who want to explore different perspectives and approaches anonymously.

Mentorship Relationships offer guidance from individuals with more experience in areas where you want to develop skills, knowledge, or wisdom, providing modeling and advice that can accelerate your growth significantly.

Spiritual and Philosophical Guidance addresses questions of meaning, purpose, values, and spiritual development through religious communities, spiritual teachers, or philosophical mentors who can help you explore life's deeper questions and develop practices that support your growth.

Building and Maintaining Support Networks

Creating sustainable support systems requires ongoing attention and investment rather than crisis-oriented help-seeking that places unrealistic demands on relationships or professional services during emergency situations.

Relationship Diversification involves building multiple sources of different types of support rather than relying on single relationships to meet all your emotional, practical, and developmental needs—a pattern that often overwhelms friendships while leaving you vulnerable if key relationships become unavailable.

Develop relationships with trusted friends for emotional support and daily life sharing, professional relationships for specialized guidance, mentor relationships for wisdom and modeling, and community connections for broader social support and contribution opportunities.

Proactive Connection Building means investing in supportive relationships during stable periods rather than only reaching out during crises, creating the trust and mutual investment that sustains relationships through difficult times while ensuring help is available when genuinely needed.

Regular check-ins with friends, ongoing professional relationships like therapy or coaching, and consistent participation in community activities build the social capital that supports you during challenging periods while allowing you to contribute to others' well-being during their difficulties.

Reciprocity and Contribution ensure that support relationships remain balanced over time through your own contributions to others' well-being, whether through practical assistance, emotional support, professional expertise, or community service that demonstrates your commitment to mutual aid rather than one-sided dependency.

Boundary Awareness helps you recognize the appropriate limits of different relationships while respecting others' boundaries and availability, preventing the burnout and resentment that can occur when support requests exceed what relationships can reasonably provide.

Geographic and Digital Integration addresses the reality that support networks may need to include both local, face-to-face relationships and remote connections through technology, particularly for specialized support or community connections that may not be available in your immediate geographic area.

Overcoming Barriers to Help-Seeking

Despite understanding the benefits of appropriate support, many men encounter internal and external obstacles that can interfere with actually reaching out when help would be beneficial, requiring conscious strategies for addressing these barriers while maintaining commitment to seeking appropriate support.

Shame and Stigma Management involves developing internal narratives and external responses that frame help-seeking as strength and wisdom rather than weakness or failure, while building relationships with others who share healthy attitudes toward interdependence and mutual support.

Practice self-compassionate internal dialogue that treats seeking help as evidence of your wisdom and commitment to growth rather than personal inadequacy. Surround yourself with people who model and support healthy help-seeking rather than those who reinforce toxic independence or shame around vulnerability.

Practical Barrier Problem-Solving addresses the realistic obstacles like cost, time, geographic access, or scheduling that might interfere with accessing appropriate support, while exploring creative solutions that make help more accessible within your circumstances.

Many communities offer sliding-scale therapy fees, support groups, peer counseling, or online resources that reduce financial barriers. Flexible scheduling, weekend options, or telehealth services can address time and transportation limitations.

Communication Skill Development helps you learn to express your needs, ask for help appropriately, and engage effectively with different types of support providers while maintaining appropriate boundaries and expectations.

Trust Building Practices help you develop discernment about identifying trustworthy support sources while gradually building confidence in your ability to receive care without exploitation or judgment.

Cultural Navigation acknowledges that help-seeking approaches may need to honor cultural values and family expectations while still accessing the support that serves your growth and well-being, finding culturally compatible resources when possible.

As we conclude this exploration of the profound strength that lies within asking for help, we celebrate your courage to consider approaches to life that honor both your individual capability and your fundamental interdependence with others who share this human journey alongside you.

Remember that developing comfort with appropriate help-seeking is itself a skill that improves with practice, requiring patience with yourself during the vulnerable moments when reaching out feels uncomfortable while celebrating each courageous step toward greater connection and support.

Your willingness to embrace help-seeking as strength rather than weakness contributes to a cultural transformation that makes it safer for others to acknowledge their own needs for support while challenging the isolation and unnecessary suffering that toxic independence creates in our communities.

The journey of authentic strength continues with each conscious choice to seek appropriate guidance when wisdom suggests it, each moment of vulnerable courage in acknowledging your limits and needs, and each decision to build the relationships and resources that enable you to contribute your gifts while receiving the support that sustains your growth and well-being.

Through your commitment to healthy interdependence, you participate in healing the wounds of isolation while modeling for others that true strength includes the wisdom to know when collaboration serves better than solitary effort, and the courage to reach out even when cultural messages suggest you should handle everything alone.

This is your invitation to a life of unprecedented support, growth, and contribution—not despite your need for help but because of your wisdom in recognizing that the greatest achievements of human civilization have always emerged through collaboration, mutual aid, and the kind of courageous vulnerability that transforms individual limitations into collective strength.

Reflection: In what ways have I adapted emotionally to meet societal or family expectations?

Chapter 15: The Healing Power of Forgiveness

Perhaps this is the most liberating chapter of your transformative journey—one that beckons you toward the profound alchemy of forgiveness, where the heaviest burdens of resentment transform into the lightest wings of freedom. It is here, where the courage to release old wounds meets the wisdom to reclaim your power from the grip of past hurts, creating space for healing that seemed impossible when anger and pain held dominion over your heart come to life.

This is your crash course on the understanding of forgiveness—not as weakness, surrender, or naive absolution of harmful behavior, but as the most sophisticated act of self-liberation and emotional intelligence available to the human spirit. Within these pages, you'll discover how forgiveness becomes not just a gift you offer to others, but the key that unlocks your own prison of resentment and opens pathways to unprecedented peace, strength, and authentic connection.

Within your capacity to forgive lies the power to transform not only your own emotional landscape but the entire trajectory of your relationships and your legacy in this world. You are taking the first steps into an understanding that honors both the reality of your pain and your magnificent potential to transcend it through conscious choice and compassionate wisdom.

Understanding Forgiveness: The Architecture of Liberation

Forgiveness stands among the most misunderstood concepts in human experience, often confused with reconciliation, excusing harmful behavior, or spiritual bypassing that minimizes legitimate pain and anger. True forgiveness, as we shall discover, represents a sophisticated process of emotional liberation that honors both your suffering and your inherent capacity to choose freedom over bondage to past hurts.

What Forgiveness Is: The Heart of Transformation

Authentic forgiveness embodies the conscious choice to release the grip of resentment, anger, and desire for revenge that keeps you energetically bound to those who have caused you pain. This release doesn't minimize the reality of harm done or suggest that painful experiences were acceptable, but rather recognizes that carrying ongoing resentment creates continued suffering that serves neither justice nor your own well-being.

Emotional Liberation lies at the core of genuine forgiveness—the recognition that resentment functions like emotional quicksand, trapping you in cycles of anger, rumination, and reactive behavior that prevent you from moving forward into the life you truly desire to create. When you choose forgiveness, you reclaim the emotional energy that resentment consumes, redirecting it toward healing, growth, and authentic contribution.

This liberation doesn't happen overnight or through simple decision, but rather unfolds as a process of gradually loosening the emotional chains that bind you to painful experiences while developing new relationships with your memories that acknowledge their reality without allowing them to control your present choices.

Reclaiming Personal Power represents another essential dimension of forgiveness, as it shifts you from the powerless position of victim to the empowered stance of conscious choice-maker who refuses to allow others' past actions to continue dictating your emotional state, life decisions, or capacity for joy and connection.

This power reclamation doesn't deny the impact of harmful experiences but rather recognizes that while you couldn't control what happened to you, you can influence how those experiences shape your future through conscious forgiveness work that transforms wounds into wisdom.

Wisdom Integration occurs as forgiveness allows you to extract learning and growth from painful experiences without remaining trapped by their emotional charge. This integration enables you to use your experiences to develop empathy, resilience, and understanding that can serve both your own continued growth and your ability to support others facing similar challenges.

Heart Opening characterizes the natural result of forgiveness work, as releasing resentment creates space for love, compassion, and authentic connection to flourish in ways that bitterness and anger cannot permit. This opening enhances not only your relationships with those you forgive but your entire capacity for intimacy and joy.

What Forgiveness Is Not: Clearing Common Misconceptions

Perhaps the greatest barrier to embracing forgiveness involves the widespread misconceptions that equate it with weakness, naivety, or the abandonment of appropriate boundaries and self-protection. Understanding what forgiveness doesn't require helps clear the pathway for authentic forgiveness work that honors both your pain and your power.

Forgiveness Is Not Reconciliation. You can forgive someone completely while maintaining appropriate boundaries that protect your well-being, including choosing to limit or eliminate contact with individuals who continue harmful behavior patterns. Forgiveness releases resentment without requiring renewed relationship or trust.

This distinction proves particularly important in cases of abuse, betrayal, or ongoing harmful behavior where reconciliation might compromise your safety or well-being. You can forgive your alcoholic father while maintaining boundaries around his drinking, forgive an unfaithful partner while choosing to end the relationship, or forgive childhood abusers while protecting yourself from further contact.

Forgiveness Is Not Excusing Harmful Behavior. Authentic forgiveness maintains clear recognition that harmful actions were wrong, inappropriate, or damaging while choosing to release ongoing resentment about those actions. This acknowledgment of wrong preserves moral clarity while preventing resentment from consuming your emotional energy.

You can forgive someone while simultaneously supporting appropriate consequences for their actions, whether through legal processes, professional accountability, or social boundaries that protect others from similar harm. Forgiveness serves justice rather than opposing it.

Forgiveness Is Not Forgetting. Healthy forgiveness includes remembering painful experiences as sources of wisdom and self-protection while releasing the emotional charge that keeps you trapped in ongoing suffering. This remembrance serves your safety and growth rather than perpetuating victimization.

Remembering without resentment allows you to maintain appropriate caution about similar situations while using your experiences to help others, make wiser choices, and develop the discrimination that protects your well-being without closing your heart to love and connection.

Forgiveness Is Not Immediate or One-Time. Authentic forgiveness typically unfolds as a gradual process that may require multiple cycles of releasing resentment as different layers of hurt surface or as life circumstances trigger old wounds. This process nature normalizes the difficulty of forgiveness while maintaining hope for eventual liberation.

Forgiveness Is Not Spiritual Bypassing. True forgiveness honors the full reality of your pain, anger, and loss while working through these emotions rather than jumping over them toward premature peace. This thorough processing ensures that forgiveness rests on solid emotional ground rather than suppressed feelings that may resurface later.

The Psychology of Resentment and Release

Understanding how resentment operates psychologically—and how forgiveness interrupts these patterns—provides crucial insight into why forgiveness proves so challenging yet ultimately liberating for emotional health and personal growth.

Trauma Bonding Through Resentment creates ongoing psychological connection to those who have hurt you, keeping their influence active in your present life through continued emotional reactivity, rumination, and decision-making based on avoiding similar harm. This bonding maintains psychological proximity to harmful experiences rather than creating genuine separation and healing.

Resentment functions like an invisible cord that energetically connects you to those who have caused pain, allowing their past actions to continue affecting your present emotional state, relationship choices, and self-concept. Forgiveness cuts these cords, creating genuine psychological freedom from others' harmful influence.

Cognitive Rumination Patterns associated with resentment create repetitive mental cycles that rehearse painful experiences, imagine revenge scenarios, or replay conversations and conflicts in ways that intensify rather than resolve emotional distress. These patterns consume mental energy while preventing the forward-focused thinking that supports healing and growth.

Identity Organization around victim status can make forgiveness feel threatening because it requires reorganizing your sense of self from someone who was wronged to someone who chooses healing and empowerment despite past pain. This identity shift, while ultimately liberating, can initially feel disorienting or like losing part of yourself.

Secondary Gains from resentment might include sympathy from others, justification for avoiding certain risks or relationships, or sense of moral superiority that provides psychological compensation for past hurt. Recognizing these hidden benefits helps address resistance to forgiveness while finding healthier ways to meet underlying needs.

The Neuroscience of Forgiveness

Modern brain research reveals that forgiveness creates specific neurological changes that enhance emotional regulation, reduce stress responses, and improve overall mental health in ways that sustained resentment cannot match.

Stress System Regulation improves dramatically through forgiveness work, as releasing resentment reduces chronic activation of fight-or-flight responses that keep your nervous system in states of tension and reactivity. This regulation enhances immune function, cardiovascular health, and overall resilience.

Prefrontal Cortex Strengthening occurs as forgiveness practices enhance activity in brain regions responsible for emotional regulation, perspective-taking, and conscious choice-making. These neurological changes improve your capacity to respond thoughtfully rather than reactively to challenging situations.

Mirror Neuron Activation associated with empathy and compassion increases through forgiveness work, enhancing your ability to understand others' perspectives while maintaining appropriate boundaries and self-care. This activation supports both forgiveness processes and improved relationship skills.

Memory Reconsolidation allows forgiveness to gradually change how traumatic memories are stored and accessed, reducing their emotional charge while preserving important learning and protective information. This process helps painful memories become sources of wisdom rather than ongoing trauma.

The Benefits of Forgiveness: The Gift That Transforms the Giver

When you courageously embark upon the journey of forgiveness, extraordinary benefits emerge that extend far beyond the immediate relief of releasing resentment to encompass profound enhancements in physical health, emotional well-being, relationship quality, and your overall capacity for joy, creativity, and authentic contribution to the world.

Physical Health and Stress Reduction

Perhaps the most immediate and measurable benefits of forgiveness involve dramatic improvements in physical health markers that demonstrate how emotional liberation translates into tangible wellness outcomes that enhance both longevity and quality of life.

Cardiovascular Health improves significantly when forgiveness reduces the chronic stress and anger that contribute to heart disease, high blood pressure, and other cardiovascular problems. Studies consistently show that individuals who practice forgiveness demonstrate lower blood pressure, reduced heart rate variability, and improved cardiovascular markers compared to those who maintain ongoing resentment.

The chronic anger and stress associated with resentment create sustained activation of fight-or-flight responses that strain cardiovascular systems while promoting inflammation throughout the body. Forgiveness interrupts these patterns, allowing your cardiovascular system to return to healthier baseline functioning.

Immune System Enhancement results from the stress reduction and emotional regulation that forgiveness provides, as chronic resentment compromises immune function while positive emotions like compassion and peace support optimal immune responses that protect against illness and disease.

Research demonstrates that individuals engaged in forgiveness work show improved immune markers, increased resistance to infection, and better recovery from illness compared to those carrying ongoing resentment and anger about past hurts.

Sleep Quality Improvement occurs naturally as forgiveness reduces the rumination and emotional activation that interfere with restful sleep. The mental rehearsal of past hurts and anger that characterizes resentment often continues during sleep attempts, preventing the deep rest necessary for physical and emotional recovery.

Pain Management Benefits emerge as forgiveness reduces the muscle tension, inflammation, and stress responses that often intensify chronic pain conditions. The relaxation and emotional peace that accompany forgiveness create optimal conditions for natural pain relief and healing.

Longevity Enhancement results from the combined effects of improved cardiovascular health, enhanced immune function, better sleep, and reduced chronic stress that forgiveness provides. Studies suggest that individuals who practice forgiveness regularly live longer, healthier lives than those who maintain ongoing resentment.

Emotional Healing and Mental Health

The emotional benefits of forgiveness extend throughout every aspect of psychological well-being, creating improvements in mood, self-esteem, emotional regulation, and overall life satisfaction that transform your entire experience of being alive.

Depression Relief occurs as forgiveness interrupts the rumination patterns and negative thought cycles that contribute to depressive episodes while creating space for positive emotions like peace, gratitude, and hope to emerge. The energy that was trapped in resentment becomes available for joy, creativity, and engagement with life.

Forgiveness doesn't eliminate appropriate sadness about losses or harm experienced, but it prevents this natural grief from becoming stuck in ongoing depression that serves no healing purpose while compromising your capacity for present-moment happiness and connection.

Anxiety Reduction results from the safety and peace that emerge when you're no longer constantly vigilant about protecting yourself from repeat harm or planning revenge against those who have hurt you. This mental and emotional relaxation reduces the hypervigilance that characterizes anxiety while building confidence in your capacity to handle future challenges.

Self-Esteem Enhancement develops as forgiveness demonstrates your strength, wisdom, and emotional sophistication while freeing you from the victim identity that can undermine self-worth and personal empowerment. Choosing forgiveness affirms your value and capability while building confidence in your emotional resilience.

Emotional Regulation Improvement emerges as forgiveness practices develop your capacity to process difficult emotions without being overwhelmed by them while building skills for choosing conscious responses rather than reactive patterns that may create additional problems in relationships and life circumstances.

Post-Traumatic Growth becomes possible when forgiveness allows traumatic experiences to be integrated as sources of strength, wisdom, and compassion rather than ongoing sources of suffering and limitation. This growth honors your pain while transforming it into gifts that can serve both your continued development and your ability to help others.

Relationship Enhancement and Social Connection

The relationship benefits of forgiveness extend beyond connections with those you forgive to enhance your entire capacity for authentic intimacy, trust, and collaborative connection with others throughout your personal and professional life.

Trust Capacity Restoration occurs as forgiveness work heals the cynicism and defensive patterns that past hurts often create, allowing you to approach new relationships with appropriate openness while maintaining healthy discernment about trustworthiness and safety.

Forgiveness doesn't make you naive about human nature or eliminate appropriate caution, but it prevents past experiences from creating blanket distrust that blocks potentially valuable and loving relationships from developing.

Communication Skills Enhancement develops through forgiveness processes that require expressing difficult emotions, setting appropriate boundaries, and navigating complex conversations about hurt and healing. These skills transfer to all your relationships, improving your capacity for honest, constructive dialogue during conflicts and challenges.

Empathy Development emerges naturally through forgiveness work as understanding others' pain, limitations, and humanity becomes possible when you're not consumed by your own resentment and anger. This empathy enhances all your relationships while building the emotional intelligence that effective connection requires.

Conflict Resolution Abilities improve dramatically as forgiveness practices develop your capacity to separate people from their behaviors, maintain care while setting boundaries, and work toward solutions that honor everyone's well-being rather than seeking to punish or control others.

Intimacy Deepening becomes possible when the walls that resentment builds around your heart come down, allowing others to see and connect with your authentic self while creating space for the vulnerability that genuine intimacy requires.

Spiritual Growth and Life Purpose

Forgiveness often catalyzes profound spiritual development and clarity about life purpose as releasing resentment creates space for deeper questions about meaning, service, and your unique contribution to healing and wholeness in the world.

Compassion Expansion develops naturally through forgiveness work as your own experience of choosing healing over resentment creates understanding and empathy for others facing similar choices. This compassion becomes a resource for service and contribution that extends far beyond personal healing.

Wisdom Integration occurs as forgiveness transforms painful experiences into sources of insight about human nature, the importance of kindness, and the preciousness of life and relationship. This wisdom becomes available for guiding your own choices while supporting others who seek similar understanding.

Purpose Clarification often emerges through forgiveness work as you discover how your experiences and healing can serve others facing similar challenges. Many individuals find that their greatest purpose involves using their wounds as sources of wisdom for helping others navigate similar difficulties.

Spiritual Connection Deepening results from the peace and openness that forgiveness creates, allowing for greater receptivity to spiritual guidance, meaning, and connection with something larger than individual concerns and grievances.

Legacy Transformation becomes possible when forgiveness breaks cycles of hurt and resentment that might otherwise pass to future generations, creating positive influence that extends through your children, students, colleagues, and communities for years to come.

Practical Steps to Practice Forgiveness: Your Journey to Freedom

The path of forgiveness requires both courage and practical wisdom, implemented through specific practices that honor the complexity of this process while providing concrete steps for moving from resentment toward liberation. These strategies respect both the difficulty of forgiveness and your inherent capacity to choose healing over continued suffering.

Forgiving Others: Releasing External Resentments

The process of forgiving those who have caused you harm involves multiple stages and approaches, each serving different aspects of the healing journey while respecting your need for safety, truth, and authentic emotional processing.

Acknowledging the Full Reality of Harm forms the essential foundation for authentic forgiveness, as premature attempts to "let go" without fully honoring your pain often result in superficial forgiveness that doesn't create genuine healing or freedom from resentment's grip.

Create safe space—perhaps through journaling, therapy, or trusted conversation—to fully acknowledge what was done to you, how it affected your life, and what losses or damage resulted from others' harmful actions. This acknowledgment validates your experience while creating solid ground for genuine forgiveness work.

Allow yourself to feel the full range of emotions associated with your pain—anger, sadness, fear, disappointment, betrayal—without immediately trying to transform or release them. These emotions contain important information and energy that need expression before genuine forgiveness becomes possible.

Understanding Without Excusing involves developing compassion for those who harmed you by recognizing their humanity, limitations, and likely pain that contributed to their harmful behavior, while maintaining clear awareness that understanding doesn't excuse their actions or eliminate appropriate consequences.

This understanding might involve recognizing that those who hurt you were likely hurt themselves, that their harmful behavior probably stemmed from their own unhealed wounds or limitations, or that they may have lacked the skills, awareness, or support necessary for better choices.

Such understanding serves forgiveness without requiring you to minimize harm done or eliminate appropriate boundaries and consequences. You can understand someone's pain while still holding them accountable for their choices and protecting yourself from further harm.

Grieving Losses and Expectations allows you to mourn not only direct harm done but also the losses of trust, innocence, safety, or life direction that harmful experiences often create. This grief work prevents these losses from becoming sources of ongoing resentment that block forgiveness.

Grieve the relationships you hoped to have but cannot due to others' limitations or harmful patterns. Mourn the childhood safety or adult security that was violated. Allow sadness about the person you might have been without certain harmful experiences, while appreciating who you've become partly through navigating these challenges.

Choosing Release Over Revenge represents the conscious decision to prioritize your own healing and freedom over desires to punish or control those who have harmed you. This choice acknowledges that revenge often perpetuates suffering while forgiveness creates possibilities for peace and growth.

This doesn't mean abandoning appropriate legal action, professional consequences, or protective boundaries, but rather releasing the emotional investment in seeing others suffer for their past actions. Focus energy on your own healing rather than monitoring whether others receive what you believe they deserve.

Compassion Practices help develop the heart opening that makes forgiveness possible by cultivating understanding and care even for those who have caused significant pain. These practices don't require feeling warm and fuzzy about people who have harmed you, but rather developing the compassion that recognizes shared humanity despite harmful behaviors.

This might involve recognizing that those who hurt you were likely doing the best they could with their current level of consciousness and skill, even if their best was far from adequate. Consider what pain or limitation might have contributed to their harmful choices without using this understanding excusing their behavior.

Self-Forgiveness: Healing Internal Resentment

Perhaps the most challenging aspect of forgiveness work involves releasing resentment toward yourself for mistakes you've made, opportunities you've missed, or ways you may have contributed to your own suffering through choices that now seem obviously harmful or inadequate.

Acknowledging Mistakes Without Self-Attack requires developing the capacity to honestly assess your role in problems or harm while maintaining the self-compassion necessary for learning and growth rather than continuing cycles of shame and self-punishment that prevent positive change.

List specific actions, choices, or patterns you regret without editing or minimizing, allowing yourself to see clearly where you contributed to difficulties in your relationships, career, health, or personal development. This honesty creates foundation for authentic change while avoiding the self-deception that prevents growth.

Simultaneously, practice responding to these mistakes with the same kindness you would offer a good friend facing similar regrets. Recognize that your harmful choices likely made sense given your level of consciousness, available information, and emotional state at the time they were made.

Understanding Your Humanity and Limitations involves recognizing that making mistakes represents normal human experience rather than evidence of fundamental inadequacy or unforgivability that sets you apart from others who deserve compassion and second chances.

Consider the circumstances that influenced your harmful choices—stress levels, available support, information you lacked, emotional wounds that affected your judgment, or skills you hadn't yet developed. This context doesn't excuse harmful behavior but helps you understand it within the larger story of your growth and development.

Making Amends Where Possible creates opportunities to address harm you may have caused others while demonstrating your commitment to different choices moving forward. These amends serve both your forgiveness process and the healing of relationships damaged by your past actions.

Sincere apologies acknowledge specific harm caused, take full responsibility without excuses or blame-shifting, express genuine remorse for pain caused, and include concrete commitments to different behavior in the future. When direct amends aren't possible or appropriate, indirect amends through service or changed behavior can serve similar healing functions.

Learning Integration and Character Development transforms regrettable experiences into wisdom and strength by extracting lessons that inform better choices while building the character qualities that prevent similar mistakes in future situations.

Identify specific lessons your mistakes have taught you about your values, the importance of certain principles, or skills you need to develop for better outcomes. Use these insights to guide current choices while sharing your learning with others who might benefit from your experience.

Commitment to Growth and Change demonstrates self-forgiveness through concrete actions that address patterns or circumstances that contributed to regrettable choices, showing yourself and others that you're serious about learning from mistakes rather than simply feeling bad about them.

This might involve pursuing therapy to address underlying emotional issues, developing new skills for handling stress or conflict, changing environments that support harmful patterns, or building support systems that encourage better choices.

Working with Complex Forgiveness Situations

Some forgiveness challenges involve particularly complex circumstances that require specialized approaches honoring the unique difficulties while maintaining commitment to eventual healing and freedom from resentment's burden.

Forgiving Those Who Haven't Apologized requires developing the strength to choose forgiveness even when others haven't acknowledged wrongdoing, taken responsibility, or expressed remorse for harm caused. This forgiveness serves your freedom rather than depending on others' cooperation or recognition.

Recognize that others' inability or unwillingness to acknowledge harm often stems from their own pain, defensiveness, or limitations rather than accurate assessment of whether harm occurred. Your healing doesn't depend on their admission of wrongdoing, though such acknowledgment might make forgiveness easier.

Focus on releasing your own resentment while maintaining appropriate boundaries and consequences that protect your well-being regardless of whether others acknowledge their role in causing harm.

Forgiving Severe Trauma and Abuse requires professional support in most cases, as the profound violations that characterize abuse often create complex trauma responses that need specialized treatment alongside forgiveness work to prevent re-traumatization or premature spiritual bypassing.

Work with trauma-informed therapists who understand both healing processes and forgiveness work, ensuring that forgiveness serves genuine liberation rather than continued victimization through premature letting go that doesn't honor the full reality of violation experienced.

Forgiving Those Who Have Died involves working through resentment toward people who are no longer available for dialogue, reconciliation, or amends, requiring internal processes that create resolution without external relationship repair possibilities.

Letter writing, empty chair exercises, or symbolic rituals can provide opportunities to express feelings and work toward forgiveness even when direct communication isn't possible. These processes honor both your need for expression and the reality that healing must occur within yourself.

Forgiving Systemic and Cultural Harms addresses the challenge of forgiving institutions, cultural patterns, or societal systems that have caused harm through discrimination, oppression, or neglect. These forgiveness challenges often require balancing personal healing with continued commitment to social justice and positive change.

Recognize that forgiving systems doesn't require abandoning efforts for justice and reform, but rather ensuring that your work for change comes from love and vision rather than hatred and resentment that may compromise your effectiveness and well-being.

Ongoing Forgiveness Processes acknowledge that forgiveness often requires multiple cycles as new layers of hurt surface or life circumstances trigger old wounds, normalizing the non-linear nature of forgiveness while maintaining hope for eventual complete release.

Develop patience with your forgiveness process, recognizing that deep wounds may require time and repeated attention before complete healing occurs. Each cycle of forgiveness work typically goes deeper and creates more lasting freedom than previous attempts.

As we conclude this sacred exploration of forgiveness, we celebrate your courage to consider releasing the burdens that may have weighed upon your heart while honoring the profound strength required to choose healing over continued resentment, freedom over bondage to past pain.

Remember that forgiveness represents not a destination you arrive at but a practice you cultivate throughout your lifetime, requiring patience with the process while maintaining faith in your inherent capacity to transform even the deepest wounds into sources of wisdom, compassion, and strength.

Your willingness to explore forgiveness contributes to healing that extends far beyond your individual experience to touch every relationship, every community, and every context where your increased capacity for love and understanding creates possibilities for greater peace and authentic connection.

The journey of forgiveness continues with each conscious choice to release resentment rather than rehearse old hurts, each moment when you choose understanding over judgment, and each decision to let love be stronger than fear in guiding your responses to life's inevitable challenges and disappointments.

Through your commitment to forgiveness, you participate in breaking cycles of pain and resentment while modeling for others the extraordinary strength that lies within choosing healing over hatred, demonstrating that forgiveness represents not weakness but the highest expression of human courage and wisdom.

This is your invitation to unprecedented freedom, peace, and authentic power—not despite the pain you've experienced but because of your magnificent capacity to transform that pain into gifts of healing that serve not only your own liberation but contribute to the healing of our wounded world through the revolutionary power of forgiveness.

Prompt: Are you compassionate with yourself in the same way you are with others?

Chapter 16: Mastering Stress Management Techniques

You can master the intricate art of navigating life's inevitable pressures with wisdom, resilience, and grace. Here, we move into the sacred territory where ancient wisdom meets modern science, where your understanding of stress evolves from seeing it as an enemy to be defeated into recognizing it as a powerful ally that, when properly understood and managed, becomes a catalyst for growth, strength, and extraordinary achievement.

Within these pages, you will discover how the cultivation of stress mastery becomes the foundation upon which optimal performance, meaningful relationships, and authentic well-being are built, transforming your relationship with challenge from one of struggle to one of confident capability.

In our rapidly changing world, stress management skills are not luxury additions to your personal development but essential competencies that determine the quality of your health, relationships, and contribution to the world around you. You are stepping into an understanding that honors both the reality of modern pressures and your magnificent capacity to meet them with increasing skill, calm, and effectiveness.

Understanding Stress: The Architecture of Human Response

Stress represents one of the most fundamental yet misunderstood aspects of human experience—a sophisticated biological and psychological response system that evolved to protect and enhance our survival, yet often becomes a source of suffering when we lack the knowledge and skills necessary to work with it constructively rather than being overwhelmed by its intensity.

The Nature and Purpose of Stress

At its core, stress embodies your body and mind's intelligent response to perceived challenges, threats, or demands that require adaptation, growth, or heightened performance. This response system represents millions of years of evolutionary refinement, designed to mobilize your resources during crucial moments while providing the energy and focus necessary to meet life's demands effectively.

Adaptive Stress Response serves essential functions that enhance your capability and performance when properly activated and managed. This positive stress, known as "eustress," provides the alertness needed for peak performance, the motivation required for growth and achievement, and the physiological arousal that enables you to rise to meet important challenges with enhanced capability and focus.

Consider how moderate stress sharpens your attention during important presentations, energizes your performance during athletic competitions, or mobilizes your resources during emergency situations. This beneficial stress response represents your nervous system's sophisticated capacity to optimize your functioning when circumstances require elevated performance or rapid adaptation.

Protective Mechanisms activated through stress responses help ensure your survival and well-being by increasing heart rate to deliver more oxygen to muscles, releasing stress hormones that enhance mental clarity and physical strength, heightening sensory awareness to detect important information, and preparing your body for either fighting threats or escaping dangerous situations.

Learning and Growth Catalyst emerges through appropriate stress exposure that challenges you just beyond your current comfort zone, stimulating neuroplasticity that creates new neural pathways, building resilience through successful navigation of difficulties, and developing confidence in your capacity to handle increasingly complex challenges.

Social Bonding Enhancement occurs through certain types of stress that activate oxytocin production, encouraging connection and cooperation during challenging times, building stronger relationships through shared difficulties, and creating the mutual support that enhances collective resilience and problem-solving capacity.

The Spectrum of Stress Experience

Understanding stress requires recognizing its diverse manifestations and intensities, from the subtle pressures of daily life to the overwhelming challenges that can exceed your current coping capacity, each requiring different approaches and management strategies.

Acute Stress represents brief, intense responses to immediate challenges or threats—situations like job interviews, medical procedures, public speaking, or emergency situations that activate your stress response temporarily before returning to baseline functioning. This type of stress, while uncomfortable, typically resolves quickly and may even provide beneficial effects like enhanced performance or valuable learning experiences.

Chronic Stress develops when stressful conditions persist over extended periods without adequate recovery time, keeping your stress response systems chronically activated in ways that begin to compromise rather than enhance your health and performance. This sustained activation can result from ongoing work pressures, relationship conflicts, financial difficulties, health concerns, or caregiving responsibilities that continue for months or years.

Traumatic Stress emerges from experiences that overwhelm your natural capacity to cope, creating lasting changes in how your nervous system responds to perceived threats while potentially affecting your sense of safety, trust, and stability in the world. These experiences might include accidents, violence, natural disasters, loss of loved ones, or other events that exceed your psychological and emotional resources.

Developmental Stress occurs during major life transitions or growth periods that require significant adaptation—career changes, relationship transitions, parenthood, aging processes, or spiritual development phases that challenge existing identity structures while demanding new skills and perspectives.

The Physiology of Stress Response

Modern science reveals stress as a complex orchestration of neurological, hormonal, and physical processes that affect every system in your body, creating both immediate performance enhancement and, when chronic, potential health challenges that require conscious management and recovery practices.

The HPA Axis (hypothalamic-pituitary-adrenal axis) serves as your body's primary stress response system, initiating when your brain perceives threats or challenges. The hypothalamus releases corticotropin-releasing hormone (CRH), which signals the pituitary gland to produce adrenocorticotropic hormone (ACTH), which then triggers the adrenal glands to release cortisol and other stress hormones.

Sympathetic Nervous System Activation creates the immediate "fight-or-flight" response that prepares your body for action through increased heart rate and blood pressure, heightened alertness and sensory awareness, increased muscle tension and strength, elevated blood glucose levels for quick energy, and reduced activity in non-essential systems like digestion and immune function.

Hormonal Cascade Effects include cortisol release that provides sustained energy and reduces inflammation, adrenaline (epinephrine) that creates immediate energy and alertness, noradrenaline that enhances focus and motivation, and various other hormones that coordinate your body's response to challenge while affecting mood, energy, sleep, and overall functioning.

Recovery and Restoration occur through parasympathetic nervous system activation that returns your body to baseline functioning, allowing heart rate and blood pressure to normalize, restoring digestive and immune function, processing stress hormones through liver metabolism, and enabling the cellular repair and recovery that maintain long-term health.

Modern Stressors and Their Impact

Contemporary life presents unique stressors that our evolutionary stress response systems weren't designed to handle, creating challenges that require conscious awareness and skillful management to prevent chronic activation that compromises health, relationships, and performance.

Information Overload from constant connectivity, social media, news cycles, and digital communication creates continuous low-level stress activation through fragmented attention, comparison with others' curated lives, exposure to global crises and conflicts, and the pressure to maintain constant availability and responsiveness to others' communications and demands.

Time Pressure and Scheduling Demands characteristic of modern life create chronic stress through overpacked schedules that provide insufficient recovery time, conflicting priorities and commitments that create internal tension, commuting and transportation stresses that consume energy without providing satisfaction, and the cultural emphasis on productivity and achievement that can make rest feel guilty or inadequate.

Social and Cultural Pressures include expectations for success and achievement that may exceed realistic possibilities, social comparison facilitated by social media and cultural messaging, economic pressures and financial insecurity that affect basic survival needs, and cultural changes that challenge traditional identity structures and social support systems.

Work-Related Stressors encompass job insecurity and economic uncertainty, workplace conflicts and toxic organizational cultures, work-life balance challenges that blur boundaries between professional and personal time, and career advancement pressures that may conflict with personal values or family priorities.

Relationship and Family Dynamics create stress through communication challenges and unresolved conflicts, caregiving responsibilities for children, aging parents, or family members with special needs, social isolation and loneliness that compromise emotional support, and the complexity of maintaining authentic connections in increasingly busy and distracted social environments.

Stress Impact on Physical Health

Chronic stress creates measurable effects throughout your body's systems, demonstrating why stress management represents not luxury self-care but essential health maintenance that affects every aspect of your physical well-being and longevity.

Cardiovascular Effects include elevated blood pressure that strains heart and blood vessels, increased risk of heart disease and stroke through chronic inflammation, irregular heart rhythms that can affect cardiac function, and compromised circulation that affects organ function and healing capacity throughout your body.

Immune System Suppression results from chronic cortisol elevation that reduces white blood cell effectiveness, increases susceptibility to infections and illnesses, slows wound healing and recovery processes, and may contribute to autoimmune conditions where your immune system begins attacking healthy tissues.

Digestive System Impact encompasses reduced digestive efficiency that affects nutrient absorption, increased risk of ulcers and gastrointestinal problems, changes in gut bacteria that affect mood and immune function, and appetite changes that may lead to weight gain or loss and nutritional imbalances.

Sleep Disruption creates cycles where stress interferes with sleep quality while sleep deprivation increases stress reactivity, compromised memory consolidation and learning that occurs during quality sleep, reduced physical recovery and cellular repair processes, and hormonal disruptions that affect mood, energy, and stress resilience.

Musculoskeletal Tension includes chronic muscle tension that can cause pain and restricted movement, headaches and jaw tension from prolonged stress activation, postural changes that affect spinal health and breathing efficiency, and increased risk of injury due to muscle imbalances and reduced flexibility.

Stress Impact on Emotional and Mental Health

The relationship between stress and emotional well-being creates complex interactions where chronic stress can contribute to mental health challenges while mental health difficulties can increase stress reactivity, requiring integrated approaches that address both stress management and emotional healing.

Mood Disorders can develop or worsen under chronic stress, including depression that emerges from prolonged stress hormone elevation, anxiety disorders that develop from chronic hypervigilance and threat detection, mood swings and emotional instability that result from hormonal fluctuations, and emotional numbness or disconnection that represents protective responses to overwhelm.

Cognitive Function Changes include memory problems and difficulty concentrating that result from chronic stress hormone exposure, reduced creative thinking and problem-solving capacity during stress activation, decision-making impairment that affects judgment and choices, and learning difficulties that compromise personal and professional development.

Relationship Impact encompasses increased irritability and conflict in personal relationships, reduced empathy and emotional availability for others' needs, social withdrawal and isolation that compromise support networks, and communication difficulties that arise from stress-related emotional reactivity and defensive patterns.

Behavioral Changes might include increased use of alcohol, drugs, or other substances to manage stress, compulsive behaviors like overeating, shopping, or gambling as stress relief attempts, procrastination, and avoidance that create additional stress through delayed responsibilities, and aggressive or passive-aggressive behaviors that strain relationships and professional situations.

The Benefits of Effective Stress Management: The Gift of Conscious Mastery

When you develop sophisticated skills for managing stress effectively, extraordinary benefits emerge that extend throughout every aspect of your life experience, creating improvements in health, relationships, performance, and overall life satisfaction that compound over time to create a fundamentally different quality of existence.

Enhanced Physical Health and Vitality

Perhaps the most immediate and measurable benefits of stress management involve dramatic improvements in physical health markers that demonstrate how emotional and psychological skills translate into tangible wellness outcomes that enhance both longevity and quality of life.

Cardiovascular Health Improvement occurs through stress management practices that reduce blood pressure, lower resting heart rate, and improve heart rate variability—indicators of cardiovascular resilience and health. Regular stress management practices have been shown to reduce heart disease risk by up to 40% while improving circulation and reducing inflammation throughout the cardiovascular system.

Effective stress management also reduces the chronic inflammation that contributes to atherosclerosis and heart disease, while improving cholesterol profiles and reducing the risk of blood clots that can cause heart attacks and strokes.

Immune System Enhancement results from stress management that allows immune function to operate optimally rather than being suppressed by chronic stress hormone elevation. Well-managed stress correlates with increased resistance to infections, faster recovery from illness and injury, reduced autoimmune reactions, and better vaccine effectiveness.

Research consistently demonstrates that individuals with effective stress management skills experience fewer colds and infections, recover more quickly from surgical procedures, and show better immune responses to various health challenges throughout their lives.

Sleep Quality Optimization emerges naturally as stress management reduces the hypervigilance and rumination that interfere with restful sleep while creating the relaxation necessary for deep, restorative rest. Quality sleep, in turn, enhances stress resilience, creating positive cycles where better sleep improves stress management while effective stress management improves sleep.

Energy and Vitality Enhancement develops as stress management prevents the chronic fatigue that results from sustained stress response activation while optimizing the recovery processes that restore and maintain your energy reserves. Individuals with strong stress management skills report higher energy levels, greater physical endurance, and more consistent vitality throughout their days.

Pain Management Benefits occur as stress reduction decreases muscle tension, reduces inflammation that contributes to pain, and improves the body's natural pain management systems. Chronic pain conditions often improve significantly when stress management becomes part of comprehensive treatment approaches.

Emotional Regulation and Mental Health

The emotional and psychological benefits of stress management extend throughout every aspect of mental health and emotional well-being, creating improvements in mood, resilience, and overall psychological functioning that enhance life satisfaction and relationship quality.

Anxiety and Depression Reduction results from stress management practices that interrupt the physiological and psychological patterns that contribute to these common mental health challenges. Regular stress management can be as effective as medication for mild to moderate anxiety and depression while providing lasting skills rather than temporary symptom relief.

Stress management practices help regulate neurotransmitters like serotonin and dopamine that affect mood, while reducing cortisol levels that contribute to depression and anxiety when chronically elevated.

Emotional Regulation Enhancement develops through stress management practices that strengthen your capacity to experience emotions without being overwhelmed by them while maintaining choice about how to respond rather than reacting automatically to emotional activation.

Cognitive Function Improvement includes enhanced memory, concentration, and decision-making capacity that results from reduced stress hormone interference with brain function. Stress management literally improves brain function by protecting neural connections while promoting neuroplasticity that supports continued learning and adaptation.

Resilience Building occurs as successful stress management creates confidence in your capacity to handle life's challenges while developing the emotional and psychological resources that support you during difficult periods. This resilience becomes a sustainable resource that grows stronger through practice and successful application.

Self-Esteem and Confidence Enhancement emerge naturally as stress management demonstrates your capability and wisdom while creating the emotional stability that supports positive self-regard and confidence in your ability to navigate life's complexities successfully.

Relationship Quality and Social Connection

Stress management skills dramatically improve relationship quality by enhancing your capacity for authentic connection while reducing the irritability, withdrawal, and defensive patterns that stress often creates in interpersonal interactions.

Communication Enhancement develops as stress management provides the emotional regulation necessary for clear, compassionate communication during conflicts and challenges while reducing the defensive reactivity that often escalates relationship tensions unnecessarily.

When you can maintain calm and clarity during relationship stress, you're able to listen more effectively, express your needs without blame or attack, and work collaboratively toward solutions rather than getting stuck in defensive or aggressive patterns.

Empathy and Compassion Development occur naturally when stress management reduces your own emotional overwhelm, creating space to understand and respond to others' experiences with care and wisdom rather than being consumed by your own stress responses.

Conflict Resolution Skills improve dramatically as stress management provides the emotional regulation and clear thinking necessary for navigating disagreements constructively while maintaining care and respect for all parties involved.

Intimacy and Vulnerability Capacity expand when stress management creates the emotional safety necessary for sharing authentic thoughts and feelings while being present for others' vulnerability without being overwhelmed or activated by emotional intensity.

Social Contribution Enhancement emerges as stress management creates emotional and energetic capacity for contributing to others' well-being, participating in community activities, and offering support during challenging times rather than being consumed by personal stress management needs.

Professional Performance and Achievement

The workplace benefits of stress management extend throughout every aspect of professional effectiveness, from daily task performance to leadership capacity and career advancement opportunities that require sustained excellence under pressure.

Productivity and Focus Enhancement result from stress management that prevents the scattered attention and mental fog that chronic stress creates while optimizing the cognitive resources necessary for sustained, high-quality work performance.

Creativity and Innovation flourish when stress management creates the psychological safety and mental clarity necessary for thinking outside conventional approaches while maintaining the confidence to propose and implement new ideas that might involve risk or uncertainty.

Leadership Effectiveness improves dramatically when stress management provides the emotional regulation and clear judgment necessary for inspiring and guiding others during challenging periods while maintaining the calm presence that others can rely on during organizational stress and change.

Decision-Making Quality enhances significantly when stress management prevents the impulsivity and tunnel vision that stress often creates while providing access to both rational analysis and intuitive wisdom that inform effective choices in complex situations.

Career Advancement Opportunities often increase for individuals with strong stress management skills, as organizations increasingly value employees who can maintain high performance during pressure while contributing to positive organizational culture and team effectiveness.

Life Satisfaction and Purpose

The broader life benefits of stress management encompass improvements in overall life satisfaction, sense of purpose, and capacity for joy and meaning that transform your entire experience of being alive while creating positive influence that extends to everyone whose life you touch.

Present-Moment Awareness develops naturally through stress management practices that interrupt the rumination about past problems and anxiety about future challenges that prevent full engagement with current experiences and opportunities for satisfaction and connection.

Joy and Pleasure Capacity expand when stress management creates the relaxation and openness necessary for appreciating life's simple pleasures while building the emotional space that allows happiness to emerge naturally rather than being blocked by chronic tension and worry.

Purpose Clarity often emerges through stress management work as reduced overwhelm creates space for reflecting on what matters most deeply to you while connecting with values and goals that provide meaning and direction for your life choices and activities.

Spiritual Connection may deepen as stress management practices create the peace and openness necessary for spiritual awareness and connection while reducing the mental noise that often blocks access to deeper sources of wisdom and guidance.

Legacy and Contribution Enhancement develop as stress management creates capacity for thinking beyond immediate survival needs toward how your life can serve purposes larger than personal comfort and security while contributing positively to others' well-being and growth.

Practical Stress Management Techniques: Your Comprehensive Toolkit

The mastery of stress requires a diverse repertoire of evidence-based techniques that can be adapted to different situations, stress levels, and personal preferences, providing you with reliable tools for both immediate stress relief and long-term resilience building that serves your health and effectiveness throughout your lifetime.

Mindfulness and Present-Moment Awareness Practices

Mindfulness-based stress management represents one of the most thoroughly researched and effective approaches for both immediate stress relief and long-term stress resilience, providing techniques that can be applied anywhere, anytime, without requiring special equipment or extensive time commitments.

Basic Breath Awareness forms the foundation of mindfulness-based stress management through simple practices that anchor your attention in present-moment experience while activating your parasympathetic nervous system to counteract stress response activation.

Begin with the 4-7-8 breathing technique: breathe in through your nose for 4 counts, hold your breath for 7 counts, and exhale through your mouth for 8 counts. This pattern naturally activates relaxation responses while providing immediate stress relief that can be used anywhere, anytime.

Practice diaphragmatic breathing by placing one hand on your chest and one on your belly, breathing deeply enough that only the bottom hand moves. This breathing pattern optimizes oxygen exchange while reducing the shallow, rapid breathing that often accompanies stress activation.

Body Scan Meditation involves systematically directing attention throughout your body to identify and release tension while developing awareness of how stress manifests physically so you can address it before it becomes overwhelming or creates physical problems.

Start with a brief 5-minute body scan: lie down or sit comfortably, close your eyes, and slowly move your attention from the top of your head down through each part of your body, noticing any tension, discomfort, or relaxation without trying to change anything immediately.

As you identify areas of tension, practice breathing into those areas while gently inviting release and relaxation. This practice builds awareness of your stress patterns while providing practical tools for physical stress relief.

Mindful Movement Practices integrate present-moment awareness with gentle physical activity that releases stress while building the mind-body connection that enhances overall stress resilience and emotional regulation.

Walking meditation involves choosing a quiet route and maintaining attention on the physical sensations of walking—the feeling of your feet touching the ground, the movement of your legs, the rhythm of your steps—while allowing thoughts to come and go without getting caught up in mental activity.

Gentle stretching with mindful attention combines the physical benefits of releasing muscle tension with the mental benefits of present-moment awareness, creating integrated stress relief that addresses both physical and psychological aspects of stress response.

Mindful Daily Activities transform routine activities into opportunities for stress relief and present-moment awareness by bringing full attention to simple activities like eating, showering, or commuting rather than multitasking or allowing mental preoccupation with stressors.

Practice mindful eating by paying complete attention to the taste, texture, and aroma of your food while eating slowly enough to notice satisfaction and fullness cues. This practice provides stress relief while often improving digestion and preventing overeating that might result from stress-related mindless consumption.

Loving-Kindness Practice specifically addresses the relational aspects of stress while building emotional resources that support resilience during challenging interpersonal situations or when stress includes feelings of isolation or conflict with others.

Begin by offering genuine wishes for your own well-being: "May I be happy, may I be healthy, may I be at peace, may I live with ease." Gradually extend these same wishes to loved ones, neutral people, difficult people, and eventually all beings, building the emotional resources that support stress resilience.

Physical Exercise and Movement Techniques

Physical activity provides one of the most effective and immediate approaches to stress management by metabolizing stress hormones while releasing endorphins that create natural mood elevation and stress relief that can last for hours after exercise completion.

Cardiovascular Exercise offers powerful stress relief through activities that increase heart rate and breathing while providing outlets for the physical energy that stress response activation creates. Regular cardiovascular exercise also builds long-term stress resilience by improving cardiovascular health and increasing stress hormone metabolism.

Walking, jogging, cycling, swimming, or dancing for 20-30 minutes provides immediate stress relief while building cardiovascular fitness that enhances your capacity to handle future stressors without becoming overwhelmed or compromising your health.

High-intensity interval training (HIIT) can provide significant stress relief in shorter time periods by alternating brief periods of intense activity with recovery periods, creating efficient workouts that fit busy schedules while providing substantial stress management benefits.

Strength Training addresses stress through focused physical effort that requires present-moment attention while building confidence and physical resilience that translates into improved stress management capacity in all areas of life.

Resistance training with weights, resistance bands, or body weight exercises provides outlets for stress-related tension while building physical strength that often correlates with improved emotional resilience and confidence in handling life's challenges.

Yoga and Stretching combine physical movement with breath awareness and present-moment attention, creating integrated stress relief that addresses physical tension while building the mind-body awareness that supports overall stress management skills.

Gentle yoga practices that emphasize breathing and relaxation provide accessible stress relief for individuals with varying fitness levels while building flexibility and strength that support overall physical health and stress resilience.

Martial Arts and Disciplined Movement offer structured approaches to stress management that combine physical activity with mental discipline and philosophical frameworks that support comprehensive stress management and personal development.

Tai chi and qigong provide gentle, meditative movement practices that build balance, flexibility, and inner calm while offering philosophical frameworks for understanding and working with life's challenges and stressors.

Nature-Based Physical Activities combine the stress relief benefits of exercise with the additional benefits of natural environments that have been shown to reduce cortisol levels and improve mood more effectively than indoor exercise alone.

Hiking, outdoor cycling, gardening, or simply walking in natural settings provide enhanced stress relief while connecting you with natural rhythms and environments that support psychological well-being and perspective on life's challenges.

Time Management and Organizational Strategies

Effective time management reduces stress by creating sense of control and accomplishment while preventing the overwhelming results from disorganization, poor planning, or unrealistic expectations about what can be accomplished in available time.

Priority Setting and Goal Clarification help focus energy on activities that matter most while reducing stress that comes from spreading attention across too many competing demands without clear criteria for making choices about time and energy allocation.

Use the Eisenhower Matrix to categorize tasks based on urgency and importance: focus primarily on important but not urgent activities that prevent crisis management while delegating or eliminating activities that are neither urgent nor important.

Planning and Scheduling Systems provide structure that reduces decision fatigue while creating realistic expectations about time requirements for various activities, preventing the stress that comes from underestimating time needs or overcommitting to more than can be accomplished effectively.

Weekly and daily planning sessions help you anticipate challenges and allocate time appropriately while building in buffer time for unexpected demands and adequate time for rest and recovery that maintains stress resilience.

Boundary Setting and Saying No represent crucial stress management skills that protect your time and energy for priorities that align with your values and goals while preventing resentment and overwhelm that result from overcommitment to others' agendas.

Practice declining requests that don't serve your priorities: "I appreciate you thinking of me, but I'm not able to take this on right now" or "That sounds interesting, but it doesn't fit with my current commitments."

Delegation and Support Systems reduce stress by recognizing that you don't need to handle everything personally while building collaborative relationships that provide mutual support and shared responsibility for achieving goals and managing demands.

Identify tasks that others could handle effectively, whether family members, colleagues, or professional services, freeing your time and energy for activities where your unique contributions provide the greatest value.

Technology Management addresses the stress that comes from constant connectivity and information overload by establishing boundaries around technology use while using technological tools to enhance rather than complicate organization and time management.

Set specific times for checking email and social media rather than allowing constant interruptions that fragment attention and increase stress while reducing productivity and present-moment awareness.

Relaxation and Recovery Techniques

Systematic relaxation practices provide essential recovery from stress activation while building the physiological and psychological resources necessary for sustained stress resilience and optimal performance across all areas of life.

Progressive Muscle Relaxation involves systematically tensing and releasing muscle groups throughout your body to identify and release physical tension while building awareness of the difference between tension and relaxation that helps you recognize and address stress earlier.

Start with your toes and work upward through each muscle group: tense each area for 5-10 seconds, then release and notice the contrast between tension and relaxation. This practice provides immediate stress relief while building body awareness that supports ongoing stress management.

Visualization and Guided Imagery use your imagination to create relaxing mental experiences that activate parasympathetic nervous system responses while building mental resources for handling stressful situations with greater calm and confidence.

Create detailed mental images of peaceful, safe places—whether real locations you've enjoyed or imaginary environments that provide comfort and calm. Engage all your senses in these visualizations while allowing your nervous system to respond to these peaceful images with natural relaxation.

Hot Baths and Hydrotherapy provide physical relaxation through warm water that soothes muscles while creating dedicated time for rest and recovery away from daily demands and stimulation that contributes to stress accumulation.

Add Epsom salts or essential oils like lavender to enhance relaxation benefits while creating rituals that signal to your nervous system that it's time to shift from activity and alertness toward rest and recovery.

Massage and Bodywork address the physical components of stress through professional or self-massage techniques that release muscle tension while activating healing and relaxation responses through therapeutic touch.

Self-massage techniques using foam rollers, massage balls, or simply your hands can provide accessible stress relief while professional massage offers deeper therapeutic benefits for comprehensive stress management and recovery.

Sleep Optimization Practices recognize quality sleep as perhaps the most important recovery practice for stress management while addressing the sleep disruptions that stress often creates through consistent sleep hygiene and relaxation routines.

Create consistent bedtime routines that signal your body to prepare for sleep: dim lights, avoid screens, practice relaxation techniques, and maintain consistent sleep and wake times even on weekends to support natural circadian rhythms that enhance stress resilience.

Ensure your sleep environment supports quality rest through comfortable temperature, minimal noise and light, and comfortable bedding that promotes the deep sleep necessary for stress hormone processing and physical recovery.

As we conclude this comprehensive exploration of stress management mastery, we celebrate your commitment to developing these essential life skills that serve not only your immediate well-being but your capacity for sustained excellence and contribution throughout your lifetime.

Remember that stress management represents not a destination you arrive at but a set of skills you continue developing and refining throughout your life, adapting your approaches to different circumstances while building the resilience that serves you during both everyday challenges and major life transitions.

Your willingness to invest in stress management skills creates ripple effects that extend throughout every relationship and community you're part of, as your increased calm and resilience contribute to collective well-being while modeling healthy approaches to life's inevitable challenges for others who may benefit from your example.

The journey of stress mastery continues with each conscious breath during moments of pressure, each choice to prioritize recovery and self-care, and each decision to apply these evidence-based techniques rather than relying on less effective coping strategies that might provide temporary relief while creating long-term problems.

Through your commitment to stress management excellence, you participate in creating a culture that values sustainable approaches to achievement and success while demonstrating that true strength includes the wisdom to care for yourself in ways that maintain your capacity for excellence and service over the long term.

This is your invitation to unprecedented resilience, effectiveness, and life satisfaction—not despite life's inevitable stressors but because of your sophisticated capacity to meet them with skills, wisdom, and grace that transform challenges into opportunities for growth, connection, and meaningful contribution to the world around you.

Prompt: Is anger a default emotion for you? What might lie beneath it?

Chapter 16.5: Mastering Anxiety Management

An extended chapter that extends a compassionate hand to those who know the weight of worry, the racing heart that speaks louder than reason, and the persistent whispers of "what if" that can transform even the simplest moments into landscapes of uncertainty. This is tender territory where understanding meets action, where your relationship with anxiety transforms from one of helpless struggle to one of informed mastery and gentle self-compassion.

It is here you will become the master the understanding of anxiety not as an enemy to be vanquished, but as a complex messenger that, when properly understood and skillfully managed, can become a source of valuable information about your needs, boundaries, and the very care your nervous system requires. As one of the millions that suffers with anxiety we venture forward where, you'll discover how anxiety, though challenging, carries within it the seeds of deeper self-awareness and the potential for cultivating unprecedented inner peace.

The recognition that within the landscape of your own experience lies both the wisdom to understand your anxiety and the inherent capacity to develop the skills that transform overwhelming worry into manageable awareness. You are entering into a space where your struggles are honored, your strength is recognized, and your potential for healing and growth is held as sacred truth.

Understanding Anxiety: The Architecture of Worry

Anxiety represents one of the most universal yet misunderstood aspects of human emotional experience—a sophisticated alarm system that evolved to protect us from genuine threats, yet often becomes overactive in ways that create suffering rather than safety. Understanding anxiety in its full complexity opens pathways to working with rather than against this fundamental aspect of your nervous system's protective intelligence.

The Nature and Purpose of Anxiety

At its essence, anxiety embodies your nervous system's anticipatory response to perceived threats or challenges, designed to prepare you for potential difficulties before they fully materialize. This forward-looking protective mechanism represents millions of years of evolutionary refinement, intended to enhance your survival by mobilizing resources and attention when future dangers seem likely.

Adaptive Anxiety Functions serve essential purposes that can enhance your safety and performance when operating within appropriate parameters. Healthy anxiety sharpens your attention during important events, motivates preparation for significant challenges, alerts you to potential problems that require attention, and provides energy for meeting demanding situations that exceed your normal capacity requirements.

Consider how moderate anxiety before a job interview helps you prepare thoroughly, how concern about a presentation motivates practice and organization, or how worry about a loved one's safety prompts you to check in and offer support. This beneficial anxiety represents your nervous system's sophisticated capacity to help you navigate life's complexities with enhanced awareness and preparation.

Threat Assessment and Survival occurs through anxiety's rapid evaluation of potential dangers, scanning your environment and future scenarios for signs of threat while preparing your body and mind for protective action. This assessment process operates largely below conscious awareness, processing thousands of subtle cues to determine whether situations warrant increased vigilance or preparation.

Future-Focused Protection distinguishes anxiety from fear by its orientation toward potential rather than immediate threats, allowing you to prepare for challenges that haven't yet occurred while building resilience for difficulties that may never actually materialize but could benefit from advance consideration and planning.

Social Connection and Safety can be enhanced through certain types of anxiety that motivate you to maintain important relationships, consider others' needs and responses, and navigate social situations with appropriate care and attention to maintaining harmony and mutual support.

The Spectrum of Anxiety Experience

Understanding anxiety requires recognizing its diverse manifestations and intensities, from the subtle unease that accompanies minor uncertainties to the overwhelming terror that can paralyze decision-making and daily functioning, each requiring different approaches and management strategies.

Normal Anxiety represents appropriate responses to genuinely uncertain or challenging situations—feeling nervous before important events, worrying about loved ones during difficult times, or experiencing concern about significant life transitions. This anxiety typically resolves when situations become clear or challenges are successfully navigated.

Generalized Anxiety involves persistent, excessive worry about multiple areas of life that continues even when specific stressors are absent or resolved. This chronic anxiety often includes physical symptoms like muscle tension, fatigue, and sleep disturbance while creating ongoing emotional distress that interferes with daily functioning and life satisfaction.

Social Anxiety emerges around interpersonal situations, creating intense fear of judgment, embarrassment, or rejection that can severely limit social and professional opportunities. This anxiety might manifest as fear of public speaking, discomfort in group settings, or avoidance of situations where performance or social competence might be evaluated.

Panic and Acute Anxiety represent intense episodes of overwhelming fear accompanied by physical symptoms like rapid heartbeat, shortness of breath, sweating, and feelings of impending doom or death. These experiences can be so intense that they create secondary anxiety about having future panic episodes.

Performance Anxiety specifically relates to situations where your competence or skills will be evaluated, creating fear of failure, mistakes, or inadequate performance that can interfere with your ability to demonstrate your actual capabilities in important situations.

The Physiology of Anxiety Response

Modern science reveals anxiety as a complex orchestration of neurological, hormonal, and physical processes that affect every system in your body, creating both the uncomfortable symptoms of anxiety and the protective responses that anxiety attempts to provide.

The Amygdala and Threat Detection serve as your brain's alarm system, constantly scanning for potential threats while initiating anxiety responses before conscious awareness of danger occurs. The amygdala can trigger anxiety responses to situations that remind it of previous threats, even when current circumstances are actually safe.

Nervous System Activation creates the physical sensations of anxiety through sympathetic nervous system arousal that increases heart rate and blood pressure, accelerates breathing and creates shortness of breath, increases muscle tension and creates physical restlessness, and heightens sensory awareness while creating hypervigilance to potential threats.

Hormonal Cascade includes adrenaline release that creates energy and alertness alongside feelings of agitation, cortisol elevation that provides sustained stress response while potentially creating fatigue and mood changes, and various other hormones that coordinate your body's preparation for dealing with perceived threats.

Cognitive Changes accompany anxiety through increased focus on potential threats while reducing attention to positive or neutral information, accelerated thinking that can feel like racing thoughts or mental loops, and difficulty concentrating on tasks unrelated to anxious concerns while memory may become impaired for positive experiences.

Common Anxiety Triggers and Patterns

Contemporary life presents numerous triggers that can activate anxiety responses, many of which represent modern stressors that our evolutionary anxiety systems weren't designed to handle, requiring conscious awareness and skillful management to prevent chronic activation.

Uncertainty and Unpredictability represent primary anxiety triggers as your brain attempts to prepare for unknown challenges while lacking sufficient information to develop specific plans or responses. This uncertainty might involve career changes, relationship situations, health concerns, or global events that feel beyond your control.

Social Evaluation and Performance situations activate anxiety through fear of judgment, criticism, or rejection while creating pressure to meet others' expectations or demonstrate competence in areas where you may feel insecure or unprepared. These situations might include work presentations, social gatherings, dating, or any context where others might evaluate your performance.

Responsibility and Decision-Making can trigger anxiety when you feel accountable for outcomes that affect others or when choices seem to carry significant consequences for your future well-being. This responsibility anxiety often intensifies around parenting decisions, career choices, financial planning, or relationship commitments.

Change and Transition activate anxiety through disruption of familiar routines and predictable patterns while requiring adaptation to new circumstances that may feel overwhelming or threatening to your sense of security and competence. Major life transitions like moving, job changes, or relationship shifts commonly trigger anxiety responses.

Health and Safety Concerns can create anxiety through worry about physical symptoms, medical procedures, or potential threats to your well-being or that of loved ones. This anxiety might focus on specific health conditions or generalize to broad concerns about safety and mortality.

Anxiety vs. Normal Worry: Important Distinctions

Understanding the difference between normal worry that serves protective functions and anxiety that becomes problematic helps you assess when your anxiety responses deserve attention and professional support versus when they represent appropriate responses to genuinely challenging circumstances.

Duration and Intensity differ significantly between normal worry and problematic anxiety. Normal worry typically resolves when situations become clear or problems are addressed, while chronic anxiety persists even when specific stressors are absent and often seems disproportionate to actual threats or challenges.

Functional Impact helps distinguish whether anxiety enhances or impairs your effectiveness. Healthy worry motivates appropriate preparation and problem-solving while maintaining your ability to function normally, whereas problematic anxiety interferes with sleep, work performance, relationships, and daily activities.

Reality Testing remains intact with normal worry, allowing you to accurately assess threat levels and respond proportionally to actual risks. Anxiety becomes problematic when it creates catastrophic thinking, overestimation of dangers, or inability to recognize when situations are actually safe or manageable.

Physical Symptoms associated with normal worry are typically mild and resolve when stressors are addressed, while chronic anxiety creates persistent physical symptoms like muscle tension, headaches, digestive problems, and sleep disturbances that continue even during relaxed periods.

Control and Management represent key differences between normal and problematic anxiety. Healthy worry responds to problem-solving efforts and rational evaluation, while chronic anxiety often feels uncontrollable and may worsen despite logical attempts to address concerns or evidence that fears are unfounded.

The Impact of Anxiety: Understanding the Ripple Effects

When anxiety becomes a persistent presence in your life, its influence extends far beyond momentary discomfort to create profound effects throughout every dimension of your existence—from your physical health and emotional well-being to your relationships, career performance, and overall life satisfaction. Understanding these impacts helps validate your experience while motivating commitment to effective anxiety management.

Physical Health Consequences

Perhaps the most immediate and measurable impacts of chronic anxiety involve significant effects on physical health that demonstrate how emotional distress translates into tangible wellness challenges that require attention and care to prevent long-term complications.

Cardiovascular System Stress results from anxiety's chronic activation of fight-or-flight responses that increase heart rate and blood pressure while creating irregular heartbeat patterns that can feel frightening and create additional anxiety. Over time, this cardiovascular stress contributes to increased risk of heart disease, hypertension, and other cardiac complications.

The rapid heartbeat and chest tightness that accompany anxiety can create fears of heart problems, leading to emergency room visits and medical tests that often reveal no cardiac abnormalities but significant anxiety-related symptoms that require psychological rather than purely medical intervention.

Respiratory System Impact includes the shallow, rapid breathing that anxiety creates, often leading to feelings of shortness of breath or inability to get enough air that can escalate into panic responses. This breathing pattern can create dizziness, light headedness, and tingling sensations that feel alarming and create additional anxiety about physical symptoms.

Digestive System Disruption occurs as anxiety redirects energy away from digestive processes, creating symptoms like nausea, stomach pain, diarrhea, or constipation that can become chronic when anxiety persists over extended periods. Many individuals with anxiety develop irritable bowel syndrome or other digestive conditions that seem primarily physical but improve significantly with anxiety treatment.

Muscle Tension and Pain develop through chronic muscle contraction that anxiety creates, particularly in the neck, shoulders, back, and jaw, leading to headaches, jaw pain (TMJ), and chronic pain conditions that may require both physical therapy and anxiety management for effective treatment.

Sleep Disruption Patterns emerge as anxiety interferes with your ability to fall asleep due to racing thoughts and worry, stay asleep due to hypervigilance and easy awakening, or achieve restful sleep due to muscle tension and hormonal disruptions that prevent deep sleep cycles necessary for physical and emotional recovery.

Immune System Suppression results from chronic stress hormone elevation that compromises your body's ability to fight infections and illnesses while slowing healing and recovery processes. Individuals with chronic anxiety often experience frequent colds, slow wound healing, and increased susceptibility to various health problems.

Emotional and Mental Health Effects

The emotional toll of persistent anxiety extends throughout every aspect of psychological well-being, creating secondary mental health challenges while compromising your natural capacity for joy, peace, and emotional resilience.

Depression Development commonly accompanies chronic anxiety as the ongoing stress and limitation that anxiety creates gradually depletes your emotional resources while reducing your capacity for pleasure, hope, and positive engagement with life. This anxiety-depression combination requires treatment approaches that address both conditions simultaneously.

Emotional Regulation Difficulties emerge as anxiety consumes emotional energy and attention, making it harder to manage other feelings effectively while creating emotional overwhelm that can lead to irritability, mood swings, and difficulty maintaining emotional balance during daily stresses.

Self-Esteem Impact occurs as anxiety creates self-doubt about your capabilities while generating shame about your anxiety symptoms and limitations. The avoidance that anxiety often creates can lead to missed opportunities and reduced confidence in your ability to handle life's challenges effectively.

Cognitive Function Changes include difficulty concentrating on tasks unrelated to anxious concerns while memory problems develop for positive experiences and future planning becomes impaired by focus on potential negative outcomes rather than realistic goal-setting and problem-solving.

Rumination and Worry Cycles create mental loops where anxious thoughts repetitively cycle without resolution, consuming mental energy while preventing the forward-focused thinking necessary for effective problem-solving and daily functioning.

Identity and Self-Concept Shifts may occur as anxiety becomes such a prominent part of your experience that you begin identifying yourself primarily as an anxious person, potentially limiting your sense of possibilities and personal growth while affecting your willingness to take appropriate risks or pursue meaningful goals.

Relationship and Social Impact

Anxiety's effects on relationships often create some of the most painful consequences as social connections—which should provide comfort and support—become sources of additional stress while anxiety symptoms may be misunderstood by others who haven't experienced similar challenges.

Communication Difficulties arise as anxiety interferes with clear thinking and emotional regulation during conversations while creating tendency to seek excessive reassurance, avoid difficult topics, or become defensive when others express concerns about your anxiety or its effects on relationships.

Social Withdrawal Patterns develop as anxiety makes social situations feel overwhelming or threatening, leading to cancellation of plans, avoidance of group activities, and gradual isolation that deprives you of the social support that could help manage anxiety while creating loneliness that often worsens anxiety symptoms.

Intimate Relationship Challenges emerge as anxiety affects your ability to be emotionally present with partners while creating need for constant reassurance, difficulty with physical intimacy when anxiety creates body awareness and tension, and potential for partners to feel frustrated or helpless about how to provide appropriate support.

Family Dynamic Changes occur as anxiety symptoms affect your availability for family activities, your patience with family members, and your ability to fulfill family responsibilities effectively while family members may struggle to understand anxiety or may inadvertently enable avoidance patterns that maintain anxiety rather than supporting recovery.

Professional Relationship Impact includes difficulty participating in workplace social activities, challenges with assertive communication about needs and boundaries, and potential for anxiety symptoms to be misinterpreted as lack of competence or commitment rather than treatable mental health concerns.

Parenting Challenges can develop as anxiety interferes with present-moment awareness needed for responsive parenting while creating tendency toward overprotectiveness that may limit children's development or modeling of anxiety responses that children may learn and adopt.

Professional and Achievement Impact

The workplace effects of anxiety often create significant limitations on career advancement and professional satisfaction while preventing you from fully utilizing your capabilities and pursuing opportunities that align with your interests and values.

Performance Anxiety can sabotage your ability to demonstrate your actual skills and knowledge during important presentations, meetings, or evaluations while creating physical symptoms that interfere with clear thinking and confident communication during crucial professional moments.

Decision-Making Paralysis emerges as anxiety creates excessive focus on potential negative outcomes while generating difficulty weighing pros and cons objectively, leading to missed opportunities, delayed career moves, and reduced professional growth due to inability to make decisions confidently when risks are involved.

Leadership Challenges develop as anxiety interferes with the calm presence and confident decision-making that leadership requires while creating difficulty with delegation, public speaking, and the risk-taking that innovation and professional advancement typically require.

Networking and Professional Relationships become challenging as social anxiety makes professional gatherings feel overwhelming while limiting your ability to build the collegial relationships that support career advancement and job satisfaction in most professional environments.

Creative and Innovation Blocks occur as anxiety's focus on potential problems interferes with the open, exploratory thinking necessary for creative problem-solving while fear of failure or criticism may prevent you from proposing innovative ideas or solutions.

Career Limitation Patterns may develop as anxiety influences career choices toward safer, less challenging options that don't fully utilize your capabilities while preventing pursuit of opportunities that might provide greater satisfaction and advancement but involve uncertainty or increased responsibility.

Daily Life and Quality of Life Impact

Perhaps most significantly, chronic anxiety affects your overall quality of life and daily experience in ways that accumulate over time to create profound limitations on your ability to enjoy life, pursue interests, and engage fully with the experiences and opportunities that provide meaning and satisfaction.

Decision Fatigue results from the mental energy that anxiety consumes through constant worry and threat assessment, leaving less mental resources available for daily decisions and activities while creating exhaustion that affects your motivation and engagement with normal life activities.

Pleasure and Joy Limitations occur as anxiety's hypervigilance interferes with present-moment awareness needed to appreciate positive experiences while worry about future problems prevents full engagement with current opportunities for satisfaction and connection.

Activity Restriction develops as anxiety creates avoidance of situations, places, or activities that trigger anxious responses, gradually limiting your life experiences while reducing opportunities for growth, learning, and the sense of accomplishment that comes from successfully navigating challenges.

Financial Impact may result from anxiety-related work limitations, medical expenses for anxiety-related health problems, or poor financial decision-making influenced by anxiety about security while inability to take appropriate financial risks may limit long-term financial growth and stability.

Travel and Adventure Limitations emerge as anxiety makes unfamiliar situations feel threatening while creating difficulty with changes in routine, new environments, or activities that involve uncertainty, potentially limiting your experiences and personal growth through exposure to different cultures and challenges.

Spiritual and Existential Impact can occur as chronic anxiety interferes with the peace and openness often necessary for spiritual connection while creating focus on survival concerns that may limit exploration of life's deeper meanings and your connection to purposes larger than immediate anxiety management.

Practical Strategies to Manage Anxiety: Your Comprehensive Toolkit

The mastery of anxiety requires a multifaceted approach that honors both the protective intelligence of your anxiety response and your need for peace, effectiveness, and joy in daily life. These evidence-based strategies provide a comprehensive framework for transforming your relationship with anxiety from one of helpless struggle to one of informed collaboration with your nervous system's protective wisdom.

Grounding and Present-Moment Techniques

Grounding practices provide immediate relief from anxiety by interrupting the future-focused worry that anxiety creates while anchoring your attention in present-moment sensory experience where safety can be assessed accurately and nervous system activation can begin to settle naturally.

5-4-3-2-1 Sensory Grounding offers a simple yet effective technique for immediate anxiety relief that can be used anywhere without drawing attention to yourself. Identify 5 things you can see, 4 things you can touch, 3 things you can hear, 2 things you can smell, and 1 thing you can taste, engaging your senses fully with each item to bring your attention into present-moment awareness.

This technique interrupts anxious thinking by requiring attention to immediate sensory information while providing evidence of your current safety through direct perception rather than worry-based imagination about potential future threats.

Progressive Muscle Relaxation addresses the physical tension that anxiety creates while building awareness of the difference between anxiety-related muscle contraction and genuine relaxation that helps your nervous system recognize safety and begin settling naturally.

Start with your toes and systematically tense each muscle group for 5 seconds, then release while noticing the contrast between tension and relaxation. This practice provides immediate physical relief while building body awareness that helps you recognize and address anxiety symptoms earlier.

Breathing Regulation Techniques directly influence your nervous system through conscious control of breathing patterns that signal safety to your anxiety response while providing immediate relief from the shallow, rapid breathing that often accompanies anxious states.

The 4-7-8 breathing pattern proves particularly effective: breathe in for 4 counts, hold for 7 counts, and exhale for 8 counts. This extended exhale activates your parasympathetic nervous system while the counting provides mental focus that interrupts anxious thinking patterns.

Cold Water and Temperature Changes provide rapid anxiety relief through physiological mechanisms that directly calm your nervous system. Splash cold water on your face, hold ice cubes, or step outside into cool air to activate your vagus nerve and create immediate calming effects.

Movement and Physical Grounding help discharge the physical energy that anxiety creates while reconnecting you with your body's strength and capability rather than focusing only on anxiety symptoms. Simple exercises like walking, stretching, or even fidgeting can provide significant anxiety relief.

Mindful Observation involves choosing an object in your environment and observing it with complete attention—its colors, textures, shapes, and details—while allowing this focused attention to anchor you in present-moment awareness that naturally reduces anxiety's future-focused worry patterns.

Cognitive Reframing and Thought Work

Anxiety often involves specific patterns of thinking that amplify worry while reducing your confidence in your ability to handle challenges effectively. Learning to identify and modify these thought patterns provides lasting anxiety management skills that address anxiety at its cognitive roots.

Identifying Cognitive Distortions helps you recognize common thinking patterns that increase anxiety unnecessarily. Catastrophizing involves imagining worst-case scenarios as if they were likely to occur; all-or-nothing thinking creates black-and-white perspectives that increase pressure; mind reading assumes you know what others are thinking, usually negatively; and fortune-telling predicts negative futures without sufficient evidence.

Reality Testing Questions help evaluate whether anxious thoughts reflect accurate assessments of actual threats or represent anxiety-distorted thinking that needs correction. Ask yourself: "What evidence do I have that this worry is realistic? What would I tell a friend facing this same concern? What are some other possible outcomes besides the one I'm worried about?"

Worst-Case Scenario Planning paradoxically reduces anxiety by thoroughly examining feared outcomes to their logical conclusion, often revealing that even worst-case scenarios are survivable and less catastrophic than anxiety suggests while developing concrete plans for handling difficulties reduces the sense of helplessness that fuels anxiety.

Probability Assessment involves realistically evaluating the likelihood of feared outcomes occurring based on actual evidence rather than anxiety's tendency to overestimate dangers. Most events we worry about never actually happen, and those that do occur are rarely as catastrophic as anxiety predicts.

Self-Compassion Practices address the self-criticism that often accompanies anxiety while providing the emotional support necessary for working with anxiety skillfully rather than adding shame about having anxiety symptoms to your existing distress.

Talk to yourself with the same kindness you would offer a good friend facing similar challenges, recognizing that anxiety is a common human experience rather than a personal failing while offering yourself patience and understanding as you develop anxiety management skills.

Positive Coping Statements provide alternative responses to anxious thoughts that acknowledge your capability and resilience. Examples include: "I have handled difficult situations before and can handle this one too," "This feeling is temporary and will pass," "I can take this one step at a time," and "I am stronger than my anxiety."

Lifestyle Modifications and Environmental Changes

Comprehensive anxiety management often requires adjustments to daily routines, environmental factors, and lifestyle choices that either support nervous system regulation or contribute to chronic anxiety activation that makes management more difficult.

Sleep Optimization represents perhaps the most crucial lifestyle factor for anxiety management, as poor sleep both results from and contributes to increased anxiety while quality sleep provides the nervous system recovery necessary for emotional regulation and stress resilience.

Establish consistent sleep and wake times, create a relaxing bedtime routine that signals your body to prepare for rest, limit screens and stimulating activities before bedtime, and ensure your sleep environment supports quality rest through appropriate temperature, darkness, and comfort.

Caffeine and Stimulant Management becomes important as these substances can mimic and amplify anxiety symptoms while interfering with sleep quality that supports anxiety management. Consider reducing or eliminating caffeine, especially in the afternoon and evening, while being aware that caffeine withdrawal may temporarily increase anxiety before improvement occurs.

Regular Exercise and Movement provide powerful anxiety relief through multiple mechanisms: physical activity metabolizes stress hormones, releases endorphins that improve mood, provides outlets for physical energy that anxiety creates, and builds confidence in your body's strength and capability.

Even gentle activities like walking, swimming, or yoga can provide significant anxiety benefits while vigorous exercise offers more intensive stress hormone metabolism and endorphin release for individuals who enjoy higher-intensity activities.

Nutrition for Anxiety Management involves eating patterns that support stable blood sugar and neurotransmitter production while avoiding foods that may increase anxiety symptoms. Regular meals prevent blood sugar fluctuations that can trigger anxiety, while adequate protein supports neurotransmitter production necessary for mood regulation.

Environmental Modifications include creating physical spaces that feel safe and calming while reducing environmental stressors that may contribute to chronic anxiety activation. This might involve organizing living spaces to reduce visual chaos, incorporating natural elements like plants or natural lighting, and creating designated spaces for relaxation and anxiety management practices.

Technology Boundaries help manage the information overload and constant connectivity that can contribute to modern anxiety through news cycles, social media comparison, and the pressure to remain constantly available to others' communications and demands.

Consider designated phone-free times, especially before bedtime and first thing in the morning, limiting news consumption to specific times rather than continuous updates, and using technology mindfully rather than as distraction from anxious feelings.

Professional Support and Treatment Options

While self-help strategies provide valuable tools for anxiety management, professional support often proves essential for comprehensive anxiety treatment, particularly when anxiety significantly interferes with daily functioning or when self-help approaches alone aren't providing sufficient relief.

Therapy Options include cognitive-behavioral therapy (CBT) that focuses on identifying and changing thought patterns that contribute to anxiety; exposure therapy that helps reduce anxiety through gradual, controlled exposure to feared situations; and acceptance-based approaches that help you develop a different relationship with anxiety rather than trying to eliminate it completely.

Medication Considerations may be helpful for some individuals, particularly when anxiety is severe or when therapy alone isn't providing sufficient relief. Antianxiety medications can provide short-term relief while longer-term medications like antidepressants may help reduce overall anxiety levels, though medication decisions should always involve careful consultation with qualified medical professionals.

Support Groups connect you with others facing similar anxiety challenges while providing community understanding and practical strategies from people with lived experience of anxiety management. Both in-person and online support groups can provide valuable encouragement and reduce the isolation that often accompanies anxiety.

Specialized Treatments might include EMDR for anxiety related to traumatic experiences, neurofeedback for anxiety involving specific brain wave patterns, or intensive outpatient programs for individuals whose anxiety requires more comprehensive treatment approaches than weekly therapy sessions.

Crisis Resources should be identified in advance for times when anxiety becomes overwhelming or when thoughts of self-harm arise. This might include crisis hotlines, emergency mental health services, or specific mental health professionals who can provide urgent support when needed.

As we conclude this compassionate exploration of anxiety management, we honor your courage in seeking understanding and tools for working with one of humanity's most common yet challenging emotional experiences. Your willingness to learn about anxiety represents profound self-care and wisdom that serves not only your own well-being but your capacity to support others who face similar struggles.

Remember that anxiety management is not about achieving a life free from all worry or concern, but about developing the skills and understanding that allow you to work with anxiety as information about your needs while preventing it from limiting your life, relationships, and pursuit of meaningful goals and experiences.

Your journey toward anxiety mastery continues with each conscious breath during anxious moments, each choice to apply these evidence-based techniques rather than avoiding situations that trigger anxiety, and each decision to seek appropriate support when anxiety exceeds your current management skills.

Through your commitment to understanding and managing anxiety skillfully, you participate in reducing the stigma and isolation that surround anxiety while modeling healthy approaches to mental health for others in your family, community, and professional networks who may benefit from your example of courage and self-care.

This is your invitation to unprecedented peace and freedom—not despite your anxiety but because of your willingness to develop the wisdom and skills that transform anxiety from an overwhelming obstacle into manageable information that serves your growth, safety, and authentic engagement with the fullness of human experience.

Prompt: If your anxiety had a voice, what would it say? What would you say back?

Chapter 17: Mastering Depression Management

We open my arms to embrace one of the most misunderstood yet profound challenges of the human experience—the complex landscape of depression, where darkness and light interweave in ways that can transform your deepest struggles into pathways toward unprecedented wisdom, resilience, and authentic connection with life's most meaningful possibilities. It is here, where vulnerability meets strength, where the courage to face depression becomes a testament to your inherent capacity for healing and growth.

This journey signals you forward into understanding depression not as a character flaw or personal failing, but as a complex interplay of biological, psychological, and social factors that millions of men navigate daily while discovering that within depression's challenges lie opportunities for profound self-discovery, deeper empathy, and more authentic ways of engaging with yourself and the world around you.

In a culture that often expects men to "power through" emotional challenges without support or understanding, choosing to learn about depression management emerges not as weakness or admission of defeat, but as one of the most intelligent and powerful steps you can take toward creating a life of genuine fulfillment and emotional freedom.

Understanding Depression: The Nature of the Shadow

Depression represents far more than temporary sadness or life's natural disappointments—it embodies a complex constellation of symptoms that affect every dimension of your experience, from the biological processes that regulate mood and energy to the psychological patterns that shape how you perceive yourself and your place in the world. Understanding depression's nature provides the foundation for developing effective management strategies while reducing the shame and isolation that often compound depression's challenges.

The Multifaceted Nature of Depression

Depression emerges through intricate interactions between genetic predisposition, brain chemistry, life experiences, and environmental factors, creating a condition that affects each individual differently while sharing common patterns that help guide understanding and treatment approaches.

Neurobiological Foundations reveal that depression involves measurable changes in brain structure and function, particularly in areas responsible for mood regulation, stress response, and cognitive processing. These changes affect neurotransmitter systems including serotonin, dopamine, and norepinephrine—the chemical messengers that influence mood, motivation, and overall emotional well-being.

Research demonstrates that depression isn't simply a matter of "thinking negatively" but involves real alterations in brain activity and structure that can be observed through neuroimaging while responding to various treatment interventions that address both biological and psychological components of the condition.

Genetic and Hereditary Influences contribute to depression vulnerability through inherited traits that affect brain chemistry, stress sensitivity, and emotional regulation capacity, though genetic predisposition doesn't guarantee depression development and environmental factors play crucial roles in whether genetic vulnerabilities become activated.

Psychosocial and Environmental Factors including childhood experiences, trauma, chronic stress, relationship difficulties, financial problems, and major life transitions can trigger or contribute to depression development while creating ongoing stressors that complicate recovery and management efforts.

Stress and Inflammation Connections demonstrate how chronic stress creates inflammatory responses throughout the body that affect brain function and contribute to depression symptoms while creating cycles where depression increases stress sensitivity, which further affects mood and overall well-being.

Recognizing Depression's Many Faces

Depression manifests differently across individuals while sharing certain core characteristics that help distinguish clinical depression from normal sadness or temporary life difficulties that don't require professional intervention or comprehensive management approaches.

Emotional Symptoms and Patterns include persistent sadness that doesn't lift with positive events, loss of interest or pleasure in previously enjoyed activities, feelings of emptiness or numbness that replace normal emotional responses, and overwhelming hopelessness about the future that affects motivation and decision-making.

Many men experience depression through irritability and anger rather than sadness, creating confusion about whether emotional difficulties represent depression or other challenges while missing opportunities for appropriate recognition and treatment of underlying depressive conditions.

Cognitive Effects and Mental Fog encompass difficulty concentrating on tasks that previously felt manageable, memory problems that affect work and personal responsibilities, indecisiveness about both minor and major life choices, and negative thought patterns that focus on personal inadequacy, life meaninglessness, or future hopelessness.

Physical Manifestations include persistent fatigue that isn't relieved by rest, changes in sleep patterns involving either insomnia or excessive sleeping, appetite changes leading to significant weight loss or gain, and physical symptoms like headaches or body aches without clear medical causes.

Behavioral Changes and Social Withdrawal involve reducing or avoiding social activities and relationships that previously provided satisfaction, neglecting personal care and responsibilities, losing motivation for work or personal goals, and sometimes engaging in risky behaviors or substance use as attempts to manage emotional pain.

Seasonal and Situational Variations acknowledge that some individuals experience depression primarily during certain seasons—particularly winter months with reduced sunlight—while others develop depression in response to specific life circumstances like job loss, relationship changes, or major life transitions.

The Impact on Relationships and Daily Life

Depression's effects extend beyond individual experience to influence every aspect of daily functioning while affecting relationships, work performance, and overall life satisfaction in ways that can create additional stress and complications during recovery efforts.

Relationship Strain and Communication Difficulties emerge as depression affects your capacity for emotional intimacy, patience with others' needs, and energy for maintaining social connections that require consistent effort and emotional availability.

Partners, family members, and friends may struggle to understand depression's impact while feeling rejected or frustrated by changes in your availability and emotional responsiveness, creating relationship tensions that can worsen depression while reducing available support during recovery.

Work Performance and Professional Impact manifest through reduced productivity, difficulty meeting deadlines, increased sick days, and challenges with concentration and decision-making that affect job satisfaction and career advancement while creating financial stress that compounds depression symptoms.

Self-Care and Health Neglect often develop as depression reduces motivation for maintaining healthy habits including exercise, nutrition, medical care, and personal hygiene while creating cycles where poor self-care worsens depression symptoms and prolongs recovery timelines.

Identity and Self-Worth Challenges involve questioning your value and capabilities while comparing your current functioning to previous abilities and achievements, creating self-criticism and shame that can perpetuate depression cycles and resist recovery efforts.

Breaking Through Stigma and Misconceptions

Understanding depression accurately requires challenging cultural myths and personal beliefs that may prevent recognition, treatment-seeking, or effective management while building more compassionate and realistic perspectives on depression as a treatable medical condition.

Masculine Identity and Depression often conflict in cultures that equate male strength with emotional control while viewing depression as weakness or failure rather than recognizing it as a common health condition that affects successful, capable men across all backgrounds and life circumstances.

These cultural messages may prevent men from recognizing depression symptoms, seeking professional help, or accepting support from others while creating additional shame and isolation that complicate recovery and increase risk for more severe symptoms or dangerous behaviors.

Strength Redefinition involves understanding that seeking help for depression demonstrates wisdom and courage rather than weakness while recognizing that managing depression effectively requires the same dedication and skill development that you might apply to other important life challenges or goals.

Medical Model Understanding helps frame depression as a health condition similar to diabetes or heart disease that benefits from professional treatment while reducing self-blame and shame that can interfere with effective management and recovery efforts.

Strategies for Managing Depression: Your Toolkit for Recovery

Effective depression management requires a comprehensive approach that addresses the biological, psychological, and social factors contributing to your depression while building skills and resources that support both immediate symptom relief and long-term emotional resilience.

Professional Treatment and Therapeutic Approaches

Working with qualified mental health professionals provides essential foundation for depression management while offering expertise, support, and treatment modalities that individual efforts alone cannot provide, especially during severe episodes or when depression significantly impairs daily functioning.

Psychotherapy and Counseling offer evidence-based approaches for understanding and changing the thought patterns, behaviors, and relationship dynamics that contribute to depression while building coping skills and emotional regulation capacity that supports long-term recovery and growth.

Cognitive Behavioral Therapy (CBT) helps identify and modify negative thought patterns that perpetuate depression while developing problem-solving skills and behavioral strategies that increase activity levels and life satisfaction through structured, goal-oriented approaches.

Interpersonal Therapy (IPT) focuses on improving relationship patterns and communication skills that may contribute to depression while building social support networks and addressing grief, role transitions, or interpersonal conflicts that affect mood and well-being.

Medication Considerations and Management involve working with psychiatrists or primary care physicians to evaluate whether antidepressant medications might benefit your particular depression symptoms while understanding potential benefits, side effects, and the time required for medications to become effective.

Medication decisions should consider your symptom severity, previous treatment responses, other health conditions, and personal preferences while maintaining realistic expectations about medication's role as one component of comprehensive depression management rather than a complete solution.

Specialized Treatment Approaches for severe or treatment-resistant depression might include intensive outpatient programs, partial hospitalization, electroconvulsive therapy (ECT), or newer treatments like transcranial magnetic stimulation (TMS) that provide additional options when standard treatments prove insufficient.

Treatment Compliance and Collaboration involve working actively with your treatment team while communicating honestly about symptom changes, treatment concerns, and life circumstances that might affect recovery progress while maintaining consistency with agreed-upon treatment plans.

Lifestyle Modifications and Self-Care Strategies

Daily lifestyle choices significantly affect depression symptoms while providing opportunities for active participation in your recovery through behaviors that support brain health, emotional regulation, and overall well-being.

Exercise and Physical Activity provide powerful antidepressant effects through multiple mechanisms including neurotransmitter regulation, stress hormone reduction, improved sleep quality, and enhanced self-esteem from achievement and physical capability development.

Research demonstrates that regular aerobic exercise can be as effective as antidepressant medication for mild to moderate depression while providing additional benefits for physical health, sleep quality, and overall life satisfaction that medications cannot offer.

Begin with manageable activity levels that match your current energy and fitness while gradually increasing duration and intensity as depression symptoms improve and motivation increases, focusing on activities you enjoy rather than forcing yourself through exercise that feels punitive.

Nutrition and Depression Management involve eating patterns that support stable blood sugar, adequate protein for neurotransmitter production, and nutrients that support brain health while avoiding excessive alcohol, caffeine, or processed foods that can worsen depression symptoms.

Key nutrients for mood support include omega-3 fatty acids from fish and nuts, B vitamins from whole grains and leafy vegetables, vitamin D through sunlight exposure or supplementation, and magnesium from seeds and dark chocolate that support neurotransmitter function.

Sleep Hygiene and Restoration address the bidirectional relationship between depression and sleep disturbances while establishing routines that support quality rest despite depression's tendency to disrupt normal sleep patterns and circadian rhythms.

Sleep strategies include maintaining consistent sleep and wake times, creating relaxing bedtime routines, optimizing bedroom environment for rest, limiting screen exposure before bed, and addressing early morning awakening or excessive sleeping that commonly accompany depression.

Stress Reduction and Relaxation Techniques help manage the chronic stress that can trigger or worsen depression while building skills for emotional regulation and nervous system calming that support overall recovery and resilience development.

Effective techniques include deep breathing exercises, progressive muscle relaxation, meditation, yoga, or other mindfulness practices that can be learned gradually and adapted to your preferences and schedule constraints.

Building Support Systems and Community Connection

Depression often involves social withdrawal and isolation that compound symptoms while reducing access to the human connection and support that facilitate recovery and provide meaning during difficult periods.

Professional Support Network Development extends beyond primary therapists to include psychiatrists, primary care physicians, support group facilitators, and other professionals who understand depression while providing various types of assistance throughout your recovery journey.

Family and Friend Education helps loved ones understand depression's nature and effects while teaching them how to provide appropriate support without enabling or creating additional pressure that might worsen symptoms or interfere with professional treatment efforts.

This education includes explaining that depression isn't a choice or character flaw while providing guidance about helpful responses, appropriate boundaries, and when to encourage professional help or crisis intervention if symptoms worsen significantly.

Peer Support and Group Participation connect you with others who understand depression through personal experience while reducing isolation and providing hope through witnessing others' recovery stories and practical strategies that have proven effective.

Support groups exist for depression generally and for specific populations like men's depression groups, professional groups, or groups focused on particular life circumstances that may contribute to depression symptoms and recovery challenges.

Community Engagement and Purpose provide opportunities to contribute beyond your personal challenges while building social connections and sense of meaning that can counteract depression's tendency to create self-focus and hopelessness about your value and impact.

Volunteer work, community organizations, religious or spiritual communities, or professional associations offer structured ways to connect with others while contributing to purposes that provide perspective and satisfaction during recovery.

Crisis Management and Safety Planning

Understanding how to recognize and respond to severe depression symptoms ensures your safety while providing clear action plans for times when depression feels overwhelming or when thoughts of self-harm occur.

Warning Sign Recognition helps you identify escalating depression symptoms that may require immediate professional attention while building awareness of personal patterns that indicate when additional support or intervention becomes necessary.

Warning signs might include thoughts of death or suicide, inability to care for basic needs, psychotic symptoms like hallucinations or delusions, or complete inability to function in work or relationship contexts that requires crisis intervention.

Safety Planning and Crisis Resources involve developing written plans that include contact information for emergency services, trusted friends or family members, mental health professionals, and crisis hotlines while identifying strategies for managing intense suicidal thoughts or self-harm impulses.

Safety plans should be developed with professional guidance while being shared with trusted individuals who can provide support and accountability during crisis situations when your judgment might be impaired by severe symptoms.

Emergency Response and Hospitalization understanding helps you recognize when inpatient treatment might be necessary while reducing fear and stigma around psychiatric hospitalization that can provide life-saving intervention during severe episodes.

Hospitalization criteria typically include imminent danger to yourself or others, inability to care for basic needs, or psychotic symptoms that require intensive medical and psychiatric management that outpatient treatment cannot provide safely.

Long-term Resilience and Growth: Building Your Emotional Foundation

Mastering depression management extends beyond symptom relief to encompass building lasting resilience that prevents future episodes while creating life patterns that support ongoing emotional health and personal growth throughout changing life circumstances.

Developing Personal Resilience Factors

Resilience represents your capacity to navigate life's challenges while maintaining emotional equilibrium and recovering from setbacks more quickly and completely, involving both internal resources and external support systems that can be developed through conscious practice.

Emotional Intelligence and Self-Awareness build your capacity to recognize emotional changes before they become overwhelming while developing skills for understanding your emotional patterns, triggers, and the early warning signs that suggest depression symptoms may be increasing.

This awareness includes understanding how stress, relationship conflicts, work pressures, seasonal changes, or other life factors affect your mood while developing proactive strategies for managing these influences before they contribute to depression episodes.

Cognitive Flexibility and Perspective-Taking help counter depression's tendency toward rigid, negative thinking patterns while building capacity to generate alternative explanations for difficult events and maintain hope during challenging periods that might otherwise trigger depression symptoms.

These skills include challenging catastrophic thinking, identifying personal strengths and past successes, maintaining realistic optimism about future possibilities, and seeking multiple perspectives when facing difficult decisions or life circumstances.

Stress Management and Coping Skills provide practical tools for handling life's inevitable stressors without allowing them to accumulate into depression-triggering levels while building confidence in your ability to navigate challenges effectively.

Effective coping strategies include problem-solving skills for addressing practical difficulties, emotion regulation techniques for managing intense feelings, social skills for maintaining relationships during stress, and self-care practices that maintain your physical and emotional resources.

Identity and Purpose Development create stable foundations for self-worth that don't depend entirely on external achievements or others' approval while building sense of meaning and direction that can sustain motivation during difficult periods when depression affects goal pursuit.

Purpose development might involve exploring your values and how they guide life decisions, identifying ways to contribute to others or causes you care about, developing skills and expertise that provide satisfaction and identity, or building relationships that provide mutual support and meaning.

Creating Sustainable Life Patterns

Long-term depression management requires lifestyle patterns that support ongoing emotional health while being sustainable through various life circumstances and changes that might otherwise destabilize your recovery and increase depression vulnerability.

Routine and Structure Balance provide stability that supports emotional regulation while maintaining enough flexibility to accommodate life's changes without creating rigid patterns that become sources of additional stress when circumstances require adaptation.

Beneficial routines might include regular sleep and wake times, consistent meal schedules, daily exercise or movement, time for relaxation and stress management, and regular social connection that provides stability without becoming overwhelming obligations.

Work and Career Alignment involve finding professional activities that align with your values and provide appropriate challenge and satisfaction while maintaining boundaries that prevent work stress from overwhelming your emotional resources and triggering depression symptoms.

This alignment might require career changes, boundary setting with current employment, skill development that increases job satisfaction, or creating better integration between work responsibilities and personal well-being that supports rather than compromises your mental health.

Relationship Investment and Maintenance build social connections that provide ongoing support and meaning while contributing to others' well-being in ways that create mutual benefit and satisfaction rather than one-sided relationships that drain your emotional resources.

Healthy relationships involve reciprocal support where you both give and receive assistance, honest communication about needs and boundaries, shared activities that provide enjoyment and connection, and mutual respect for individual growth and changing needs over time.

Personal Growth and Learning maintain engagement with life through ongoing development of skills, interests, and understanding that provide stimulation and achievement while preventing stagnation that can contribute to depression symptoms and reduce life satisfaction.

Growth activities might include formal education, hobby development, creative pursuits, spiritual exploration, travel, or other experiences that expand your perspective and capabilities while providing goals and achievements that enhance self-esteem and life satisfaction.

Recognizing and Preventing Relapse

Understanding depression's tendency toward recurrence empowers you to recognize early warning signs while implementing preventive strategies that can interrupt developing episodes before they become severe or significantly impair your functioning.

Early Warning System Development involves identifying the subtle changes in mood, energy, sleep, appetite, or thinking patterns that typically precede full depression episodes in your particular case while creating action plans for responding quickly when these signs appear.

Warning signs might include increased irritability, social withdrawal, sleep disturbances, reduced interest in usually enjoyable activities, increased pessimism, or changes in appetite and energy that occur days or weeks before more obvious depression symptoms develop.

Preventive Intervention Strategies provide specific actions to take when early warning signs appear while having plans that can be implemented quickly before depression symptoms worsen to levels that require more intensive intervention or significantly disrupt your life functioning.

Preventive strategies might include increasing therapy frequency, medication adjustments, enhanced self-care routines, stress reduction, increased social support, or lifestyle modifications that address factors contributing to symptom recurrence.

Support System Activation involves informing trusted individuals about your warning signs while creating agreements about how they can provide assistance when you might not recognize developing symptoms or feel motivated to implement preventive strategies independently.

Professional Maintenance and Check-ins ensure ongoing access to mental health support even during stable periods while providing regular monitoring that can detect subtle changes and prevent minor setbacks from developing into major depression episodes.

Maintenance might include periodic therapy sessions, medication monitoring, annual mental health checkups, or participation in ongoing support groups that provide continuous connection and accountability for maintaining emotional health practices.

Building a Legacy of Healing

As your depression management skills mature, opportunities emerge to transform your experience into resources for helping others while contributing to broader understanding and support for men facing similar challenges.

Sharing Your Story and Experience can inspire others who may be struggling while reducing stigma and isolation that prevent many men from seeking help, creating positive impact that transforms personal struggle into community service and contribution.

This sharing might occur through formal peer support roles, informal mentoring relationships, writing or speaking about your experience, or simply being open about your journey in ways that give others permission to seek help and hope for recovery.

Community and Advocacy Involvement provide opportunities to contribute to mental health awareness and resources while working to create better support systems for others facing depression and related mental health challenges that affect men disproportionately.

Professional Development and Expertise might emerge through training in peer support, mental health education, or other roles that utilize your experience while building careers that align with your values and provide meaningful contribution to others' healing and growth.

Mentorship and Guidance for men beginning their depression management journey allows you to share practical strategies while providing hope and encouragement that recovery is possible even during the darkest periods when healing seems impossible.

As we conclude this comprehensive exploration of depression management as both personal healing and community service, we celebrate your courage to face one of life's most challenging experiences with wisdom, determination, and commitment to growth that serves both your own well-being and the healing of others who walk similar paths.

Remember that mastering depression management is not about achieving perfect emotional control but about developing skills, resources, and perspectives that enable you to navigate depression's challenges with greater ease while maintaining connection to life's meaning and possibilities even during difficult periods.

Your willingness to understand and actively manage depression creates ripple effects that extend throughout your community while contributing to cultural change that recognizes depression as a treatable condition requiring support rather than shame, professional help rather than self-criticism, and time for healing rather than pressure for quick fixes.

The journey of depression mastery continues throughout your lifetime as you refine your understanding, adapt your strategies to changing circumstances, and discover how your experience can serve purposes larger than personal recovery while building lives of unprecedented meaning, connection, and contribution.

Through your commitment to depression management excellence, you participate in healing not only your own life but contribute to collective wisdom about resilience, hope, and the remarkable human capacity for transformation that can emerge from life's most difficult challenges when approached with courage, support, and unwavering belief in the possibility of healing and growth.

This is your invitation to unprecedented emotional freedom, authentic connection, and meaningful contribution—not through avoiding depression's challenges but through mastering the skills that transform struggle into strength while building lives that honor both your own healing and your capacity to light the way for others traveling similar paths toward hope, recovery, and renewed joy in living.

Prompt: Do you give yourself permission to seek help when needed? Why or why not?

Chapter 18: The Healing Power of Nature

Congratulations on making it this far into your journey. This chapter holds one of humanity's most ancient and profound sources of healing—the sacred embrace of the natural world that surrounds us. When science meets soul, when the wisdom of millennia converges with modern understanding it reveals nature not merely as a backdrop to human experience, but as an active participant in your journey toward emotional wholeness and authentic well-being.

Rediscover what your ancestors knew instinctively—that within the rustling of leaves, the rhythm of ocean waves, and the silent strength of mountains lies medicine for the modern malaise that disconnects us from our deepest sources of peace and vitality. You'll uncover how your relationship with the natural world becomes not just a pleasant addition to your healing journey, but an essential component of emotional intelligence and resilience.

These concepts represent an act of profound wisdom—the recognition that in our increasingly digital and urbanized world, the call to reconnect with nature emerges not as nostalgic romanticism, but as essential medicine for the soul-deep hunger that modern living often creates. You are stepping into a chapter that honors both the complexity of contemporary life and the simple yet revolutionary healing that awaits in your conscious relationship with the living world around you.

Why Nature Heals: The Science of Natural Medicine

The healing power of nature extends far beyond poetic metaphor to encompass measurable, scientifically documented benefits that affect every system in your body and mind. This natural medicine operates through sophisticated mechanisms that our ancestors understood intuitively, and modern research continues to validate with increasing precision and wonder.

The Neuroscience of Natural Connection

Modern brain imaging reveals that exposure to natural environments creates specific neurological changes that enhance emotional regulation, reduce stress responses, and promote the kind of mental clarity that supports both healing and optimal performance in all areas of life.

Prefrontal Cortex Restoration occurs through what researchers call "attention restoration theory," where natural environments provide the kind of gentle, effortless attention that allows your brain's executive function centers to recover from the directed attention fatigue that characterizes modern life. Unlike urban environments that demand constant vigilance and decision-making, nature offers what scientists term "soft fascination"—engaging enough to hold your attention while allowing mental restoration to occur naturally.

Studies using brain imaging show increased activity in areas associated with empathy, emotional stability, and positive mood after time spent in natural settings, while simultaneously showing decreased activation in the subgenual prefrontal cortex—the brain region associated with rumination and depression.

Stress Response Regulation improves dramatically through nature exposure as your nervous system responds to natural environments with reduced cortisol production, lower blood pressure, and decreased activation of fight-or-flight responses. The Japanese practice of "forest bathing" (shinrin-yoku) has been extensively studied, showing that even brief periods in forested environments reduce stress hormones while boosting immune function and overall well-being.

Default Mode Network Balancing occurs as nature exposure helps regulate the brain's default mode network—the system active during rest and introspection that, when overactive, contributes to anxiety, depression, and rumination. Natural environments promote healthy default mode network function that supports self-reflection without becoming trapped in negative thought cycles.

Mirror Neuron Activation happens when you observe natural processes like flowing water, swaying trees, or animal movements, creating unconscious learning about rhythm, flow, and natural resilience that your nervous system incorporates as resources for emotional regulation and stress management.

Physiological Healing Mechanisms

The physical health benefits of nature exposure demonstrate how environmental medicine operates at cellular levels to promote healing, resilience, and optimal functioning throughout your body's interconnected systems.

Immune System Enhancement occurs through exposure to phytoncides—antimicrobial compounds released by trees and plants that boost natural killer (NK) cell activity when inhaled. These immune cells play crucial roles in fighting infections and even cancerous cells, with studies showing that forest exposure can increase NK cell activity by up to 50% while effects persist for weeks after nature experiences.

Cardiovascular Benefits include measurable reductions in blood pressure, heart rate, and arterial stiffness after time spent in natural environments. These effects occur rapidly—often within minutes of nature exposure—and contribute to long-term cardiovascular health when nature contact becomes regular practice.

Inflammatory Response Modulation demonstrates how nature exposure reduces chronic inflammation that contributes to numerous health conditions including depression, anxiety, cardiovascular disease, and autoimmune disorders. Natural environments appear to activate parasympathetic nervous system responses that promote healing and recovery while reducing inflammatory markers.

Sleep Quality Improvement results from nature's influence on circadian rhythms through natural light exposure, reduced artificial stimulation, and the nervous system regulation that nature provides. Even brief morning nature exposure helps regulate melatonin production for better sleep quality while reducing the sleep disturbances that often accompany stress and anxiety.

Pain Management Benefits emerge through natural environments' ability to reduce perception of pain while increasing pain tolerance. Hospital patients with window views of nature require less pain medication and recover more quickly than those without natural views, demonstrating nature's role in physical healing and recovery processes.

Psychological and Emotional Restoration

Beyond physical benefits, nature provides sophisticated emotional and psychological healing through mechanisms that address the root causes of modern mental health challenges while building resilience and emotional intelligence.

Rumination Interruption occurs as natural environments break the repetitive thought patterns that characterize anxiety and depression. The gentle demands of navigating natural spaces, observing wildlife, or simply taking in natural beauty interrupt the mental loops that often maintain emotional distress while providing healthier focus for attention and mental energy.

Self-Esteem and Confidence Building develop through nature experiences that demonstrate your capability to navigate challenges, appreciate beauty, and connect with something larger than immediate personal concerns. Regular nature exposure correlates with improved self-regard and reduced symptoms of depression and anxiety across diverse populations.

Emotional Regulation Enhancement emerges as natural environments provide safe spaces for processing difficult emotions while offering perspective that helps put personal challenges into larger context. The vastness of natural landscapes often creates beneficial sense of awe that reduces ego-centered concerns while connecting you with sources of strength and resilience.

Attention and Focus Improvement result from nature's restoration of directed attention capacity that modern life consistently depletes. Children with ADHD show improved attention spans after nature exposure, while adults demonstrate enhanced concentration and cognitive performance following time in natural settings.

Creativity and Problem-Solving Enhancement occur through nature's stimulation of divergent thinking and innovative approaches to challenges. The relaxation and mental space that nature provides often allow creative solutions to emerge naturally while reducing the mental pressure that blocks innovative thinking.

Spiritual and Existential Benefits

Nature connection addresses fundamental human needs for meaning, transcendence, and connection to something larger than individual existence, providing resources for spiritual growth and existential well-being that complement psychological and physical healing.

Awe and Wonder Cultivation through exposure to natural beauty and complexity creates what researchers call "awe experiences" that correlate with increased life satisfaction, reduced materialism, greater generosity, and enhanced sense of meaning and purpose in life.

Present-Moment Awareness Development occurs naturally in natural settings where the immediacy of sensory experience—bird songs, wind, sunlight, natural scents—anchors attention in present-moment awareness that interrupts worry about future or rumination about past experiences.

Connection and Belonging emerge through recognition of your place within larger ecological systems, reducing the isolation and alienation that characterize much modern emotional distress while fostering sense of interdependence and belonging that supports mental health and resilience.

Perspective and Wisdom develop through exposure to natural cycles, seasonal changes, and the timeless rhythms of natural systems that provide context for personal challenges while demonstrating the resilience, adaptation, and renewal that characterize all living systems.

Reconnecting with the Natural World: Healing Modern Disconnection

Contemporary life has created unprecedented separation from natural environments and rhythms, contributing to what researchers term "nature deficit disorder"—a constellation of physical, emotional, and spiritual symptoms that arise from insufficient contact with the natural world that shaped human evolution over millions of years.

Understanding Modern Nature Disconnection

The scope of modern nature disconnection extends beyond simply living in urban environments to encompass fundamental changes in how we structure time, attention, and daily life that systematically reduce contact with natural systems and rhythms that support human well-being.

Indoor Living Patterns characterize contemporary life, with most people spending over 90% of their time indoors, breathing recycled air, under artificial lighting, surrounded by manufactured materials that provide none of the subtle sensory richness that natural environments offer. This indoor focus affects circadian rhythms, vitamin D production, air quality exposure, and the countless subtle ways that natural environments support physical and emotional health.

Even when outdoors, modern life often involves paved surfaces, manicured landscapes, and structured activities that provide limited contact with wild or semi-wild natural systems that offer the greatest healing benefits through their complexity, unpredictability, and seasonal variations.

Artificial Light and Screen Dominance disrupts natural light exposure patterns that regulate mood, sleep, and countless physiological processes. The blue light from screens interferes with melatonin production while the constant visual stimulation prevents the kind of visual rest that natural environments provide through their patterns, colors, and gentle movements.

Scheduled and Hurried Living leaves little time for the slow, meandering relationship with nature that provides maximum benefit. Brief, goal-oriented outdoor activities often provide some benefit but lack the restorative qualities that emerge through unhurried presence in natural settings where deeper relaxation and connection can occur.

Digital Distraction Patterns mean that even when in natural settings, electronic devices often interrupt the attention and presence necessary for receiving nature's healing benefits. The constant availability of digital stimulation prevents the mental quiet and receptivity that allows natural environments to work their subtle magic on stressed nervous systems.

The Costs of Nature Disconnection

Research consistently demonstrates that nature disconnection contributes to numerous physical and mental health challenges while reducing resilience and life satisfaction in ways that affect every aspect of well-being and human flourishing.

Mental Health Impacts include increased rates of anxiety, depression, and attention difficulties in populations with limited nature access. Urban children show higher rates of behavioral problems and academic difficulties compared to children with regular nature exposure, while adults in urban environments report higher stress levels and reduced life satisfaction.

Physical Health Consequences encompass vitamin D deficiency from insufficient sunlight, compromised immune function from reduced phytoncide exposure, increased myopia in children from limited distance vision opportunities, and various stress-related health problems that nature exposure helps prevent and ameliorate.

Attention and Cognitive Effects include what researchers call "directed attention fatigue" from constant exposure to environments that demand vigilant attention without providing the restoration that natural environments offer. This fatigue contributes to reduced productivity, increased errors, and the mental exhaustion that characterizes much modern life.

Social and Community Impact emerges as nature disconnection reduces opportunities for shared outdoor experiences that build community bonds while increasing isolation and the social fragmentation that affects mental health and social support systems.

Spiritual and Existential Consequences include what many describe as spiritual emptiness or existential void that emerges from disconnection from natural systems that traditionally provided context for human meaning-making and spiritual connection.

The Evolutionary Mismatch

Understanding why nature connection feels so essential requires recognizing that human beings evolved in natural environments over millions of years, developing neurological, physiological, and psychological systems that depend on natural stimuli for optimal functioning.

Biophilia Theory suggests that humans possess innate tendency to seek connection with nature and other living systems, with this tendency representing evolutionary adaptation that supported survival and well-being in natural environments. This innate affinity explains why natural settings feel restorative even to people with limited nature experience.

Sensory System Evolution occurred in natural environments characterized by complex visual patterns, natural sounds, varied textures, seasonal scents, and three-dimensional spaces that modern built environments rarely replicate. Sensory deprivation from these natural stimuli contributes to the restlessness and seeking that many people experience in entirely artificial environments.

Circadian Rhythm Adaptation developed through exposure to natural light cycles, seasonal variations, and the subtle cues that natural environments provide for regulating sleep, mood, hormone production, and countless physiological processes. Artificial lighting and indoor living disrupt these ancient regulatory systems.

Stress Response Calibration evolved in natural environments where threats were typically immediate and physical, requiring brief activation of stress responses followed by recovery in safe natural settings. Modern chronic stressors combined with lack of natural restoration create the sustained stress activation that contributes to numerous health problems.

Cultural and Societal Factors

The disconnection from nature reflects broader cultural shifts that have systematically devalued natural connection while prioritizing technological advancement and economic productivity over human well-being and environmental health.

Urbanization and Development Patterns have created environments designed primarily for efficiency and commerce rather than human well-being, with limited green space, nature access, or integration of natural elements into built environments where most people spend their daily lives.

Educational System Changes have reduced outdoor education, nature study, and unstructured outdoor play in favor of indoor, screen-based learning that may provide academic skills while neglecting the nature connection that supports emotional regulation, creativity, and overall development.

Work Culture Shifts toward indoor, sedentary occupations provide fewer opportunities for natural light exposure, fresh air, and the movement and visual variety that outdoor work traditionally provided, while longer work hours leave less time for nature connection and outdoor activities.

Technology and Entertainment Changes offer indoor alternatives to outdoor activities that previous generations used for recreation, socialization, and stress relief, while creating entertainment options that compete with nature experiences for time and attention.

Economic Pressures often make nature access seem like luxury rather than necessity, while financial stress may reduce motivation and time availability for nature activities that require transportation, equipment, or time away from income-generating activities.

Recognizing Your Nature Hunger

Developing awareness of your own nature disconnection symptoms helps motivate and guide efforts to restore healing connection with natural environments while recognizing that nature hunger may manifest in subtle ways that aren't immediately obvious.

Physical Restlessness and Fatigue that isn't relieved by rest or entertainment may indicate need for natural stimulation and the kind of gentle physical activity that outdoor environments naturally encourage through walking, exploring, and moving through three-dimensional natural spaces.

Attention and Focus Difficulties particularly when combined with screen fatigue or mental overwhelm, often improve significantly with nature exposure that provides the attention restoration that indoor environments cannot offer regardless of how restful they might seem.

Mood and Emotional Symptoms including unexplained sadness, irritability, or sense of emptiness may reflect nature deficit, particularly when combined with excessive indoor time or limited exposure to natural light, fresh air, and the sensory richness of outdoor environments.

Sleep and Circadian Disruptions often improve with increased natural light exposure and time spent in natural settings that help regulate internal clocks while reducing artificial stimulation that interferes with natural sleep-wake cycles.

Spiritual Seeking or Existential Restlessness may reflect deep need for connection with natural systems that provide context for human existence while offering resources for meaning-making and spiritual connection that purely human-created environments rarely provide.

Practical Ways to Integrate Nature into Daily Life

Healing your relationship with nature doesn't require dramatic lifestyle changes or relocation to rural settings, but rather the cultivation of conscious practices that weave natural connection throughout your existing routine in ways that provide cumulative healing benefits over time.

Simple Daily Nature Practices

These accessible practices can be integrated into most lifestyles and living situations, providing regular doses of natural medicine that support emotional regulation, stress management, and overall well-being without requiring significant time investment or special equipment.

Morning Nature Greeting involves stepping outside first thing in the morning, even briefly, to breathe fresh air, feel natural light on your skin, and consciously acknowledge the natural world around you. This practice helps regulate circadian rhythms while setting a tone of connection and presence for your entire day.

Even urban environments offer some natural elements—sky, clouds, trees, birds, or simply fresh air—that provide benefits when received with conscious attention rather than being ignored in the rush toward indoor activities and artificial stimulation.

Window Gardening and Indoor Plants bring living natural systems into your immediate environment while providing opportunities for daily care and observation of natural growth processes. Research shows that even viewing plants and natural elements indoors reduces stress while improving air quality and providing subtle but measurable psychological benefits.

Choose plants appropriate for your lighting conditions and care capacity, focusing on the satisfaction of nurturing living systems rather than perfection in gardening skills. The process of caring for plants provides many of the benefits of gardening while being accessible regardless of outdoor space limitations.

Walking and Movement Practices in natural settings, even urban parks or tree-lined streets, provide significantly greater healing benefits than indoor exercise while combining physical activity with nature exposure for synergistic effects on mood, energy, and stress relief.

Practice mindful walking by paying attention to natural elements around you—feeling ground beneath your feet, noticing trees and plants, observing sky and weather, listening to natural sounds—rather than using outdoor time primarily for exercise goals or mental planning and problem-solving.

Nature Sounds, and Natural Elements can be incorporated into indoor environments through recorded nature sounds, natural materials like wood and stone, water features, or simply opening windows to allow fresh air and outdoor sounds to enter your living and working spaces.

Sunset and Sunrise Awareness involves periodically taking time to witness these daily natural transitions, either through direct observation or simply conscious acknowledgment of natural light changes. These practices connect you with natural rhythms while providing opportunities for reflection, gratitude, and present-moment awareness.

Seasonal Connection and Awareness

Developing conscious relationship with seasonal cycles provides deeper nature connection while supporting emotional resilience through understanding and working with natural rhythms rather than fighting against them or remaining oblivious to their influence.

Seasonal Activity Adaptation involves choosing activities that align with seasonal energy and opportunities—energetic spring cleaning and new projects, summer outdoor adventures and social activities, autumn reflection and preparation practices, winter rest and indoor contemplation—rather than maintaining identical routines year-round.

Seasonal Eating and Natural Foods connect you with natural cycles while providing optimal nutrition that supports seasonal energy needs. This might involve eating lighter, fresh foods during summer months while choosing warming, grounding foods during winter, along with attention to locally grown and seasonal produce when possible.

Weather Appreciation and Outdoor Time in various conditions develops resilience while deepening nature connection through experiencing natural diversity rather than hiding indoors during any weather that isn't perfect. Appropriate clothing and preparation allow safe enjoyment of rain, snow, wind, and seasonal variations that provide different benefits and experiences.

Natural Light Optimization throughout seasonal changes supports circadian rhythm regulation while providing mood and energy benefits that artificial light cannot replicate. This includes maximizing natural light exposure during darker months while managing light sensitivity during brighter seasons.

Seasonal Reflection and Planning using natural transitions as prompts for personal reflection, goal-setting, and life planning creates alignment between personal growth and natural rhythms while providing regular opportunities for assessing and adjusting life direction in harmony with natural cycles.

Deeper Nature Immersion Practices

These more intensive practices provide profound healing benefits while building lasting relationship with natural environments that supports ongoing emotional health and resilience through life's inevitable challenges and transitions.

Forest Bathing and Wilderness Time involves spending extended periods in natural settings with minimal agenda other than presence and receptivity to natural environments. This practice, validated by extensive research, provides immune system benefits, stress reduction, and emotional restoration that brief nature contacts cannot match.

Begin with whatever wilderness access you have—local parks, nature preserves, or undeveloped areas—focusing on unhurried presence rather than hiking goals or outdoor recreation activities. The healing comes through being rather than doing in natural settings.

Gardening and Growing Practices provide intimate connection with natural cycles while offering the satisfaction of participating in food production or beauty creation through cooperation with natural systems. Even container gardening or herb growing provides benefits while larger garden spaces offer more comprehensive nature connection.

Outdoor Meditation and Contemplation combines mindfulness practices with natural settings for enhanced benefits from both approaches. Natural environments provide gentle sensory anchors for attention while supporting the relaxation and inner awareness that meditation cultivates.

Nature Photography and Art encourage detailed observation of natural beauty while providing creative outlets that deepen appreciation and awareness of natural environments. These practices slow down outdoor time while training attention to notice details and patterns that casual observation might miss.

Camping and Overnight Nature Experiences provide immersion in natural rhythms through sleeping outdoors, cooking with fire, and extended exposure to natural light cycles and outdoor sounds. These experiences often provide breakthrough insights and emotional shifts that day trips cannot achieve.

Wildlife Observation and Interaction develops empathy and connection through watching and learning about other living beings while providing opportunities for patience, stillness, and appreciation of natural intelligence and beauty that exists independently of human concerns and activities.

Overcoming Barriers to Nature Connection

Common obstacles to nature connection can be addressed through creative solutions and realistic approaches that honor both practical limitations and the genuine importance of natural healing for emotional health and well-being.

Time Constraints can be addressed through integration of brief nature contacts into existing routines—eating lunch outdoors, walking meetings in parks, outdoor phone calls when possible, gardening during brief breaks, or simply stepping outside between activities for fresh air and sky connection.

Urban Living Limitations require creativity in finding and maximizing available natural elements—rooftop gardens, balcony plants, park visits, waterfront areas, or even single trees and small green spaces that provide some nature connection benefits despite limited wilderness access.

Weather and Seasonal Challenges can be overcome through appropriate clothing, covered outdoor spaces, seasonal activity adjustments, and developing appreciation for weather diversity rather than viewing non-ideal weather as barriers to outdoor time and nature connection.

Physical Limitations don't prevent nature benefits, as even viewing nature through windows, sitting in gardens or parks, or gentle outdoor activities provide measurable healing benefits while adaptive equipment and assistance can enable outdoor access for most physical conditions.

Safety Concerns require realistic assessment and appropriate precautions rather than complete avoidance of outdoor activities. Many nature connection practices can be enjoyed in safe, populated areas while gradually building confidence and skills for more adventurous outdoor experiences if desired.

Cost and Equipment Concerns rarely present actual barriers to basic nature connection, as most healing practices require minimal equipment while many communities provide free access to parks, trails, and natural areas that offer substantial benefits without financial investment.

As we conclude this exploration of nature's profound healing wisdom, we celebrate your openness to rediscovering what your deepest self already knows—that within the embrace of the living world lies medicine for the modern soul and balm for the wounds that contemporary life can create.

Remember that nature connection is not about becoming an outdoors expert or dramatically changing your lifestyle, but about opening your heart and attention to the natural world that surrounds you even in urban environments, offering its gifts of peace, perspective, and renewal to all who approach with receptivity and respect.

Your willingness to explore nature as healing medicine contributes to a cultural shift toward recognizing environmental health as inseparable from human health while modeling for others the wisdom of seeking balance between technological advancement and the ancient rhythms that still pulse through your cells and consciousness.

The journey of natural healing continues with each conscious breath of fresh air, each moment of appreciating natural beauty, and each choice to step outside when indoor spaces feel confining or overwhelming. These simple acts accumulate into profound transformation that affects not only your own well-being but your capacity to contribute to the healing of the larger web of life of which you are an essential part.

Through your commitment to nature connection, you participate in remembering and preserving ancient wisdom while discovering contemporary applications that serve both personal healing and the collective awakening to humanity's place within the magnificent, resilient, and endlessly generous natural world that continues offering its gifts despite all we have forgotten about receiving them.

This is your invitation to unprecedented peace, vitality, and belonging—not through complex techniques or expensive treatments, but through the simple revolutionary act of stepping outside, breathing deeply, and remembering that you are not separate from the natural world but an expression of its creativity, resilience, and endless capacity for renewal and growth.

Prompt: What does emotional freedom look and feel like to you?

Chapter 19: Cultivating Mindfulness

You are invited to one of humanity's most profound and accessible pathways to inner peace—the sacred art of mindfulness that invites you to discover the extraordinary richness hidden within each ordinary moment. Here, we venture into the uncharted territory where ancient wisdom meets modern neuroscience, where your breath becomes a bridge to presence, and where the simple act of paying attention transforms into the most powerful tool for emotional healing and authentic living.

We turn our attention to the understanding of mindfulness not as another item on your self-improvement checklist, but as a way of being that permeates every aspect of your existence with awareness, compassion, and profound acceptance. It is here, you'll discover how the cultivation of present-moment awareness becomes the foundation upon which lasting emotional health, meaningful relationships, and authentic success are built.

Within the landscape of your own awareness lies everything needed for transformation, healing, and the discovery of peace that no external circumstance can disturb. You are stepping into an understanding that honors both the complexity of modern life and the simple yet revolutionary practice that can transform your relationship with every experience, every emotion, and every moment of your precious human existence.

What Is Mindfulness: The Architecture of Present-Moment Awareness

Mindfulness represents far more than a meditation technique or stress-reduction tool—it embodies a fundamental way of relating to life that cultivates deep awareness, radical acceptance, and the kind of presence that transforms ordinary moments into opportunities for profound connection and insight. Understanding mindfulness in its full richness opens pathways to living with unprecedented freedom, peace, and authentic engagement with the fullness of human experience.

Defining Mindfulness: Beyond the Buzzword

At its essence, mindfulness encompasses the practice of paying attention to present-moment experience with openness, curiosity, and acceptance, rather than getting lost in automatic reactions, mental storytelling, or attempts to control experiences that are naturally arising and passing away. This deceptively simple practice represents one of the most sophisticated approaches to emotional health and spiritual development available to human consciousness.

Present-Moment Awareness forms the cornerstone of mindfulness practice through deliberately directing your attention to what is actually happening right now—the sensations in your body, the thoughts moving through your mind, the emotions arising and subsiding, and the immediate sensory experience of sight, sound, smell, taste, and touch that constitutes your direct encounter with reality.

This present-moment focus interrupts the mental time travel that characterizes much human suffering—the rumination about past events that cannot be changed and the anxiety about future possibilities that may never occur. When you anchor attention in present experience, you discover that this moment, whatever it contains, is the only place where peace, joy, and authentic action are actually available.

Non-Judgmental Observation distinguishes mindfulness from ordinary thinking by cultivating the capacity to witness your experience without immediately categorizing it as good or bad, right or wrong, desirable or undesirable. This witnessing stance creates space between you and your experiences, allowing for conscious response rather than automatic reaction.

This non-judgmental awareness doesn't mean becoming passive or losing your capacity for discernment, but rather developing the wisdom to see clearly what is actually happening before adding layers of interpretation, story, or emotional reactivity that often distort your perception and limit your response options.

Curious Investigation characterizes the mindful approach to all experience—pleasant, unpleasant, and neutral—with the attitude of a friendly scientist discovering something new and interesting rather than a critic judging whether experiences meet your preferences or expectations.

This curiosity extends to your own mental and emotional patterns, observing how thoughts arise and pass away, how emotions move through your body, and how your mind creates stories and interpretations that either increase or decrease your suffering and effectiveness.

The Core Principles of Mindful Living

Mindfulness practice rests upon several fundamental principles that guide both formal meditation practice and informal integration of mindful awareness into daily activities, creating a comprehensive approach to conscious living that affects every aspect of your existence.

Acceptance and Non-Resistance represent perhaps the most radical aspects of mindfulness practice—learning to allow experiences to be as they are without immediately trying to change, fix, or escape them. This acceptance doesn't mean liking everything that happens or becoming passive about problems that need addressing, but rather working with reality as it is rather than fighting against it.

When you stop fighting against uncomfortable emotions, difficult thoughts, or challenging circumstances, you free up enormous energy that was previously consumed in resistance while creating space for creative responses that can only emerge when you're fully present with what is actually happening.

Beginner's Mind involves approaching each moment and experience with fresh eyes, as if encountering it for the first time, rather than filtering everything through past experiences, expectations, or assumptions that prevent you from seeing clearly what is actually occurring right now.

This beginner's mind proves particularly valuable in relationships, where mindful presence allows you to see your partner, friends, or family members freshly rather than relating primarily to your stories and expectations about who they are or how they should behave.

Patient Allowing recognizes that insights, healing, and transformation occur in their own natural timing rather than according to your preferences or schedules. This patience creates space for organic unfolding while reducing the impatience and forcing that often interfere with natural healing and growth processes.

Trust in Natural Wisdom involves developing confidence in your innate capacity for healing, growth, and appropriate response when you create the conditions of awareness and acceptance that allow inner wisdom to emerge rather than constantly trying to figure everything out through mental analysis alone.

The Neuroscience of Mindful Awareness

Modern brain research reveals that mindfulness practice creates specific neurological changes that enhance emotional regulation, increase empathy and compassion, improve attention and focus, and build resilience in ways that transform both brain structure and function over time.

Prefrontal Cortex Strengthening occurs through regular mindfulness practice as the brain regions responsible for executive function, emotional regulation, and self-awareness become more active and better integrated with other brain areas. This strengthening improves your capacity to observe emotions without being overwhelmed by them while enhancing decision-making and impulse control.

Amygdala Regulation represents one of the most significant neurological benefits of mindfulness practice, as the brain's alarm system becomes less reactive to perceived threats while developing better communication with the prefrontal cortex that governs rational response. This regulation reduces anxiety, reactivity, and the fight-or-flight responses that often create suffering in situations that don't actually require emergency responses.

Insula Development enhances your capacity for interoception—awareness of internal bodily sensations—that forms the foundation for emotional intelligence and empathy. A well-developed insula helps you recognize your own emotional states more quickly and accurately while improving your ability to sense and respond appropriately to others' emotional experiences.

Default Mode Network Changes occur as mindfulness practice affects the brain's default mode network—the system active during rest and self-referential thinking. Regular mindfulness practice reduces excessive self-focus and rumination while promoting the kind of present-moment awareness that supports both individual well-being and authentic connection with others.

Neuroplasticity Enhancement demonstrates that mindfulness literally reshapes your brain throughout your lifetime, creating new neural pathways that support positive mental states while weakening patterns associated with anxiety, depression, and emotional reactivity.

Mindfulness vs. Mind-Wandering: Understanding the Difference

Developing clear understanding of the difference between mindful awareness and ordinary mental activity helps you recognize when you're practicing mindfulness effectively versus when your mind has returned to its habitual patterns of distraction, judgment, and automatic reaction.

Mindful Awareness Characteristics include clear recognition of present-moment experience without getting lost in mental commentary, acceptance of whatever is happening without immediately trying to change it, spacious awareness that can hold multiple experiences simultaneously without being overwhelmed, and the capacity to observe thoughts and emotions without becoming identified with their content.

When practicing mindfulness effectively, you maintain awareness of your role as the observer of experience rather than being completely consumed by whatever you're observing, creating the psychological space that allows for conscious choice about how to respond.

Mind-Wandering Patterns involve getting completely absorbed in thoughts about past or future, losing awareness of present-moment sensory experience, becoming identified with emotional states rather than observing them, and reacting automatically to experiences based on habitual patterns rather than conscious choice.

Mind-wandering isn't "wrong" or something to eliminate completely, but recognizing when it's happening allows you to gently return attention to present-moment awareness without self-criticism or judgment about having become distracted.

The Practice of Returning represents the essence of mindfulness practice—not maintaining perfect present-moment awareness at all times, which would be impossible for most humans, but noticing when attention has wandered and gently returning to mindful awareness without judgment about having become distracted.

This practice of returning strengthens mindfulness "muscles" while developing self-compassion and the understanding that becoming distracted is completely normal rather than a sign of failure or inadequacy in your practice.

Common Mindfulness Misconceptions

Clearing up widespread misunderstandings about mindfulness helps you approach the practice with realistic expectations while avoiding common pitfalls that can lead to frustration or abandonment of this profoundly beneficial practice.

Mindfulness Is Not About Stopping Thoughts or achieving a blank mind, but rather changing your relationship with thinking by observing thoughts as mental events that arise and pass away rather than absolute truths that you must believe or act upon automatically.

Attempting to stop thinking often increases mental agitation and creates frustration, while mindful observation of thinking gradually reduces the compulsive quality of mental activity while increasing your freedom to choose which thoughts deserve attention and which can be allowed to pass by naturally.

Mindfulness Is Not Passive Acceptance of harmful situations or behaviors, but rather clear seeing that enables more effective action by reducing the emotional reactivity and mental confusion that often lead to ineffective or counterproductive responses to genuine problems.

Mindful awareness often reveals more skillful ways to address difficulties while building the emotional regulation and clear thinking necessary for effective action in challenging situations.

Mindfulness Is Not Always Relaxing and isn't primarily intended as a relaxation technique, though relaxation often occurs as a natural byproduct. Sometimes mindfulness involves staying present with uncomfortable emotions or difficult experiences, which may initially increase rather than decrease tension as you learn to be with what you've been avoiding.

Mindfulness Is Not Spiritual Bypassing or using meditation to avoid dealing with practical problems, psychological issues, or interpersonal difficulties that require active engagement. True mindfulness enhances your capacity for appropriate action rather than creating spiritual detachment from ordinary responsibilities and relationships.

The Benefits of Mindfulness: Transforming Life Through Awareness

When you commit to cultivating mindfulness as a way of life rather than merely a stress-reduction technique, extraordinary benefits emerge that extend throughout every dimension of your existence, creating improvements in physical health, emotional well-being, relationship quality, and professional effectiveness that compound over time to fundamentally transform your experience of being alive.

Emotional Health and Regulation Benefits

Perhaps the most profound and immediately noticeable benefits of mindfulness practice involve dramatic improvements in emotional intelligence, regulation, and overall mental health that create the foundation for authentic well-being and resilience in the face of life's inevitable challenges.

Emotional Awareness Enhancement develops naturally through mindfulness practice as you learn to recognize emotional states as they arise rather than being overwhelmed by them or remaining unconscious of their influence on your thoughts and behavior. This early recognition allows for conscious choice about how to respond rather than automatic emotional reactions that may create additional problems.

Mindful awareness helps you distinguish between different emotional states with greater precision—recognizing the difference between sadness and depression, anger and frustration, anxiety and excitement—enabling more appropriate responses that address the actual emotion you're experiencing rather than reacting based on vague emotional discomfort.

Anxiety and Stress Reduction occur through mindfulness practice that interrupts the rumination and future-focused worry that characterize anxiety while teaching your nervous system that present-moment experience is typically safe even when your mind is generating fearful stories about potential problems.

Research consistently demonstrates that regular mindfulness practice reduces symptoms of generalized anxiety disorder, panic disorder, and stress-related health problems while building resilience that prevents future stress from becoming overwhelming or unmanageable.

Depression Prevention and Recovery happen through mindfulness practices that interrupt the negative thought cycles and rumination patterns that maintain depressive episodes while building awareness of the difference between temporary sadness and clinical depression that requires additional support.

Mindfulness-based cognitive therapy has proven as effective as antidepressant medications for preventing depression relapse while providing lasting skills rather than temporary symptom management through external interventions.

Emotional Resilience Building emerges as mindfulness practice develops your capacity to experience difficult emotions without being destroyed by them while building confidence in your ability to handle whatever life presents without losing your essential well-being or life direction.

This resilience doesn't mean becoming emotionally numb or invulnerable, but rather developing the strength and flexibility to bend without breaking during emotional storms while maintaining connection to your values and capacity for joy even during challenging periods.

Self-Compassion Development naturally accompanies mindfulness practice as you learn to observe your struggles and mistakes with the same kindness you would offer a good friend facing similar difficulties, rather than the harsh self-criticism that often accompanies emotional challenges.

Self-compassion proves more effective than self-criticism for motivating positive change while reducing the secondary suffering that comes from attacking yourself for having normal human struggles and limitations.

Physical Health and Stress Response Benefits

The physical health benefits of mindfulness practice demonstrate how emotional and mental well-being translate into tangible improvements in bodily health, immune function, and overall vitality that enhance both longevity and quality of life.

Stress Response Regulation improves dramatically through mindfulness practice that activates your parasympathetic nervous system—the "rest and digest" response that promotes healing and recovery—while reducing chronic activation of fight-or-flight responses that characterize much modern stress.

Regular mindfulness practice reduces cortisol levels, lowers blood pressure, and improves heart rate variability—indicators of nervous system balance and cardiovascular health that reduce risk of stress-related illness while enhancing your capacity to handle future stressors effectively.

Immune System Enhancement occurs through stress reduction and the positive emotional states that mindfulness cultivates, as research shows that mindfulness practice increases antibody production, enhances vaccine effectiveness, and reduces inflammation that contributes to numerous health conditions.

Sleep Quality Improvement develops naturally as mindfulness practice reduces the rumination and anxiety that interfere with restful sleep while teaching relaxation and letting-go skills that support natural sleep cycles and deeper rest.

Pain Management Benefits emerge as mindfulness practice changes your relationship with physical discomfort, reducing the secondary suffering that comes from fighting against pain while often reducing actual pain perception through relaxation and acceptance that prevent pain-related muscle tension and stress.

Mindfulness-based stress reduction programs consistently show effectiveness for chronic pain management that equals or exceeds pharmaceutical interventions while providing additional benefits for overall well-being and life satisfaction.

Digestive Health Enhancement results from stress reduction and nervous system regulation that optimize digestive function while reducing stress-related gastrointestinal problems like irritable bowel syndrome, acid reflux, and digestive inflammation.

Relationship and Social Connection Benefits

Mindfulness practice profoundly enhances relationship quality and social connection through developing the presence, empathy, and communication skills that create authentic intimacy while reducing the reactivity and defensiveness that damage relationships.

Present-Moment Presence in relationships allows you to truly listen to others rather than planning your response or being distracted by mental activity, creating the quality of attention that others experience as love, respect, and genuine care.

When you're fully present with someone, they feel seen and valued in ways that scattered, distracted attention cannot provide, deepening intimacy and trust while reducing the loneliness that can exist even within relationships when partners aren't emotionally present.

Empathy and Compassion Development occur naturally through mindfulness practice that builds your capacity to sense and respond appropriately to others' emotional experiences without becoming overwhelmed or defensive, creating the emotional intelligence that supports healthy relationships.

Communication Enhancement develops as mindfulness practice improves your ability to speak from clarity rather than emotional reactivity while listening with openness rather than defensive judgment, transforming conflicts into opportunities for deeper understanding and connection.

Mindful communication involves pausing before responding to check your motivations and choose words that serve connection and understanding rather than winning arguments or protecting your ego, creating conversations that build rather than damage relationships.

Conflict Resolution Skills improve dramatically when mindfulness allows you to remain present during disagreements rather than becoming activated by perceived threats, enabling collaborative problem-solving rather than adversarial fighting that creates winners and losers.

Boundary Setting and Maintenance become more skillful when mindfulness helps you recognize your own needs and limits clearly while communicating them with kindness rather than aggression or passive-aggressive manipulation that confuses relationship dynamics.

Parenting Enhancement emerges as mindfulness practice improves your capacity to remain calm and responsive during children's emotional storms while modeling emotional regulation and present-moment awareness that supports children's healthy development.

Professional Performance and Leadership Benefits

The workplace benefits of mindfulness practice extend throughout every aspect of professional effectiveness, from daily task performance to leadership capacity and the kind of innovative thinking that drives career advancement and organizational success.

Focus and Attention Enhancement develop naturally through mindfulness training that strengthens your capacity for sustained attention on chosen tasks while reducing the distractibility and mental scattered-ness that compromise productivity and work quality.

Mindful attention allows you to enter "flow states" more easily—periods of effortless concentration where peak performance occurs naturally—while reducing the mental effort required for focusing on important tasks and projects.

Creativity and Innovation flourish when mindfulness creates the mental spaciousness and openness necessary for new ideas to emerge while reducing the mental rigidity and habitual thinking that block creative problem-solving and innovative approaches to challenges.

Decision-Making Quality improves significantly when mindfulness provides access to both rational analysis and intuitive wisdom while reducing the emotional reactivity and mental confusion that often lead to poor choices with negative consequences.

Mindful decision-making involves taking time to consider multiple perspectives and potential outcomes while remaining connected to your values and long-term goals rather than making impulsive choices based on immediate emotional reactions.

Leadership Presence and Effectiveness develop as mindfulness creates the calm confidence and authentic presence that inspire trust and followership while providing the emotional regulation necessary for skillful guidance during organizational stress and change.

Mindful leaders demonstrate better listening skills, more effective communication during conflicts, and the kind of visionary thinking that emerges when you're not constantly distracted by mental noise and emotional reactivity.

Stress Management and Burnout Prevention occur naturally when mindfulness practice provides tools for working with work pressure skillfully while maintaining perspective and balance that prevent the exhaustion and cynicism that characterize professional burnout.

Team Collaboration Enhancement emerges as your increased presence and empathy improve your ability to work effectively with diverse colleagues while contributing to positive team dynamics that enhance collective productivity and job satisfaction.

Spiritual Growth and Life Purpose Benefits

Beyond practical benefits, mindfulness practice often catalyzes profound spiritual development and clarity about life purpose as present-moment awareness creates space for deeper questions about meaning, service, and your unique contribution to the healing and wholeness of the world.

Meaning and Purpose Clarity often emerge through mindfulness practice as reduced mental noise allows you to hear the subtle guidance about what matters most deeply to you while connecting with values and aspirations that transcend immediate personal comfort and security.

Spiritual Connection Deepening occurs naturally as mindfulness creates the inner quiet and receptivity necessary for spiritual awareness while reducing the ego-driven concerns that often block access to transcendent experiences and wisdom.

Wisdom and Insight Development happen through mindfulness practice that reveals the impermanent nature of all experience while building understanding of the patterns and principles that govern emotional well-being and authentic living.

Service Orientation Enhancement emerges as mindfulness practice reduces self-centered preoccupation while increasing awareness of your connection to others and the ways your healing and growth can serve the collective well-being of your community and world.

Gratitude and Appreciation develop naturally through present-moment awareness that reveals the extraordinary richness and beauty available in ordinary experiences while building appreciation for the precious opportunity of conscious human existence.

Practical Mindfulness Practices: Your Toolkit for Present-Moment Living

The cultivation of mindfulness requires consistent practice across multiple domains of life, implemented gradually and sustainably through specific techniques that can be adapted to your individual circumstances, preferences, and schedule while providing cumulative benefits that transform your overall relationship with experience.

Foundation Meditation Practices

Formal meditation provides concentrated training in mindful awareness that builds the mental "muscles" necessary for maintaining presence during daily activities, creating a strong foundation for integrating mindfulness throughout all aspects of your life.

Basic Breath Awareness Meditation offers the most accessible entry point for mindfulness practice through focusing attention on the natural rhythm of breathing while developing the capacity to notice when attention wanders and gently return focus to the present moment.

Begin with 5-10 minute sessions, sitting comfortably with your spine straight but not rigid, eyes closed or softly focused downward. Simply observe the sensations of breathing—the air entering and leaving your nostrils, the rise and fall of your chest or belly—without trying to control or change your breath in any way.

When you notice your mind wandering to thoughts, plans, or concerns, gently acknowledge "thinking" and return attention to breathing sensations without judgment or frustration about having become distracted. This practice of returning strengthens mindfulness while building self-compassion.

Body Scan Meditation develops intimate awareness of physical sensations while building the mind-body connection that supports emotional intelligence and stress management. This practice also provides deep relaxation while teaching you to observe physical experience with acceptance rather than immediate attempts to change or fix discomfort.

Lie down comfortably and systematically move attention through different parts of your body, starting with your toes and gradually working upward through legs, torso, arms, and head. Notice whatever sensations are present—warmth, coolness, tension, relaxation, tingling, or numbness—without trying to change anything, simply observing with curious acceptance.

Walking Meditation combines gentle movement with mindful awareness, making meditation accessible for people who find sitting meditation difficult while providing practice in maintaining present-moment awareness during activity rather than just while sitting still.

Choose a quiet path 10–20 steps long and walk slowly while focusing attention on the physical sensations of walking—the lifting, moving, and placing of each foot, the shifting of weight from one leg to the other, the movement of muscles and joints involved in walking.

When your mind wanders, simply stop, acknowledge the distraction, and return attention to walking sensations. This practice builds the capacity to remain present during daily activities while providing gentle physical activity that supports overall well-being.

Loving-Kindness Meditation specifically cultivates compassion and goodwill toward yourself and others while addressing the self-criticism and interpersonal difficulties that often accompany stress and emotional challenges.

Begin by offering genuine wishes for your own well-being: "May I be happy, may I be healthy, may I be at peace, may I live with ease." Notice any resistance or discomfort with self-directed kindness, exploring these responses with gentle curiosity rather than judgment.

Gradually extend these same wishes to loved ones, neutral people, difficult people, and eventually all beings, building the emotional resources that support both personal healing and improved relationships.

Mindful Daily Activities

Integrating mindfulness into routine activities transforms ordinary moments into opportunities for present-moment awareness while making mindfulness practice accessible without requiring additional time in your already busy schedule.

Mindful Eating Practices provide excellent opportunities for present-moment awareness while often improving digestion and preventing overeating that results from distracted consumption. Begin with one mindful meal or snack each day, eating slowly while paying attention to tastes, textures, temperatures, and the experience of chewing and swallowing.

Notice hunger and satisfaction cues that are often missed during hurried or distracted eating, while appreciating the colors, aromas, and complexity of your food. This practice builds appreciation while creating natural portion control through awareness of actual hunger and fullness.

Mindful Household Activities transform chores and routine tasks into meditation opportunities by bringing full attention to physical sensations, movements, and immediate experience rather than rushing through activities while planning or worrying about other concerns.

Practice mindful dishwashing by paying attention to water temperature, soap bubbles, the feeling of dishes becoming clean, and the simple satisfaction of completing a useful task. Similarly, mindful cleaning, laundry, or gardening can become opportunities for present-moment awareness and stress relief.

Mindful Technology Use addresses the distraction and overstimulation that electronic devices often create by establishing conscious boundaries and practices around screen time while using technology as occasional mindfulness bell rather than constant source of distraction.

Practice taking three conscious breaths before checking email or social media, setting specific times for technology use rather than constant availability, and occasionally using phone notifications as reminders to return to present-moment awareness rather than immediately reacting to digital demands.

Mindful Commuting transforms travel time into opportunities for present-moment awareness whether driving, walking, or using public transportation, creating calm transitions between home and work while building mindfulness skills during routine activities.

When driving, practice attention to physical sensations of steering, the feeling of your body in the seat, and visual awareness of your surroundings while maintaining safe focus on traffic and road conditions. When walking or using public transportation, pay attention to physical sensations of movement while observing your environment with gentle curiosity.

Mindful Breathing Techniques

Conscious breathing provides immediate access to present-moment awareness while offering powerful tools for emotional regulation, stress management, and the kind of nervous system balance that supports overall health and well-being.

Three-Part Breathing (dirgha pranayama) promotes deep relaxation while building awareness of breath capacity and the calming effects of complete breathing that engages your entire respiratory system rather than the shallow breathing that often accompanies stress.

Place one hand on your chest and one on your belly, breathing slowly and deeply enough that your belly rises first, followed by your ribcage expanding, and finally your chest rising slightly. Exhale slowly, reversing the process. This complete breathing activates relaxation responses while providing immediate stress relief.

Box Breathing (sama vritti) creates mental focus while promoting nervous system balance through equal counts for inhaling, holding, exhaling, and holding, creating rhythmic breathing that calms mental activity while building concentration.

Breathe in for 4 counts, hold for 4 counts, exhale for 4 counts, hold for 4 counts, repeating this pattern for several minutes. Adjust the count to whatever feels comfortable while maintaining equal timing for each phase of the breath cycle.

Extended Exhale Breathing directly activates your parasympathetic nervous system through making exhales longer than inhales, providing immediate anxiety relief while promoting the relaxation response that supports healing and recovery from stress.

Try breathing in for 4 counts and exhaling for 6–8 counts, or whatever ratio feels comfortable while ensuring exhales are longer than inhales. This technique proves particularly effective for falling asleep or managing anxiety episodes.

Natural Breath Observation simply involves paying attention to breathing without changing it in any way, building awareness of your natural breathing patterns while developing the fundamental mindfulness skill of observing experience without trying to control or improve it.

Notice the pauses between breaths, the temperature of air entering and leaving your body, and the subtle movements throughout your torso that accompany breathing, allowing breath to be exactly as it is while using breathing sensations as anchors for present-moment awareness.

Mindful Movement Practices

Combining mindfulness with physical activity provides integrated benefits for both mental and physical health while making meditation accessible for people who find sitting practices challenging or insufficient for their temperament and needs.

Mindful Walking involves walking at a natural pace while maintaining attention on physical sensations of movement rather than getting lost in mental activity about destinations or problems you're trying to solve through walking.

Pay attention to the contact between your feet and the ground, the coordination required for balanced movement, and the rhythm of walking while remaining aware of your surroundings through sight, sound, and other senses that connect you with your immediate environment.

Yoga and Stretching provide structured approaches to mindful movement that combine physical benefits of flexibility and strength with mental benefits of present-moment awareness and breath coordination that characterize effective yoga practice.

Focus on the sensations of stretching, the coordination of movement with breathing, and the balance between effort and ease that effective yoga practice requires, rather than striving for perfect poses or comparing your flexibility with others.

Tai Chi and Qigong offer gentle, flowing movement practices specifically designed to integrate mindfulness with physical activity while building energy, balance, and the kind of inner calm that supports both health and emotional well-being.

Swimming and Water Activities provide unique opportunities for mindful movement through the sensory richness of water contact, the rhythm of swimming strokes coordinated with breathing, and the meditative qualities that water activities often naturally provide.

Running and Aerobic Exercise can become mindfulness practices through attention to physical sensations of movement, breathing rhythms, and the immediate environment rather than using exercise primarily as distraction from mental concerns or purely for fitness goals.

Integration Strategies and Habit Building

Sustainable mindfulness practice requires thoughtful integration into your existing lifestyle rather than dramatic changes that might prove difficult to maintain, while building habits gradually through consistent small practices that accumulate into significant transformation over time.

Start Small and Be Consistent rather than attempting long meditation sessions that might feel overwhelming or impossible to maintain with your current schedule and responsibilities. Five minutes of daily practice proves more beneficial than occasional longer sessions that happen sporadically.

Link Mindfulness to Existing Habits by practicing brief moments of mindful awareness before or after activities you already do consistently—three conscious breaths before meals, mindful attention while brushing teeth, or present-moment awareness while waiting for coffee to brew.

Use Environmental Cues to remind yourself to return to mindful awareness throughout the day—setting phone reminders for breathing breaks, placing visual cues in frequently seen locations, or using routine activities like doorway crossings as prompts for brief present-moment awareness.

Track Your Practice without becoming obsessive about perfect consistency, noting how mindfulness affects your mood, stress levels, and relationship quality while celebrating small improvements rather than focusing on missed sessions or imperfect practice.

Find Community and Support through meditation groups, mindfulness classes, or online communities that provide encouragement, guidance, and the social support that helps sustain long-term practice while learning from others' experiences and insights.

Adapt Practices to Your Lifestyle rather than trying to force yourself into traditional meditation formats that might not suit your temperament, schedule, or circumstances. Mindfulness can be practiced anywhere, anytime, in whatever form serves your actual life situation and needs.

As we conclude this exploration of mindfulness as a transformative practice for emotional health and authentic living, we celebrate your courage to slow down in a world that often demands constant acceleration, to pay attention in a culture of distraction, and to find peace within whatever circumstances life presents.

Remember that mindfulness is not about achieving a perpetual state of calm or eliminating all mental activity, but about developing a fundamentally different relationship with your experience—one characterized by presence, acceptance, and the kind of wise responsiveness that serves both your own well-being and your capacity to contribute positively to the lives of others.

Your commitment to cultivating mindfulness creates ripple effects that extend far beyond personal benefits to influence every relationship, every interaction, and every community you're part of, as your increased presence and emotional regulation contribute to collective healing while modeling possibilities for conscious living that others may find inspiring and hopeful.

The journey of mindfulness continues with each conscious breath, each moment of returning from distraction to presence, and each choice to meet your experience with curiosity and kindness rather than judgment and resistance. These simple yet profound acts accumulate into a transformation that touches the very core of what it means to be fully, authentically human.

Through your dedication to present-moment awareness, you participate in an ancient yet urgently contemporary movement toward greater consciousness, compassion, and wisdom that serves not only your individual healing and growth but contributes to the collective awakening that our world desperately needs during these complex and challenging times.

This is your invitation to unprecedented peace, clarity, and authentic engagement with life—not through achieving some future state of perfection, but through the radical act of fully inhabiting this moment, this breath, this precious opportunity to be consciously alive in a world that needs your presence, your wisdom, and your compassionate participation in the grand adventure of human existence.

Reflection: What are some early emotional wounds that may still influence me today?

Chapter 20: The Importance of Sleep

Chapter 20 is what may prove to be the most powerful chapter of your healing journey—one that beckons you toward understanding the profound sanctuary of sleep, where your body and mind perform their most essential work of restoration, integration, and renewal. Here, we venture into the sacred territory where consciousness meets unconsciousness, where the day's experiences transform into tomorrow's wisdom, and where the very architecture of your emotional resilience is built night after night in the quiet depths of restorative slumber.

Sleep not as merely time lost to unconsciousness, but as active participation in your body's most sophisticated healing processes—a nightly journey of cellular repair, memory consolidation, and emotional regulation that determines the quality of every waking moment. Within these pages, you'll uncover how your relationship with sleep becomes the cornerstone upon which all other aspects of emotional health ultimately rest.

Recognizing that in our culture of constant productivity and endless stimulation, understanding and prioritizing sleep emerges not as laziness or self-indulgence, but as perhaps the most practical and powerful intervention available for emotional healing and optimal functioning. This knowledge that honors both the complexity of sleep science and the simple yet revolutionary truth that quality rest transforms everything.

Why Sleep Matters: The Foundation of Emotional Wellness

Sleep represents far more than a biological necessity or temporary escape from daily pressures—it embodies a sophisticated orchestration of physiological and psychological processes that serve as the foundation for emotional regulation, mental clarity, and the resilience that enables you to navigate life's challenges with grace and effectiveness.

The Architecture of Restorative Sleep

Understanding sleep's profound importance begins with recognizing the intricate processes that unfold during your nightly journey through different sleep stages, each serving essential functions that directly impact your emotional health and overall well-being during waking hours.

Non-REM Sleep Stages provide the foundation for physical restoration and memory consolidation through increasingly deep levels of unconsciousness that allow your body and brain to perform essential maintenance and repair functions. Stage 1 represents the transition from wakefulness to sleep, lasting only minutes as your brain activity begins to slow and your muscles relax, preparing for deeper restoration.

Stage 2 encompasses the majority of your sleep time, characterized by further decreases in heart rate and body temperature while your brain begins consolidating memories and clearing metabolic waste that accumulates during waking hours. This stage proves crucial for learning retention and emotional processing of daily experiences.

Deep Sleep (Stage 3) represents the most physically restorative period, when growth hormone release peaks, immune system repair accelerates, and your brain clears toxic proteins associated with neurodegenerative diseases while strengthening memories and integrating learning from the previous day.

REM Sleep provides essential psychological restoration through the vivid dreaming that characterizes this stage, during which your brain processes emotions, consolidates complex memories, and integrates experiences in ways that support emotional regulation and creative problem-solving during waking hours.

The cyclical nature of these stages throughout the night ensures comprehensive restoration, with each cycle lasting approximately 90 minutes and the proportion of deep sleep versus REM sleep shifting throughout the night to provide different types of restoration at optimal times.

Physiological Benefits of Quality Sleep

The physical health benefits of adequate, quality sleep extend throughout every system in your body, creating the biological foundation necessary for emotional stability, mental clarity, and the resilience that supports your capacity to handle stress and maintain positive relationships.

Immune System Strengthening occurs primarily during sleep as your body produces infection-fighting cells, antibodies, and protective proteins that defend against illness while clearing damaged cells and toxins that accumulate during daily activities. Adequate sleep has been shown to improve vaccine effectiveness while reducing susceptibility to viruses and infections.

Sleep deprivation compromises immune function within just one night, reducing natural killer cell activity by up to 70% while increasing inflammatory markers that contribute to various health problems including depression, anxiety, and cardiovascular disease.

Hormonal Balance Restoration happens through sleep's regulation of crucial hormones including cortisol, which should naturally decrease during sleep to allow recovery from daily stress; growth hormone, which peaks during deep sleep to support tissue repair and regeneration; and leptin and ghrelin, which regulate appetite and metabolism.

Cardiovascular Health Maintenance occurs as sleep allows heart rate and blood pressure to decrease, giving your cardiovascular system essential recovery time while reducing inflammation and oxidative stress that contribute to heart disease, stroke, and other cardiovascular complications.

Brain Detoxification Processes activate during sleep through the glymphatic system, which clears metabolic waste and toxic proteins from brain tissue, including amyloid-beta and tau proteins associated with Alzheimer's disease and other neurodegenerative conditions.

Cellular Repair and Regeneration accelerate during sleep as your body produces proteins necessary for cell growth and repair while DNA damage from daily oxidative stress is corrected and tissues throughout your body undergo essential maintenance and restoration.

Psychological and Emotional Benefits

Perhaps most relevant to your emotional health journey, sleep provides crucial psychological benefits that directly impact mood regulation, stress resilience, and your capacity for authentic relationships and meaningful life engagement.

Emotional Regulation Enhancement occurs through sleep's consolidation of emotional memories and restoration of brain regions responsible for emotional control, particularly the prefrontal cortex that governs rational decision-making and the amygdala that processes emotional responses and threat detection.

Research consistently demonstrates that sleep deprivation increases emotional reactivity while reducing your ability to accurately read others' emotions or respond appropriately to emotional situations, making conflicts more likely and resolution more difficult.

Stress Hormone Regulation happens primarily during sleep as cortisol levels naturally decrease, allowing your nervous system to shift from stress response activation toward rest and recovery states that build resilience for handling future challenges with greater calm and effectiveness.

Memory Consolidation and Learning occur through sleep's transfer of information from short-term to long-term memory while strengthening neural connections that support skill development, problem-solving capacity, and the integration of new experiences with existing knowledge and wisdom.

Mood Stabilization results from sleep's regulation of neurotransmitters including serotonin, dopamine, and norepinephrine that directly affect mood, motivation, and emotional well-being while supporting the brain chemistry necessary for positive outlook and emotional resilience.

Creative Problem-Solving Enhancement emerges through REM sleep's unique ability to forge new neural connections between disparate pieces of information, often leading to breakthrough insights and innovative solutions that conscious thinking alone cannot achieve.

Sleep's Role in Mental Health

The relationship between sleep and mental health represents a complex interplay where sleep problems can both result from and contribute to emotional difficulties, making sleep optimization a crucial component of comprehensive mental health care and emotional healing.

Depression and Sleep Connection reveals bidirectional relationships where sleep disturbances often precede depressive episodes while depression frequently disrupts sleep patterns, creating cycles that must be addressed simultaneously for effective treatment and lasting recovery.

Studies show that treating insomnia can significantly reduce depression symptoms even without direct depression treatment, while improving sleep quality enhances the effectiveness of traditional depression therapies including medication and psychotherapy.

Anxiety and Sleep Interactions demonstrate how worry and rumination interfere with sleep initiation and maintenance while sleep deprivation increases anxiety sensitivity and reduces your capacity to cope with stressful situations that might otherwise be manageable.

Trauma Processing and Integration occur primarily during REM sleep as your brain works to process traumatic experiences and integrate them into your overall life narrative in ways that reduce their emotional charge and disruptive impact on daily functioning.

Sleep disturbances represent common symptoms of post-traumatic stress disorder, while improving sleep quality often significantly reduces trauma symptoms and enhances the effectiveness of trauma-focused therapies.

Cognitive Function and Mental Clarity depend heavily on adequate sleep for optimal performance in attention, concentration, decision-making, and problem-solving—all essential components of emotional intelligence and effective stress management.

The Evolutionary Perspective on Sleep

Understanding sleep's evolutionary importance provides context for why modern sleep disruptions create such significant problems while highlighting the fundamental role that quality sleep has played in human development and survival throughout our species' history.

Survival and Adaptation Functions include memory consolidation that allowed our ancestors to learn from experiences and adapt to changing environments, immune system strengthening that provided resistance to infections and diseases, and energy conservation that optimized resource utilization during periods of vulnerability.

Social and Emotional Development occurred through sleep's role in processing social interactions and emotional experiences while supporting the empathy and cooperation that enabled human communities to thrive through collaborative efforts and mutual support.

Brain Development and Learning throughout human evolution depended on sleep's role in neural plasticity and skill acquisition, allowing our species to develop increasingly sophisticated tools, languages, and social systems that required complex learning and adaptation.

Modern Sleep Challenges emerge from environments and lifestyle patterns that differ dramatically from the conditions in which human sleep systems evolved, including artificial lighting, electronic stimulation, irregular schedules, and chronic stress that our sleep systems weren't designed to handle.

The Consequences of Sleep Deprivation: Understanding the Cost

When sleep becomes compromised through insufficient quantity, poor quality, or disrupted timing, the consequences ripple throughout every aspect of your life—from immediate effects on mood and cognitive function to long-term impacts on physical health, relationships, and overall life satisfaction that accumulate over time to create significant challenges.

Immediate Mental Health Impact

The acute effects of sleep deprivation on mental and emotional functioning appear quickly and intensify with continued sleep loss, creating immediate challenges that affect your capacity to handle daily responsibilities and maintain emotional equilibrium.

Mood Disruption and Irritability represent perhaps the most immediately noticeable effects of sleep loss, as insufficient sleep increases emotional reactivity while reducing your capacity to regulate responses to frustrating or challenging situations that you might normally handle with patience and wisdom.

Even one night of poor sleep significantly increases negative emotions while reducing positive mood states, making you more likely to experience irritation, sadness, anxiety, and stress while less likely to feel joy, gratitude, or emotional contentment throughout the following day.

Cognitive Impairment and Mental Fog emerge rapidly with sleep deprivation as attention, concentration, and working memory become compromised while decision-making capacity decreases and reaction times slow, affecting everything from work performance to driving safety.

Emotional Regulation Difficulties manifest as increased difficulty controlling emotional responses, greater sensitivity to criticism or setbacks, and reduced capacity to maintain perspective during challenging situations that require emotional intelligence and measured responses.

Increased Anxiety and Worry often accompany sleep deprivation as tired brains tend toward threat-focused thinking and catastrophic interpretation of neutral events while your capacity to challenge anxious thoughts and maintain realistic perspective becomes impaired.

Social Interaction Challenges develop as sleep deprivation affects your ability to read others' emotions accurately, respond appropriately to social cues, and maintain the patience and empathy that healthy relationships require while increasing likelihood of conflicts and misunderstandings.

Long-Term Mental Health Consequences

Chronic sleep deprivation creates cumulative effects that significantly increase risk for serious mental health conditions while making existing emotional challenges more severe and resistant to treatment approaches that might otherwise prove effective.

Depression Development and Severity show strong correlations with chronic sleep problems, with persistent insomnia increasing depression risk by up to 10 times while sleep disturbances often precede depressive episodes and predict more severe symptoms and longer recovery times.

Anxiety Disorder Vulnerability increases substantially with chronic sleep loss as your nervous system remains in heightened activation states while your capacity to cope with normal life stressors becomes progressively compromised through exhaustion and emotional depletion.

Cognitive Decline and Memory Problems accelerate with persistent sleep deprivation as the brain's ability to clear toxic proteins becomes impaired while memory consolidation processes suffer, potentially contributing to early cognitive decline and increased dementia risk.

Emotional Intelligence Erosion occurs gradually as chronic sleep loss impairs your ability to understand your own emotions, empathize with others, and navigate social situations with the wisdom and sensitivity that meaningful relationships require.

Stress Sensitivity Increases develop as sleep-deprived individuals show heightened cortisol responses to stressors while recovering more slowly from stressful experiences, creating vulnerability to chronic stress that further disrupts sleep and perpetuates harmful cycles.

Physical Health Deterioration

Sleep deprivation creates serious physical health consequences that extend far beyond fatigue to encompass increased disease risk and accelerated aging processes that affect both quality and quantity of life.

Cardiovascular Disease Risk increases significantly with chronic sleep loss as blood pressure remains elevated, inflammatory markers rise, and stress on the heart and blood vessels accumulates while the protective effects of sleep's cardiovascular recovery are lost.

Immune System Compromise becomes severe with persistent sleep deprivation, increasing susceptibility to infections, reducing vaccine effectiveness, and impairing the body's ability to fight off illnesses while slower healing and recovery from injuries and illnesses become common.

Metabolic Dysfunction and Weight Gain result from sleep loss's disruption of hormones regulating appetite, metabolism, and blood sugar while increasing cravings for high-calorie foods and reducing motivation for physical activity that supports healthy weight maintenance.

Accelerated Aging Processes occur at cellular levels as sleep deprivation increases oxidative stress and inflammation while reducing growth hormone production and cellular repair processes that maintain youthful functioning and appearance.

Increased Accident and Injury Risk develops as reaction times slow, attention becomes impaired, and judgment suffers while drowsy driving creates risks comparable to drunk driving and workplace accidents increase substantially among sleep-deprived individuals.

Relationship and Social Consequences

Sleep deprivation significantly affects your capacity for healthy relationships and social connection, creating patterns that can damage important relationships while reducing your ability to build new connections and maintain social support networks.

Communication Impairment emerges as sleep loss affects language processing, emotional expression, and listening skills while increasing likelihood of misunderstandings and reducing your ability to engage in the kind of meaningful conversation that builds and maintains intimate relationships.

Empathy and Compassion Reduction occur as tired brains become more self-focused while losing capacity to understand and respond to others' emotional needs, creating relationship dynamics where partners, family members, and friends feel unsupported or misunderstood.

Conflict Escalation Patterns develop as sleep deprivation increases irritability and emotional reactivity while reducing patience and problem-solving capacity, making disagreements more likely to become heated conflicts rather than opportunities for mutual understanding and resolution.

Social Withdrawal Tendencies emerge as exhaustion makes social activities feel burdensome while reduced emotional capacity makes it difficult to engage authentically with others, leading to isolation that further compromises mental health and relationship satisfaction.

Parenting Challenges intensify dramatically with sleep deprivation as the patience, emotional regulation, and consistent energy that effective parenting requires become compromised while modeling poor sleep habits and stress management for children who learn from your example.

Professional and Achievement Impact

The workplace consequences of sleep deprivation extend throughout every aspect of professional performance while affecting career advancement opportunities and overall work satisfaction in ways that can have lasting effects on financial security and professional fulfillment.

Productivity and Performance Decline manifest through reduced concentration, increased errors, slower task completion, and diminished creative problem-solving capacity while the quality of work output suffers even when quantity is maintained through increased effort.

Decision-Making Impairment becomes particularly problematic in leadership roles as sleep deprivation affects risk assessment, strategic thinking, and the judgment necessary for complex decisions that affect multiple people and organizational outcomes.

Innovation and Creativity Blocks emerge as sleep loss impairs the kind of flexible thinking and novel connection-making that innovation requires while reducing motivation to pursue challenging projects that might advance career goals and professional development.

Leadership Effectiveness Reduction occurs as sleep-deprived leaders show decreased emotional intelligence, reduced inspirational capacity, and impaired ability to manage team dynamics effectively while their own stress and irritability affect team morale and performance.

Safety and Liability Concerns increase substantially in professions requiring attention to detail, quick reflexes, or safety consciousness as sleep deprivation creates conditions similar to intoxication in terms of impaired judgment and delayed reaction times.

Economic and Life Satisfaction Costs

The broader life impacts of sleep deprivation include significant economic consequences and reduced overall life satisfaction that affect long-term goals and your capacity to create the kind of life that provides meaning and fulfillment.

Healthcare Costs Increase substantially among sleep-deprived individuals who show higher rates of illness, injury, and chronic disease while requiring more medical interventions and missing more work days due to health-related problems.

Lost Productivity and Income result from reduced work performance, increased sick days, and potential job loss or career limitations that sleep problems create while the economic impact extends beyond individual consequences to affect families and communities.

Quality of Life Deterioration encompasses reduced capacity for enjoyment, diminished energy for pursuing interests and hobbies, and decreased satisfaction with relationships and life circumstances while overall sense of well-being and life fulfillment suffer significantly.

Goal Achievement Difficulties emerge as sleep deprivation reduces motivation, persistence, and the sustained effort necessary for achieving meaningful personal and professional goals while impairing the learning and skill development that growth requires.

Life Expectancy Reduction represents the ultimate cost of chronic sleep deprivation, with studies showing that persistent sleep loss increases mortality risk while contributing to earlier onset of age-related diseases and reduced healthy lifespan.

Practical Strategies for Better Sleep: Your Guide to Restorative Rest

Achieving consistently restorative sleep requires a comprehensive approach that addresses not only the immediate environment and habits surrounding sleep, but also the daytime behaviors, stress management practices, and lifestyle choices that set the stage for quality rest throughout each 24-hour cycle.

Sleep Hygiene Fundamentals

Establishing excellent sleep hygiene creates the foundation for quality rest through consistent practices that signal to your body and mind that sleep time approaches while optimizing your environment for deep, uninterrupted restoration.

Consistent Sleep Schedule represents perhaps the most important factor in sleep quality, involving going to bed and waking up at the same times every day—including weekends—to strengthen your natural circadian rhythm and make falling asleep and waking up feel natural and effortless.

Your internal clock responds to consistency by releasing sleep and wake hormones at appropriate times while adjusting body temperature and other physiological processes to support your sleep schedule, but this synchronization requires several weeks of consistent timing to establish fully.

Optimized Sleep Environment creates conditions that promote deep, uninterrupted rest through attention to temperature, lighting, noise, and comfort factors that either support or interfere with your brain's natural sleep processes.

Keep your bedroom cool (65-68 °F), as your body temperature naturally decreases during sleep and cooler environments support this process while overheated rooms interfere with sleep initiation and maintenance throughout the night.

Minimize light exposure through blackout curtains or eye masks, as even small amounts of light can disrupt melatonin production and interfere with deep sleep while artificial light from electronics proves particularly disruptive to natural sleep processes.

Evening Routine Development involves creating consistent pre-sleep activities that signal your nervous system to begin transitioning from active daytime states toward rest and restoration while providing buffer time between daily stressors and sleep onset.

Begin your wind-down routine 1–2 hours before desired sleep time with calming activities like reading, gentle stretching, meditation, or listening to soothing music while avoiding stimulating activities, work-related tasks, or emotionally intense conversations.

Electronic Device Management requires limiting screen exposure in the evening as blue light suppresses melatonin production while the stimulating content of television, social media, or work emails keeps your brain in alert states that interfere with sleep preparation.

Consider using blue light filtering glasses or apps that reduce blue light emission from devices if evening screen use is necessary, while establishing device-free zones and times that protect your sleep preparation from digital stimulation.

Bedroom Sanctity Preservation means using your bedroom exclusively for sleep and intimate relationships, avoiding work, eating, or entertainment in the space associated with rest, so your brain learns to associate the bedroom environment with sleep rather than alertness.

Lifestyle Factors for Better Sleep

Comprehensive sleep improvement requires attention to daytime behaviors and lifestyle choices that either support or undermine your capacity for quality rest, recognizing that sleep quality reflects the cumulative effect of choices made throughout each 24-hour period.

Exercise and Physical Activity provide powerful sleep benefits when timed appropriately, with regular physical activity improving sleep quality, reducing sleep onset time, and increasing deep sleep duration while helping regulate circadian rhythms and reducing stress and anxiety.

Aim for moderate exercise earlier in the day while avoiding vigorous workouts within 3–4 hours of bedtime, as intense physical activity close to sleep time can increase alertness and body temperature in ways that interfere with sleep initiation.

Nutrition and Eating Patterns significantly affect sleep quality through their influence on blood sugar stability, neurotransmitter production, and digestive processes that either support or interfere with restful sleep throughout the night.

Avoid large meals, spicy foods, or excessive liquids close to bedtime while considering light snacks containing tryptophan (turkey, milk, bananas) or complex carbohydrates that may support sleep onset through their effects on sleep-promoting brain chemistry.

Caffeine and Stimulant Management proves crucial as these substances can interfere with sleep for 6–8 hours after consumption, with individual sensitivity varying considerably while age increases sensitivity to caffeine's sleep-disrupting effects.

Consider eliminating caffeine after 2 PM or earlier if you're particularly sensitive, while being aware that caffeine appears in chocolate, some medications, and various beverages beyond obvious sources like coffee and tea.

Alcohol Considerations require understanding that while alcohol may initially help you fall asleep, it significantly disrupts sleep architecture by reducing REM sleep and causing more frequent awakenings while creating rebound alertness as alcohol metabolizes during the night.

Stress Management Integration throughout the day prevents the accumulation of tension and worry that interfere with sleep onset while building resilience that reduces the likelihood of stress-related sleep disruptions during challenging periods.

Practice stress reduction techniques like meditation, deep breathing, or progressive muscle relaxation during the day rather than waiting until bedtime when accumulated stress may prove difficult to release quickly enough for timely sleep onset.

Managing Common Sleep Disorders

Understanding and addressing specific sleep disorders requires recognizing symptoms that indicate problems beyond simple poor sleep habits while seeking appropriate professional evaluation and treatment for conditions that may require specialized intervention.

Insomnia Recognition and Management involves identifying patterns of difficulty falling asleep, staying asleep, or waking too early that persist for several weeks and significantly impact daytime functioning while ruling out underlying medical or psychological causes.

Cognitive-behavioral therapy for insomnia (CBT-I) represents the gold standard treatment approach, involving techniques like sleep restriction therapy, stimulus control, and cognitive restructuring that address both behaviors and thoughts that perpetuate sleep difficulties.

Sleep Apnea Awareness requires recognizing symptoms like loud snoring, gasping during sleep, morning headaches, excessive daytime fatigue, and frequent nighttime awakening that may indicate breathing disruptions requiring medical evaluation and treatment.

Risk factors include being overweight, having a thick neck, family history, age over 40, and certain anatomical features while untreated sleep apnea significantly increases cardiovascular disease risk and can be life-threatening.

Restless Leg Syndrome Management involves addressing uncomfortable sensations in the legs that create irresistible urges to move while lying down, often accompanied by periodic limb movements that disrupt sleep throughout the night.

Lifestyle modifications including regular exercise, avoiding caffeine, and addressing iron deficiency may help while severe cases may require medical treatment with specific medications designed to reduce symptoms and improve sleep quality.

Shift Work Sleep Disorder affects individuals whose work schedules conflict with natural circadian rhythms, requiring special strategies like strategic light exposure, melatonin supplementation, and careful sleep environment optimization to maintain health despite irregular schedules.

Circadian Rhythm Disorders involve disruptions to your internal clock that can result from travel, irregular schedules, or medical conditions while requiring specialized treatment approaches that may include light therapy, melatonin, or schedule adjustments.

Natural Sleep Aids and Relaxation Techniques

Various natural approaches can support better sleep quality when combined with good sleep hygiene and healthy lifestyle practices, though it's important to understand both benefits and limitations of different natural interventions.

Herbal Sleep Supports include chamomile tea, valerian root, passionflower, and lavender that may provide mild sedating effects while creating bedtime rituals that psychologically support sleep preparation, though effects are typically gentle and individual responses vary.

Melatonin Supplementation can be helpful for circadian rhythm disruptions like jet lag or shift work while generally being less effective for insomnia caused by stress, anxiety, or poor sleep habits, with optimal timing and dosage varying by individual and situation.

Progressive Muscle Relaxation involves systematically tensing and releasing muscle groups throughout your body to reduce physical tension while building awareness of the difference between tension and relaxation that supports overall stress management and sleep preparation.

Deep Breathing Techniques like the 4-7-8 breathing pattern (inhale 4 counts, hold 7 counts, exhale 8 counts) activate parasympathetic nervous system responses that promote relaxation while providing mental focus that interrupts worry and rumination that interfere with sleep onset.

Meditation and Mindfulness Practices specifically designed for sleep help quiet mental chatter while building present-moment awareness that reduces anxiety about sleep itself, with guided sleep meditations providing structured approaches for those new to mindfulness practices.

Aromatherapy and Environmental Enhancements through lavender, vanilla, or other calming scents may provide subtle relaxation benefits while creating sensory cues that support bedtime routines and sleep environment optimization.

When to Seek Professional Help

Recognizing when sleep problems require professional evaluation and treatment prevents the development of more serious complications while ensuring access to specialized interventions that self-help approaches alone cannot provide.

Persistent Sleep Problems lasting more than several weeks despite consistent sleep hygiene improvements warrant professional evaluation to rule out underlying sleep disorders, medical conditions, or mental health issues that require specialized treatment approaches.

Daytime Functioning Impact from sleep problems that significantly affects work performance, relationships, safety, or overall quality of life indicates need for professional help regardless of how long sleep problems have persisted.

Mental Health Symptom Connections require integrated treatment when sleep problems occur alongside depression, anxiety, trauma symptoms, or other mental health concerns that may both contribute to and result from sleep disturbances.

Medical Symptom Associations including cardiovascular problems, frequent illness, chronic pain, or other physical health issues that may be related to sleep disorders require medical evaluation to address both sleep and health concerns comprehensively.

Sleep Study Evaluation may be recommended for suspected sleep apnea, restless leg syndrome, or other sleep disorders that require objective measurement and diagnosis through overnight monitoring in specialized sleep laboratories or home testing equipment.

As we conclude this essential exploration of sleep's profound importance, we honor your commitment to understanding one of the most powerful yet undervalued aspects of emotional health and overall well-being. Your willingness to prioritize sleep represents wisdom that serves not only your own healing but your capacity to show up authentically for everyone whose life you touch.

Remember that improving sleep quality is not about perfection but about creating consistent practices and conditions that support your natural capacity for restorative rest while being patient with the process as your sleep patterns gradually improve and stabilize over time.

Your commitment to sleep optimization creates ripple effects that enhance every aspect of your emotional health journey while providing the foundation of energy, clarity, and resilience that makes all other growth and healing work more effective and sustainable.

The journey toward restorative sleep continues with each conscious choice to prioritize rest over productivity pressure, each evening routine that honors your need for transition and preparation, and each recognition that caring for your sleep is not self-indulgence but essential self-care that serves your highest potential.

Through your dedication to sleep wellness, you model for others the revolutionary understanding that rest is productive, that sleep is medicine, and that honoring our natural cycles of activity and restoration represents wisdom rather than weakness in a world that often celebrates exhaustion as achievement.

This is your invitation to unprecedented vitality, emotional stability, and life satisfaction—not through doing more, but through embracing the profound healing that occurs each night when you surrender to sleep's ancient wisdom and allow it to restore you for whatever tomorrow may bring.

Challenge: Track your sleep for 5 days:

- Hours of sleep
- Sleep quality (scale 1–10)
- Mood upon waking
  At the end, **reflect on patterns.** How does your emotional state shift with better (or worse) sleep?

Goal: Build awareness of the connection between sleep and emotional resilience.

Chapter 21: The Transformative Power of Exercise and Movement

The profound alchemy that occurs when you set your body in motion with intention and purpose. Here, we venture into sacred territory where ancient wisdom meets modern science, where the simple act of moving your body becomes a gateway to emotional liberation, mental clarity, and the kind of vibrant vitality that transforms not just how you feel, but who you become in the world.

This exploration invites you to rediscover movement not as another item on your endless to-do list, but as a fundamental expression of your aliveness—a conversation between your deepest self and the physical vessel that carries you through this remarkable journey of being human. Within these pages, you'll uncover how exercise and movement become not mere physical activities, but profound practices of self-care that honor both your body's need for vitality and your soul's hunger for authentic expression.

In our increasingly sedentary world, choosing to move your body is not vanity or obligation, but a revolutionary act of self-love that ripples through every dimension of your emotional, mental, and spiritual well-being. You are stepping into an understanding that honors both the complexity of modern life and the simple yet transformative truth that your body is designed to move, and in that movement lies extraordinary healing.

Why Movement Matters: The Foundation of Holistic Well-Being

Movement represents far more than a means to physical fitness or weight management—it embodies a sophisticated orchestration of biological, psychological, and spiritual processes that serve as the cornerstone for emotional regulation, mental clarity, and the resilient vitality that enables you to navigate life's challenges with grace and authentic strength.

The Neuroscience of Movement and Mood

Modern brain research reveals that physical activity creates specific neurological changes that enhance emotional well-being, cognitive function, and stress resilience in ways that no other intervention can match, providing both immediate mood benefits and long-term protection against mental health challenges.

Endorphin Release and Natural Euphoria occur through sustained physical activity that triggers your body's production of these natural opioids, creating the phenomenon often called "runner's high" but available through any form of movement that elevates your heart rate and engages large muscle groups for extended periods.

These endorphins provide natural pain relief while creating feelings of euphoria and well-being that can last for hours after exercise completion, offering a healthy and accessible alternative to external substances or activities that might provide temporary mood elevation but lack exercise's comprehensive benefits.

BDNF (Brain-Derived Neurotrophic Factor) Production increases dramatically through regular exercise, supporting the growth of new neurons and strengthening existing neural connections while protecting against age-related cognitive decline and enhancing learning, memory, and emotional regulation capacity.

This "miracle grow for the brain" proves particularly beneficial for men dealing with depression, anxiety, or trauma, as BDNF supports the brain's ability to adapt, heal, and develop new patterns of thinking and responding that support emotional health and resilience.

Neurotransmitter Balance Optimization occurs through exercise's influence on serotonin, dopamine, and norepinephrine—the brain chemicals that regulate mood, motivation, and attention while providing natural antidepressant effects that often prove as effective as medication for mild to moderate depression and anxiety.

Stress Hormone Regulation improves significantly through regular physical activity that helps metabolize cortisol and adrenaline while teaching your nervous system to activate and recover from stress responses more efficiently, building the kind of stress resilience that protects against burnout and chronic overwhelm.

Neuroplasticity Enhancement through movement supports your brain's capacity for change and adaptation throughout your lifetime, enabling healing from trauma, development of new skills and perspectives, and the kind of mental flexibility that supports continued growth and emotional intelligence.

Physical Health Benefits That Support Emotional Well-Being

The physical health improvements that result from regular movement create a foundation of vitality and bodily confidence that profoundly affects emotional state, self-esteem, and your capacity for engaging fully with life's opportunities and challenges.

Cardiovascular Health Enhancement through aerobic exercise strengthens your heart while improving circulation, blood pressure, and overall cardiovascular fitness that provides the physical energy and endurance necessary for sustained emotional resilience and active engagement with life's demands.

Immune System Strengthening occurs through moderate exercise that boosts your body's ability to fight infections and illnesses while reducing chronic inflammation that contributes to depression, anxiety, and various physical health problems that can affect emotional well-being.

Sleep Quality Improvement results from physical activity's influence on circadian rhythms, stress hormone regulation, and the natural fatigue that promotes deep, restorative sleep essential for emotional regulation and mental clarity during waking hours.

Bone and Muscle Strength Development provides the physical foundation for confidence and capability while preventing the weakness and frailty that can contribute to anxiety about physical limitations or concerns about aging and mortality.

Energy and Vitality Enhancement emerge paradoxically through expending energy in physical activity, as regular exercise improves mitochondrial function and overall metabolic efficiency, providing more sustained energy for daily activities and emotional resilience during challenging periods.

Emotional and Psychological Benefits

Perhaps most relevant to your emotional health journey, exercise provides direct psychological benefits that address the root causes of many mental health challenges while building the emotional resources necessary for authentic relationships and meaningful life engagement.

Anxiety Reduction and Stress Relief occur through movement's ability to discharge the physical energy that anxiety creates while providing healthy outlets for tension and worry that might otherwise accumulate and interfere with daily functioning and emotional well-being.

Physical activity interrupts the rumination and worry cycles that characterize anxiety while providing concrete evidence of your capability and strength that builds confidence in your ability to handle life's challenges effectively.

Depression Prevention and Treatment through exercise rival the effectiveness of antidepressant medications for many individuals, providing natural mood elevation while addressing the fatigue, hopelessness, and inactivity that often characterize depressive episodes.

Self-Esteem and Confidence Building develop naturally through exercise achievements, physical improvements, and the sense of accomplishment that comes from setting and reaching fitness goals while building trust in your body's capabilities and resilience.

Emotional Regulation Enhancement emerges through exercise's influence on brain chemistry and stress response systems while providing healthy outlets for difficult emotions like anger, frustration, or sadness that might otherwise be suppressed or expressed destructively.

Body Image and Self-Acceptance Improvement occur not primarily through appearance changes but through developing appreciation for your body's strength, capability, and resilience while building the kind of embodied confidence that affects every aspect of self-regard and authentic expression.

Social and Relational Benefits

Movement and exercise often provide opportunities for social connection and community building that support emotional health through relationship development while offering contexts for shared goals and mutual encouragement that enhance overall life satisfaction.

Community and Belonging develop through group fitness activities, sports participation, or shared outdoor adventures that create bonds with others who value health and vitality while providing social support and accountability for maintaining active lifestyles.

Leadership and Team Building skills often emerge through sports, group fitness, or athletic challenges that require cooperation, communication, and mutual support while building confidence in your ability to contribute to collective goals and achievements.

Modeling and Inspiration for family members, friends, and colleagues occur when your commitment to physical activity demonstrates the possibility and benefits of active living while potentially influencing others to prioritize their own health and well-being.

Relationship Enhancement through shared physical activities with partners, friends, or family members creates opportunities for connection and mutual support while building memories and experiences that strengthen bonds and provide ongoing sources of satisfaction and meaning.

Spiritual and Existential Dimensions

Movement can serve as a form of moving meditation and spiritual practice that connects you with your body's wisdom while providing pathways to transcendent experiences and deeper understanding of your place in the larger web of life.

Mind-Body Connection Deepening occurs through conscious movement that builds awareness of physical sensations, internal rhythms, and the intimate relationship between mental states and physical experience while fostering the kind of embodied presence that supports overall well-being.

Present-Moment Awareness develops naturally through physical activity that requires attention to breathing, form, and immediate physical experience while interrupting the mental preoccupation with past regrets or future worries that characterize much mental suffering.

Flow States and Peak Experiences emerge through challenging physical activities that require complete attention and skill integration, creating the kind of transcendent experiences that provide meaning, inspiration, and connection to something larger than everyday concerns and limitations.

Nature Connection and Environmental Awareness through outdoor activities build appreciation for the natural world while providing the grounding and perspective that come from recognizing your place within larger ecological systems that support all life.

Purpose and Meaning Enhancement often develop through physical challenges and achievements that demonstrate your capacity for growth and accomplishment while providing goals and activities that contribute to sense of purpose and life direction.

Overcoming Barriers to Movement: Navigating the Obstacles

The path toward establishing a sustainable movement practice often encounters significant obstacles that can derail your progress or prevent you from beginning altogether. Understanding these common barriers and developing strategies for addressing them empowers you to create realistic, sustainable approaches to physical activity that honor both your limitations and your potential for growth.

Time Constraints and Scheduling Challenges

Perhaps the most universal barrier to regular exercise involves the perception that movement requires large blocks of time that compete with work responsibilities, family obligations, and other pressing demands of contemporary life.

Time Perception Shifts help you recognize that exercise doesn't require hours of daily commitment, as research demonstrates that even brief periods of physical activity—as little as 10-15 minutes—provide measurable health benefits while longer sessions can be scheduled less frequently to accommodate busy periods.

Integration Strategies involve weaving movement into existing activities rather than adding exercise as separate obligations. This might include taking walking meetings, using stairs instead of elevators, parking farther from destinations, or incorporating stretching and movement breaks into work routines.

Efficiency Focus through high-intensity interval training (HIIT) or compound exercises that work multiple muscle groups simultaneously can provide comprehensive fitness benefits in 15–30 minutes, making effective exercise accessible even during the busiest periods of your life.

Priority Assessment helps distinguish between legitimate time limitations and habits or commitments that might be adjusted to accommodate the physical activity that supports your overall effectiveness and well-being in all other areas of life.

Morning Movement practices take advantage of the time before daily obligations begin while building energy and mood benefits that enhance your capacity for handling subsequent challenges and responsibilities throughout the day.

Motivation and Consistency Struggles

Maintaining regular physical activity requires ongoing motivation that can fluctuate with mood, energy levels, and life circumstances, making consistency one of the most challenging aspects of establishing sustainable movement practices.

Intrinsic Motivation Development involves connecting exercise with personally meaningful goals and values rather than external pressures or expectations, focusing on how movement makes you feel rather than primarily on appearance changes or performance metrics that may provide less sustainable motivation.

Start Small Philosophy prevents overwhelm and builds momentum through achievable goals that create success experiences rather than attempting dramatic lifestyle changes that may prove unsustainable and lead to discouragement and abandonment of exercise altogether.

Habit Stacking connects new movement practices with existing routines, such as exercising immediately after morning coffee or taking evening walks after dinner, using established habits as cues for physical activity that gradually becomes automatic rather than requiring constant decision-making.

Accountability Systems through workout partners, fitness tracking, or commitment to others provide external support for consistency while recognizing that sustainable motivation ultimately must come from internal recognition of exercise benefits rather than external pressure or expectation.

Flexible Approaches accommodate varying energy levels, schedules, and circumstances through multiple exercise options that can be adapted to different situations rather than rigid routines that may be abandoned when perfect conditions aren't available.

Physical Limitations and Health Concerns

Many men avoid exercise due to current physical limitations, past injuries, or health conditions that seem to make physical activity impossible or dangerous, often creating cycles where inactivity contributes to continued weakness and health problems.

Medical Consultation and Clearance provide essential foundation for safe exercise when health concerns exist, ensuring that physical activity plans align with medical recommendations while identifying appropriate modifications and precautions that enable safe participation.

Adaptive Exercise Approaches recognize that movement can be modified to accommodate virtually any physical limitation while still providing significant health benefits, from chair exercises for mobility limitations to gentle swimming for joint problems or walking programs for cardiovascular concerns.

Progressive Development involves starting with current capacity rather than pre-injury or ideal fitness levels, building strength and capability gradually while respecting healing processes and avoiding the re-injury or setbacks that can result from attempting too much too quickly.

Pain vs. Discomfort Distinction helps navigate the difference between harmful pain that signals potential injury and the normal discomfort of muscle fatigue or cardiovascular challenge that accompanies beneficial exercise, building confidence in your ability to exercise safely.

Professional Guidance through physical therapists, exercise physiologists, or fitness professionals with experience in adaptive exercise provides expertise for creating safe, effective programs that address specific limitations while supporting overall health and fitness goals.

Psychological and Emotional Barriers

Internal obstacles like fear, shame, perfectionism, or past negative experiences with exercise can create powerful resistance to physical activity that requires compassionate attention and gradual healing rather than forcing yourself through psychological barriers.

Body Image and Gym Anxiety affect many men who feel self-conscious about their current fitness level, appearance, or exercise competence while comparing themselves to others who seem more fit or experienced, creating avoidance of public exercise venues or activities.

Perfectionism and All-or-Nothing Thinking create patterns where exercise must be perfect, comprehensive, or maintained consistently, or it's viewed as failure, preventing the realistic, flexible approach that sustainable fitness requires while creating shame and discouragement during inevitable lapses.

Past Negative Experiences with exercise, sports, or physical education may create lasting associations between movement and failure, embarrassment, or physical discomfort that require gentle healing and positive experiences to overcome gradually.

Fear of Injury or Physical Harm can be realistic concerns that require appropriate precautions or may be anxiety-based worries that exceed actual risk levels, requiring education about safe exercise practices and gradual exposure to build confidence in your body's capabilities.

Identity and Masculine Concerns might involve worry that certain types of exercise don't align with masculine identity or concerns about appearing weak or incompetent while learning new movement skills or building fitness from low starting points.

Practical and Environmental Obstacles

External barriers like cost, access to facilities, weather, or equipment limitations can significantly affect your ability to maintain regular physical activity while requiring creative problem-solving and resourcefulness to overcome effectively.

Cost and Financial Concerns often prevent gym memberships or expensive equipment purchases while overlooking the many effective, no-cost exercise options including walking, running, bodyweight exercises, and outdoor activities that provide comprehensive fitness benefits without financial investment.

Equipment and Space Limitations in small living spaces or without access to traditional exercise equipment can be addressed through body weight exercises, resistance bands, or creative use of household items while recognizing that effective exercise requires minimal equipment when approached thoughtfully.

Weather and Seasonal Challenges require backup plans for maintaining activity during periods when preferred outdoor activities aren't possible, including indoor alternatives, weather-appropriate gear, or seasonal activity adjustments that maintain consistency despite changing conditions.

Travel and Schedule Disruptions challenge routine maintenance but can be accommodated through portable exercise options, hotel room workouts, or local activity exploration that maintains movement habits while adapting to changing circumstances and environments.

Safety and Neighborhood Concerns about exercising outdoors in certain areas require realistic assessment and appropriate alternatives, including indoor options, safer locations, or group activities that provide security while maintaining access to physical activity.

Practical Ways to Incorporate Movement: Your Sustainable Action Plan

Creating a lasting relationship with movement requires practical strategies that integrate seamlessly with your existing lifestyle while honoring your individual preferences, limitations, and goals. These actionable approaches provide flexible frameworks for building consistent physical activity that enhances rather than complicates your daily life.

Starting Simple: Foundation Movement Practices

Building a sustainable movement practice begins with accessible activities that require minimal time, equipment, or experience while providing immediate benefits that motivate continued participation and gradual expansion of your physical activity repertoire.

Walking as Medicine represents perhaps the most accessible and beneficial form of exercise, requiring no equipment or special skills while providing cardiovascular benefits, mood enhancement, and opportunities for mindfulness, social connection, or solitary reflection depending on your preferences and needs.

Begin with 10-15 minute daily walks, focusing on consistency rather than intensity while gradually increasing duration or pace as your fitness improves and walking becomes a cherished part of your routine rather than another obligation to manage.

Bodyweight Exercise Foundations provide comprehensive strength training using your body's own resistance through exercises like push-ups, squats, lunges, and planks that can be performed anywhere while being easily modified for different fitness levels and physical limitations.

Start with basic versions of each exercise, performing as many repetitions as possible with proper form while focusing on gradual improvement rather than comparing yourself to others or attempting advanced variations before mastering fundamental movements.

Stretching and Flexibility Routines address the muscle tension and reduced mobility that often accompany sedentary lifestyles while providing gentle introduction to physical activity for those who find vigorous exercise overwhelming or intimidating initially.

Breathing and Movement Integration through simple practices like conscious breathing during walking or gentle stretching helps develop the mind-body awareness that enhances all forms of physical activity while providing immediate stress relief and emotional regulation benefits.

Daily Movement Integration involves finding opportunities to move within your existing routine—taking stairs, parking farther away, doing household chores with energy and intention, or having walking conversations—rather than viewing exercise as separate from daily life.

Creating Sustainable Routines

Establishing consistent movement patterns requires developing routines that fit naturally within your lifestyle while providing enough structure to maintain regularity without becoming rigid obligations that create guilt or stress when circumstances require flexibility.

Time-Based Approaches help you identify the most realistic and consistent times for physical activity within your schedule, whether morning movement to start your day with energy, lunch break activities that provide midday renewal, or evening exercise that helps transition from work to personal time.

Habit Linking connects new movement practices with established routines, using existing habits as cues for physical activity while building automatic patterns that require less conscious decision-making and willpower to maintain over time.

Weekly Planning Strategies involve scheduling specific movement activities just as you would important appointments, while maintaining flexibility to adjust plans based on energy levels, weather, or other circumstances that might affect your preferred activities.

Progressive Development Plans build gradually from your current fitness level toward more challenging goals, preventing the overwhelm and injury risk that can result from attempting dramatic increases in activity while maintaining motivation through achievable milestones and consistent improvement.

Seasonal and Cyclical Approaches acknowledge that your activity preferences and capacity may vary throughout the year, allowing for seasonal sports, weather-appropriate activities, and natural fluctuations in energy and motivation that require program adjustments rather than rigid consistency.

Creative Movement Solutions

Expanding beyond traditional exercise approaches opens possibilities for physical activities that feel more like play or creative expression while providing comprehensive fitness benefits and addressing the boredom that can develop with repetitive exercise routines.

Dance and Rhythmic Movement provide cardiovascular benefits while engaging creativity and self-expression through various styles from formal dance classes to free movement in your living room, offering both physical and emotional benefits through embodied creative expression.

Outdoor Adventure Activities like hiking, cycling, rock climbing, or water sports combine fitness benefits with nature exposure and adventure satisfaction while providing goals and experiences that extend beyond mere physical improvement to include skill development and exploration.

Sports and Recreational Games offer social interaction and competitive enjoyment while providing comprehensive physical activity through basketball, tennis, golf, martial arts, or recreational leagues that combine fitness with community and goal-oriented achievement.

Functional Movement Practices focus on movements that enhance daily life activities through exercises that improve balance, coordination, strength, and flexibility for tasks like lifting, carrying, climbing, or maintaining good posture during sedentary work.

Mind-Body Practices including yoga, tai chi, or Qigong integrate physical movement with mental focus and spiritual awareness while providing comprehensive benefits for strength, flexibility, balance, and stress reduction through ancient movement traditions.

Technology and Tracking Integration

Modern technology offers valuable tools for supporting movement consistency while providing motivation and information that can enhance your exercise experience and help maintain long-term commitment to physical activity.

Fitness Apps and Programs provide structured workouts, progress tracking, and instructional guidance for home exercise while offering variety and progression that can prevent boredom and ensure continued challenge as your fitness improves over time.

Wearable Device Benefits through step counters, heart rate monitors, or comprehensive fitness trackers provide immediate feedback about your activity levels while gamifying movement through goals, achievements, and progress visualization that can enhance motivation.

Online Communities and Support through fitness apps, social media groups, or virtual challenges provide accountability and encouragement while connecting you with others who share similar health goals and can offer support, advice, and inspiration.

Virtual Classes and Instruction make professional fitness guidance accessible regardless of location or schedule while providing variety and expert instruction for activities you might not have access to locally or feel comfortable trying in person initially.

Progress Documentation through photos, measurements, performance metrics, or journal entries helps you recognize improvements that might not be immediately obvious while providing motivation during periods when progress feels slow or inconsistent.

Overcoming Plateaus and Maintaining Interest

Long-term success with physical activity requires strategies for navigating the inevitable periods when progress slows, motivation wanes, or activities begin to feel routine rather than engaging and beneficial.

Variety and Cross-Training prevent boredom and overuse injuries while ensuring comprehensive fitness development through different types of activities that challenge your body in various ways while maintaining interest through novelty and skill development.

Goal Setting and Achievement provide direction and motivation through short-term objectives that lead toward longer-term aspirations while celebrating accomplishments and using success experiences to fuel continued commitment and effort.

Social Integration and Accountability through workout partners, group activities, or fitness communities provide external motivation and support while making exercise more enjoyable through shared experiences and mutual encouragement during challenging periods.

Professional Guidance and Instruction through personal trainers, group fitness instructors, or specialized coaches can provide expertise for breaking through plateaus while ensuring safe progression and introducing new challenges that reignite enthusiasm for physical activity.

Mindset and Perspective Shifts help maintain long-term commitment by focusing on how exercise makes you feel rather than just appearance changes while viewing physical activity as self-care and investment in overall life quality rather than punishment or obligation.

As we conclude this exploration of movement's transformative power, we celebrate your courage to consider physical activity not as another burden in an already full life, but as a profound gift you give yourself—one that ripples through every aspect of your emotional, mental, and spiritual well-being.

Remember that beginning or returning to movement is not about perfection or dramatic transformation, but about honoring your body's need for activity while building the kind of relationship with physical exercise that supports your overall healing and growth throughout your lifetime.

Your willingness to embrace movement as medicine contributes to a cultural shift that recognizes physical activity as essential self-care rather than vanity or luxury while modeling for others the wisdom of investing in the body that carries you through this precious life experience.

The journey of embodied vitality continues with each conscious step you take, each moment you choose movement over sedentary comfort, and each decision to honor your body's design for activity and strength. These choices accumulate into profound transformation that affects not only your physical health but your capacity for emotional resilience, mental clarity, and authentic engagement with life's opportunities.

Through your commitment to movement, you participate in reclaiming the birthright of physical vitality while demonstrating that caring for your body is not selfish but essential—a foundation that supports your ability to show up fully for yourself, your relationships, and your meaningful contribution to the world.

This is your invitation to unprecedented energy, confidence, and joy—not through complex fitness regimens or extreme challenges, but through the simple revolutionary act of moving your body with intention, respect, and appreciation for the magnificent vessel that enables every experience of beauty, connection, and purpose that makes life worth living.

Challenge: Move intentionally every day for 7 days. This could include:

- A 20-minute walk
- Stretching or yoga
- Strength training
- Dancing or active play with kids

Goal: Use movement as an emotional outlet, not just physical fitness.

Chapter 22: The Role of Nutrition in Emotional Health

We begin an exploration that invites you to one of the most intimate and transformative relationships in your life—the profound connection between what you choose to nourish your body with and the emotional landscape that unfolds within your mind and heart each day. Here, we venture into sacred territory where ancient wisdom meets cutting-edge science, where the simple act of choosing wholesome foods becomes a powerful declaration of self-care that reverberates through every dimension of your emotional well-being.

Rediscover nutrition not as a collection of rules and restrictions, but as a compassionate conversation between your body's deepest needs and your conscious choices to honor the remarkable vessel that carries you through this precious human experience. As you explore these pages, you'll uncover how the foods that grace your plate become the building blocks not only of physical vitality but of emotional resilience, mental clarity, and the stable foundation upon which authentic happiness can flourish.

The recognition that in our world of convenience foods and dietary confusion, understanding the relationship between nutrition and emotional health emerges not as another burden to bear, but as one of the most empowering tools available for creating lasting change from the inside out. You are stepping into knowledge that honors both the complexity of nutritional science and the beautifully simple truth that how you feed your body directly influences how you experience life itself.

Why Nutrition Matters: The Foundation of Emotional Vitality

The relationship between nutrition and emotional health extends far beyond the temporary mood changes we might notice after eating certain foods—it encompasses a sophisticated network of biochemical processes that literally construct the neural pathways, neurotransmitter systems, and cellular structures that determine your capacity for joy, resilience, and emotional balance throughout each day of your life.

The Neuroscience of Nutritional Mood

Modern research reveals that your brain, despite representing only 2% of your body weight, consumes approximately 20% of your daily caloric intake while requiring specific nutrients to manufacture the chemical messengers that regulate every aspect of your emotional experience. Understanding this relationship transforms nutrition from dietary preference into essential medicine for mental health.

Neurotransmitter Production depends entirely on the raw materials you provide through food choices, with serotonin—your primary mood-regulating neurotransmitter—being synthesized from the amino acid tryptophan found in protein-rich foods, while requiring adequate B vitamins, magnesium, and zinc as cofactors for optimal production and function.

Nearly 90% of your body's serotonin is actually produced in your digestive system, creating a direct pathway between the foods you consume and your capacity for emotional stability, happiness, and overall psychological well-being. This gut-brain axis represents one of the most important discoveries in modern neuroscience.

Dopamine and Motivation Chemistry emerges from the amino acid tyrosine found in fish, eggs, cheese, and nuts, working in concert with iron, folate, and vitamin B6 to create the neurotransmitter responsible for motivation, pleasure, and the drive to pursue meaningful goals and experiences that provide life satisfaction.

GABA Production for Calm and Relaxation relies on adequate intake of complex carbohydrates and specific amino acids that support your brain's primary inhibitory neurotransmitter, helping to counter anxiety and create the inner peace that allows for authentic self-expression and genuine connection with others.

Blood Sugar and Emotional Stability

Perhaps no aspect of nutrition affects emotional health more immediately than blood sugar regulation, as your brain's primary fuel source directly influences mood stability, anxiety levels, and your capacity to handle stress and interpersonal challenges with grace and wisdom.

Glucose Stability and Mood Regulation create the foundation for emotional balance, as dramatic fluctuations in blood sugar levels trigger stress hormone release while creating the irritability, anxiety, and depression-like symptoms that many men attribute to personality traits rather than recognizing as nutritional influences that can be addressed through dietary choices.

Insulin Sensitivity and Mental Clarity affect not only physical health but cognitive function and emotional regulation, as insulin resistance—often resulting from excessive sugar and refined carbohydrate consumption—impairs brain function while contributing to the brain fog and emotional instability that can affect relationships and professional performance.

Stress Response Amplification occurs when blood sugar instability triggers cortisol and adrenaline release, creating cycles where nutritional choices increase stress sensitivity while stress hormones further disrupt blood sugar regulation, creating compound effects on emotional well-being that require dietary intervention to resolve.

Energy and Vitality Patterns throughout your day reflect blood sugar stability, with steady energy levels supporting emotional resilience while energy crashes create vulnerability to negative emotions, conflict, and the poor decision-making that can damage relationships and undermine personal goals and values.

Inflammation and Mental Health

The connection between dietary choices and inflammation throughout your body extends directly to brain health, with chronic inflammation now recognized as a major contributor to depression, anxiety, and other mental health challenges that affect millions of men worldwide.

Neuroinflammation and Depression show strong correlations in research, with inflammatory markers often elevated in individuals experiencing depression while anti-inflammatory dietary patterns demonstrate significant protective effects against depressive episodes and support recovery from existing mental health challenges.

Inflammatory Foods and Emotional Reactivity include processed foods, excessive sugar, trans fats, and highly refined products that trigger inflammatory responses while contributing to the emotional volatility, irritability, and reduced stress tolerance that can strain relationships and undermine emotional intelligence.

Anti-Inflammatory Protection emerges through consumption of omega-3 fatty acids, colorful fruits and vegetables, herbs and spices, and whole foods that actively reduce inflammation while supporting the brain health necessary for optimal emotional regulation and mental clarity.

Gut Health and Emotional Well-Being

The emerging field of nutritional psychiatry reveals your digestive system as a "second brain" that produces more neurotransmitters than your actual brain while hosting trillions of bacteria that directly influence mood, anxiety, and overall mental health through complex biochemical communication pathways.

Microbiome Diversity and Mental Health demonstrate clear connections, with greater bacterial diversity in your gut correlating with better emotional resilience, reduced anxiety, and improved stress management capacity while poor gut health contributes to depression and emotional instability through multiple biological pathways.

Probiotic Foods and Mood Enhancement through fermented foods like yogurt, kefir, sauerkraut, and kimchi provide beneficial bacteria that support both digestive health and emotional well-being while reducing inflammation and improving the production of mood-regulating neurotransmitters.

Prebiotic Fiber and Emotional Stability from fruits, vegetables, and whole grains feed beneficial gut bacteria while supporting the production of short-chain fatty acids that reduce inflammation and support brain health, creating sustainable improvements in emotional regulation and mental clarity.

Specific Nutrients and Emotional Function

Understanding how individual nutrients affect emotional health empowers you to make informed choices about supplementation and food selection while recognizing that optimal mental health requires a comprehensive approach rather than focusing on single nutrients in isolation.

Omega-3 Fatty Acids and Brain Health provide essential building blocks for brain cell membranes while reducing inflammation and supporting the neurotransmitter function necessary for emotional stability, with research showing significant benefits for depression, anxiety, and overall cognitive function.

B Vitamin Complex and Energy Production at the cellular level supports both physical energy and mental clarity while playing crucial roles in neurotransmitter synthesis, with deficiencies in B vitamins often manifesting as depression, anxiety, fatigue, and cognitive difficulties that improve with appropriate supplementation.

Magnesium and Stress Response regulation helps calm the nervous system while supporting healthy sleep patterns and reducing the physical tension that often accompanies emotional stress, with magnesium deficiency contributing to anxiety, depression, and poor stress tolerance in many individuals.

Vitamin D and Seasonal Mental Health affects mood regulation and overall mental well-being, with deficiencies contributing to seasonal depression and general mood disorders while adequate levels support emotional resilience and cognitive function throughout all seasons.

Zinc and Cognitive Function supports both immune system health and neurological function, with zinc deficiency contributing to depression and anxiety while adequate intake supports emotional regulation and stress resilience through multiple biological pathways.

Common Nutritional Pitfalls: Recognizing the Saboteurs

Despite good intentions and growing awareness of nutrition's importance, many men unknowingly engage in dietary patterns that undermine their emotional health and create unnecessary obstacles to mental well-being. Understanding these common pitfalls empowers you to make conscious changes that support rather than sabotage your emotional healing and growth.

The Sugar Trap: Blood Sugar Rollercoaster

Perhaps no dietary pattern creates more havoc with emotional stability than the consumption of excessive refined sugars and processed carbohydrates that trigger dramatic blood sugar fluctuations throughout the day, creating cycles of energy crashes and mood instability that affect every aspect of life.

Hidden Sugar Sources extend far beyond obvious sweets to include breakfast cereals, flavored yogurts, salad dressings, pasta sauces, and countless processed foods that contain surprising amounts of added sugars, often consuming 2–3 times the recommended daily intake without conscious awareness.

Addiction-Like Patterns develop around sugar consumption as it triggers dopamine release in brain reward centers while creating tolerance that requires increasing amounts to achieve the same satisfaction, leading to cycles of craving, consumption, temporary satisfaction, and inevitable crashes that affect mood and decision-making.

Energy and Mood Crashes following sugar consumption create vulnerability to irritability, anxiety, depression-like symptoms, and poor stress tolerance while triggering cravings for more sugar or caffeine to restore energy levels, perpetuating cycles that undermine emotional stability.

Sleep Disruption Patterns result from blood sugar fluctuations that can cause middle-of-the-night awakenings as your body releases stress hormones to stabilize glucose levels, disrupting the restorative sleep necessary for emotional regulation and stress resilience.

Relationship and Performance Impact emerges as sugar-induced mood swings affect your interactions with others while energy crashes reduce productivity and the sustained attention necessary for meaningful work and authentic connection with family and friends.

Processed Food Dependency

The convenience of processed and packaged foods often comes at a significant cost to emotional health, as these products typically contain additives, preservatives, and artificial ingredients while lacking the nutrients necessary for optimal brain function and emotional regulation.

Nutrient Depletion Consequences occur when processed foods replace whole foods in your diet, creating deficiencies in essential vitamins, minerals, and phytonutrients while providing empty calories that contribute to weight gain without supporting the nutritional needs that emotional health requires.

Chemical Additives and Brain Function include artificial colors, flavors, preservatives, and other synthetic compounds that can affect neurotransmitter function while contributing to hyperactivity, mood swings, and cognitive difficulties in sensitive individuals.

Inflammatory Ingredients common in processed foods include trans fats, high amounts of omega-6 oils, artificial sweeteners, and various chemical additives that promote inflammation throughout your body while contributing to the neuroinflammation associated with depression and anxiety.

Convenience Trap Psychology develops when busy lifestyles make processed foods seem like the only viable option, creating dependency patterns that make whole food preparation feel overwhelming or impossible despite the significant benefits for emotional and physical health.

Caffeine and Stimulant Overuse

While moderate caffeine consumption can provide benefits, many men rely on excessive amounts of coffee, energy drinks, or other stimulants to manage fatigue and low energy that may actually result from nutritional deficiencies or poor sleep patterns that caffeine ultimately worsens.

Anxiety and Jitters Amplification occurs as excessive caffeine stimulates your nervous system while potentially triggering panic attacks or heightened anxiety in susceptible individuals, creating cycles where caffeine use to combat fatigue actually increases the anxiety and stress that further disrupt sleep and energy levels.

Sleep Disruption Cycles develop when caffeine consumed later in the day interferes with sleep quality and duration while creating dependence on morning caffeine to compensate for poor sleep, perpetuating patterns that undermine the natural energy and emotional stability that quality sleep provides.

Adrenal Stress and Burnout can result from chronic stimulant use that pushes your stress response systems beyond their healthy capacity while masking underlying fatigue and nutritional needs that require rest and proper nutrition rather than continued stimulation.

Withdrawal and Dependency Issues create additional emotional challenges when regular caffeine users attempt to reduce consumption, experiencing headaches, irritability, and depression-like symptoms that make dietary changes feel more difficult than necessary.

Alcohol and Emotional Self-Medication

Many men use alcohol as a way to manage stress, anxiety, or depression, not realizing that while alcohol may provide temporary relief, it ultimately worsens emotional health while interfering with sleep, nutrition absorption, and the healthy coping mechanisms that sustainable emotional well-being requires.

Depression and Anxiety Amplification occur through alcohol's effects on neurotransmitter systems, as it initially increases GABA activity to create relaxation but then causes rebound anxiety and depression as alcohol leaves your system, often creating worse emotional states than existed before drinking.

Sleep Quality Deterioration results from alcohol's interference with REM sleep and deep sleep stages, creating fatigue and emotional instability the following day while disrupting the sleep patterns necessary for emotional regulation and stress resilience.

Nutritional Depletion Effects include alcohol's interference with vitamin and mineral absorption while depleting B vitamins, magnesium, and other nutrients essential for brain health, creating deficiencies that contribute to depression, anxiety, and cognitive difficulties.

Coping Mechanism Displacement occurs when alcohol becomes the primary strategy for managing difficult emotions, preventing the development of healthy coping skills like exercise, meditation, social support, or professional help that provide lasting emotional resilience.

Extreme Dieting and Restriction

Restrictive eating patterns, whether motivated by weight loss goals or health concerns, can create nutritional deficiencies and psychological stress that significantly impact emotional well-being while often leading to unsustainable cycles of restriction and overeating.

Nutrient Deficiency Consequences for overly restrictive diets can create deficiencies in essential fatty acids, vitamins, minerals, and amino acids necessary for neurotransmitter production while contributing to depression, anxiety, irritability, and cognitive difficulties.

Metabolic Stress Response triggered by extreme calorie restriction activates your body's stress response systems while increasing cortisol production, which can contribute to anxiety, depression, and the difficulty losing weight that makes restrictive dieting counterproductive.

Social and Relationship Impact emerges when rigid dietary rules interfere with social eating, family meals, and the flexibility necessary for maintaining relationships while creating stress and isolation that affect emotional well-being and social connection.

Psychological Restriction Backlash often leads to episodes of overeating or binge-eating that create guilt, shame, and emotional distress while reinforcing unhealthy relationships with food that may require professional support to resolve effectively.

Hydration Neglect and Its Emotional Consequences

Chronic mild dehydration affects millions of people while contributing to fatigue, headaches, irritability, and cognitive difficulties that are often attributed to other causes rather than recognizing inadequate water intake as a simple yet crucial factor in emotional well-being.

Cognitive Function Impact from dehydration includes difficulty concentrating, memory problems, and reduced mental clarity that affect work performance and decision-making while contributing to the frustration and stress that can strain relationships and professional success.

Mood and Energy Effects of inadequate hydration include increased irritability, fatigue, and reduced stress tolerance while proper hydration supports energy levels and emotional stability throughout the day.

Hunger and Fullness Confusion often occurs when dehydration signals are misinterpreted as hunger, leading to overeating and poor food choices while adequate hydration helps maintain accurate appetite regulation and supports healthy eating patterns.

Practical Strategies for Healthy Eating: Your Nutritional Action Plan

Transforming your relationship with food requires practical strategies that honor both your nutritional needs and the realities of daily life, creating sustainable approaches to healthy eating that support emotional well-being while fitting realistically within your schedule, preferences, and circumstances.

Meal Planning and Preparation Fundamentals

Successful nutrition for emotional health begins with thoughtful planning that ensures consistent access to nourishing foods while preventing the decision fatigue and convenience food reliance that can derail healthy eating intentions during busy or stressful periods.

Weekly Planning Sessions involve dedicating 15-30 minutes each week to plan meals and snacks that provide balanced nutrition while considering your schedule, preferences, and any special circumstances that might affect your eating patterns during the upcoming week.

Create simple meal templates that include a protein source, colorful vegetables, healthy fats, and complex carbohydrates rather than planning elaborate recipes that may prove overwhelming or time-consuming to execute consistently throughout busy weeks.

Batch Cooking Strategies maximize efficiency by preparing larger quantities of staple foods like grains, proteins, and roasted vegetables that can be combined in different ways throughout the week while ensuring healthy options are always readily available without daily cooking requirements.

Emergency Food Planning prevents nutritional derailment during stressful periods by maintaining supplies of healthy convenience foods like nuts, seeds, protein bars, frozen vegetables, and other options that support good nutrition even when time and energy for food preparation are limited.

Shopping List Organization based on planned meals ensures you have necessary ingredients while preventing impulse purchases of processed foods that may undermine your nutritional goals, organizing lists by store sections to maximize efficiency and reduce shopping stress.

Mindful Eating Practices

Developing conscious awareness around eating transforms meals from rushed necessities into opportunities for nourishment and self-care while improving digestion, satisfaction, and your ability to recognize hunger and fullness cues that support healthy weight management.

Present-Moment Eating involves minimizing distractions like television, phones, or work during meals while focusing attention on the tastes, textures, and aromas of your food, creating greater satisfaction from smaller portions while supporting healthy digestion through relaxed eating.

Hunger and Fullness Recognition develops through paying attention to physical signals before, during, and after eating while distinguishing between physical hunger and emotional or habitual eating patterns that may not serve your nutritional needs or emotional well-being.

Gratitude and Appreciation Practices around food acknowledge the sources of your nourishment while creating positive emotional associations with healthy eating that support long-term dietary changes through appreciation rather than restriction or deprivation.

Eating Pace Awareness involves slowing down your eating speed to allow adequate time for digestion and satiety signals while improving nutrient absorption and reducing the overeating that often occurs when meals are consumed rapidly during busy schedules.

Building Balanced Meals and Snacks

Creating meals that support stable energy and mood throughout the day requires understanding how different macronutrients work together while ensuring adequate protein, healthy fats, complex carbohydrates, and micronutrients in appropriate portions.

Protein Prioritization at each meal provides amino acids for neurotransmitter production while supporting stable blood sugar and sustained energy levels, aiming for palm-sized portions of fish, poultry, eggs, legumes, or other high-quality protein sources.

Healthy Fat Integration through avocados, nuts, seeds, olive oil, and fatty fish supports brain health and hormone production while providing satisfaction and stable energy that reduces cravings for processed snacks and supports emotional well-being.

Complex Carbohydrate Selection from vegetables, fruits, whole grains, and legumes provides steady glucose for brain function while avoiding the blood sugar spikes and crashes associated with refined carbohydrates that can affect mood stability throughout the day.

Colorful Vegetable Emphasis ensures adequate micronutrient intake while providing antioxidants and anti-inflammatory compounds that support brain health, aiming to include vegetables of different colors to maximize nutritional diversity and phytonutrient intake.

Portion Awareness using visual cues rather than strict measuring helps create appropriate serving sizes while maintaining flexibility and reducing the obsessive behaviors that can develop around food measurement and calorie counting.

Nutrient Timing and Frequency

Understanding when and how often to eat supports optimal energy levels and mood stability while working with your natural circadian rhythms and daily schedule to maximize the emotional and physical benefits of good nutrition.

Breakfast Optimization provides essential fuel for morning energy and cognitive function while setting the tone for stable blood sugar throughout the day, emphasizing protein and healthy fats to support sustained energy rather than relying on sugar-heavy breakfast foods.

Regular Meal Timing every 3–4 hours prevents extreme hunger that can lead to poor food choices while maintaining steady blood sugar levels that support emotional stability and cognitive function throughout daily activities and responsibilities.

Pre- and Post-Workout Nutrition optimizes exercise benefits while supporting recovery and energy levels, combining carbohydrates for energy with protein for muscle recovery in timing that supports your specific activity patterns and fitness goals.

Evening Eating Guidelines balance the need for adequate nutrition with sleep quality considerations, avoiding heavy meals close to bedtime while ensuring adequate nutrition throughout the day to prevent late-night cravings or hunger that can disrupt sleep.

Supplementation and Special Considerations

While whole foods provide the foundation for optimal nutrition, strategic supplementation can address specific deficiencies or support particular health goals while recognizing that supplements complement rather than replace a healthy dietary foundation.

Essential Supplement Assessment might include vitamin D, omega-3 fatty acids, vitamin B12, and magnesium—nutrients commonly deficient in modern diets while playing crucial roles in emotional health and brain function that may benefit from supplementation under professional guidance.

Individual Needs Recognition acknowledges that optimal nutrition varies based on age, activity level, health conditions, medications, and other individual factors that may require personalized approaches rather than one-size-fits-all recommendations.

Quality and Safety Considerations in supplement selection involve choosing third-party tested products from reputable companies while consulting healthcare providers about potential interactions with medications or existing health conditions.

Whole Foods First Philosophy prioritizes getting nutrients from natural food sources whenever possible while using supplements to address specific gaps rather than relying on pills and powders to replace the complex nutrition that whole foods provide.

Creating Sustainable Lifestyle Changes

Long-term success with nutritional changes requires approaches that honor your preferences, circumstances, and realistic capacity for change while building gradually toward more optimal eating patterns that support emotional well-being without creating additional stress.

Gradual Implementation Strategies introduce one or two changes at a time rather than attempting complete dietary overhauls that may prove overwhelming and unsustainable, allowing new habits to become established before adding additional modifications.

Flexible Approach Development accommodates social events, travel, and life circumstances that may temporarily disrupt optimal eating while maintaining overall healthy patterns without perfectionism or guilt that can undermine long-term success.

Support System Building through family involvement, cooking partners, or professional guidance provides encouragement and accountability while making healthy eating more enjoyable and sustainable through shared commitment and mutual support.

Progress Tracking and Adjustment monitors how dietary changes affect energy, mood, sleep, and overall well-being while making modifications based on results rather than rigid adherence to plans that may not serve your individual needs and circumstances.

As we conclude this nourishing exploration of nutrition's profound role in emotional health, we celebrate your courage to recognize food as medicine and your commitment to honoring your body's needs through conscious nutritional choices that support not just physical health but emotional vitality and mental clarity.

Remember that transforming your relationship with food is not about perfection or rigid adherence to complex rules, but about developing awareness, making conscious choices, and gradually building eating patterns that support your overall well-being while bringing joy and satisfaction to one of life's essential pleasures.

Your willingness to prioritize nutritional health creates ripple effects that enhance every aspect of your emotional healing journey while providing the stable foundation of physical vitality that makes all other growth work more effective and sustainable over time.

The journey of nutritional wellness continues with each conscious food choice, each meal prepared with intention and care, and each recognition that nourishing your body is not obligation but gift—an act of self-love that honors the remarkable vessel that carries you through this precious human experience.

Through your commitment to nutritional awareness, you model for others the wisdom of caring for yourself comprehensively while demonstrating that true strength includes the intelligence to fuel your body in ways that support optimal functioning and authentic well-being.

This is your invitation to unprecedented vitality, emotional stability, and life satisfaction—not through complex dietary rules or expensive supplements, but through the simple revolutionary act of choosing foods that love you back, nourishing every cell and supporting every emotion with the care and wisdom your magnificent body and precious life deserve.

Challenge: For 5 days, track how your meals affect your energy and emotions. Note:

- What you ate
- How you felt physically and emotionally 1 hour later
  At the end, identify patterns and adjust accordingly.

Goal: Link food to emotional wellness, not just physical health.

Chapter 23: The Strength in Setting Healthy Boundaries

In this chapter we beckon you toward one of the most transformative acts of self-respect and emotional wisdom—the sacred art of establishing and maintaining healthy boundaries that honor both your deepest needs and your authentic relationships with others. Here, we venture into territory where courage meets compassion, where saying "no" becomes an act of profound love for yourself and ultimately for those whose lives you touch with your presence and care.

This exploration invites you to rediscover boundaries not as walls that separate you from meaningful connection, but as bridges that create the safety and clarity necessary for authentic intimacy to flourish. Within these pages, you'll uncover how the conscious establishment of personal limits becomes not an act of selfishness or rigidity, but one of the most generous gifts you can offer to yourself and to every relationship that graces your life.

Your willingness to explore these concepts represents an act of profound wisdom—the recognition that in a world that often demands endless availability and limitless giving, choosing to honor your own needs and limits emerges not as weakness or failure, but as the foundation upon which genuine strength and sustainable love are built. You are stepping into an understanding that celebrates both your inherent worth and your responsibility to protect the precious resources of energy, time, and emotional capacity that enable you to show up authentically for what matters most.

Understanding Boundaries: The Architecture of Emotional Safety

Boundaries represent far more than simple rules about what you will and won't accept—they embody the fundamental framework that defines where you end and others begin, creating the psychological safety and emotional clarity necessary for authentic relationships, sustainable well-being, and the kind of self-respect that enables you to contribute your gifts to the world without depleting your essential resources.

The Nature of Healthy Boundaries

At their essence, healthy boundaries function as invisible lines that delineate your personal space, emotional capacity, values, and limits while simultaneously respecting others' right to their own boundaries and choices. These protective parameters serve not to isolate you from meaningful connection, but to create the conditions under which genuine intimacy and mutual respect can flourish naturally.

Personal Space and Physical Boundaries encompass your right to determine who may touch you, how they may touch you, and under what circumstances physical contact feels comfortable and appropriate. These boundaries honor your body's wisdom while recognizing that physical safety forms the foundation for all other forms of emotional and relational well-being.

Physical boundaries extend beyond touch to include your personal environment, possessions, and living space, acknowledging your right to privacy and the importance of having sanctuary spaces where you can restore and rejuvenate without intrusion or unwanted demands on your attention and energy.

Emotional Boundaries and Energy Protection involve recognizing where your emotions end and others' emotions begin, developing the capacity to empathize and care without taking responsibility for others' emotional states or allowing their emotional turbulence to destabilize your own inner equilibrium and well-being.

These boundaries enable you to offer genuine support and compassion while maintaining the emotional clarity necessary for wise decision-making and authentic self-expression that serves both your growth and your capacity to contribute meaningfully to others' lives.

Time and Energy Boundaries acknowledge that your time and energy represent finite resources that require conscious stewardship, giving you permission to prioritize commitments and activities that align with your values and goals while declining demands that would overextend your capacity or compromise your well-being.

Values and Belief Boundaries protect your right to hold and express your own opinions, beliefs, and moral convictions without requiring others to agree while simultaneously respecting others' right to their own perspectives and choices, even when they differ significantly from your own.

The Psychology of Boundary Development

Understanding how boundaries develop throughout your life provides insight into why boundary-setting might feel challenging while recognizing that learning to establish healthy limits represents a natural part of emotional maturation and psychological health.

Childhood Boundary Formation occurs through interactions with caregivers who ideally model appropriate boundaries while respecting your emerging autonomy and teaching you to respect others' limits. When childhood experiences include boundary violations, overly rigid boundaries, or complete absence of limits, adult boundary-setting often requires conscious learning and practice.

Cultural and Social Influences shape your understanding of appropriate boundaries through family traditions, cultural norms, and social expectations that may emphasize individual autonomy or collective harmony, requiring you to develop boundaries that honor both cultural values and personal needs.

Masculine Identity and Boundaries can be complicated by cultural messages about male strength, self-reliance, and emotional control that might discourage boundary-setting seen as weakness while encouraging boundary violations that demonstrate power or control over others.

Healthy masculine identity includes the strength to protect your own well-being while respecting others' autonomy, recognizing that genuine strength involves knowing your limits and honoring them consistently rather than pushing through every challenge regardless of personal cost.

Trauma and Boundary Disruption often results from experiences that violate your physical, emotional, or psychological boundaries, potentially creating confusion about where appropriate limits should be drawn while making boundary-setting feel dangerous or threatening to important relationships.

Types of Boundaries and Their Functions

Different types of boundaries serve various protective and organizational functions in your life, each contributing to overall emotional health while addressing specific aspects of your relationships and daily experience.

Rigid Boundaries involve walls that keep others at significant distance, potentially protecting you from harm but also preventing the vulnerability and openness that authentic intimacy requires. While temporary rigid boundaries might be necessary during healing from trauma or toxic relationships, long-term rigidity can create isolation and loneliness.

Flexible Boundaries adapt to different relationships and circumstances while maintaining core principles about respect and safety, allowing you to be more open with trusted friends while maintaining professional distance with colleagues, or offering more support during others' crises while protecting your energy during your own difficult periods.

Porous Boundaries offer little protection from others' emotions, demands, or intrusions, often resulting in feeling overwhelmed, taken advantage of, or losing sense of your own needs and identity within relationships that become unbalanced and potentially harmful to your well-being.

Professional Boundaries maintain appropriate relationships within work contexts while balancing friendliness and competence with the professional distance necessary for effective collaboration and ethical behavior that protects both you and others from complications that blur professional relationships.

Digital and Social Media Boundaries address the unique challenges of maintaining privacy and emotional well-being in an interconnected world where personal information, opinions, and availability can be constantly accessible to others without your conscious consent or control.

The Connection Between Boundaries and Self-Worth

Perhaps most fundamentally, your ability to establish and maintain healthy boundaries reflects and reinforces your sense of self-worth, creating cycles where boundary-setting builds self-respect while healthy self-regard makes boundary maintenance feel natural and necessary rather than selfish or difficult.

Self-Respect and Boundary Courage develop together as you recognize that protecting your well-being serves not only your own interests but also your capacity to contribute authentically to others' lives without resentment or depletion that ultimately harms all your relationships.

Identity Clarity and Limit Setting emerge through understanding your values, needs, and goals, providing the foundation for boundary decisions that align with your authentic self rather than being driven by guilt, fear, or desire to please others at your own expense.

Worthiness and Saying No often challenge men who have been taught that their value depends on their usefulness to others, requiring the radical recognition that your worth exists independently of your ability to meet others' needs or expectations.

The Benefits of Setting Boundaries: Transforming Life Through Healthy Limits

When you courageously commit to establishing and maintaining healthy boundaries, extraordinary benefits emerge that extend throughout every aspect of your life experience, creating improvements in relationships, stress levels, self-respect, and overall life satisfaction that compound over time to create fundamental shifts in how you experience yourself and your connections with others.

Enhanced Relationship Quality and Authentic Connection

Perhaps counterintuitively, establishing clear boundaries often dramatically improves relationship quality by creating the safety and clarity necessary for genuine intimacy while preventing the resentment and depletion that can poison even well-intentioned connections.

Reduced Resentment and Emotional Clarity emerge when boundaries prevent the accumulation of unexpressed anger and frustration that often builds when you consistently give more than feels sustainable or accept treatment that doesn't align with your values and self-respect.

Clear boundaries help others understand your expectations while preventing the guessing games and misunderstandings that can create conflict and distance in relationships where limits and expectations remain unclear or inconsistently enforced.

Increased Mutual Respect develops naturally when you model self-respect through boundary-setting while demonstrating respect for others' boundaries, creating relationships characterized by equality and consideration rather than patterns of exploitation or emotional manipulation.

Deeper Intimacy Through Safety emerges when boundaries create the psychological security necessary for vulnerability and authentic sharing, as people feel safer being genuine when they trust that their limits will be respected and their well-being protected.

Healthier Communication Patterns develop through the practice of expressing your needs and limits clearly while learning to respect others' expressions of their boundaries, building skills that enhance all forms of interpersonal communication and conflict resolution.

Stress Reduction and Energy Management

Healthy boundaries serve as powerful stress management tools by preventing the overwhelming commitments and energy drains that often characterize lives without clear limits, creating space for the restoration and self-care necessary for sustained well-being.

Overwhelm Prevention occurs when boundaries help you recognize your capacity limits while providing frameworks for making decisions about commitments that honor your energy and time constraints rather than leading to chronic overextension and burnout.

Energy Conservation and Distribution improve dramatically when boundaries protect your physical and emotional resources from unnecessary depletion while ensuring that your energy goes toward activities and relationships that align with your values and provide genuine satisfaction.

Decision-Making Clarity emerges through boundary-based frameworks that simplify choices about how to spend your time and energy, reducing decision fatigue while providing clear criteria for evaluating opportunities and requests that compete for your attention.

Stress Response Regulation improves when boundaries reduce exposure to situations that trigger anxiety or overwhelm while creating predictable environments where your nervous system can maintain equilibrium rather than remaining in chronic states of defensive activation.

Self-Respect and Personal Empowerment

The act of setting and maintaining boundaries builds fundamental self-respect while creating experiences of personal agency and empowerment that enhance confidence and self-efficacy across all areas of your life.

Self-Worth Validation occurs through the repeated experience of honoring your own needs and limits, demonstrating to yourself that your well-being matters while building the internal conviction necessary for continued boundary maintenance even when others resist or challenge your limits.

Personal Agency and Control develop through boundary-setting experiences that prove your ability to influence your life circumstances while creating the sense of empowerment that comes from taking responsibility for your own well-being rather than hoping others will respect limits you haven't clearly established.

Identity Clarity and Authenticity strengthen as boundaries help you discover and express your genuine preferences, values, and needs while reducing the people-pleasing and self-abandonment that can obscure your authentic identity and life direction.

Confidence Building occurs naturally through successful boundary-setting experiences that prove your capability to navigate challenging conversations and maintain your position despite potential pushback or disapproval from others.

Professional Growth and Career Development

Workplace boundaries significantly enhance professional effectiveness while protecting against the burnout and exploitation that can derail career advancement and job satisfaction, creating sustainable approaches to professional excellence.

Workload Management and Productivity improve when clear boundaries prevent the overwhelming commitments that reduce quality and efficiency while ensuring that your professional energy goes toward high-impact activities that advance your career goals and demonstrate your value.

Professional Relationship Quality benefits from boundaries that maintain appropriate distance while enabling effective collaboration, preventing the complications that can arise when professional and personal boundaries become blurred or undefined.

Leadership Development often requires strong boundary-setting skills that enable you to make difficult decisions, delegate appropriately, and maintain the perspective necessary for strategic thinking rather than becoming overwhelmed by operational details or others' emotional reactions.

Career Advancement Opportunities may increase when boundaries demonstrate your professionalism and self-respect while preventing the overcommitment and burnout that can make you appear unreliable or limit your availability for new challenges and responsibilities.

Physical Health and Well-being

The stress reduction and self-care that healthy boundaries enable create significant physical health benefits while protecting against the illness and exhaustion that often result from chronic boundary violations and overextension.

Sleep Quality Enhancement occurs when boundaries create clear separations between work and rest time while protecting your evening and weekend hours from demands that can interfere with the restoration necessary for physical and emotional recovery.

Immune System Support improves through the stress reduction that boundaries provide, as chronic stress from boundary violations suppresses immune function while healthy limits support the relaxation necessary for optimal physical health and healing.

Energy and Vitality Preservation result from boundaries that prevent energy depletion while ensuring adequate time and space for the activities and relationships that restore and rejuvenate your physical and emotional resources.

Pain and Tension Reduction often occur when boundaries reduce the stress and conflict that contribute to physical symptoms like headaches, muscle tension, and digestive problems while creating space for self-care activities that support physical well-being.

Spiritual Growth and Life Purpose

Healthy boundaries create the clarity and space necessary for connecting with your deeper values and life purpose while protecting against the distractions and obligations that can prevent the reflection and growth that spiritual development requires.

Values Alignment and Integrity strengthen when boundaries ensure that your time and energy go toward activities that reflect your authentic priorities and beliefs rather than being scattered among obligations that don't serve your deeper purpose or meaning.

Spiritual Practice Protection emerges when boundaries preserve time and mental space for meditation, reflection, or other practices that nourish your spiritual development while preventing the busyness that can crowd out activities essential for inner growth.

Service and Contribution Balance develop through boundaries that enable sustainable giving while preventing the martyrdom and self-sacrifice that can lead to resentment and burnout rather than the joyful service that emerges from overflow rather than depletion.

Life Purpose Clarity often emerges when boundaries create space for the reflection and exploration necessary for discovering your authentic calling while protecting against the external pressures that might lead you away from your genuine path and interests.

Practical Steps to Establish and Maintain Boundaries: Your Implementation Guide

Creating and sustaining healthy boundaries requires both internal work to clarify your limits and external skills for communicating and maintaining those boundaries effectively, even when others resist or challenge your efforts to protect your well-being and authentic self-expression.

Identifying Your Personal Limits and Values

The foundation of effective boundary-setting lies in developing clear awareness of your own needs, values, and limits while understanding the difference between preferences that might be negotiable and non-negotiable requirements for your well-being and self-respect.

Values Clarification Exercises help identify the principles and priorities that should guide your boundary decisions while providing frameworks for evaluating whether specific situations align with your authentic self and life direction.

Create a list of your top 5-10 core values—such as integrity, family time, health, creativity, or service—and use these as criteria for boundary decisions, asking whether particular commitments or relationships support or compromise these fundamental priorities.

Limit Recognition and Assessment involves paying attention to physical and emotional signals that indicate when you're approaching or crossing your healthy limits while developing sensitivity to the early warning signs that suggest boundary adjustments may be necessary.

Notice patterns of resentment, exhaustion, anxiety, or physical symptoms that might indicate boundary violations while tracking which relationships, activities, or commitments tend to create these experiences most consistently.

Need Identification and Prioritization help distinguish between wants that might be flexible and genuine needs that require protection through boundaries, creating clarity about which limits are essential for your well-being versus those that might be preferences you could negotiate.

Energy and Time Audits involve honestly assessing how you currently spend your time and energy while identifying areas where boundaries might create better alignment between your actual activities and your stated values and priorities.

Boundary Violation Recognition builds awareness of past and present experiences where your limits have been crossed while understanding how these violations have affected your well-being and relationships, providing motivation and clarity for future boundary-setting.

Communicating Boundaries Effectively

Successfully establishing boundaries requires clear, consistent communication that expresses your limits with confidence and respect while providing others with the information they need to honor your boundaries without creating unnecessary conflict or misunderstanding.

Direct and Clear Expression involves stating your boundaries explicitly rather than hoping others will guess your limits or interpret subtle hints about your needs and preferences, reducing confusion while demonstrating your seriousness about maintaining your boundaries.

Use "I" statements that express your needs and decisions without attacking or blaming others: "I need to leave work by 6 PM to spend time with my family" rather than "You always expect me to stay late" or "This company doesn't respect work-life balance."

Timing and Context Considerations help ensure that boundary conversations happen when both parties can listen and respond thoughtfully rather than during emotional or stressful moments when defensive reactions might prevent productive dialogue.

Confidence and Consistency in boundary communication demonstrate your commitment to maintaining your limits while helping others understand that your boundaries are serious decisions rather than temporary preferences they might be able to negotiate or ignore.

Respectful Firmness maintains kindness and consideration for others while clearly expressing that your boundaries are non-negotiable, avoiding both aggressive confrontation and passive expressions that might be dismissed or misunderstood.

Explanation Boundaries involve deciding when and how much to explain your reasons for particular limits while recognizing that you don't always need to justify your boundaries with detailed explanations that might be used to argue against your limits.

Handling Pushback and Resistance

When you begin setting boundaries, particularly in relationships where limits haven't existed before, others may resist your changes through various tactics that test your commitment to maintaining your newly established limits.

Understanding Common Resistance Patterns helps you recognize guilt trips, manipulation attempts, anger, or withdrawal as potentially normal responses to boundary changes rather than evidence that your boundaries are wrong or harmful to others.

Some people may escalate their demands or become more persistent when you first establish boundaries, testing whether your limits are genuine or temporary preferences they can overcome through increased pressure or emotional manipulation.

Guilt and Manipulation Management involves recognizing when others use guilt, obligation, or fear to pressure you into abandoning your boundaries while maintaining your limits despite emotional pressure that might make boundary maintenance feel selfish or harmful.

Develop standard responses to common manipulation attempts: "I understand you're disappointed, but my decision stands" or "I care about you and that's why I need to maintain this boundary for our relationship's health."

Emotional Regulation During Confrontation helps you maintain calm and clarity when others react strongly to your boundaries while avoiding the emotional reactivity that might lead you to abandon your limits or engage in defensive arguments.

Consequences and Follow-Through ensure that your boundaries have meaning by implementing appropriate responses when boundaries are violated while maintaining consistency that demonstrates your serious commitment to your limits.

Support System Utilization provides encouragement and perspective when boundary-setting feels difficult while helping you maintain resolve during periods when others' resistance might make you question your decisions or limits.

Maintaining Boundaries Over Time

Long-term boundary maintenance requires ongoing attention and refinement while adapting your limits to changing circumstances and relationships without abandoning the core principles that protect your well-being and self-respect.

Regular Boundary Review and Adjustment involves periodically assessing whether your current boundaries still serve your well-being while making modifications based on life changes, relationship developments, or new insights about your needs and limits.

Consistency Across Relationships maintains similar standards in different contexts while avoiding the confusion and resentment that can develop when boundaries vary dramatically between relationships without clear reasons for different treatment.

Boundary Flexibility Without Compromise allows for appropriate adjustments during special circumstances or emergencies while maintaining your core limits and returning to normal boundaries once temporary situations resolve.

Self-Care and Boundary Energy ensure that you have the physical and emotional resources necessary for maintaining boundaries while recognizing that boundary-setting requires energy and supporting yourself through adequate rest, nutrition, and stress management.

Celebrating Boundary Success involves acknowledging and appreciating the positive changes that result from healthy boundary-setting while reinforcing your commitment to continued limit-setting through recognition of its benefits for your life and relationships.

Professional Support When Needed recognizes that some boundary challenges may require help from therapists, coaches, or other professionals while seeking appropriate assistance when boundary violations involve abuse, addiction, or other serious issues that exceed self-help approaches.

As we conclude this empowering exploration of boundary-setting as essential life skill, we celebrate your courage to recognize that protecting your well-being through healthy limits represents not selfishness but wisdom—the kind of self-respect that enables you to show up authentically for yourself and others without depletion or resentment.

Remember that learning to set and maintain boundaries is a gradual process that improves with practice while requiring patience with yourself during the learning curve and the inevitable challenges that arise when you begin honoring your limits more consistently and courageously.

Your commitment to healthy boundary-setting creates ripple effects that enhance every aspect of your life while modeling for others the possibility of relationships based on mutual respect rather than exploitation or people-pleasing that serves no one's authentic well-being in the long term.

The journey of boundary mastery continues with each conscious choice to honor your limits despite pressure to abandon them, each conversation where you express your needs clearly and respectfully, and each decision to prioritize your well-being alongside your care for others.

Through your dedication to healthy boundaries, you participate in creating a culture that values authentic relationships over convenient ones while demonstrating that genuine love includes respect for limits and that true strength includes the wisdom to know when to say no in service of what matters most.

This is your invitation to unprecedented freedom, respect, and authentic connection—not through rigid walls that separate you from others, but through the clear, loving boundaries that create safety for your true self to emerge and flourish in relationships that honor both your needs and the dignity of every person whose life intersects with your own precious journey.

Prompt: What is strength to you, and how does it effect how you handle stress, grief, or anxiety?

Chapter 24: Building Supportive Communities

We step into a chapter that beckons you toward one of the most profound realizations of the human experience—that within the tapestry of authentic community lies not merely companionship, but the very architecture upon which emotional resilience, personal transformation, and lasting well-being are constructed. Here, we venture into sacred territory where individual healing meets collective strength, where your journey of emotional growth becomes interwoven with the journeys of others who share the courage to seek authenticity, connection, and mutual support.

This exploration invites you to rediscover community not as an optional addition to your emotional health journey, but as an essential element that amplifies every aspect of your healing while providing the witnessing, encouragement, and shared wisdom that individual effort alone cannot fully provide. Within these pages, you'll uncover how the conscious cultivation of supportive relationships becomes both a gift you offer to others and a wellspring of strength that sustains you through every challenge and celebration that life presents.

Your willingness to explore these insights represents an act of profound wisdom—the recognition that in our increasingly connected yet paradoxically isolated world, choosing to build and participate in authentic community emerges not as dependency or weakness, but as one of the most powerful interventions available for emotional healing and sustained well-being. You are stepping into an understanding that honors both your individual uniqueness and your fundamental need for belonging, connection, and the kind of mutual support that transforms isolated struggle into shared strength.

The Importance of Community: The Foundation of Emotional Resilience

Community represents far more than a collection of individuals sharing common interests or circumstances—it embodies a living ecosystem of mutual support, shared wisdom, and collective resilience that provides the psychological safety and emotional nourishment essential for authentic personal growth and sustained well-being throughout life's inevitable challenges and transitions.

The Psychology of Belonging and Connection

At the deepest level of human psychology lies a fundamental need for belonging that shapes our emotional development, stress resilience, and capacity for authentic self-expression in ways that extend far beyond conscious awareness to influence every aspect of mental health and personal fulfillment.

Neurobiological Foundations of Connection reveal that our brains are literally wired for social interaction, with neural networks dedicated to reading social cues, forming attachments, and regulating emotions through relationship connections. When these systems receive adequate social nourishment through supportive community relationships, they enhance emotional regulation while promoting the neuroplasticity that supports continued learning and adaptation throughout your lifetime.

The vagus nerve, which plays crucial roles in emotional regulation and stress response, is significantly influenced by social connection quality. Positive community interactions activate the parasympathetic nervous system, creating the calm alertness that supports both emotional well-being and optimal cognitive function while building resilience against stress and trauma.

Attachment Security and Community Healing demonstrate how supportive community relationships can provide corrective experiences that heal attachment wounds from earlier life experiences while building the internal sense of safety and worth that enables authentic vulnerability and genuine intimacy with others.

Even individuals who experienced insecure attachment patterns in childhood can develop earned security through consistent, supportive community relationships that demonstrate reliability, acceptance, and unconditional positive regard that gradually builds trust in both others and oneself.

Identity Formation and Validation occur significantly through community interactions that reflect back your authentic self while providing feedback about your growth, strengths, and areas for continued development. These social mirrors help you understand yourself more clearly while building confidence in your unique contributions and inherent worth.

Social Learning and Skill Development accelerate through community participation as you observe others navigating similar challenges, learn from their experiences and strategies, and practice new emotional and interpersonal skills within supportive contexts that encourage growth while providing safety for experimentation and occasional mistakes.

Collective Resilience and Shared Strength

The power of community extends beyond individual support to create collective resilience that enables groups to weather challenges that might overwhelm individuals while building shared resources of wisdom, strength, and hope that benefit all community members.

Stress Buffering and Resource Sharing occur naturally within supportive communities where individual challenges are met with collective resources, whether through practical assistance, emotional support, or shared problem-solving that distributes the burden of difficulties while multiplying available solutions and perspectives.

Research consistently demonstrates that individuals with strong social support networks show lower cortisol levels, better immune function, and improved recovery from both physical and emotional challenges compared to those facing difficulties in isolation.

Witnessing and Validation provide essential healing elements that can only occur within relationship contexts, as your experiences are seen, acknowledged, and validated by others who can offer perspective, encouragement, and the kind of understanding that transforms isolated suffering into shared human experience.

Accountability and Growth Support emerge through community relationships that gently challenge you to grow while providing encouragement during difficult periods and celebration during times of progress and accomplishment, creating external motivation that supplements internal commitment during challenging phases of personal development.

Wisdom Transmission and Cultural Healing occur as communities become repositories of collective knowledge about navigating life's challenges while preserving and sharing insights that can benefit current and future community members facing similar struggles or opportunities.

The Healing Power of Shared Experience

Perhaps most profoundly, community provides the irreplaceable gift of shared experience that transforms isolation into connection while demonstrating that your struggles, questions, and aspirations are part of the universal human experience rather than evidence of personal inadequacy or uniqueness that separates you from others.

Normalization and De-Stigmatization happen naturally within communities where individuals share vulnerabilities and challenges, revealing the common humanity underlying seemingly unique personal struggles while reducing shame and isolation that often accompany emotional health difficulties.

When men discover that others share similar experiences with depression, anxiety, trauma, or relationship challenges, the stigma and self-criticism that often compound these difficulties begin to dissolve, replaced by self-compassion and hope for healing and growth.

Hope and Inspiration Through Modeling emerge as you witness others who have navigated similar challenges successfully, providing living proof that growth, healing, and positive change are possible while offering concrete examples of strategies and approaches that have proven effective.

Meaning-Making and Purpose Discovery often develop through community service and contribution opportunities that connect your personal healing journey with purposes larger than individual well-being, creating sense of significance and direction that enhances motivation and life satisfaction.

Celebration and Joy Amplification occur when positive experiences are shared within supportive communities that can appreciate and celebrate your growth, achievements, and moments of happiness in ways that multiply joy while creating positive memories and associations with community connection.

Breaking the Isolation Cycle

Modern life often creates patterns of isolation that compound emotional health challenges while preventing access to the natural healing and growth that supportive relationships provide, making conscious community building essential for comprehensive emotional well-being.

Digital Connection Limitations demonstrate that while technology enables unprecedented global communication, virtual interactions often lack the depth, nuance, and physiological benefits of in-person connection, requiring intentional effort to build face-to-face community relationships alongside digital communication.

Geographic and Social Barriers in contemporary society can make community building challenging through factors like frequent relocation, suburban isolation, work demands, or cultural differences that require creative approaches and persistent effort to overcome while building meaningful connections.

Masculine Socialization and Community often presents unique challenges as cultural messages about male self-reliance and emotional control can discourage the vulnerability and mutual support that authentic community requires, necessitating conscious efforts to redefine strength in ways that include interdependence and emotional openness.

Fear and Vulnerability Resistance naturally arise when considering deeper community involvement, as authentic connection requires the courage to be seen and known while risking rejection or judgment that may have caused pain in previous relationship experiences.

Identifying and Creating Supportive Networks: Your Community Blueprint

Building supportive community requires both the wisdom to recognize existing communities that align with your values and emotional needs, and the courage to create new community connections when existing options don't fully serve your desire for authentic belonging and mutual support.

Assessing Your Community Needs and Values

The foundation of meaningful community building lies in understanding your own authentic needs, values, and preferences while recognizing that supportive communities can take many forms, each offering different benefits and requiring different levels of commitment and vulnerability.

Values Alignment Assessment helps identify what principles and priorities should guide your community choices while ensuring that the groups you join or create support rather than compromise your authentic self and personal growth goals.

Consider whether you're drawn to communities focused on spiritual growth, professional development, creative expression, physical fitness, service to others, or specific shared experiences like parenting, recovery, or life transitions, recognizing that multiple community connections can serve different aspects of your emotional and social needs.

Support Needs Identification involves honest assessment of what types of support would most benefit your emotional health journey, whether through accountability partnerships, emotional processing opportunities, practical assistance during challenges, or celebration and encouragement during growth and achievement.

Intimacy and Privacy Preferences help determine what level of emotional sharing and vulnerability feels comfortable while recognizing that different communities can offer varying degrees of depth, from casual social connections to deeply intimate emotional support that requires careful consideration of trust and safety.

Time and Energy Investment Capacity realistically assesses what level of community involvement feels sustainable given your current life circumstances while recognizing that community building requires investment but ultimately provides returns that often exceed the energy invested.

Geographic and Accessibility Considerations acknowledge practical factors like location, transportation, scheduling, and physical accessibility that affect your ability to participate consistently in community activities and relationships.

Exploring Existing Community Options

Before creating new communities, exploring existing options can provide valuable connections while offering insights into what community elements serve your needs and what aspects might benefit from different approaches or additional development.

Professional and Therapeutic Communities include support groups, therapy groups, men's groups, or professional organizations that provide structured environments for personal growth while offering expert facilitation and established frameworks for healthy community interaction.

These communities often provide excellent starting points for community building as they include built-in safety measures, clear boundaries, and professional guidance while focusing explicitly on emotional health and personal development goals.

Interest-Based Communities around hobbies, sports, creative pursuits, or volunteer activities offer opportunities for connection through shared activities while potentially developing into deeper relationships as trust and familiarity build over time through consistent interaction.

Spiritual and Philosophical Communities including religious congregations, meditation groups, philosophical societies, or spiritual study groups provide frameworks for exploring life's deeper questions while building connections with others seeking meaning, growth, and authentic living.

Professional and Career Networks can evolve beyond purely professional purposes to include personal support and friendship while offering opportunities for mentorship, collaboration, and mutual assistance in both professional and personal growth endeavors.

Online and Digital Communities provide access to global networks of individuals sharing similar experiences while offering opportunities for connection that transcend geographic limitations, though these require conscious effort to develop beyond surface-level interaction.

Creating New Communities and Initiatives

When existing community options don't fully meet your needs, creating new community initiatives provides opportunities to design supportive environments that align precisely with your values while serving others who share similar needs for authentic connection and mutual support.

Community Vision and Purpose Development involves clarifying the specific focus and goals for your community initiative while ensuring that the vision serves collective needs rather than just personal preferences, creating foundations for sustainable growth and meaningful impact.

Structure and Format Considerations help determine whether your community will function as informal gatherings, structured meetings, activity-based groups, or combination approaches that balance flexibility with enough organization to support consistent connection and growth.

Safety and Boundaries Establishment creates guidelines that protect all community members while encouraging authentic sharing and vulnerability, including confidentiality agreements, communication guidelines, and procedures for addressing conflicts or inappropriate behavior.

Leadership and Facilitation Models determine whether community leadership will be shared, rotational, or designated while ensuring that leadership serves the community's growth rather than individual ego needs or power dynamics that could undermine trust and safety.

Growth and Evolution Planning acknowledges that healthy communities naturally change and develop over time while building flexibility and adaptability into community structures that can accommodate growth, member changes, and evolving needs without losing core purpose and values.

Overcoming Barriers to Community Participation

Many men encounter internal and external barriers to meaningful community participation that require conscious attention and strategic approaches to overcome while maintaining authenticity and personal boundaries throughout the community building process.

Social Anxiety and Fear Management often arise when considering deeper community involvement, requiring gradual exposure approaches that build confidence while honoring your emotional comfort zones and natural pacing for relationship development.

Start with lower-risk community activities that align with your interests while gradually building toward deeper sharing and vulnerability as trust and comfort develop naturally through positive experiences and consistent connection.

Time Management and Priority Balancing help integrate community involvement with existing responsibilities while recognizing that community connection ultimately supports rather than competes with other life priorities by providing stress relief, emotional support, and practical assistance.

Masculine Identity and Vulnerability Concerns may require redefining strength to include emotional openness and mutual support while recognizing that authentic masculine identity encompasses the full range of human experience including sensitivity, interdependence, and emotional intelligence.

Trust and Safety Building acknowledge past relationship wounds while taking appropriate risks for connection that honor both your need for safety and your desire for authentic relationship, gradually building trust through consistent, positive community experiences.

Geographic and Practical Limitations can be addressed through creative approaches including online components, flexible meeting arrangements, or community activities that accommodate varying schedules and transportation needs while maintaining consistent connection opportunities.

Sustaining and Nurturing Community Connections: The Art of Mutual Support

Creating supportive community represents only the beginning of a lifelong practice of nurturing relationships that provide mutual benefit while contributing to collective well-being through your presence, participation, and commitment to others' growth and flourishing alongside your own.

Building Trust and Emotional Safety

The foundation of sustainable community lies in creating and maintaining emotional safety that allows all members to bring their authentic selves while feeling protected from judgment, exploitation, or betrayal that could damage the trust essential for meaningful connection.

Consistency and Reliability form the bedrock of trust through showing up consistently for community activities while following through on commitments and maintaining presence during both celebration and difficulty that demonstrates your genuine investment in others' well-being.

Confidentiality and Discretion protect the vulnerable sharing that deepens community bonds by maintaining appropriate boundaries around sensitive information while ensuring that personal disclosures remain within the community context rather than becoming topics for outside conversation or gossip.

Empathetic Listening and Non-Judgment create safety through offering presence and understanding without immediately trying to fix, advise, or minimize others' experiences while demonstrating acceptance and care that encourages continued authenticity and vulnerability.

Emotional Regulation and Conflict Navigation contribute to community safety through managing your own emotional reactions skillfully while addressing interpersonal challenges directly and respectfully rather than allowing resentments or misunderstandings to fester and damage community trust.

Boundary Respect and Communication honor both your own and others' limits while expressing needs and concerns clearly and respectfully, creating community norms that support individual well-being alongside collective connection and mutual support.

Contributing to Community Culture and Growth

Sustainable community requires active participation from all members who contribute their unique gifts while supporting collective values and goals that serve everyone's growth and well-being rather than just individual needs or preferences.

Reciprocity and Mutual Support ensure that community benefits flow in multiple directions through offering assistance, encouragement, and resources to others while receiving support gracefully when you face challenges or need community assistance and care.

Skill Sharing and Resource Contribution utilize your unique knowledge, abilities, and resources to benefit community members while learning from others' expertise and experience, creating collaborative environments where everyone both teaches and learns.

Conflict Resolution and Problem-Solving approach community challenges as opportunities for growth and learning while working collaboratively toward solutions that honor everyone's needs and maintain the relationships that form community foundation.

Celebration and Recognition acknowledge others' growth, achievements, and contributions while creating positive community culture that highlights successes and milestones rather than focusing only on problems and challenges that require attention.

Mentorship and Guidance offer support and wisdom to newer community members while remaining open to learning from others regardless of their experience level, creating intergenerational exchange that benefits everyone involved.

Adapting to Change and Community Evolution

Healthy communities naturally evolve over time as members grow, circumstances change, and collective needs shift, requiring flexibility and adaptability while maintaining core values and purposes that provide continuity and stability.

Life Transition Support acknowledges that community members will face changes in career, family, health, or other circumstances that affect their participation while maintaining connection and support through these transitions rather than losing valuable relationships.

New Member Integration welcomes newcomers while maintaining community culture and values, providing orientation and support that helps new members contribute meaningfully while learning community norms and building relationships with existing members.

Leadership Transition and Succession ensures community sustainability through developing multiple leaders and shared responsibility rather than depending on single individuals whose departure could compromise community continuity and effectiveness.

Conflict and Challenge Navigation treats community difficulties as opportunities for deepening trust and understanding while developing skills for addressing problems directly and compassionately rather than avoiding conflict or allowing issues to damage relationships.

Purpose Evolution and Renewal allows community focus and activities to evolve as members grow and collective needs change while maintaining connection to core values that provide identity and direction throughout natural development and maturation.

Creating Lasting Legacy and Impact

Mature communities develop capacity to influence and serve purposes beyond immediate member needs while creating positive impact that extends to families, workplaces, and broader society through the transformed lives and relationships of community participants.

Ripple Effect Recognition acknowledges how community participation affects all your relationships while creating positive influence that spreads through your family, professional, and social networks as you bring community-developed skills and perspectives to other contexts.

Intergenerational Transmission shares community values and practices with children, students, or younger colleagues while preserving wisdom and approaches that have proven beneficial for emotional health and authentic relationship building.

Community Service and Outreach extends community benefits beyond immediate membership through service projects, educational initiatives, or support for other groups seeking to build similar communities while contributing to collective social healing.

Documentation and Sharing preserves community wisdom and experience through recording insights, practices, and lessons learned while sharing approaches and resources with others seeking to build supportive communities in their own contexts.

Cultural and Social Impact participates in broader cultural shifts toward emotional intelligence, authentic masculinity, and community-based approaches to well-being while modeling alternatives to individualistic approaches that often increase isolation and emotional distress.

As we conclude this profound exploration of community building as essential medicine for the human soul, we celebrate your courage to recognize that your emotional health journey flourishes not in isolation but within the sacred container of authentic relationships that honor both your individual uniqueness and your fundamental need for belonging.

Remember that building supportive community is not a destination to be reached but a lifelong practice of showing up authentically for yourself and others while contributing to collective well-being through your presence, vulnerability, and commitment to mutual growth and support.

Your willingness to invest in community creates ripple effects that extend far beyond your immediate experience to touch every life that intersects with your transformed relationships while contributing to cultural healing that serves generations beyond your own lifetime.

The journey of community building continues with each brave step toward authentic connection, each moment of vulnerability that deepens trust, and each act of service that demonstrates your commitment to collective flourishing alongside personal growth and healing.

Through your dedication to supportive community, you participate in weaving the social fabric that enables all individuals to thrive while modeling for others the revolutionary understanding that strength includes interdependence, wisdom encompasses emotional intelligence, and true success involves lifting others as you rise.

This is your invitation to unprecedented belonging, mutual support, and shared strength—not through perfect communities free from challenge, but through authentic relationships that embrace both the beauty and difficulty of human experience while creating together the kind of world where emotional health and genuine connection can flourish for all.

Reflection: Where am I emotionally thriving—and where am I emotionally stuck?

Chapter 25: Building Successful Relationships

This is a profound exploration of one of life's most essential yet intricate endeavors—the art of building relationships that not only survive but truly flourish, becoming wellsprings of mutual growth, authentic connection, and enduring joy. Within these pages, we will explore the sacred territory where individual healing meets relational wisdom, where the emotional intelligence you've been cultivating transforms into the foundation for connections that honor both your authentic self and the precious humanity of those who walk alongside you on this remarkable journey.

Within these pages, you'll discover how the principles of emotional health you've been developing become the very building blocks for relationships. Which can withstand life's challenges while fostering the intimacy and partnership that enriches the human experience infinitely.

The recognition that investing in relationship skills serves not only your own emotional well-being but contributes to the healing and flourishing of everyone whose life intersects with yours. You are stepping into wisdom that honors both the complexity of human connection and the simple yet transformative truth that meaningful relationships require both heart and skill, both love and learned competency in the delicate dance of authentic partnership.

The Foundation of Successful Relationships: Building on Bedrock

Successful relationships rest upon fundamental pillars that must be consciously constructed and continuously maintained, forming the bedrock upon which all other aspects of connection can flourish. Understanding and developing these foundational elements transforms relationship building from hopeful chance into skillful practice that creates lasting bonds capable of supporting both individual growth and mutual fulfillment.

Trust as the Cornerstone of Connection

Trust represents the invisible foundation upon which all meaningful relationships are built. Encompassing far more than simple honesty to include reliability, emotional safety, and the deep confidence that your partner or friend will honor both the explicit and implicit agreements that hold relationships together through both joyful and challenging times.

Reliability and Consistency form the daily building blocks of trust through following through on commitments, showing up when expected, and maintaining consistent behavior patterns that allow others to predict and depend upon your responses and availability. These seemingly small acts accumulate into profound security that enables deeper intimacy and vulnerability to develop naturally over time.

Trust builds through countless small moments—arriving when you say you will, calling when promised, remembering important details about others' lives, and maintaining emotional stability that others can rely upon during both ordinary and extraordinary circumstances that test relationship resilience.

Emotional Safety and Respect create the psychological container within which trust can flourish. Ensuring that personal vulnerabilities shared in moments of intimacy will be honored rather than used as weapons during conflicts or shared inappropriately with others outside the relationship boundary.

This safety includes respecting boundaries, maintaining confidentiality about personal information, and responding with compassion rather than judgment when others reveal their struggles, fears, or imperfections that require delicate handling and unconditional acceptance.

Honesty and Transparency provide the clear communication foundation that prevents the erosion of trust through deception, omission, or manipulation while creating relationships characterized by authentic sharing rather than performative presentations designed to maintain false impressions or avoid difficult conversations.

Authentic honesty includes sharing your genuine thoughts and feelings while delivering truth with kindness and timing that serves relationship growth rather than using brutal honesty as justification for insensitive communication that damages rather than strengthens connection.

Forgiveness and Repair acknowledge that trust violations will inevitably occur in long-term relationships. It is by developing skills for addressing breaches through sincere apology, changed behavior, and the gradual rebuilding process that can actually strengthen relationships when handled with wisdom and commitment from both parties.

The ability to repair trust after violations often distinguishes relationships that grow stronger through challenges from those that remain fragile or dissolve when difficulties arise, making repair skills essential for relationship longevity and depth.

Communication as the Bridge Between Hearts

Effective communication serves as the bridge that connects individual inner worlds while creating understanding, intimacy, and collaborative problem-solving capacity that transforms potential conflicts into opportunities for deeper connection and mutual growth.

Active Listening and Presence form the foundation of meaningful communication through offering complete attention to others' expressions while seeking to understand rather than immediately formulating responses or solutions that may miss the deeper emotional content beneath surface words.

True listening involves hearing not only what is said but what remains unspoken—the emotions, needs, and concerns that may be difficult to articulate—while providing the patience and presence that allows others to explore and express their inner experience without rushing toward premature closure or advice.

Emotional Expression and Vulnerability enable authentic communication through developing capacity to identify and share your inner emotional landscape while creating space for others to do the same without judgment or immediate problem-solving that can shut down emotional exploration and sharing.

Learning to express emotions skillfully includes distinguishing between feelings and thoughts, owning your emotional experience without blaming others, and timing emotional sharing in ways that invite connection rather than creating defensiveness or overwhelm.

Conflict Navigation and Resolution transform disagreements from relationship threats into opportunities for understanding different perspectives while developing collaborative approaches to addressing differences that honor both parties' needs and strengthen rather than damage relational bonds.

Healthy conflict resolution involves staying focused on specific issues rather than attacking character, expressing needs and concerns clearly while listening for underlying interests, and working together toward solutions that serve the relationship's well-being rather than individual victory.

Nonverbal Communication Awareness recognizes that body language, tone of voice, facial expressions, and energy levels communicate as powerfully as words while developing sensitivity to these subtle channels that often convey the emotional truth underlying verbal content.

Developing nonverbal awareness includes monitoring your own body language and tone to ensure they align with your intended message while reading others' nonverbal cues as information about their emotional state and receptivity to different types of communication.

Emotional Intelligence in Relationships

Emotional intelligence provides the sophisticated understanding of emotional dynamics that enables you to navigate relationship complexities with wisdom. Supporting both your own emotional well-being and that of others through conscious, skillful responses to the inevitable emotional challenges that intimate relationships present.

Self-Awareness and Emotional Regulation enable you to understand your own emotional patterns, triggers, and reactions. By managing your responses in ways that serve relationship health rather than simply expressing whatever emotions arise without consideration for timing, intensity, or impact on others.

This self-awareness includes recognizing when your emotional state might be influenced by factors outside the relationship—stress, fatigue, hormonal fluctuations, or past experiences—while taking responsibility for your emotional contribution to relationship dynamics without blame or projection.

Empathy and Perspective-Taking develop your capacity to understand others' emotional experiences while responding with compassion even when their reactions or needs differ significantly from your own preferences or natural responses to similar situations.

Empathy involves temporarily setting aside your own perspective to genuinely understand how situations feel from others' viewpoints while maintaining your own emotional boundaries and avoiding the emotional fusion that can lead to codependency or loss of individual identity.

Social Skills and Relationship Navigation encompass the practical abilities needed for building and maintaining healthy relationships while adapting your communication and behavior to different relationship contexts and the varying needs of different individuals in your life.

These skills include reading social situations accurately, timing sensitive conversations appropriately, offering support in ways that truly help rather than simply expressing good intentions, and maintaining multiple relationships without neglecting any while honoring the unique needs each relationship requires.

Emotional Support and Validation provide the nourishing responses that help others feel seen, understood, and accepted while building the emotional climate that encourages continued vulnerability and growth within relationship contexts.

Effective support includes distinguishing between times when others need empathy versus practical advice while offering presence and understanding without trying to fix problems that may simply require witnessing and emotional processing rather than immediate solutions.

Overcoming Common Challenges: Navigating Relationship Obstacles

Even the strongest relationships encounter predictable challenges that test commitment and skill while providing opportunities for deeper understanding and increased intimacy when approached with wisdom, patience, and collaborative problem-solving that transforms obstacles into growth experiences.

Understanding and Resolving Conflict

Conflict represents a natural and potentially beneficial aspect of intimate relationships when approached as information about differences that need attention rather than threats to relationship survival that must be avoided or won through dominance and control.

Conflict as Growth Opportunity reframes disagreements as chances to understand each other more deeply while developing collaborative skills that strengthen relationship resilience and create more satisfying solutions than either party could develop independently.

Healthy conflict involves curiosity about differences rather than immediately attempting to prove your perspective correct while exploring underlying needs and concerns that may not be obvious from initial positions or demands that seem incompatible on the surface.

Common Conflict Patterns and Triggers help you recognize recurring themes that emerge in your relationships while identifying the underlying issues—often involving needs for respect, understanding, autonomy, or security—that create repetitive conflicts when left unaddressed.

Understanding your personal conflict style—whether you tend toward aggressive confrontation, passive withdrawal, or assertive collaboration—enables conscious choice about responses while developing flexibility to adapt your approach based on what serves relationship health rather than simply following automatic patterns.

De-escalation and Emotional Regulation provide essential skills for preventing conflicts from escalating beyond productive levels while maintaining connection and respect even during disagreements that involve strong emotions or deeply held convictions.

De-escalation techniques include taking breaks when emotions become too intense for productive conversation, speaking more softly when others become loud, focusing on specific behaviors rather than character attacks, and seeking understanding before insisting on being understood.

Resolution and Repair Strategies transform conflicts into relationship strengthening experiences through collaborative problem-solving that addresses underlying needs while creating agreements and understanding that prevent similar conflicts from recurring unnecessarily.

Effective resolution involves acknowledging each person's contribution to conflicts without keeping score, focusing on future solutions rather than past blame, and creating specific agreements about behavior changes that both parties commit to implementing going forward.

Addressing Miscommunication and Assumptions

Miscommunication represents one of the most common relationship challenges, often arising not from ill intent but from different communication styles, unspoken expectations, or assumptions that prevent clear understanding and collaborative problem-solving.

Communication Style Differences acknowledge that individuals naturally vary in directness, emotional expression, processing time, and preferred communication methods while developing flexibility to adapt your approach for effective connection with different personality types and preferences.

Some people process externally through talking while others need internal reflection time before sharing, some prefer direct confrontation while others need gentle approaches, and some communicate primarily through actions while others rely heavily on verbal expression.

Assumption Identification and Checking prevents many relationship problems through developing habits of verifying understanding rather than assuming you know what others mean or what they need from you in various situations.

This includes asking clarifying questions, reflecting back what you've heard to ensure accuracy, and explicitly discussing expectations rather than assuming others share your assumptions about how relationships should function or what specific situations require.

Cultural and Background Differences recognize that family of origin experiences, cultural backgrounds, and personal histories create different relationship expectations and communication patterns that require understanding and negotiation rather than judgment about right and wrong approaches.

These differences might involve expectations about gender roles, family involvement in relationships, financial management, conflict resolution, or emotional expression that seem natural to each person but may conflict without conscious discussion and mutual accommodation.

Repair and Reconnection After Misunderstandings provide pathways back to intimacy after miscommunications create distance or hurt feelings while building resilience and trust through successful navigation of relationship ruptures and repairs.

Repair involves acknowledging your contribution to misunderstandings, expressing genuine remorse for any hurt caused regardless of intent, and working together to prevent similar miscommunications through clearer communication agreements and increased understanding of each other's needs and sensitivities.

Managing Differing Expectations and Needs

Relationships inevitably involve individuals with different backgrounds, personalities, and life goals who must negotiate their differences while creating shared vision and collaborative approaches that honor individual authenticity alongside relationship commitment.

Expectation Exploration and Negotiation involve explicit conversations about hopes, needs, and assumptions regarding relationship functioning while creating mutual agreements that honor both parties' core needs without requiring either person to abandon their authentic self.

This process includes discussing expectations about time together and apart, communication frequency and methods, physical and emotional intimacy, household responsibilities, financial management, social activities, and future goals that affect relationship direction and daily functioning.

Individual Needs Within Relationship Context balance personal autonomy with partnership commitment while ensuring that relationship involvement enhances rather than diminishes individual well-being and authentic self-expression.

Healthy relationships support individual growth and interests while creating shared experiences and goals that benefit from partnership without requiring either person to lose their identity or sacrifice their core values and aspirations.

Compromise and Creative Problem-Solving develop collaborative approaches to differences that create solutions serving both parties rather than win-lose dynamics where one person's needs are met at the other's expense, creating resentment and relationship imbalance.

Effective compromise involves identifying underlying needs behind specific positions while brainstorming creative solutions that meet core needs even when surface preferences seem incompatible, often leading to better outcomes than either party originally envisioned.

Boundary Setting and Respect within relationships maintain individual integrity while honoring the interdependence that intimate relationships require, creating clear agreements about personal limits and mutual responsibilities that support both individual well-being and relationship health.

Healthy boundaries include maintaining friendships and interests outside the relationship, having privacy about some personal matters, and retaining decision-making authority over personal choices while consulting with partners about decisions that significantly affect the relationship.

Practical Strategies for Nurturing Relationships: Your Connection Toolkit

Building and maintaining successful relationships requires ongoing attention and skill development through practical strategies that can be applied consistently to create deeper intimacy, stronger trust, and more satisfying connection that enriches both individual lives and shared partnership experiences.

Fostering Deeper Connection and Intimacy

Intimacy develops through intentional practices that create emotional safety while encouraging vulnerability and authentic sharing that allows individuals to be truly known and accepted within relationship contexts.

Quality Time and Presence involve creating regular opportunities for focused attention and meaningful interaction while minimizing distractions that prevent deep connection and genuine engagement with each other's experiences and inner worlds.

This includes establishing device-free times for conversation, creating regular date nights or friendship activities, and offering complete presence during daily interactions rather than multitasking through relationship time that dilutes connection quality.

Emotional Intimacy Building develops through practices that encourage deeper sharing about thoughts, feelings, dreams, fears, and experiences while creating safety for vulnerability that might feel risky but ultimately strengthens relational bonds.

Intimacy practices include asking meaningful questions that go beyond surface topics, sharing your own vulnerabilities to model openness, expressing appreciation for others' authentic sharing, and creating rituals or traditions that deepen connection over time.

Physical Affection and Touch (appropriate to relationship type) provide important connection through appropriate physical expressions of care and affection while respecting personal boundaries and preferences that vary between individuals and relationship contexts.

This includes hugs, hand-holding, shoulder touches, or other appropriate physical expressions that communicate care and affection while recognizing that physical affection needs and preferences require explicit discussion and ongoing consent.

Shared Experiences and Adventures create positive memories and common ground while providing opportunities for mutual discovery and growth that strengthen relational bonds through overcoming challenges together or exploring new interests collaboratively.

Shared experiences might include travel, learning new skills together, participating in community service, pursuing creative projects, or simply exploring each other's interests and hobbies to better understand different perspectives and passions.

Maintaining Healthy Boundaries Within Relationships

Healthy relationships require clear boundaries that protect individual well-being while supporting relational intimacy through mutual respect for personal limits and autonomous decision-making within partnership contexts.

Individual Identity Preservation maintains personal interests, friendships, and goals while participating fully in relationship without losing authentic self-expression or sacrificing core values and aspirations to maintain harmony or meet others' expectations.

This includes maintaining friendships outside the relationship, pursuing individual hobbies and interests, making personal decisions about career and lifestyle choices, and retaining the right to privacy about some personal matters while sharing appropriately about relationship-relevant issues.

Communication Boundaries and Respect establish agreements about timing, methods, and content of difficult conversations while ensuring that communication serves connection rather than becoming pressure, manipulation, or emotional dumping that overwhelms or damages relationship trust.

Communication boundaries include agreeing on appropriate times for serious conversations, respecting requests for processing time before responding to important issues, and maintaining respectful tone even during disagreements that involve strong emotions or conflicting perspectives.

Time and Space Boundaries balance together time with individual space and external relationships while ensuring that both partnership needs and personal autonomy needs, receive appropriate attention and respect.

This includes negotiating schedules that honor both shared activities and individual pursuits, respecting needs for solitude and reflection, and maintaining appropriate relationships with family and friends without excluding partners inappropriately or including them beyond their comfort level.

Emotional Responsibility and Support distinguish between offering appropriate support and taking responsibility for others' emotions while maintaining your own emotional well-being and avoiding codependent patterns that create unhealthy relationship dynamics.

Healthy emotional boundaries include offering empathy without trying to fix others' problems, supporting without enabling, and maintaining your emotional stability without suppressing authentic reactions or sacrificing your needs to manage others' emotional states.

Growing Together While Honoring Individual Paths

Successful long-term relationships require balancing shared growth and goals with individual development while creating partnership that enhances rather than limits personal evolution and authentic self-expression.

Shared Vision and Goal Setting create common direction and purpose while ensuring that partnership activities align with both parties' values and aspirations rather than requiring one person to sacrifice their authentic path for relationship maintenance.

This involves regular conversations about individual and shared goals while looking for ways to support each other's dreams and aspirations even when they require significant time, energy, or resources that might temporarily affect relationship dynamics or shared activities.

Individual Growth Support celebrates and encourages each other's personal development while recognizing that individual growth may sometimes create temporary relationship stress as people change and evolve in ways that require relationship adaptation and renegotiation.

Supporting individual growth includes encouraging pursuit of personal interests and challenges, celebrating achievements and milestones, offering practical support during difficult growth periods, and adapting relationship expectations as individuals develop new capacities and interests.

Change Navigation and Adaptation develop resilience for handling the inevitable changes that occur in long-term relationships while maintaining connection and commitment through life transitions that test relationship flexibility and mutual support capacity.

This includes anticipating and discussing how major life changes—career transitions, health challenges, family additions, aging, or spiritual development—might affect relationship dynamics while creating agreements about mutual support during transition periods.

Legacy Building and Shared Contribution create meaning and purpose through collaborative service to others while building shared values and activities that extend relationship benefits beyond immediate partnership to contribute to family, community, or causes that reflect mutual values and aspirations.

Legacy building might include mentoring other couples, contributing to community organizations, creating family traditions that strengthen extended relationships, or collaborating on creative or service projects that utilize both parties' strengths and interests for purposes larger than individual fulfillment.

Sustaining Relationships Through Life's Seasons

Long-term relationship success requires understanding and preparing for the natural seasons and cycles that affect all relationships while developing resilience and adaptation skills that maintain connection through various life phases and challenges.

Relationship Seasons and Cycles acknowledge that relationships naturally experience periods of closer connection alternating with more distant phases while understanding these cycles as normal rather than signs of relationship failure or inadequacy.

These seasons might be influenced by work stress, family demands, health challenges, personal growth phases, or simply the natural ebb and flow of intimacy that occurs in all long-term relationships. When viewed from broader perspectives that encompass years rather than weeks or months.

Crisis Navigation and Support prepare for handling major challenges—health problems, job loss, family crises, or other significant stressors—through mutual support that strengthens rather than weakens relationship bonds during difficult periods.

Crisis preparation includes discussing potential challenges and support strategies, maintaining individual and relationship resources that provide resilience during difficulties, and developing communication and problem-solving skills that function effectively under pressure.

Renewal and Revitalization Practices prevent relationship stagnation through regular attention to keeping connection fresh while introducing new experiences, deepening intimacy, and adapting relationship practices to accommodate growth and changing needs over time.

Renewal practices might include regular relationship check-ins, periodic retreats or special trips, learning new activities together, seeking counseling or workshops for relationship enrichment, or simply maintaining curiosity about each other's continuing development and evolution.

Long-term Commitment and Vision maintain relationship stability through challenging periods while keeping sight of long-term goals and shared vision that provide motivation for working through temporary difficulties rather than abandoning relationships when challenges arise.

This commitment includes understanding that all relationships require ongoing effort and attention while maintaining realistic expectations about relationship satisfaction that acknowledge both wonderful periods and challenging seasons as normal aspects of long-term partnership.

As we conclude this profound exploration of relationship building as both art and skill. We celebrate your commitment to investing in the connections that provide life's greatest joys while acknowledging that meaningful relationships require both heart and learned competency in the delicate dance of authentic partnership.

Remember that building successful relationships is not about achieving perfect harmony but about developing the skills and commitment necessary for navigating life's inevitable challenges together. It is by maintaining mutual respect, individual authenticity, and shared growth that enriches both individual lives and collective partnership experience.

Your willingness to prioritize relationship skills creates ripple effects that extend throughout your entire social network while contributing to cultural healing through modeling healthy relationship patterns for others who may benefit from witnessing authentic connection and mutual support in action.

The journey of relationship mastery continues with each conscious choice to show up authentically for others. Each moment of vulnerability that deepens trust, and each decision to invest time and energy in nurturing the connections that provide life's most meaningful experiences and lasting satisfaction.

Through your commitment to relationship excellence, you participate in healing not only your own capacity for connection but contribute to collective understanding that successful relationships require both love and skill. Both a commitment and continuous learning that serves individual flourishing alongside mutual growth and support.

This is your invitation to unprecedented intimacy, mutual fulfillment, and lasting partnership—not through perfect relationships free from challenge, but through skilled navigation of life's complexities alongside others who share the courage to grow, heal, and create together the kinds of connections that make the human journey infinitely more meaningful, joyful, and complete.

Prompt: In what ways do you tie your self-worth to what you do, rather than who you are?

Chapter 26: How to Manage Grief and Loss

Easily one of the most profound and universal aspects of the human journey—the sacred territory where love meets loss, where the depth of our connections is revealed through the magnitude of our mourning, and where the courage to grieve becomes a testament to our capacity for meaningful attachment. In this section, we explore the tender landscape where sorrow and healing interweave, where the process of grieving transforms from an unbearable burden into a pathway toward deeper understanding of both love and resilience.

Understanding grief not as a problem to be solved or weakness to be overcome, but as a natural and necessary response to loss that honors the significance of what has been taken from your life. Within these pages, you'll discover how grief, though painful beyond measure, carries within it the seeds of healing, growth, and a more profound appreciation for the precious nature of all connections that grace our lives with meaning and purpose.

You are continuing this transformative journey it represents an act of extraordinary courage—the recognition that in a culture that often rushes past pain or attempts to fix what cannot be mended, choosing to understand and honor your grief emerges not as self-indulgence or weakness, but as one of the most authentic expressions of love and humanity available to the human heart. You are stepping into wisdom that celebrates both the reality of loss and your inherent capacity to navigate grief's complex terrain with grace, dignity, and hope for renewed connection to life's beauty and possibility.

Understanding Grief: The Nature of Love's Shadow

Grief represents one of love's most profound expressions—the emotional and physical response that emerges when something or someone precious to us is no longer accessible in the ways we have known and cherished. Understanding grief's nature, patterns, and manifestations provides essential foundation for navigating loss with compassion while recognizing that your grief experience reflects the depth and significance of your capacity for meaningful attachment.

The Essence and Purpose of Grief

Grief embodies the natural psychological and physiological response to loss that serves essential functions in human emotional processing. Providing the necessary time and space for adjusting to life without someone or something that held significant meaning and importance in your daily experience and future aspirations.

Evolutionary and Adaptive Functions of grief have developed over millennia to serve important survival and social cohesion purposes, including motivating search behaviors for lost loved ones. Signaling need for support from community members, and processing the reality of loss in ways that eventually enable renewed engagement with life and relationships.

Grief's intensity often corresponds directly to the significance of what has been lost, demonstrating that profound grief indicates profound love rather than personal inadequacy or inability to cope with life's natural transitions and inevitable losses.

Attachment and Bonding Expressions through grief reveal the sophisticated human capacity for forming deep emotional connections that transcend physical presence while demonstrating that love creates lasting neural pathways and emotional patterns that require time and care to reorganize after loss occurs.

The pain of grief reflects your brain's attempt to maintain connection with someone or something no longer available through familiar channels, creating the disorientation and longing that characterize early grief experiences while your system gradually adjusts to new reality.

Meaning-Making and Life Integration emerge through grief's process of reviewing, remembering, and integrating the significance of what has been lost. Gradually developing new ways of carrying forward the love, lessons, and memories that continue to provide meaning even after physical presence has ended.

Common Types of Loss and Grief

Grief extends beyond death to encompass numerous forms of loss that can create significant emotional disruption while requiring similar processes of acknowledgment, processing, and gradual adjustment to changed circumstances and altered life trajectories.

Death and Bereavement represent perhaps the most recognized form of grief, involving the permanent physical separation from loved ones including family members, friends, pets, or other significant relationships that provided companionship, support, and meaning in daily life experiences.

Grief following death often involves not only mourning the person who has died but also grieving the loss of shared future experiences, daily interactions, support systems, and the unique role that person played in your life story and identity formation.

Relationship Losses through divorce, separation, or relationship endings create grief responses that may be complicated by anger, guilt, or relief. Still requiring processing of attachment disruption and the loss of shared dreams, daily companionship, and the identity that existed within that particular relationship dynamic.

Life Transition Losses include retirement, children leaving home, job loss, moving away from familiar communities, or health changes that alter capabilities and lifestyle, creating grief for previous life stages, roles, or abilities that provided identity and satisfaction.

Anticipatory Grief emerges when facing impending losses such as terminal illness diagnoses, watching loved ones deteriorate through progressive diseases, or facing inevitable life changes that allow time to begin grief processing before actual loss occurs.

Ambiguous Loss involves situations where loss is unclear or incomplete, such as missing persons, estranged family relationships, or loved ones with conditions like dementia that create partial presence but fundamental changes in the relationship's nature and mutual recognition.

The Physical and Emotional Landscape of Grief

Grief affects every aspect of human functioning, creating physical, emotional, cognitive, and spiritual symptoms that can feel overwhelming while representing normal responses to significant loss that require patience, self-care, and appropriate support during the healing process.

Physical Grief Manifestations include fatigue and exhaustion that seem disproportionate to activity levels, changes in appetite and sleep patterns that disrupt normal routines, headaches and body aches without clear medical causes, and susceptibility to illness as grief affects immune system functioning.

Many people experience what feels like physical pain in their chest or heart area during intense grief, leading to the accurate description of "heartbreak" as grief creates measurable stress on cardiovascular systems while the body processes emotional trauma.

Emotional Grief Responses encompass profound sadness and yearning for what has been lost. Anger at circumstances or people perceived as responsible for the loss. Guilt about things said or unsaid, relief when suffering has ended, and fear about facing life without familiar sources of support or meaning.

These emotions often occur in waves of varying intensity rather than steady states, creating the unpredictable emotional landscape that characterizes grief processing while gradually becoming less frequent and overwhelming over time.

Cognitive Grief Effects include difficulty concentrating on daily tasks or responsibilities, memory problems and forgetfulness. That can be frightening or frustrating, confusion about identity and life direction without familiar reference points, and difficulty making decisions as mental energy focuses on grief processing.

Spiritual and Existential Questions often emerge during grief as loss confronts basic assumptions about meaning, fairness, divine presence, or life purpose while creating opportunities for deeper exploration of values, beliefs, and what provides genuine significance and hope.

Grief Patterns and Individual Variations

Understanding that grief experiences vary significantly between individuals helps normalize your particular grief expression while recognizing that cultural background, personality, relationship with the deceased, and life circumstances all influence how grief unfolds and what approaches prove most helpful for healing.

Cultural and Social Influences shape grief expression through family traditions, religious or spiritual beliefs, cultural norms about emotional expression, and community expectations about mourning rituals and time frames that may or may not align with your natural grief processing needs.

Some cultures encourage open emotional expression while others emphasize Stoic acceptance, some provide elaborate mourning rituals while others prefer private processing, requiring you to find approaches that honor both cultural connections and personal authenticity.

Personality and Coping Style Differences affect how individuals naturally approach grief processing, with some people preferring social support and shared processing while others need solitary reflection, some benefiting from structured activities while others requiring unstructured emotional exploration.

Complicated Grief Patterns may develop when grief becomes stuck or prolonged beyond typical healing timelines; often involving intense grief reactions that don't decrease over time, inability to accept loss reality, or grief that significantly impairs daily functioning for extended periods requiring professional support.

Disenfranchised Grief occurs when losses aren't socially recognized or supported, such as grief over miscarriage, pet death, ex-partner death, or other relationships that may not receive the same validation and support as more recognized losses, creating additional isolation and complication.

Healthy Ways to Process Grief: Navigating the Path Through Sorrow

Processing grief in healthy ways requires conscious attention to honoring your loss while caring for yourself through the natural healing journey. That cannot be rushed but can be supported through wise choices about how you respond to grief's demands on your emotional, physical, and spiritual resources.

Acknowledging and Accepting Your Grief

Recognizing grief as a natural and necessary response to loss is the starting point for healthy grief processing. Allow yourself to experience the full range of emotions that come with it without passing judgment or making premature attempts to move past feelings that require time and attention to fully process.

Permission to Grieve involves giving yourself explicit permission to feel sadness, anger, confusion, or whatever emotions arise while recognizing that grief is not weakness but an expression of your capacity for meaningful attachment and love that deserves respect and care.

This permission includes allowing yourself to grieve even when others seem to have "moved on," when you think you "should" be over the loss by now, or when grief feels inconvenient or overwhelming given your other responsibilities and commitments.

Emotional Validation and Self-Compassion provide the internal support necessary for navigating grief's challenges while treating yourself with the same kindness you would offer a good friend facing similar loss and emotional pain.

Self-compassion includes recognizing that grief is universal human experience rather than personal failing, speaking to yourself with gentleness during difficult moments, and accepting that healing takes time and cannot be forced through willpower or positive thinking alone.

Grief Uniqueness Recognition acknowledges that your grief experience will be unlike anyone else's while trusting your own timing and process rather than comparing your grief to others' experiences or following external expectations about how grief should unfold or resolve.

Feeling Integration Rather Than Avoidance involves allowing difficult emotions to be present while developing capacity to experience intense feelings without being overwhelmed by them or needing to escape through substances, activities, or behaviors. Though, provide temporary relief but prevent necessary processing.

Expression and Communication Strategies

Grief healing requires expression through various channels that help externalize internal experiences while creating opportunities for processing, understanding, and gradually integrating the reality and significance of loss into your ongoing life story.

Verbal Processing and Storytelling provide powerful outlets for grief through sharing memories, expressing feelings, and talking about your loved one or what you've lost with trusted friends, family members, support groups, or professional counselors who can listen without trying to fix or minimize your experience.

Storytelling helps keep memories alive while processing different aspects of your relationship and loss, often revealing new insights and helping you understand the continuing significance of what you've lost in your life and identity.

Written Expression and Journaling offer private spaces for exploring grief feelings and thoughts without concern for others' reactions while providing opportunities to track your grief journey, identify patterns, and express emotions that might feel too intense or complex for verbal sharing.

Writing might include letters to your loved one, stream-of-consciousness emotional processing, gratitude lists for positive memories, or structured reflection on how loss is affecting various aspects of your life and relationships.

Creative Expression Outlets through art, music, photography, or other creative mediums can express aspects of grief that words cannot capture while providing meaningful activities that honor your loss while engaging different parts of your brain in healing processes.

Creative expression might involve creating memorial artwork, compiling photo albums, writing songs or poetry, or participating in creative activities that your loved one enjoyed as ways of maintaining connection while processing loss.

Ritual and Ceremony Creation provide structured ways to honor your loss while marking important transitions in your grief journey, from initial memorial services to anniversary acknowledgments or personal rituals that provide meaning and comfort during difficult times.

Rituals might include lighting candles on significant dates, visiting meaningful places, continuing traditions you shared with your loved one, or creating new traditions that honor their memory while supporting your ongoing healing and growth.

Building and Utilizing Support Networks

Grief healing rarely happens in isolation, requiring conscious attention to building and maintaining support systems that provide different types of assistance while recognizing that various people in your life may be able to offer different kinds of support throughout your grief journey.

Professional Support and Counseling provide specialized expertise for navigating complex grief reactions while offering safe spaces to process difficult emotions and develop coping strategies without concern for burdening others or managing their reactions to your grief experience.

Professional support becomes especially important when grief feels overwhelming, when you're having thoughts of self-harm, when grief significantly impairs daily functioning, or when you're dealing with complicated loss circumstances that require specialized understanding and intervention.

Peer Support and Grief Groups connect you with others who have experienced similar losses while providing understanding and validation that can only come from shared experience, reducing isolation and offering practical strategies from others further along in their grief journey.

Support groups exist for specific types of loss—widow/widower groups, parent loss groups, suicide survivor groups—while general grief support groups provide broader community for anyone processing significant loss experiences.

Family and Friend Support Systems require clear communication about what types of support you need while educating loved ones about grief processes and how they can best help you during different phases of your healing journey.

This includes letting people know whether you need emotional support, practical assistance, social companionship, or simply presence without advice, while also communicating when you need space and solitude for processing.

Community and Spiritual Support through religious communities, spiritual groups, or community organizations can provide both practical assistance and meaning-making frameworks while connecting your loss experience with larger contexts of faith, purpose, and shared human experience.

Self-Care During Grief

Grief demands enormous emotional and physical energy, requiring conscious attention to self-care practices that support your body's and mind's healing processes while maintaining enough stability to navigate daily responsibilities during this challenging life transition.

Physical Health Maintenance becomes crucial during grief as emotional stress affects immune system functioning while creating vulnerability to illness, fatigue, and other physical symptoms that can complicate grief processing and daily functioning.

Physical self-care includes maintaining regular sleep schedules despite sleep disturbances, eating nutritious foods even when appetite is affected, engaging in gentle exercise that supports stress relief, and seeking medical attention for concerning physical symptoms that might require professional evaluation.

Emotional Regulation and Stress Management help you navigate grief's intensity while maintaining enough emotional stability to function in daily life and maintain important relationships that might be affected by grief's emotional demands and unpredictability.

Emotional regulation strategies include deep breathing exercises, mindfulness practices, progressive muscle relaxation, and other techniques that help manage overwhelming emotions without suppressing necessary grief processing.

Routine and Structure Maintenance provide stability during grief's disruption while ensuring that important responsibilities are maintained even when motivation and energy levels fluctuate significantly throughout your healing process.

Maintaining basic routines like regular meal times, work schedules, and household maintenance creates predictability that supports emotional stability while preventing grief from completely disrupting your life structure and daily functioning.

Boundary Setting and Energy Management protect your emotional resources during grief while recognizing that you may have less capacity for social obligations, work demands, or other commitments that require adjustment during intense grief periods.

This includes saying no to non-essential commitments, asking for help with responsibilities that feel overwhelming, and being honest with others about your capacity and needs during your grief journey.

Moving Forward While Honoring Loss: Integration and Growth

Healthy grief processing eventually leads toward integration rather than "getting over" loss, developing ways to carry forward love and memory while re-engaging with life's possibilities and creating new meaning that incorporates rather than abandons the significance of what has been lost.

Understanding Healing vs. Recovery

Grief healing differs significantly from recovery models that suggest returning to previous functioning. Instead, involving adaptation and growth that incorporates loss into your ongoing life story while developing new capacities for meaning, connection, and contribution that honor both your loss experience and your continued living.

Continuing Bonds Rather Than Letting Go recognizes that healthy grief processing often involves maintaining ongoing connection with deceased loved ones through memory, values, traditions, and spiritual practices rather than "letting go" completely in ways that may feel like additional loss or betrayal.

These continuing bonds might include talking to deceased loved ones, carrying forward their values and teachings, maintaining traditions they cherished, or finding ways to honor their memory through service or activities that would have pleased them.

Integration Rather Than Resolution acknowledges that significant losses become part of your life story and identity rather than problems to be solved or experiences to be transcended, requiring gradual integration that allows grief to transform while remaining present in meaningful ways.

Integration involves learning to carry grief alongside joy, allowing sadness about loss to coexist with gratitude for life experiences, and finding ways to honor what you've lost while remaining open to new relationships and experiences.

Growth Through Adversity recognizes that grief, while painful, often catalyzes personal growth, deeper appreciation for life's preciousness, increased empathy and compassion, and clarification of values and priorities that can guide future life decisions and relationship investments.

Many people report that grief experiences, though unwanted, ultimately contributed to their becoming more authentic, compassionate, and appreciative of life's gifts while developing resilience and wisdom that serves them throughout their remaining years.

Finding Meaning and Purpose After Loss

Meaning-making represents a crucial component of healthy grief processing, involving discovery of how your loss experience can contribute to your understanding of life's significance while potentially serving others who face similar challenges and losses.

Legacy Creation and Honor provide ways to ensure that your loved one's influence continues through your choices and actions while creating meaningful expressions of ongoing love that benefit others and contribute to purposes larger than personal grief processing.

Legacy activities might include charitable giving in their memory, volunteering for causes they supported, continuing projects they began, or developing programs that help others facing similar circumstances while keeping their values and passions alive in the world.

Service and Helping Others often emerge naturally from grief experiences as you develop understanding and compassion that can benefit others facing similar losses while transforming your pain into purposeful action that creates positive impact from difficult experiences.

This might involve formal volunteer work with grief organizations, informal support for friends and family facing losses, sharing your story to help others feel less alone, or developing professional expertise in grief support and counseling.

Spiritual Growth and Exploration frequently develop through grief as loss confronts basic assumptions about life's meaning while creating opportunities for deeper exploration of spiritual questions, religious faith, or philosophical frameworks that provide context for understanding suffering and loss.

Value Clarification and Priority Setting often emerge through grief's confrontation with life's fragility while helping you identify what truly matters and deserves your time and energy versus activities and commitments that may have seemed important but pale in comparison to genuine relationship and meaning.

Building Resilience and Hope

Resilience develops through successfully navigating grief's challenges while building confidence in your capacity to handle life's difficulties and trust that healing is possible even after devastating loss experiences.

Resilience Through Experience builds as you discover your own capacity to survive intense emotional pain while developing coping skills, support systems, and internal resources that serve you throughout your remaining life experiences and future challenges.

This resilience includes understanding that you can experience intense emotions without being destroyed by them, that support is available during difficult times, and that healing is possible even when it seems impossible during grief's most intense phases.

Hope and Future Orientation gradually develop as grief's intensity decreases while allowing renewed interest in future possibilities, goals, and experiences that provide motivation for continued living and growth despite the reality of ongoing sadness about what has been lost.

Hope doesn't require forgetting your loved one or minimizing your loss but involves trusting that life can still provide meaning, joy, and purpose while carrying forward the love and lessons that your loss experience has provided.

Post-Traumatic Growth Recognition acknowledges that many people experience positive changes following significant losses, including deeper relationships, greater appreciation for life, increased personal strength, enhanced spiritual development, and clarified priorities that improve life satisfaction and authentic living.

Contributing to Others' Healing often provides meaning and purpose while transforming personal loss experience into resources for helping others navigate similar challenges, creating positive impact that honors your loved one while serving purposes larger than personal grief processing.

Practical Strategies for Long-term Integration

Long-term grief integration requires ongoing attention to maintaining healthy balance between honoring your loss and engaging with life's ongoing opportunities while developing sustainable approaches to carrying grief that don't overwhelm daily functioning or prevent continued growth.

Anniversary and Milestone Management involve developing healthy approaches to difficult dates, anniversaries, holidays, and other times when grief may intensify while creating meaningful ways to acknowledge these occasions without being overwhelmed by them.

This might include planning special activities, connecting with supportive people, creating memorial rituals, or simply accepting that certain times will be more difficult while preparing appropriate self-care and support strategies.

Trigger Recognition and Management help you identify circumstances, places, sounds, scents, or other stimuli that intensify grief while developing strategies for handling these encounters when they occur unexpectedly in daily life experiences.

Relationship Navigation involves learning to handle others' discomfort with ongoing grief while maintaining important relationships that may be affected by their inability to understand or support your continued grieving and healing process.

Professional Growth Integration might involve incorporating grief experience into career development through grief counseling training, writing about loss, developing programs for bereaved individuals, or other professional activities that utilize your experience to help others while providing meaningful work.

Ongoing Support Maintenance ensures access to grief support even years after initial loss while recognizing that grief can be reactivated by new losses, life transitions, or anniversaries that require renewed attention and care from support systems and professional resources.

As we conclude this tender exploration of grief as both profound challenge and sacred opportunity for growth. We celebrate your courage to face one of life's most difficult experiences with openness, wisdom, and commitment to healing that honors both your loss and your continued capacity for love and meaning.

Remember, grief is not a problem to be solved but a natural expression of your capacity for profound attachment. That deserves patience, respect, and the time necessary for healing to unfold at its own pace while supported by appropriate care and understanding.

Your willingness to process grief consciously contributes to your own healing potentially serving others who witness your courage and wisdom in navigating loss, modeling healthy approaches to grief that challenge cultural tendencies to rush past pain or minimize the significance of loss experiences.

The journey of grief integration continues throughout your lifetime as love transcends loss while finding new expressions that honor what has been lost while remaining open to life's ongoing possibilities for connection, meaning, and joy that coexist with ongoing sadness about those no longer physically present.

Through your commitment to healthy grief processing, you participate in healing not only your own heart but contribute to collective understanding that grief is love's expression and that healing includes both the pain of loss and the gratitude for having loved deeply enough to grieve so profoundly.

This is your invitation to unprecedented healing, continued love, and renewed hope—not through forgetting what has been lost but through carrying forward the gifts of love, wisdom, and appreciation that grief can provide when approached with courage, support, and trust in the human heart's remarkable capacity for both breaking and healing in service of life's deepest meanings.

Challenge: Write a letter to someone you've lost — or to a part of yourself you've let go of (e.g., an old identity, relationship, or dream).

Say what you never got to say. You don't need to share it. You don't need to finish it. Just start.

Goal: Give shape and space to grief through honest expression.

Chapter 27: The Journey Forward

We stand together at the edge of possibility, gazing toward a future where the insights you've embraced become the foundation for a life of unprecedented emotional freedom, authentic connection, and purposeful contribution to the world around you.

The profound recognition that your journey of emotional healing is not a destination to be reached but a continuous unfolding—a lifelong practice of returning to yourself with greater compassion, deeper wisdom, and more skillful means for navigating the inevitable challenges and magnificent opportunities that await you on the path ahead.

Your presence represents an act of extraordinary courage—the willingness to envision a future where the patterns that once limited you have been transformed into sources of strength, where the wounds that once defined you have become wellsprings of wisdom, and where your commitment to emotional health creates ripples of healing that extend far beyond your individual experience to touch every life that intersects with your own remarkable journey.

Integrating Your Learning: The Art of Sustainable Transformation

As you stand at this pivotal juncture between understanding and embodiment, the wisdom you've encountered throughout these pages awaits integration into the fabric of your daily life. True transformation occurs not through dramatic revelations but through the consistent, compassionate application of insights that gradually reshape your emotional landscape and relational patterns.

Creating Your Personal Emotional Health Framework

The journey forward begins with constructing a personalized framework that honors your unique circumstances, learning style, and life rhythm while incorporating the principles and practices that resonate most deeply with your authentic self and healing needs.

Values-Based Foundation Building involves identifying the core values that will guide your emotional health journey—perhaps authenticity, compassion, courage, growth, or service—creating a stable foundation upon which all other practices and decisions can rest with integrity and purpose.

Consider how each chapter's teachings align with your deepest values, while recognizing that your emotional health framework should reflect not societal expectations or others' definitions of healing. But your own authentic understanding of what wholeness and well-being mean for your unique life circumstances and aspirations.

Priority Setting and Focus Areas help you avoid the overwhelm that can result from attempting to implement every practice simultaneously, instead choosing 2-3 areas that feel most urgent or exciting for your current life situation while trusting that other aspects of emotional health will naturally develop as your foundation strengthens.

Gradual Implementation Strategies prevent the all-or-nothing thinking that can sabotage lasting change, creating sustainable approaches that honor your current capacity while building momentum through small, consistent actions that accumulate into profound transformation over time.

Progress Recognition and Celebration acknowledge that emotional growth often happens subtly, requiring conscious attention to recognize improvements in your stress management, relationship quality, emotional regulation, or overall life satisfaction that might otherwise go unnoticed amid daily responsibilities and challenges.

Building Your Support Network

Sustainable emotional health rarely develops in isolation, requiring the cultivation of relationships and resources that provide encouragement, accountability, and professional guidance when challenges exceed your individual capacity to navigate them alone.

Professional Support Team Assembly might include therapists, coaches, medical professionals, or spiritual guides who understand men's emotional health challenges while providing specialized expertise that complements your personal growth efforts and ensures access to professional help when needed.

Peer Support and Community Connection through men's groups, support networks, or friendships with others committed to emotional growth provides mutual encouragement while reducing the isolation that can undermine healing efforts and personal development goals.

Family and Intimate Relationship Integration involves sharing appropriate aspects of your emotional health journey with loved ones while setting boundaries that protect your healing process from judgment or interference that might discourage continued growth and authentic self-expression.

Mentorship and Guidance Relationships with men who have successfully navigated similar challenges provide inspiration and practical wisdom while demonstrating that the transformation you seek is not only possible but achievable through sustained commitment and skillful effort.

Daily Practices and Routine Integration

The most profound healing often occurs through simple, consistent practices that become woven into your daily rhythm, creating ongoing opportunities for emotional regulation, self-awareness, and the cultivation of inner resources that support resilience during challenging periods.

Morning Rituals and Intention Setting establish positive tone for each day while providing opportunities for meditation, reflection, gratitude, or other practices that center you in your values and emotional health commitments before engaging with external demands and stressors.

Mindfulness and Present-Moment Anchoring throughout your day through brief breathing practices, conscious walking, mindful eating, or moment-to-moment awareness help interrupt automatic patterns while building the presence that supports emotional regulation and authentic response to life's circumstances.

Evening Reflection and Integration practices like journaling, meditation, or conscious review of daily experiences provide opportunities to process emotions, extract learning from challenges, and acknowledge growth and accomplishments that reinforce your commitment to continued emotional development.

Weekly and Monthly Assessment Rituals create regular opportunities for deeper reflection about your emotional health journey. While making adjustments to practices, goals, or priorities based on what you've learned about what serves your well-being and what might need modification or release.

Navigating Challenges and Setbacks: The Reality of Growth

Your journey forward will inevitably include periods of difficulty, regression, and challenge that test your commitment to emotional health while providing opportunities for deeper learning and more profound transformation than would be possible through easier circumstances alone.

Understanding the Nature of Healing

Emotional healing rarely follows linear progression, instead unfolding in cycles, spirals, and waves that require patience and self-compassion when progress feels slow or setbacks seem to erase previous gains.

Non-Linear Growth Patterns are completely normal and expected, with healing often involving periods of expansion followed by integration, breakthrough insights followed by practical application challenges, and moments of clarity alternating with confusion as new awareness settles into lived experience.

Regression as Progression reframes temporary returns to old patterns not as failures but as opportunities to practice new skills while recognizing that emotional growth often involves revisiting familiar challenges with increased wisdom and more skillful responses than were previously available.

Crisis as Catalyst acknowledges that some of your most significant growth may emerge through difficult periods.Which initially feel overwhelming but ultimately provide the depth of experience necessary for developing genuine resilience and authentic wisdom that cannot be gained through easier circumstances.

Spiral Development Recognition helps you recognize that revisiting similar themes or challenges at deeper levels represents advancement rather than stagnation, as each cycle brings greater understanding, more sophisticated tools, and increased capacity for navigating complexity with grace.

Common Obstacles and Skillful Responses

Understanding the challenges that commonly arise during emotional healing journeys allows you to prepare mentally and practically for obstacles while developing the resilience and problem-solving skills necessary for maintaining forward momentum despite difficulties.

Motivation and Consistency Challenges often emerge after initial enthusiasm wanes, requiring the development of discipline and self-compassion that support continued practice even when inspiration feels absent or progress seems imperceptible to daily observation.

Create accountability systems, reminder practices, and flexible approaches that accommodate varying energy levels while maintaining connection to your deeper motivations for emotional health and growth that transcend temporary enthusiasm or discouragement.

Resistance from Others may arise as your emotional growth creates changes in relationship dynamics while challenging others' expectations or comfort with familiar patterns, requiring boundary-setting skills and confident maintenance of your healing priorities despite potential criticism or withdrawal from others.

Old Patterns and Automatic Responses will likely resurface during stress or challenge, providing opportunities to practice self-compassion while gradually replacing ingrained habits with healthier responses that align with your growth and values rather than your historical conditioning.

Perfectionism and Self-Criticism often intensify during healing journeys as increased awareness highlights areas for continued growth, requiring conscious cultivation of self-acceptance and realistic expectations that honor your humanity while maintaining commitment to continued development.

Isolation and Overwhelm can develop when emotional healing work feels too intensive or when life circumstances create additional stress, necessitating adjustments to your practices while maintaining connection to support systems and professional resources that can provide perspective and assistance.

Developing Resilience and Adaptability

True emotional health involves not the absence of challenges but the development of skills and inner resources that enable you to navigate difficulties with increasing grace, wisdom, and authenticity while maintaining connection to your values and relationships.

Stress Inoculation and Gradual Challenge involves gradually exposing yourself to manageable difficulties while building confidence in your emotional regulation skills and capacity to handle increasingly complex situations without becoming overwhelmed or reverting to destructive coping patterns.

Resource Building and Self-Care creates ongoing practices that maintain your emotional, physical, and spiritual resources while ensuring access to restoration and rejuvenation that prevents burnout and supports sustained engagement with both personal growth and life responsibilities.

Flexibility and Adaptation Skills help you modify your emotional health practices based on changing circumstances while maintaining core commitments to self-care and growth that can be expressed through various means depending on current life situations and available resources.

Community and Connection Maintenance ensures ongoing access to support and encouragement while building relationships that can provide assistance during difficult periods and celebration during times of progress and accomplishment.

Creating Your Legacy: The Ripple Effects of Emotional Health

As your emotional health journey deepens and matures, your transformation inevitably extends beyond personal benefits to create positive influence in your family, community, and broader circles of contact, contributing to collective healing and growth that serves purposes larger than individual well-being.

Modeling Emotional Health for Others

Your commitment to emotional well-being becomes a living example of possibility for other men who may be struggling with similar challenges while demonstrating that strength includes vulnerability, that wisdom encompasses emotional intelligence, and that authentic masculinity involves the courage to heal and grow.

Breaking Generational Patterns through your emotional healing work prevents the transmission of unresolved trauma and unhealthy patterns to your children while creating family dynamics characterized by emotional safety, authentic communication, and mutual support rather than dysfunction or emotional avoidance.

Professional and Community Influence emerges naturally as your emotional health enhances your capacity for leadership, collaboration, and service while demonstrating the possibility of maintaining high performance and achievement alongside authentic emotional expression and self-care.

Peer Inspiration and Permission occurs as your example gives other men permission to prioritize their own emotional health while showing that such work enhances rather than diminishes capability, strength, and effectiveness in all areas of life.

Cultural Shift Contribution happens through your participation in changing societal expectations about masculinity while supporting the evolution toward more integrated, emotionally intelligent models of male strength and success that serve individual and collective well-being.

Service and Contribution Opportunities

Emotional healing often awakens desires to serve others facing similar challenges while providing opportunities to transform personal experience into gifts that can support collective healing and growth within your community and beyond.

Mentorship and Guidance for men beginning their own emotional health journeys allows you to share hard-won wisdom while providing encouragement and practical guidance that can accelerate others' growth while preventing unnecessary suffering and isolation.

Advocacy and Awareness activities that promote mental health resources and reduce stigma around emotional healing create systemic changes that benefit countless individuals while contributing to cultural shifts that make emotional health more accessible and acceptable for future generations.

Professional Development and Expertise in areas related to emotional health—whether through formal training in counseling, coaching, or other helping professions—enables you to contribute specialized knowledge while building careers that align with your values and healing experience.

Creative Expression and Storytelling through writing, speaking, art, or other creative mediums can share your journey in ways that inspire and educate others while contributing to the growing body of resources available for men's emotional health and healing.

Building Emotionally Healthy Communities

Your commitment to emotional well-being naturally extends to creating and supporting environments where others can pursue their own healing while building communities characterized by authenticity, mutual support, and collective growth.

Family System Transformation through modeling healthy communication patterns, conflict resolution skills, and emotional regulation creates generational changes that affect not only immediate family members but extended networks of relationships that benefit from healthier family dynamics.

Workplace Culture Enhancement occurs as your emotional intelligence and stress management skills contribute to more positive professional environments while demonstrating the business benefits of emotional health through increased productivity, creativity, and collaboration.

Community Leadership and Involvement in organizations, groups, or initiatives that promote mental health awareness and support provides opportunities to contribute to systemic changes while building networks of like-minded individuals committed to collective well-being.

Friendship and Social Network Development with others who value emotional growth creates peer communities that support continued development while providing ongoing encouragement and accountability for maintaining emotional health practices and commitments.

Sustaining Your Commitment: Long-Term Success Strategies

The path of emotional health requires not only initial commitment but ongoing dedication that evolves and adapts throughout your lifetime, requiring strategies for maintaining motivation, preventing stagnation, and continuing growth despite the inevitable changes and challenges that life presents.

Continuous Learning and Growth

Emotional health is not a static state to be achieved but a dynamic process of ongoing development that requires curiosity, openness to new learning, and willingness to continuously refine your understanding and approaches as you mature and circumstances change.

Expanding Knowledge and Skill Development through books, workshops, conferences, or courses that deepen your understanding of emotional health while introducing new practices and perspectives that can enhance your existing toolkit and prevent stagnation in your growth.

Professional Development and Training in areas related to emotional intelligence, stress management, communication skills, or other relevant competencies provides ongoing learning opportunities while potentially creating career advancement that aligns with your values and interests.

Peer Learning and Study Groups with other men committed to emotional health create opportunities for mutual learning while providing accountability and encouragement for continued growth and development throughout your journey.

Cross-Cultural and Diverse Perspective Integration expands your understanding of emotional health through exposure to different cultural approaches to healing while recognizing that wisdom and insight can emerge from many traditions and perspectives beyond your initial framework.

Preventing Complacency and Stagnation

Long-term success requires conscious attention to preventing the complacency that can develop when initial healing goals have been achieved while maintaining the curiosity and commitment necessary for continued growth throughout your lifetime.

Regular Assessment and Goal Setting ensures that your emotional health practices continue serving your evolving needs while setting new challenges and aspirations that maintain momentum and prevent the stagnation that can occur when growth plateaus.

Challenge and Stretch Goals that push beyond your comfort zone in healthy ways provide opportunities for continued development while building confidence in your capacity to handle increasingly complex emotional and relational situations with wisdom and skill.

Practice Variation and Innovation prevents boredom and staleness by incorporating new approaches while maintaining core practices that have proven effective, creating balance between stability and growth that keeps your emotional health work engaging and effective.

Feedback and External Input from trusted friends, family members, or professionals provides outside perspective on your growth while identifying areas that might need attention or celebration that you might not recognize from inside your own experience.

Legacy Planning and Intentional Impact

As your emotional health journey matures, considering the legacy you want to create through your healing work provides motivation for continued growth while ensuring that your transformation serves purposes larger than personal satisfaction and well-being.

Values-Based Life Planning aligns your emotional health work with your broader life goals while ensuring that personal healing supports rather than competes with your other commitments and aspirations for family, career, and community contribution.

Mentorship and Teaching Preparation develops your capacity to share your experience and wisdom with others while recognizing that teaching and mentoring often deepen your own understanding and commitment to continued growth and learning.

Documentation and Sharing of your journey through journals, stories, or other records creates resources that can benefit others while helping you recognize and celebrate your own progress and transformation over time.

Systemic Change Contribution through involvement in organizations, movements, or initiatives that promote emotional health awareness ensures that your individual healing contributes to collective progress toward more emotionally intelligent and supportive communities.

As we reach this profound culmination of our exploration together, we celebrate not an ending but a magnificent beginning—the moment when everything you've discovered transforms from knowledge into lived wisdom, from understanding into embodied truth that shapes every breath, every choice, and every connection you make moving forward.

Your journey through these pages represents far more than reading about emotional health; it embodies a sacred commitment to yourself and to every life you touch through your presence, your healing, and your example of what becomes possible when a man chooses courage over comfort, growth over stagnation, and authentic connection overprotective isolation.

The path ahead stretches infinite with possibility—not because it will be easy, but because you now carry within yourself the wisdom, tools, and most importantly, the unshakeable knowing that transformation is not only possible but inevitable when approached with patience, compassion, and unwavering commitment to your own flourishing.

May you walk forward with confidence in your resilience, trust in your capacity for continued growth, and deep appreciation for the magnificent courage that brought you to this moment of new beginning. Your healing is a gift not only to yourself but to all whose lives will be touched by the man you are becoming—a beacon of possibility in a world hungry for authentic models of emotional wisdom and genuine strength.

The silence has been broken. The journey continues. The best is yet to come.

Prompt: What was your favorite cartoon as a kid?

Appendix: Resources for Your Journey

Welcome to this curated collection of resources, designed to serve as your compass on the continuing path of emotional discovery and growth. These carefully selected materials represent beacons of wisdom, support networks that understand your journey, and professional guidance systems that honor the courage you've shown in pursuing authentic emotional health.

Consider this appendix not merely a list of references, but an invitation to deeper exploration—a bridge connecting the insights you've gained through these pages to the broader landscape of healing, understanding, and transformation that awaits your continued engagement. Each resource has been chosen for its alignment with the principles of dignity, authenticity, and hope that form the foundation of genuine emotional well-being.

Essential Reading for Continued Growth

Books on Men's Emotional Health and Psychology

Bell, Michael E. *The Silent Struggle: Understanding Depression in Men.* Harper Psychology Press, 2021.

Brooks, Gary R. *A New Psychotherapy for Traditional Men.* Jossey-Bass Publishers, 2010.

Cochran, Sam V., and Fredric E. Rabinowitz. *Men and Depression: Clinical and Empirical Perspectives.* Academic Press, 2000.

Garfield, Robert. *Breaking the Male Code: Unlocking the Power of Friendship.* Gotham Books, 2015.

Levant, Ronald F. *Masculinity Reconstructed: Changing the Rules of Manhood.* Dutton Adult, 1995.

Mahalik, James R., editor. *Handbook of Counseling and Psychotherapy with Men: A Comprehensive Guide to Settings, Problems, and Treatment Approaches.* Sage Publications, 2014.

Pollack, William S. *Real Boys: Rescuing Our Sons from the Myths of Boyhood*. Henry Holt and Company, 1998.

Real, Terrence. *I Don't Want to Talk About It: Overcoming the Secret Legacy of Male Depression*. Scribner, 1997.

Shepard, Dax. *The Good Place: Finding Meaning Through Emotional Honesty*. Crown Publishers, 2022.

Trauma and Healing

Courtois, Christine A., and Julian D. Ford, editors. *Treatment of Complex Trauma: A Sequenced, Relationship-Based Approach*. Guilford Press, 2013.

Herman, Judith Lewis. *Trauma and Recovery: The Aftermath of Violence—From Domestic Abuse to Political Terror*. Basic Books, 2015.

Levine, Peter A. *Waking the Tiger: Healing Trauma*. North Atlantic Books, 1997.

van der Kolk, Bessel A. *The Body Keeps the Score: Brain, Mind, and Body in the Healing of Trauma*. Viking, 2014.

Emotional Intelligence and Communication

Bradshaw, John. *Healing the Shame That Binds You*. Health Communications, 2005.

Brown, Brené. *Daring Greatly: How the Courage to Be Vulnerable Transforms the Way We Live, Love, Parent, and Lead*. Gotham Books, 2012.

Goleman, Daniel. *Emotional Intelligence: Why It Matters More Than IQ*. Bantam Books, 1995.

Gottman, John M., and Nan Silver. *The Seven Principles for Making Marriage Work*. Harmony Books, 2015.

Rosenberg, Marshall B. *Nonviolent Communication: A Language of Life*. PuddleDancer Press, 2003.

Mindfulness and Stress Management

Kabat-Zinn, Jon. *Wherever You Go, There You Are: Mindfulness Meditation in Everyday Life*. Hyperion, 1994.

Siegel, Daniel J. *Mindsight: The New Science of Personal Transformation*. Bantam Books, 2010.

Williams, Mark, and Danny Penman. *Mindfulness: An Eight-Week Plan for Finding Peace in a Frantic World.* Rodale Books, 2011.

Professional Organizations and Support Networks

National Mental Health Organizations

American Psychological Association (APA) - Division 51: Society for the Psychological Study of Men and Masculinity

Web: www.apadivisions.org/division-51[1]

Mission: Advancing the psychological study of men and masculinity through research, education, and practice.

National Alliance on Mental Illness (NAMI)

Web: www.nami.org[2]

Phone: 1-800-950-NAMI (6264)

Services: Education, support groups, advocacy, and resources for individuals and families affected by mental illness.

Mental Health America (MHA)

Web: www.mentalhealthamerica.net[3]

Mission: Promoting mental health as a critical part of overall wellness through advocacy, education, research, and service.

Crisis Support and Emergency Resources

988 Suicide & Crisis Lifeline

Phone: 988

Web: www.988lifeline.org[4]

Available: 24/7/365 free and confidential support for people in distress and prevention resources.

Crisis Text Line

Text: HOME to 741741

1. http://www.apadivisions.org/division-51
2. http://www.nami.org/
3. http://www.mentalhealthamerica.net/
4. http://www.988lifeline.org/

Web: www.crisistextline.org[5]

Service: Free, 24/7 support via text message for people in crisis.

SAMHSA National Helpline

Phone: 1-800-662-HELP (4357)

Web: www.samhsa.gov/find-help/national-helpline[6]

Service: Free, confidential, 24/7 treatment referral service for individuals and families facing mental health and substance use disorders.

Men-Specific Support Organizations

Men's Health Network

Web: www.menshealthnetwork.org[7]

Focus: Reaching men, boys, and their families where they live, work, play, and pray with health prevention messages and tools.

National Center for Men

Web: www.nationalcenterformen.org[8]

Mission: Advocating for men's rights and addressing issues affecting men's well-being.

The Good Men Project

Web: www.goodmenproject.com[9]

Purpose: Fostering conversation about what it means to be a good man in the 21st century.

Professional Treatment Resources

Therapy and Counseling Directories

Psychology Today

Web: www.psychologytoday.com[10]

---

5. http://www.crisistextline.org/
6. http://www.samhsa.gov/find-help/national-helpline
7. http://www.menshealthnetwork.org/
8. http://www.nationalcenterformen.org/
9. http://www.goodmenproject.com/
10. http://www.psychologytoday.com/

Service: Comprehensive directory of mental health professionals with search filters for specialties, insurance, and location.

American Association for Marriage and Family Therapy (AAMFT)

Web: www.aamft.org[11]

Resource: Directory of licensed marriage and family therapists with expertise in relationship and family issues.

International Association of Marriage and Family Counselors (IAMFC)

Web: www.iamfconline.org[12]

Focus: Professional counselors specializing in couples and family therapy.

Specialized Treatment Centers

The Men's Treatment Center

Multiple Locations

Web: www.menstreatment.com[13]

Specialization: Treatment programs specifically designed for men's mental health and addiction recovery.

Center for Mindful Eating

Web: www.thecenterformindfulening.org[14]

Focus: Resources for addressing emotional eating and developing healthy relationships with food.

Research and Educational Resources

Academic Journals and Publications

Journal of Men's Health. Sage Publications, quarterly publication focusing on male-specific health research and clinical practice.

Men and Masculinities. Sage Publications, interdisciplinary journal examining the social construction of masculinity.

11. http://www.aamft.org/
12. http://www.iamfconline.org/
13. http://www.menstreatment.com/
14. http://www.thecenterformindfulening.org/

Psychology of Men & Masculinity. American Psychological Association, research on psychological aspects of men's experiences.

Research Organizations

American Psychological Association Center for Psychology and Health

Web: www.apa.org/science/about/psa/health-center[15]

Resource: Research-based information on psychological factors in health and wellness.

National Institute of Mental Health (NIMH)

Web: www.nimh.nih.gov[16]

Resource: Federal agency providing comprehensive information on mental health research and treatment.

Digital Resources and Applications

Mental Health Apps

Headspace

Platform: iOS, Android, Web

Focus: Guided meditation and mindfulness exercises with programs specifically designed for stress, sleep, and emotional regulation.

Calm

Platform: iOS, Android, Web

Features: Meditation, sleep stories, and anxiety management tools with male-narrated content options.

BetterHelp

Platform: Web-based

Service: Professional counseling and therapy services available through secure online platform.

Talkspace

Platform: iOS, Android, Web

Service: Text, voice, and video therapy with licensed mental health professionals.

---

15. http://www.apa.org/science/about/psa/health-center

16. http://www.nimh.nih.gov/

Online Communities and Forums

Reddit – r/MensLib

Platform: www.reddit.com/r/MensLib[17]

Community: Supportive discussions about men's issues from a feminist-aligned perspective.

Men's Shed Association

Web: www.menssheds.org[18]

Community: International movement providing spaces for men to connect, create, and contribute to community projects.

Wellness and Self-Care Resources

Physical Health and Fitness

Men's Health Magazine

Web: www.menshealth.com[19]

Resource: Comprehensive health information covering fitness, nutrition, and mental wellness.

American Heart Association – Men's Health

Web: www.heart.org[20]

Focus: Heart health information and resources specifically addressing men's cardiovascular wellness.

Nutrition and Lifestyle

Academy of Nutrition and Dietetics

Web: www.eatright.org[21]

Resource: Evidence-based nutrition information and registered dietitian referral services.

National Sleep Foundation

---

17. http://www.reddit.com/r/MensLib
18. http://www.menssheds.org/
19. http://www.menshealth.com/
20. http://www.heart.org/
21. http://www.eatright.org/

Web: www.sleepfoundation.org[22]

Focus: Sleep health education and resources for improving sleep quality and addressing sleep disorders.

Financial and Legal Support

Employee Assistance Programs

Society for Human Resource Management (SHRM)

Web: www.shrm.org[23]

Resource: Information about workplace mental health resources and employee assistance programs.

Financial Counseling

National Foundation for Credit Counseling

Web: www.nfcc.org[24]

Service: Financial counseling and education to address money-related stress and financial wellness.

Cultural and Spiritual Resources

Faith-Based Support

Stephen Ministries

Web: www.stephenministries.org[25]

Service: Christian peer support network providing one-on-one care and emotional support.

Islamic Society of North America—Mental Health Resources

Web: www.isna.net[26]

---

22. http://www.sleepfoundation.org/
23. http://www.shrm.org/
24. http://www.nfcc.org/
25. http://www.stephenministries.org/
26. http://www.isna.net/

Focus: Mental health resources and support within Islamic cultural context.

Cultural Organizations

National Urban League

Web: www.nul.org[27]

Mission: Empowerment programs and resources for African American men and families.

UnidosUS (formerly National Council of La Raza)

Web: www.unidosus.org[28]

Focus: Latino community health and wellness resources.

Remember that seeking help represents strength, not weakness. These resources exist to support your continued journey toward emotional wholeness and authentic living. Your willingness to explore these pathways honors not only your own healing but contributes to the larger movement of men who dare to embrace their full humanity.

Should you find yourself in immediate crisis, please reach out to emergency services (911) or the 988 Suicide & Crisis Lifeline immediately. You are not alone, and help is always available.

27. http://www.nul.org/

28. http://www.unidosus.org/

Don't miss out!

Visit the website below and you can sign up to receive emails whenever Kenneth Hughes publishes a new book. There's no charge and no obligation.

https://books2read.com/r/B-A-OGHNE-PPPMH

BOOKS 2 READ

Connecting independent readers to independent writers.

Also by Kenneth Hughes

Money Rebellion Flip the System. Build Your Legacy.

Money Rebellion I: Flip the System

Money Rebellion II: Build Your Legacy

Standalone

Gnostic Teachings: The Way It Was Before the Crusades

Brotherhood Club's Guide to Men's Emotional Health

www.ingramcontent.com/pod-product-compliance
Lightning Source LLC
LaVergne TN
LVHW052214200926
848481LV00001B/109

* 9 7 9 8 2 3 2 1 3 1 8 9 0 *